The Spiritual-Industrial Complex

The Spiritual-Industrial Complex

America's Religious Battle against Communism in the Early Cold War

JONATHAN P. HERZOG

OXFORD
UNIVERSITY PRESS

OXFORD

UNIVERSITY PRESS

Oxford University Press, Inc., publishes works that further
Oxford University's objective of excellence
in research, scholarship, and education.

Oxford   New York
Auckland   Cape Town   Dar es Salaam   Hong Kong   Karachi
Kuala Lumpur   Madrid   Melbourne   Mexico City   Nairobi
New Delhi   Shanghai   Taipei   Toronto

With offices in
Argentina   Austria   Brazil   Chile   Czech Republic   France   Greece
Guatemala   Hungary   Italy   Japan   Poland   Portugal   Singapore
South Korea   Switzerland   Thailand   Turkey   Ukraine   Vietnam

Published by Oxford University Press, Inc.
198 Madison Avenue, New York, NY 10016

www.oup.com

Oxford is a registered trademark of Oxford University Press

Library of Congress Cataloging-in-Publication Data
Herzog, Jonathan P., 1981–
The spiritual-industrial complex : America's religious battle against communism
in the early Cold War / Jonathan P. Herzog.
p. cm.
ISBN 978-0-19-539346-0
1. United States—Foreign relations—1945–1989.
2. World politics—1945–1989. 3. Cold War.
4. Communism and Christianity. I. Title.
E744.H486   2011
973.921—dc22   2010053172

For my Grandpa,
Arthur N. Jensen
(1927–2010)

CONTENTS

PREFACE

If what undergraduates tell me is true, that Stanford's beauty has a way of breaking their concentration, then late winter must be the cruelest time of all. The days grow warm, the orange California poppies multiply, and the brown hillsides give way to an impossible green. The afternoons are a time to hike or simply lounge on the quad. But this was not always an option in the late winter of 2006 for those enrolled in my colloquium on modern American conservatism. They spent Tuesday and Thursday afternoons discussing, among other things, the intellectual inheritance of Edmund Burke, Barry Goldwater's *Conscience of a Conservative*, and the impact of California's Proposition 13.

Of all the speeches, books, and tracts we examined that quarter, one modest pamphlet sparked the most unexpected and fruitful debate. Written by a Chinese American conservative in 1960, it was entitled "Why a Christian Cannot Be a Communist." The students were accustomed to thinking about Communism as a political or economic system, and to them the argument seemed strange. What I originally thought would be a brief discussion ended up consuming the entire class period. We listed the reasons why Communism might be antithetical to Christianity, eventually producing a catalog far exceeding the author's original argument. And then we began drawing out his logic, searching for its unspoken assumptions. Finally I asked: "If a Christian can't be a Communist, can a non-Christian be an American?" The group began considering the deeper implications of a Cold War divided along religious lines.

Was this pamphlet an isolated argument? Was it a claim monopolized by the Right, or did it transcend political ideology? Did American leaders act upon this conclusion? While Communism, as we've long known, was atheistic, the pamphlet argued something more. It did not only construe Communism as a philosophy hostile to religion but also as a powerful religious system itself. I resolved to learn more.

This work is the result of that inquiry. I learned that the 1960 pamphlet was but one piece of a worldview, widely accepted and acted upon by American leaders in the early Cold War. I learned that my parents remember asking God to convert Russia as Catholic school children in the 1950s, that my grandmother prayed in 1946 for the release of a Croatian cardinal from an Iron Curtain jail, and that my grandfather signed the religiously inspired Freedom Scroll in 1950. They did these things for two reasons. First, such actions marshaled faith against faith. But more importantly, these deeds displayed their religious convictions and, in turn, their Americanism. They did not act alone. Millions of Americans, from presidents on down, participated in a spiritual crusade—not with bullets or bayonets but with patriotic and religious affirmations.

My curiosity about Cold War constructions of Communism intersects in *The Spiritual-Industrial Complex* with another interest: the relationship between religion and society. For better or worse, the march of Western civilization has coincided with a general decrease in the role, influence, and authority of religion. This is not to say that religion has become unimportant. People still attend religious services, pray, and profess a belief in higher powers. But in Western, industrialized nations, religious ideas and institutions are no longer as dominant a linchpin of social order as they were in the year 1900, much less the year 1300.

Maybe this decrease in the role and influence of religion, labeled secularization by sociologists, is not as uniform and inexorable as some think. Perhaps there are times and circumstances where even the most modern of Western societies conclude they require the unique contributions of religion. For American society, the early Cold War represented one such instance.

Seventeenth-century salon regular François de la Rochefoucauld quipped that "gratitude is simply the hope for future favors." Such cynicism often finds a warm place in my kindred heart, and while I hope to continue reaping the benefaction of all involved with this project, acknowledgments as merited and heartfelt as these can bear no guile.

Thanks to David M. Kennedy, the wordsmith and master historian, who possesses an uncanny ability to understand my arguments and recapitulate them with lean clarity and rhetorical splendor. He has given me opportunities, honest criticism, and something even more valuable: his time. David has a quick anecdote for any of the little crises of graduate school existence—words of comforting wisdom—and I am much the better for having known him.

Thanks to Jack Rakove, the eternal skeptic, jovial counselor, and first-rate scholar, who always seems to know the difference between my best work and imitation. Thanks to other scholars who have read part or all of this work, including David Brady, David Foglesong, John T. McGreevy, Margaret Pugh O'Mara, and the anonymous reviewers for Oxford University Press.

Thanks to Stanford University and its history department for not only giving me a free education but also subsidizing my living expenses. Thanks to the librarians and archivists who made my research possible, especially at Stanford Libraries, the Hoover Institution, the Library of Congress, the National Archives, and the Catholic University of America. And special thanks to Herb Pankratz at the Eisenhower Library and Randy Sowell at the Truman Library for their time and guidance.

Thanks to Susan Ferber, executive editor at Oxford University Press, who fielded a multitude of sometimes dazed and deficient questions from me throughout this process. Her wit and unsparing edits made this a much more comprehensible book.

Thanks to the history department faculty at the University of Oregon, who supported this book in its final stages. Thanks especially to Ellen Herman and John McCole for understanding that sometimes a career change is the best option.

Last, thanks to my family. Thanks to my grandparents for your recollections of days I will never know, and our Tuesday trips to local sites of historical interest. You were my first, and best, history books. Thanks to my parents and brother for constant encouragement and much needed diversions. And thanks to my wife, Beth. Thanks for insisting upon reading everything I write, even when it's boring. Thanks for listening attentively to my chapter ideas on long hikes, even when you'd rather talk about something else or nothing at all. Thanks for everything.

The views expressed in this book are the author's and do not necessarily reflect those of the State Department or U.S. Government.

The Spiritual-Industrial Complex

Introduction

> "You can divide geographically. You can share economically. You can endure politically. But no system has yet been devised for cutting the human soul in twain and making it serve two masters."
> —Representative Victor L. Anfuso, 1955

U.S. Army instructors in the 1950s could not tell new recruits when the Cold War would end. They could not tell them to where it would spread. But they did tell them this: that the world was divided into three kinds of nations. There were "demonic" nations that attacked both organized religion and belief in higher powers. There were "secular" nations that enforced a strict separation between church and state. And then there were "covenant" nations that recognized their dependence upon God.[1] This left little room for nuance. With respect to religion, a nation could kill it, coddle it, or let it fend for itself.

Finding the undertakings of a demonic nation in the early Cold War was simple enough. Recruits might have looked to the village of Peredel, a three-hour drive west of Moscow. There once was a small chapel there, old and uncared for. Its roof was cracked and its walls were crumbling. All around it new buildings were rising—a state-owned farm, a middle school, even a hospital. There is no record of when it was built. It may have stood when Peter the Great modernized Russia or when Napoleon's troops burned their way across the steppe. It certainly survived the German Wehrmacht's occupation of the region during World War II. Historians may never know when the small church was born, but they know when it died. On September 6, 1956, a Soviet committee labeled it a "building" and not a "church," since it no longer held religious services. Progress, they decided, needed bricks, and so they demolished the church and used its stones to build a brighter, secular future. Villagers, they thought, needed food, education, and healthcare more than the dusty pews and even dustier promises of the Russian Orthodox Church.[2]

Such demolitions were not uncommon. The Soviet Union had been engaged in a carefully managed program of religious destruction since its inception. This was no small task, for religion was more than some superstructure. Its roots were deep, reaching to a time long before industrialization or the Russian state itself. As a result, the policy had two directives. First, the Soviets discredited religion. During the early Cold War a typical laborer in the USSR could visit the Museum of the History of Religion and Atheism in Leningrad, housed in the shell of Our Lady of Kazan Cathedral. There he could peruse an exhibit scientifically rejecting Noah's Ark or laugh with other visitors at the supposed bones of some long dead saint. He and his wife could take in a movie like *The End of the World*, in which a con man claimed to be a living saint, only to disappoint his foolish followers. In school, his children might be assigned the essay topic "Why is it necessary to combat religion?" Depending on the year—and the mood of the current Soviet premier—his family may have been able to worship in a government-licensed church, but such practice could cost him a promotion at work, make his children vulnerable to schoolyard bullying, or earn his wife a stint in a psychiatric ward.[3]

Second, the Soviets offered a substitute system of belief. This laborer could pray at the altar of the "Promethean man" and accept the tenets of "scientific atheism." He could celebrate the Days of Industrialization on December 25 and 26 each year, place a "New Year's tree" in his living quarters, and tell tales of "Grandfather Frost." His children could become "Little Octobrists" in lieu of being baptized, and any deaths in the family could be consecrated with a "Red funeral." If he was a man of strong conviction, he could wait in line for hours to glorify Lenin's Tomb or join one of the many atheist brigades and clubs that met in the larger cities to create antireligious propaganda.[4]

As for the other two kinds of nations, it would be reasonable to assume that the U.S. Army considered America secular. After all, the Constitution regulated state interference in religious affairs, and tax dollars were not a church prop. But Americans and their leaders in the early Cold War knew differently. According to the army, secular nations were places like France—lands of spiritual indifference, ennui, and rising rates of skepticism. Secular nations were not opposed to their demonic counterparts. Frankly, they did not care enough. No, the United States was a covenant nation.

The signs of this covenant nation were equally apparent in the early Cold War as local committees in America also discussed the future of churches in 1956. Consider Chicago's suburbs, where, during the week that the church in Peredel died, four new churches were born. In Lansing, Illinois, Baptists announced plans to build a new $225,000 sanctuary. North of there, in Highland Park, Lutherans celebrated the completion of their own church. Several miles west, in Park Ridge, Catholics broke ground on a half-million-dollar structure with an adjoining grade school. And a few miles to the northwest, Methodist women in Arlington Heights sold cookies and cakes to raise funds for a new church building.[5] Each of these churches still stands today—monuments to one of the greatest periods of religious growth in American history.

When it came to the relationship between religion and society, a typical American housewife in the early Cold War would have had an entirely different experience from the Soviet laborer. If she watched television, listened to the radio, or read a newspaper, she knew that her local, state, and national leaders wanted her to pray and attend religious services. If she drove her children to school, she would see large billboards paid for by the Advertising Council telling her that true Americans had religious faith. If her husband belonged to a veterans club, he may have been involved in "Back to God" campaigns or the installation of memorials to the Ten Commandments in village parks and city courthouses. Her family could go to a movie theater and see *The Ten Commandments* or *Quo Vadis*. Or they could visit traveling exhibitions like the Freedom Train, which housed a special car devoted to America's religious heritage. On Independence Day, she probably heard church bells ringing, reminding her to pray. In school, her children likely said a prayer at the beginning of each day, and, after 1954, they pledged allegiance to a nation "under God." By the late 1950s, when she bought clothes at the department store, groceries at the supermarket, or gasoline at the local filling station, she would pay with paper money bearing the new national motto, "In God We Trust."

One might think that this almost frantic promotion of religion within American society was nothing new. Indeed, the nation was settled in part for religious reasons. Presidents have long called the citizenry to prayer. Americans have always been God loving (and God fearing). But these exhortations—films, speeches, mottos—were anything but organic. They were planned, often carefully. Just as the Soviet elites during the Cold War considered traditional religious faith a hindrance to national interest and worked to destroy it, American elites considered religious faith a bulwark and worked to promote it. The Soviets thought progress required bricks; the Americans thought it required faith. In this way, the experiences of the Russian laborer and American housewife were not so different after all.

Americans after World War II faced a theologically alien enemy. Just as Edmund Burke had assessed the dangers of democratic revolution nearly two centuries earlier, American leaders recognized that Communism was an "armed doctrine," a disease of the psyche and spirit that arms alone could not defeat. Intellectuals, journalists, and theologians who studied Communism in the decades after the Russian Revolution began to conclude that it stood for more than atheism and the destruction of organized religion. They saw it also as a powerful religion of materialism, complete with its own scripture, prophets, and eschatology. Whereas other religious traditions placed faith in the divine, Communism held that people could perfect themselves through an inevitable historical process. In the early years of the Cold War, the Soviets did little to disabuse Americans of this conviction. Each martyred priest and closed church in the Eastern Bloc became yet another confirmation of religion's centrality to the unfolding conflict. American leaders understood the menace of Soviet troops, but they recognized as well that the Cold War would be won or lost not only at the barrel of a gun but also within conflicted souls at home and around the world.[6]

Worried that the spread of Communist ideas would undermine the home front, these leaders concluded that religious faith was one of the most potent arrows in the quiver of domestic security. They did not hesitate to call the Cold War a holy crusade. They fought faith with faith. Religion in America, having had its political, social, and cultural meaning circumscribed for the preceding several decades, could fulfill a function no other institution could. During the first half of the twentieth century, the United States boasted unequaled economic power, but government, business, and religious leaders wondered if their nation was becoming too materialistic and religiously bankrupt to win a holy war. In speeches and advertisements, in pledge drives and military training facilities, in schools and movie theaters, the engineers of spiritual mobilization set out to create a citizenry immune to the atheistic, immoral, and corporeal siren song of Communist ideology. Through their efforts religious faith became the bedrock of freedom and the lodestone of Americanism.

There was no single, convenient committee of religious affairs issuing reports and brainstorming ways to create a more spiritually grounded society. Nor was there a single leader who coordinated such efforts. Instead, when President Dwight D. Eisenhower emphasized the military-industrial complex in his farewell address, he might also have mentioned the spiritual-industrial complex.[7] This nation still wrestles with its legacy. Like its more material cousin, the spiritual-industrial complex was born of assumption and urgency. And like its counterpart, it would have a profound and enduring, though largely underappreciated, effect upon the trajectory of postwar America. The spiritual-industrial complex represented the deliberate and managed use of societal resources to stimulate a religious revival in the late 1940s and 1950s. It was an amalgam of institutions that straddled two worlds—one within the realm of policy decisions and the other within the realm of theological conjecture.

The term is vague, but each word encapsulates an important truth. "Spiritual" emphasizes the fact that just as America mobilized for the Cold War in body, its leaders sought to energize the soul. It signals that American leaders thought that secular institutions and beliefs alone were insufficient to meet society's Cold War needs. American leaders participated in the spiritual-industrial complex to reendow religion with social, cultural, and political meaning. The word also conveys a certain ambivalence, for "spiritual" is vaguer than "religious," and this ambiguity became a topic of increasingly heated argument throughout the 1950s.

The word "industrial" underscores the factory-made approach and contrived feel that emblematized some of the spiritual rhetoric and policies of the early Cold War. The spiritual-industrial complex was the beneficiary of state sanction and commercial talent. It worked to foment a religious revival that was conceived in boardrooms rather than camp meetings, steered by Madison Avenue and Hollywood suits rather than traveling preachers, and measured with a statistical precision that old-time revivalists like Charles Grandison Finney or Dwight Moody would have envied. Its importance came not from the fact that for a brief time in the 1950s record numbers of Americans attended religious services but instead from those institutional interests who eagerly measured such statistics. In this case the impulses of the "saved" were far less instructive than the motives of the "saviors."

Finally, the word "complex" highlights the effort's interwoven motives, actors, and actions. Leaders formed a series of committees, organizations, and advisory boards that put the resources of American bureaucracy behind religious revival and spiritual rededication. At first glance, the endeavor seemed to succeed. Church attendance swelled, sales of the Bible reached all-time highs, and Billy Graham filled Madison Square Garden with a sea of born-again followers. Radios blared religious hits like "The Man Upstairs," "Vaya con Dios," and "Big Fellow in the Sky." A popular toy company developed a doll that could kneel in prayer, and railroads printed grace on their dining-car menus.[8] Visible faith served as an inoculation against the Communist epidemic, and Americans mounted Decalogue monuments in public space as if they were military installations.

Still, a troubling paradox lay within the heart of early Cold War religiosity. Previous religious revivals in American history, like the celebrated Second Great Awakening, had been groundswells managed by well-known religious leaders but carried out largely by local preachers and the flocks they tended. The revivals of the early nineteenth century were in this sense democratized exercises of the religious free market.[9] Far from killing off American spirituality, as some had predicted, the lack of government interference in religion created an incentive for theological originality and compromise as new denominations competed for adherents against well-established competitors. Yet whereas earlier awakenings spread from the bottom up, important components of the 1950s revival came from the top down. In some ways, it resembled an orchestrated makeover painting a veneer of faith across the social and cultural landscape.[10] The irony of the spiritual-industrial complex was that by trying to spark and manage a religious revival, secular leaders may have unwittingly harmed what they sought to protect. They concerned themselves not with the particularities of religious belief but instead with promoting religion in the broadest terms possible. By injecting God into everything from national pledges to currency, they risked weakening religion on the individual and institutional levels. By binding religious faith to the ebb and flow of the Communist peril, they also ensured that if the perceived threat of Communism receded, so too would the urgent need for revival.

Not all theologians, sociologists, and journalists were swept away in the ebullience of 1950s religiosity. Some characterized the revival as "bland" or "directionless." They worried that, by promoting faith for faith's sake, spiritual mobilization had bled American religion of its vigor. Eisenhower's oft-cited assertion, "Our form of government makes no sense unless it is founded in a deeply religious faith, and I don't care what it is," seemed to confirm these fears. As the immediate concerns of Communist victory dissipated and Americans proved safe from Marxist conversion, many lost interest in the spiritual dimensions of anti-Communism. By 1965, less than a third of Americans believed that religion was still increasing its influence upon society.[11]

The most visible signs of national piety so evident in the 1950s may have disappeared in the social turmoil of the 1960s, but the social and cultural residue of the spiritual-industrial complex proved far more indelible. Cold War leaders did not invent this connection between religion and nationalism, but they reified it. The statutes, monuments, and sentiments live on as bulwarks against secularism and reminders that the nation rests upon the groundwork of religious faith. They help explain the growth of religious and political conservatism and continue to serve as valuable tools for those defending the place of religion in American life.

This is a story of two conflicts. Much has been written on the Cold War—its causes, turning points, scoundrels, heroes, and mistakes. In a way, these histories probe a larger, more contentious question: what was the *essence* of the conflict? Was it a battle of narrow state interests or an ideological quest? Did it hinge on the personality quirks of great men or on the impersonal forces of military-industrial complexes? Most works tell us the Cold War was a contest between rival economic and political systems, of humming factories, nuclear submarines, and great technological fortresses carved into mountainsides. Such works suggest that religion played at most a modest role—more of a foil for reasoned belligerency than a starring part. Often in this sense religion comes to represent the worst kind of hysterical anti-Communism. It seems a symptom of early Cold War irrationality that people actually believed religious faith could be a valuable weapon in a conflict typified by red telephones, ballistic missiles, and backyard fallout shelters. Still, for American leaders from Harry S. Truman to Eisenhower and beyond, the employment of spiritual means to achieve Cold War ends was not only rational but essential.[12]

Recently a small but growing collection of studies explore the conflict's religious dimensions. Their point is not to make religion the dominant prism through which the Cold War can be understood but rather to draw attention to the role that religious considerations played within it.[13] This valuable effort has been part of a larger attempt to connect religion to major themes in modern American history.[14] Works on religion and the Cold War often begin *in medias res*, which is to say that they start only after American leaders concluded Communism was a dangerous spiritual adversary. They also tend to focus primarily or even exclusively on foreign policy. While they place religious solutions within the context of the Cold War, they do not place the spiritual battle against Communism in the wider context of religion's ever-changing relationship with American society. This book contributes to this growing field of research by providing a detailed background to Cold War religious solutions, focusing on domestic policies and institutions, offering a wide context through which the spiritual-industrial complex—born of Cold War agitation but conceived in the muddiness of older arguments—can be better understood, and exploring the political and cultural effects of such an effort.

An even broader conflict is addressed in the pages that follow: the conflict between America the secular nation and America the covenant nation. This tension is as old as the country itself. It has played out with different words in different times during the debates of Thomas Jefferson and John Adams, H. L. Mencken and William Jennings Bryan, and Sam Harris and James Dobson. The difference does not turn on court cases or pulpit pleas or whether children pray before class. It is a state of mind best articulated in a simple question: does society need religion? Americans have never agreed on the answer, but during the early Cold War, they came closer to consensus than at any other time in modern history.[15]

The distinction between secular and covenant nations does not lie in the height of walls between church and state. That is perhaps the narrowest accounting, and even during the spiritual-industrial complex's brightest bloom, few American leaders thought it wise to tear down such barriers entirely. Rather, they understood that the best gauge was the degree to which society depended upon religion, despite the impossibility of precise calculations. The famed mythologist Joseph Campbell once suggested that the answer could be found by simply staring at the skylines of world cities. During the Middle Ages, he observed, the tallest buildings were churches—a physical manifestation of the church's importance in ordering society. But churches gave way to the towers of politicians, and those structures were eventually overshadowed by the growth of businessmen's skyscrapers.

The history of religion's relationship to society in Western Europe more or less supports Campbell's simple conclusion. It has been the story of covenanted societies becoming secular ones. Religion was once the primary explainer of the unknown, reliever of the sick, sustainer of the poor, patron of the arts, ruler of the state, teacher of the young, and "sacred canopy."[16] But as society developed, new secular institutions emerged that specialized in satisfying these basic needs. Science furnished explanations for the unknown, social-service agencies succored the indigent, and secular schools entered the field of education. With its function and meaning increasingly constricted, religion slowly lost its influence upon society. The gilded sanctuaries of Western Europe ministered to an ever dwindling flock, and where once the church shaped policy in Old World capitals, it became a political vestige.[17] The process of secularization remains the most fruitful theory for explaining the effect of modernization upon religion. On its simplest level, secularization theory posits that as societies develop, the significance of religion will decline.[18] The theory is not without its critics, though, and the American religious experience, in which the last several decades have punctuated the power, organization, and resilience of religion, has proven a jarring anomaly.[19]

Perhaps there is more to secularization than empty pews. Religious vitality can be measured in different ways.[20] Americans may attend church and believe in God at a constant rate, but these measurements do not entail that religion's function within society has remained unchanged. A steepled sanctuary may stand for centuries in the same New England village, but its meaning and place in society have not been constant. Some have proposed a theory of "multiple modernities" to explain why the process of secularization sometimes follows disparate trajectories in particular cultural environments. Others have objected to the linear concept of secularization altogether, arguing that the process is cyclical.[21] One new theory argues that, instead of being the handmaiden for modernization, secularization is "the outcome of a struggle between contending groups of conflicting interests seeking to control social knowledge and institutions."[22] As a process influenced by individuals, social changes, and historical events, it incorporates a modicum of chance and uncertainty. More importantly, this approach views secularization as a conscious social act, not simply as an unstoppable social force.

This book treats secularization as the process by which the perceived role of religion diminishes, making religious ideas and institutions less a part of any solution to societal problems. Religion is not rendered meaningless, and it may retain meaning in the lives of individuals. Some denominations may grow during even the most pronounced periods of secularization. More important, if conducive social environments and specific actions can make religion seem increasingly vestigial to society, another set of circumstances and decisions can reendow religion with meaning, particularly when the secular alone is particularly unequipped to solve a major problem. Not only can it slow or stop, the process of secularization can reverse, a process labeled "sacralization." Like secularization, the reendowment of religion with perceived political, social, economic, or intellectual value on the societal level is often the product of deliberate action.[23] Scholars have often studied the process by which covenant societies become secular ones, but there is value also in examining a secular society that strives to become a covenant nation. America tried to do exactly that in the early Cold War.

The Spiritual-Industrial Complex is divided into three parts, though many of the movements, ideas, and individuals discussed in one section invariably reappear in the others. Part One examines the circumstances and perceptions that led American leaders to the conclusion that sacralization was an important condition for Cold War victory. The first chapter uses the story of three communities to illustrate early twentieth-century secularization—a time when a host of secular institutions began assuming functions once the primary domain of religious institutions. Chapter 2 traces the birth and development of the idea that Communism was more than a political and economic system. References to "atheistic Communism" appear often in Cold War rhetoric, but American leaders came to understand the Marxist doctrine as much more than the lack of belief in God. Without a religious understanding of Communism, Americans would have still found themselves in an ideological struggle, but one in which religion would have been peripheral.

Part Two focuses upon the rhetoric, policies, and actions of institutions that made up the spiritual-industrial complex, with each chapter concentrating upon different groups of American leaders. The third chapter centers upon political institutions. It examines how popular ideas of Communism as a rival religious system of belief impacted early Cold War political rhetoric and how this rhetoric translated into policy decisions. Chapter 4 canvasses the thoughts and deeds of national security institutions. Security experts recognized that America could not win a war of "asymmetric zeal." They feared the messianic fanaticism of the Soviets and openly questioned whether the American fight for simple state interest was enough. Along these lines, the military implemented new training techniques that emphasized religion. At the same time, American propagandists began recognizing that religious belief could be highly instrumental in the Cold War. Chapter 5 analyzes another set of institutions, including education, the media, corporations, voluntary associations, and entertainment. As these erstwhile agents of secularization recognized the importance of religion in the Cold War, they lent their social and cultural influence to the cause of spiritual mobilization in American society.

Part Three analyzes the outcome of the spiritual-industrial complex. Chapter 6 appraises the revival of religious interest that coincided with the sacralization of American society, paying particular attention to critics of the spiritual-industrial complex and explaining why the endeavor had faded by the dawn of the 1960s. The final chapter explores the spiritual-industrial complex's legacy by detailing a 1962 controversy in one Southern California suburb. It shows how religious arguments marshaled against Communism during the 1950s provided a platform from which both modern religious and political conservatism grew.

Pick up a newspaper or peruse the latest edition of the World Values Survey, and you are likely see some variation of a simple question: why is America so religious? Often concealed within such a query are assumptions of both permanence and inevitability. From Puritan dreams to evangelical rallies, from Alexis de Tocqueville's observations to the recently lauded Baylor Religious Survey, from Jonathan Edwards to Billy Graham, it seems that religion has remained a constant force in America's national journey. The structure of church-state relations may have ensured the vitality of American religious expression, but the process by which religious faith has been fused with popular conceptions of Americanism was not brought about by some movement of destiny's hand. The early Cold War period covers only one stretch of this evolution, but an important one nonetheless, since for millions constantly bombarded with the message that the religious could not be Communists, it was a short logical step to the authoritative axiom that the irreligious could not be true Americans.

If what follows is construed as a religious history, to some it will seem peculiar. Secular, not religious, leaders and institutions are the main actors, and that is the point. This is not a tale of how individuals found faith, how religion affected their daily lives, or how denominations adapted and competed over time. Throughout American history, religious institutions have been the greatest advocates of religion's importance to American society. During the early Cold War, much the same could be said. But this book focuses upon the religious advocacy of other, more unlikely, institutions. Rare are the moments when so many organizations unite in an effort to make a country more religious. Why did they act? What did they do? Did it work?

The first answer lies in the decades before the Cold War. The final answer is still a matter of debate.

PART ONE

ROOTS

1

A Colossus of Straw

"The jack-of-all-trades cannot compete with the specialist."
—Eduard C. Lindeman, 1929

The messenger of spiritual warning came to America in 1947 not as a fiery preacher or glib politician but rather in the guise of a graying, bushy-browed, and tweedy English historian. Halfway through the completion of his mammoth twelve-volume study of the rise and fall of civilizations, Arnold J. Toynbee embarked on a U.S. speaking tour, warning that Western Civilization, including the United States, was on the verge of collapse.

His was a work of astounding analytical idiosyncrasy, not only a work of history, but a jeremiad as well.[1] His magnum opus, *A Study of History*, combined psychology and theology with historical inquiry, downplaying national borders in favor of societal groupings based on religious belief. It asserted that the energies of God and Satan formed the dialectic upon which civilizations prospered and collapsed. It painted a bleak picture of decline but rejected the determinism of forebears like Edward Gibbon and Oswald Spengler. Of the twenty-six civilizations Toynbee identified in world history, he argued that only five remained active in the twentieth century: Western, Orthodox, Islamic, Hindu, and Far Eastern. According to the prophetic professor, all were in varying stages of death.[2]

The unstoppable and often disastrous decline of a civilization is somehow more captivating than its slow ascent. Toynbee fascinated Americans by offering them a front-row seat to their own demise. He argued that the decline of civilizations began not with economic or military overreach but instead with a "schism in the soul." Spiritual insolvency preceded material collapse. As the wave of spiritual sickness reached its peak, Toynbee believed, two kinds of saviors appeared. The "savior-archaist" promised salvation through a return to an imagined past, while the "savior-futurist" promised salvation through a leap to an imagined

15

future. For Toynbee, Gandhi represented the savior-archaist and Lenin the savior-futurist. But both were false messiahs. For him, the one true savior in world history was Jesus Christ. More importantly, he contended, there was a connection between spiritual breakdown at the individual and societal levels. The schism in the soul began with individuals, and healing had to start there as well.

Toynbee owed his sudden popularity to shameless promotion and careful argumentative streamlining by Henry R. Luce's publishing empire. The professor appeared on the cover of *Time* in March 1947 accompanied by an obsequious article proclaiming that all history would henceforth be dated "B.T." and "A.T."— Before Toynbee and After Toynbee.[3] The issue coincided with the release of an abridged version of *A Study of History*. But at nearly six hundred pages, this "layman's version" was still too dense to leave a lasting imprint on the American psyche. *Time*'s editors, most notably Whittaker Chambers, condensed Toynbee's arguments into a four-thousand-word cover story, and in doing so they struck a nerve. America and its spiritual health became central elements of Toynbee's conclusions, a manipulation that served Luce's ends but distorted the nuance of the professor's volumes.[4] Nevertheless, church leaders, educators, politicians, and businessmen flooded the offices of Time, Inc. with congratulatory notes and requests for reprints. The Englishman went on to deliver public addresses to overflowing crowds.[5]

The spiritual-industrial complex took root at the confluence of two streams of thought. The first, embodied by these interpretations of Toynbee, watered it with notions that American society had become too secularized—a conclusion drawn from observations across society large and small. American leaders, both secular and religious, wondered if their nation's spiritual growth had not kept pace with its material development. They came to comprehend power as both physical and spiritual. While they acknowledged the United States was indeed reaching the height of its material power, they also worried that such victories of the flesh were purchased with retreats of the soul. Some called it "psychic lethargy" or "spiritual bankruptcy." Few articulated the dilemma better than Brigadier General C. T. Lanham, director of the staff and Personnel Policy Board for the Defense Department. "Over and over again," he reflected in 1949, "gigantic concentrations of physical power have gone down in defeat before a lesser strength propelled by conviction. . . . The Goliaths have perished at the hands of the Davids." He continued:

> Therefore, without deprecating our armed might and the evil circumstances that make it necessary, I contend that we must be increasingly vigilant lest we come to evaluate our strength and our security exclusively in terms of material power. . . . To do otherwise is to build a colossus of straw.[6]

Fears that America might become a colossus of straw seem particularly strange given the immense industrial and military capacity that the United States enjoyed immediately after World War II. In 1946 Winston Churchill informed his transatlantic allies that their nation stood at the "pinnacle of world power." This was no expression of back-patting flattery but a sober calculation. Not only did America have sole possession of atomic weaponry, it contained half the world's industrial capacity, held two-thirds of all gold reserves, produced twice as much oil as the rest of the planet combined, harbored the largest merchant marine with the most powerful navy to protect it, and had developed a dazzling array of technology. The United States was the only major nation to raise its standard of living during the war.[7]

Such warnings of secularization may also seem ill conceived and overwrought. Church membership in America remained relatively high throughout the decades before the Cold War. Swelled by the influx of immigrants from southern and eastern Europe, America's Catholic Church grew into the nation's largest religious institution. While immigrant Catholics built an urban empire, preachers set the rural nights afire with charismatic revivals. The Holiness movement sprouted quickly, and fundamentalism battled modernism in Protestant pulpits throughout the land. Church membership rosters and contributions to religious organizations show that, if anything, Americans had managed to become even more religious by the eve of World War II.[8]

Yet for those Americans who participated in and observed the spiritual-industrial complex, its most remarkable feature was a sharp contrast with the recent past. For them, religion as a societal institution was losing its capstone quality in several important ways. Religious leaders knew it. Political leaders knew it. Journalists knew it. And many citizens knew it too.

In order to appreciate an early Cold War America in which religion was considered a solution to the problems facing society, one must first comprehend an early twentieth-century America where religion was not. Whether paranoid or prescient, this sense of secularization and fear of its consequences is essential to understanding the spiritual-industrial complex. Reconstructing such a mindset requires the retelling of American religious history in the early twentieth century using the perceptions of observers interested in religion—a catalog, however impressionistic, of the events and trends that led to such a mood.

In the decades before the Cold War, the process of secularization was noted in communities across the nation. Three of them—a small city, a town, and the national capital—have been chosen to provide entry points into the hopes, fears, and realities of secularization. Though separated by distance, demographics, and culture, these places help explain why the Cold War seemed so dangerous, why the spiritual-industrial complex seemed so fresh, and why a tame academic like Toynbee seemed so prophetic.

This colossus-of-straw image reached maturity in the early Cold War, but it was born decades earlier in places like Muncie, Indiana. During the 1920s, more than 35,000 people called Muncie home. Many of their parents and grandparents had come there from the industrial centers of the East after coal miners struck a rich deposit of natural gas a few miles north of town. A boom town in the 1880s, by the 1920s it resembled less a kinetic hive than a placid, fattened setting for a Sinclair Lewis novel. The working class spent their days in the foundries and plants. The business class spent their days in the banks and offices. No matter their social stratus, children there were better educated and generally more secure than their parents had been. People in Muncie worked hard, and for good reason, since a typical household required nearly $2,000 per year to remain solvent. They did not work constantly, though. Weekends in Muncie were a time for leisure, whether watching movies, swimming in community pools, or exploring simple country roads.[9]

These aspects of life in Muncie are well known because of an experiment that was conducted there during the 1920s. Together with a staff of researchers, sociologists Robert and Helen Lynd descended upon the city with the mission of analyzing all of its cultural facets. Social surveys were nothing new, but the Lynds were not content to conduct a garden-variety investigation. They and their research team would become part of the community—entering homes, asking personal questions, and attending club meetings all around town. It was unprecedented in scope. Five years and hundreds of interviews later, they published the groundbreaking book *Middletown: A Study in American Culture*, which detailed the rapid transformation of American culture over a thirty-five-year period.[10]

The Lynds devoted a sizable portion of their study to religion. A cursory inspection revealed healthy signs of religious devotion, with forty-two churches punctuating the city's modest skyline. But beneath this veneer of visible piety, they concluded, the position of religion in society had changed significantly since 1890. Muncie's ministers resigned themselves to falling rates of attendance. Only 11 percent of men and 18 percent of women attended weekly religious services. When the researchers interviewed those who did not attend church, many said that they were too tired, wanted to rest, or enjoyed other activities on Sundays. Some argued that recent scientific developments had mortally wounded religious belief.[11] This trend was echoed in the findings of other social scientists.

Despite religious census data that demonstrated increased church membership throughout the Progressive Era, sociologists conducting community studies in the early 1900s noted the decay of religion as a linchpin institution within society. The erosion was most conspicuous in the rural Northeast, Midwest, and West. In a time before opinion polls and detailed studies like *Middletown*, researchers focused on rates of religious participation. The eminent

Progressive Gifford Pinchot noted a 35 percent decrease in the church attendance of Tompkins County, New York, between 1890 and 1910. In Windsor County, Vermont, average attendance hovered near 19 percent of the total population in 1910 and fell to 10 percent by 1921. The Great Plains fared little better. In Sedgwick County, Kansas, less than a quarter of all residents belonged to a church. Regular church attendance of Protestants and Catholics in one Rocky Mountain county was fewer than 2 percent by the 1920s. A comprehensive study of six different geographic regions funded by the Institute of Social and Religious Research concluded that the role of religion within rural society was disintegrating. Outside the South, rural America rapidly lost places of worship in the early twentieth century, leaving many communities churchless. These observed problems extended to America's growing cities. Often cited as examples of religious vitality, they contained large numbers of inhabitants devoid of religious association. In 1920s Columbus, Ohio, for example, nearly four in ten adults denied affiliation with any church.[12]

Beneath simple declines in attendance, the Lynds recognized an even more ominous trend, noting that the position and role of religion within society had rapidly eroded in a little more than a generation. "As changes proceed at accelerating speed in other sections of the city's life," they observed, "the lack of dominance of religious beliefs becomes more apparent." They concluded that while in theory religious beliefs retained their prominence, "actually, large regions of Middletown's life appear uncontrolled by them."[13] Ministers who once paid frequent pastoral calls to the sick found their role supplanted by secular charity bureaus and the new visiting nurse service. Citizens devoted their time and energy to men's and women's clubs rather than the church. Secular marriages were on the rise. Although there were still many churches in Muncie, in many cases drawing increased contributions and building new additions, the Lynds believed that religion was becoming an ever fainter voice in the growing chorus of modern America. These observations were not unique to one city in Indiana.

By the early twentieth century, the manifold roles of religion in society were increasingly played by a host of other developing institutions. Eduard C. Lindeman, a churchman who studied American religion in the 1920s, concluded that "the church need not do what other institutions are already doing well." He sounded an even starker warning: "The jack-of-all-trades cannot compete with the specialist. The church which operates cafeterias, theatres, gymnasiums, nurseries, cooking-classes, et cetera, may become a useful social center, but it will thereby risk losing its capacity for ministering to religious needs."[14] One study in 1916, for instance, concluded that religious leaders who broadened the function of their churches to advocate for social justice suffered significant losses in attendance, while those whose ministers stuck to theology enjoyed fuller pews on Sunday.[15] When religion increasingly competed against other institutions specifically designed to carry out its formerly uncontested functions, its role in society changed. As Lindeman recognized, American secularization from 1900 to 1945 was primarily driven by the process of differentiation—the growth of institutions and outlets that specialized in performing tasks once the province of religion.

Of all its functions in American society, the historical role of religion as the incubator and guardian of public morality was paramount. Speaking beneath the canvas of a Chautauqua tent, a minister in Muncie invoked the timelessness of religious wisdom and morality. "All human philosophy, reasoning, is alike," he opined; "it is no more than the newspaper—just for the hour; but the Bible, read as a child would read it, is for the ages."[16] From the early days of the republic, the fledgling nation's elite looked for a bond that would fortify society against forces of individualism. Morality served as this societal glue, and America's religious institutions were its essential guardians and propagators. In his farewell address, George Washington noted that, "of all the dispositions and habits which lead to political prosperity, Religion and morality are indispensable supports." "Reason and experience," he continued, "both forbid us to expect that national morality can prevail in exclusion of religious principle."[17] In much of the century that followed, religious leaders remained at the forefront of social cohesion and necessary reform.[18]

In a century of rapid economic, social, and cultural change, religious institutions could offer American society an anchor. But shortly after the Civil War, the theories of philosophers like Herbert Spencer cast a long shadow over both religion and academia. Spencer was most famous for coining the term "survival of the fittest," but his conceptualization of society as a social organism proved significant as well. If society and its institutions were akin to living creatures, they would adapt and evolve over time. This brought with it a pressing question: how could religious institutions claim guardianship of eternal truths if they themselves were constantly evolving?[19]

American sociologists absorbed Spencer's conclusions. In December 1909, William Graham Sumner created a minor sensation when he delivered his presidential address to the American Sociological Society, entitled "Religion and the Mores." He argued that the environment, not religious institutions, was most critical in establishing moral codes. "Nobody has ever done what the Bible says," Sumner said. "What men have always done, if they tried to do right, was to conform to the mores of the group and the time." The argument had profound implications. Morality was not the product of absolute and eternal truth emanating from a powerful institution. "Everything must change," said Sumner, "Religion is no exception."[20]

Sumner's conception was part of a larger paradigm shift in the social sciences that began in the late nineteenth century. He and other giants in American sociology like Lester Ward, Albion Small, and Edward A. Ross came from devoutly religious families, but in time they became evangelists for secularization and the triumph of science.[21] Some of their colleagues analyzed the Bible through a sociological lens, arguing that the idea of God was a mere "incident of social process." Others contended that human conscience seemed fluid rather than fixed by religious doctrine. At the same time, economists like Simon N. Patten, a professor at the University of Pennsylvania's Wharton School, argued that the evolution of morality was intimately tied to economic laws rather than religious truths.[22]

In 1929, Walter Lippmann, America's foremost journalist, appraised his nation's moral economy and found it deficient. In his book *A Preface to Morals*, he composed a bittersweet elegy to the old American faith—a faith which had operated with certainty and provided indisputable facts. As this ancestral religious order broke down in the early twentieth century, he observed, religious leaders no longer wielded moral authority within society. "This is the first age, I think," Lippmann wrote, "when the circumstances of life have conspired with the intellectual habits of the time to render any fixed and authoritative belief unfeasible to large masses of men." The "acids of modernity" worked continuously to render traditional religious morality obsolete. According to Lippmann, Americans did not feel liberated from the confines of religious dogmatism. They craved moral guideposts, but found themselves pulled apart by the modern cacophony of exhortations.[23] No longer could religious leaders claim the same authority as guardians, inculcators, and disseminators of morals.

If people in Muncie, and by extension America, looked less to religious teachings for a moral order or code of conduct, where might they turn? Muncie's business class, the Lynds observed, eagerly circumscribed the role of religion in the community, blocking religious leaders from membership in civic organizations like the Rotary Club and subscribing to a "go-getter" ethos in which progress could be achieved without dependence on religion. They attended church less frequently, and some of them considered religion a relic of the past. The ministry, they thought, had "played out." Speaking of religious training, one businessman was particularly forceful. "I'd never advise a boy to go into it," he said.[24]

Nor were observations like these specific to Muncie. When Christian Gauss, dean of the college at Princeton and a renowned literature professor, surveyed America's religious landscape in early 1934, he noted that "the church has been crowded out of its central position and is invariably overtopped by the skyscraper which houses our business men and lawyers." His observations turned from physical comparison to psychological transformation. Most remarkable for Gauss was the evolution of the American role model. Instead of looking to religious leaders for inspiration and guidance, twentieth-century Americans turned to the biographies and words of industrialists like Henry Ford for wisdom and virtue.[25]

Advertising executive Bruce Barton's best-selling *The Man Nobody Knows* illustrated well the transformation Gauss articulated. His 1925 work claimed to discover the real Jesus—not the "pale young man with flabby forearms and a sad expression" nailed to Sunday-school walls across the nation, but instead the dynamic youthful go-getter who "built the greatest organization of all." In this new account, Jesus was a powerful executive, organizer, socialite, advertising wizard, and outdoor enthusiast who was born poor but built a business empire through hard work. Barton turned the New Testament into a Horatio Alger tale. The message was well suited to the middle-class in Middletowns across America, and by making Jesus relevant to twentieth-century America, Barton underscored the growing influence of businessmen as moral leaders.[26]

No business leader loomed larger over the American moral landscape than Henry Ford. The father of the American automobile industry and the assembly line, Ford, with his self-made success, humanitarian policies, and penchant for publicity, was at the center of national attention for much of the early twentieth century. The automaker's celebrity catapulted to new heights on January 5, 1914, when he announced the Ford Motor Company was doubling the paychecks of all workers. The five-dollar day cemented Ford's credentials as the nation's foremost industrial reformer and folk hero.[27]

That year Ford established himself as a moral leader with the publication of his anticigarette pamphlet *The Case Against the Little White Slaver*, which associated smoking with moral erosion. He had already forbidden salesmen at his dealerships from smoking, a habit he viewed as dirty and an obstacle to success. Ford reserved more ire for alcohol. He argued that drinking destroyed character, hampered individual liberty, created poverty, and ruined families. On a more practical level, alcoholism made workers less productive. "The executive who drinks cannot so plan that high wages will result in low prices," Ford wrote, "while the workman who drinks cannot work intelligently enough to earn high wages."[28] Beliefs like these were shared by other business leaders like John D. Rockefeller and George Perkins. Indeed, Prohibition was as much a triumph of corporate clamor as it was religious fervor.[29]

But Ford did more than simply campaign against vice. He developed and propagated a distinctive moral worldview independent of traditional religious institutions. Machinery was "the new Messiah," and the industrialist optimistically claimed that technology was "accomplishing in the world what man has failed to do by preaching, propaganda, or the written record." Moral progress did not come from religion, revivals, or awakenings. Rather, for Ford, the rules of economics forced change and compelled progress. During the Cold War viewpoints like these were labeled communistic, but in the 1920s they curried favor.

Ford recognized the influence of businessmen on society. "Business men do not think of themselves as leaders in social movements, but they are," he wrote. "They have more influence on society than politicians, schoolmasters, or clergymen, because their contact is constant and their influence unavoidable."[30]

It was probably no coincidence that the minister at the Muncie Chautauqua deprecated the evanescent nature of newspapers. One of his colleagues summed up the feeling best when he sadly noted that "in the old days people went to their preachers for consolation, information, and inspiration. They still come to us for consolation, but go to the newspapers for information and inspiration."[31] In the late 1870s American universities began offering courses in modern journalism, and professional organizations proliferated.[32] The number of American cities with a daily newspaper leaped from 353 in 1900 to 913 in 1930. Monthly periodicals nearly doubled in circulation over the same period, and quarterlies tripled. By 1931, nine of the nation's most popular women's magazines claimed subscriptions of over one million. As secular magazine and newspaper subscriptions exploded, advertisers looked less to the religious press.[33]

The professionalization of journalism coincided with significant changes in the media's relationship to religion. In his contribution to the government-sponsored study *Recent Social Trends*, Hornell Hart noted significant losses of readership by religious periodicals and impressive gains by scientific journals. Protestant magazine circulation fell from a peak of 371,000 in 1910 to 276,000 in 1930. Over the same period, circulation of popular scientific magazines increased from 392,000 to 1,243,000.[34] Even more telling was the frequency with which popular magazines discussed religious topics. Between 1905 and 1909, 17.1 percent of all articles in women's magazines discussed church work. By 1930 this proportion fell to less than 1 percent.[35] Beyond the diminishing frequency of religious articles was the more striking trend of decreasing favorability toward religion. A random sampling revealed that while 78 percent of all articles were favorable toward Christianity in 1905, only 33 percent remained so in 1930. In intellectual magazines such as the *Atlantic Monthly*, the percentage of approval dropped to a paltry 18 percent.[36] Statistics like these are no doubt open to interpretation, but they nonetheless point to a major trend in secularization. More Americans received information from the media than ever before, and the information they obtained increasingly minimized and assailed the authority of American religion.[37]

Few journalists cast larger shadows upon the relationship between American society and religion than H. L. Mencken. Journalist, satirist, iconoclast, hero, and villain, he became perhaps the country's favorite pundit and critic.[38] From his perch at the Baltimore *Evening Sun*, Mencken proudly used his influence to wage a continual battle against the role of religion in American society. His most comprehensive and blistering attack came in his 1930 book *Treatise on the Gods*. Like William Graham Sumner, he construed religion less as a fixed truth than an institution continually shaped by society. In its steadfast refusal to adapt to changing truths, Mencken argued, Christianity bore an "unyielding hostility . . . to all true human progress." As with Lippmann and other intellectuals, he seriously addressed the diminishing role of religion as moral custodian. Unlike Lippmann, he contended that American religion was an obstacle to a morally sound society. "The priest," Mencken once wrote, "is the most immoral of men, for he is always willing to sacrifice every other sort of good to the one good of his Arcanum."[39]

Journalists were not the only opinion makers offsetting their pens against religion. While the Lynds were still conducting their research, Sinclair Lewis, America's leading author in the 1920s, informed his good friend Mencken that he would write a novel on American religion. His rendering of the crass, alcoholic, womanizing, and opportunistic preacher Elmer Gantry was censured by the *New York Times* for operating as propaganda rather than a work of fiction. The work specifically targeted fundamentalists, but liberal Protestant leaders recognized it as an assault on religion in general. Still, in the words of *Literary Digest*, *Elmer Gantry* sold like "peanuts at a circus."[40] Lewis's hostility toward religion, like Mencken's, stemmed from its opposition to progress. He criticized the way that organized religion turned "young, fresh emotion-charged thought from reality to devotion . . . while a whole world of nobility and need waits outside."[41] Elmer Gantry's ethos was made more despicable by comparison to one of Lewis' earlier protagonists—the scientist Martin Arrowsmith. Though *Arrowsmith* skewered the American medical profession, for the first time Lewis rendered an admirable character. Readers recognized Arrowsmith as an idealistic hero, a prototypical young and energetic mind who lent his talents to progress, and a far cry from the cynical and senseless devotion of Gantry. Through these portrayals, Lewis offered Americans a fictional version of the choice that journalists formulated during the Scopes trial. They could follow Gantry or Arrowsmith, but not both.

For those who feared spiritual attenuation, the colossus of straw matured in towns like Dayton, Tennessee. As the crow flies, it is 325 miles from Muncie. Both were boom towns during the late nineteenth century. But while Muncie grew into a small city, Dayton dwindled beside the banks of the Tennessee River. At one point the town boasted a population of 3,000, but by 1925 only 1,800 souls lived there. Guarantees of industrialization and markets connected by railroad seemed little more than whispered promises from another generation by then. The local economy ran on iron and coal from the nearby mines and strawberries picked from the surrounding valley. For a town of its small size, Dayton did boast an impressive three-story courthouse made of red bricks. Shaded by oaks, it stood in the village center, flanked by empty store fronts of businesses that never came.

It was in this courthouse that one of the most important microcosms of early twentieth-century secularization played out. In a crowded courtroom heated by the July sun, the smoldering controversies of modern America burst into flames before a worldwide audience. Three-time presidential candidate William Jennings Bryan called the faithful to battle. Clarence Darrow, America's most famous defense attorney, stood in the opposite corner. Here was a battle of science against religion, liberal theology versus fundamentalism, and modernity against tradition.[42]

In towns like Dayton during the days of Prohibition, the closest thing to a saloon was the local drugstore. It made perfect sense, then, that the entire episode began in the spring of 1925 inside Robinson's drugstore on Main Street with a group of local lawyers, school officials, and a diminutive Yankee engineer who oversaw the sputtering mines. They came to discuss the Butler Bill, which passed the Tennessee legislature earlier that year and made it illegal for teachers in public schools to teach any doctrine that denied the biblical story of creation. After receiving a promise of legal support from the American Civil Liberties Union, the conspirators drafted a young high school teacher named John T. Scopes who openly taught the theory of evolution in his biology classes. Scopes volunteered to be arrested on charges brought by the drugstore cabal.[43] The Associated Press carried the story the following day.[44]

Scopes only faced a fine for his actions, but his opponents and supporters soon drew imposing battle lines. On July 7, William Jennings Bryan, perhaps the nation's best known defender of the "old time religion," arrived in Dayton wearing a pith helmet, slurped an ice cream soda at Robinson's drugstore, and proclaimed that the trial would be a "duel to the death." Bryan's words conveyed growing disillusionment with secularization. For him the authority of religion in America was at stake. He feared that progressive education and the recent scientific breakthroughs were teaching society to view religion as a superstition. While in Dayton, he preached to local congregations, attended community events, and gave frequent interviews.[45]

The case's outcome was never in doubt, but this did not prevent the trial from descending into a carnival of the absurd. For eight days a local judge presided over a raucous court.[46] Darrow and Bryan spoke in a small, crowded courtroom, but both men knew they were performing before a national audience. Each morning their speeches appeared in newspapers across the country, particularly Darrow's famous examination of Bryan on the witness stand during which the Boy Orator of the Platte asserted that Jonah was swallowed by a whale, Joshua made the sun stand still, and the world was only five thousand years old. Darrow derided these beliefs as a "fool religion."[47] Nonetheless, on

Tuesday, July 21, 1925, the jury found Scopes guilty, and the judge imposed a $100 fine. Five days later Bryan died of a stroke while taking a nap.

Legally the Scopes trial accomplished nothing. The case never made it to the U.S. Supreme Court, as the ACLU had hoped, and Tennessee's highest court refused to overturn the law. But in broader terms, the trial portended the colossus of straw. It seemed to confirm the secularization of information dissemination and opinion making that the Lynds observed in Muncie. John Scopes's travails would have been an interesting but isolated case if not for the media. In less than one month, an army of journalists wired more than two million words to presses around the nation as twenty-two telegraphers worked nonstop in a sweat-drenched Nashville storeroom.[48] Over the course of the trial, major American newspapers printed hundreds of articles and excerpts from the case. Columnists assailed the South and rural America but reserved the greatest indignation for the role of religion in Dayton.

Most critically, the press painted the Scopes trial as a case of religion attempting to reassert control over the state. A piece for the *Nation* noted that a change in American government from democracy to theocracy was not as farfetched as many believed. Even Robert R. McCormick's archconservative *Chicago Daily Tribune* rebuked the religious "zealots who . . . clamp custom and opinion down on the nation by constitutional amendment and by statute." Other editorials expressed fear that the Tennessee law was the first salvo in a coming war between religion and the state.[49] In his last dispatch from Tennessee, Mencken warned the nation to guard against religious fanaticism. "It serves notice on the country," he wrote, "that Neanderthal man is organizing in these forlorn backwaters of the land, led by a fanatic, rid of sense, and devoid of conscience."[50]

At its heart the Scopes trial was about the collision of two trends that affected the role of religion within early twentieth-century American society: progressive education and scientific developments. At the time of the trial, there were fifty thousand high school students in Tennessee and two million nationwide. These numbers would seem small were it not for the fact that only ten thousand had been enrolled in Tennessee high schools in 1910, with only 200,000 in high schools nationwide in 1890.[51] The same was true for Muncie, where high school enrollment climbed from 8 percent to 25 percent between 1890 and 1924.[52]

The history of American education is also the story of religion's changing role in society. In colonial times education was the domain of the Church, and religious groups founded many of America's early schools and colleges to educate youth in the reading of scripture and provide adequate training for future ministers. In 1837, Massachusetts secretary of education Horace Mann began a public campaign for adoption of the common school, the world's first system of publicly funded education. Mann thought free public education necessary to the preservation of American democracy. The common-school movement followed on the heels of disestablishment throughout New England, and Mann knew that public taxes could not support specific religious beliefs. At the same time he conceived of public schools as inculcators of national virtue and morality, an enterprise in which religion would be indispensable. The solution was nonsectarianism. Students would read the Bible and receive instruction in general Protestant principles.[53]

Catholics established their own parallel educational system, but Mann's marriage of Protestantism and education remained largely unchallenged for much of the nineteenth century. In an 1859 address, the vice president of the National Teachers Association argued that "the place of Christianity in education . . . is first and foremost."[54] Educational elites widely believed that religious instruction in schools was the only means of endowing pupils with the character and virtue necessary to benefit society. In 1859, the year that Darwin published *Origin of the Species*, the National Teachers Association adopted a resolution declaring that "the inculcation of the Christian religion is necessary to the happiness of the people and the perpetuity of our institutions."[55]

In the waning years of the nineteenth century, public educators began to rethink their once bold assertions. Gone were the bumbling Ichabod Cranes of the early republic and the Horace Manns of antebellum society, replaced by a new professional class of teachers and administrative progressives who shared the belief that education was a science.[56] Instruction in all things sacred rapidly vanished from the classroom, leading the U.S. Commissioner of Education to conclude in his 1892 report that "religious education has almost ceased in the public schools, and it is rapidly disappearing from the program of colleges and preparatory schools."[57] The president of Northwestern University observed twelve years later that "it is perfectly evident that this country will never permit the church as such to control in any vital way . . . the higher education of the community."[58] Students began to profess growing doubts about religious truth. A 1924 study conducted at the University of Washington revealed that more than a third of students believed that Jesus was only human, and nearly two-thirds viewed the Bible as a mythological account. The same research found that an astounding 62 percent of seniors believed that Jesus was but a man.[59]

This trend was not the result of some carefully crafted scheme by American educators to subvert religion.[60] Rather, the place of religion in schools faded due the decline of classical education, a demand for more rigorous scholarship, and the growing fears of sectarianism and religious irrationality in public institutions.[61] For the president of the University of Chicago, divorcing religion from education was obvious for two simple reasons: "The public schools belong to all the people," and "theology . . . can by no means be disassociated from sectarianism."[62] The U.S. commissioner of education was more forceful. In a 1903 discussion before the National Education Association convention, he argued that "the principle of religious instruction is authority; that of secular instruction is demonstration and verification. It is obvious that these two principles should not be brought into the same school, but separated as widely as possible."[63] Even George U. Wenner, the preeminent advocate for religious instruction in public schools, recognized the primacy of these arguments when he wrote that "we must have public schools, open to all children without regard to creed."[64]

Had public educators abandoned Mann's vision altogether, they would have fallen victim to what religious leaders came to call secularism. But educators continued to believe that the inculcation of morality and virtue was the chief task of public schools, an end that could be achieved in a classroom devoid of religion. The conviction that public schools could become society's most important moral custodians was expressed by the title of character education. In 1907 the National Education Association Executive Committee on Moral Training concluded that "the end aim of all education is the development of character; education is growth toward intellectual and moral perfection," a particularly jarring conclusion considering the stance of the National Education Association fifty years earlier.[65] Schools went from being partners in the quest for moral development to acting as instruments of its perfection. Swept up in this wave, Pennsylvania's deputy superintendent of education declared a year later that "the common school is the best possible image of society. It is a larger edition of the home and a smaller edition of the nation."[66] With sentiments like these, public schools moved ever closer to taking over the role Washington bestowed upon American religion as the glue of society.

Public educators had been moving toward moral instruction years earlier. Wilson L. Gill's "School Republic" program, which organized each school into a mini-society with the hope of building character and virtue, spread in the early 1900s to cities like Washington, DC, and Philadelphia. In 1901, Jane Brownlee developed a popular moral training program where students began each morning with a five-minute talk on a specific virtue like kindness, cleanliness, or obedience. The Lexington, Kentucky, schools embarked upon a new curriculum in 1903 in which students wrote short stories illustrating morals, and this program, known as Golden Deeds, became a model for many other districts. By 1910, many districts had developed grading rubrics that emphasized conduct and character, as opposed to strict academics.[67] More crucially, public schools increasingly employed secular examples when teaching morals. High school students in Lexington, for instance, read Plato's *Republic* rather than scripture. The character-building program of the Character Development League of New York used the biographies of famous Americans to illustrate morality and virtue. Children studied secular heroes instead of Biblical prophets, and the popular textbook *Parables for School and Home* avoided religious allusions entirely.[68]

Progressive educators pointed to an important difference between religious and educational moral training. Religion, they thought, inculcated morality and virtue by command and authority. Education, on the other hand, was an organic process whereby students absorbed lessons and formulated their own ethical consciousness. Children were thus organisms conditioned by their environment, a conclusion well aligned with the emergent worldview of intellectuals like Sumner.[69]

Some educators still viewed religion as a complementary institution. Others, like Stanford professor and educational reformer Ellwood P. Cubberly, were devout Christians.[70] When in 1905 the Inter-Church Conference adopted a resolution calling upon public schools to let pupils leave the classroom for one afternoon a week to receive religious instruction, many districts implemented such plans. Released time, as the practice was known, thrived in thirty-three states and 27 percent of all public districts.[71] The National Education Association consistently admitted that families and churches were needed to attain the promise of a moral America.[72] Although educators did not seek to usurp the role of religion as moral steward, the removal of religious instruction from classrooms and the entrance of public schools into the field of character education contributed to the process of early twentieth-century secularization.

The Scopes trial also highlighted the growing conflict between the roles of science and religion. Science and the technological advances it spawned cut deeply into one of religion's most important societal functions—the elucidator of mysteries and wellspring of ultimate truth. It promised to shine light on darkened uncertainties and guaranteed the progress of mankind. For much of the nineteenth century, religious leaders believed that scientific and religious truth were one and the same. Science and religion were not always considered diametrically opposed entities in America. Theologians at Princeton and elsewhere applied the Baconian ideal of induction to both nature and scripture. This "common sense" philosophy, rooted in the Scottish Enlightenment, argued that ultimate and eternal truths could not be understood through reason but rather through empirical observation. In keeping with this view, religious leaders assumed that all theologians and scientists applying the proper method of induction would reach identical conclusions.

But American citizens, scientists, and religious leaders increasingly believed that one needed to choose between the two worldviews.[73] Charles Darwin's work, coupled with the theories of Herbert Spencer, divided America's religious leaders. Liberal Protestants sought to incorporate theories of evolution into a new theology. Conservatives assailed the blasphemies of Darwinian science.[74] Just as people like Bryan doubted scientific legitimacy, as the pace of discovery quickened, America's scientists found religious belief incompatible

with scientific truth. By 1934, 83 percent of the nation's major physicists and 88
percent of it biologists disbelieved or doubted the existence of God. Among
psychologists, the level of doubt reached 98 percent.[75]

Despite the ongoing debate among religious leaders, most Americans rallied
behind the prospect of scientific progress and the technological advances it
made possible.[76] Air conditioners, skyscrapers, airplanes, automobiles, radios,
and telephones heralded the arrival of a new age. It was the dawn of Ford's "new
Messiah." Scientists expanded the limits of natural truth. Ernest Rutherford discovered the atomic nucleus, and in 1913 Niels Bohr proposed the quantum
atomic model. Three years later Albert Einstein's general theory of relativity
rocked the scientific community, and meanwhile William Johannsen coined the
term "genes" to describe the carriers of inherited traits. On January 9, 1929, Stuart Craddock, a patient of Dr. Alexander Fleming, became the first human to
undergo penicillin treatment. His infection cleared, representing the triumph of
science over nature's finger of death.[77]

As Americans recognized the promise of science to explain the unknown,
religion ceded its influence over yet another societal role. Writing in the aftermath of the Scopes trial, Harry Emerson Fosdick saw religion's loss of authority
to science as an inescapable fact. Fosdick, a Baptist minister, was a leading figure
in the modernist movement and became one of America's most famous contem-
porary theologians after his contentious 1922 sermon "Shall the Fundamentalists Win?" In poetic prose, he reflected on the irony of history, focusing on the
parched lands of an ancient empire:

> This would have been a famine year in Egypt in the olden time; so low a
> Nile would have meant starvation to myriads. One stands amid the ruins
> of Karnak and reconstructs in imagination the rituals, sacrifices, prayers
> offered before Amon-Ra seeking for help in such a famished year. But no
> one went to Karnak this year for fear of starving, or to any Coptic church
> or Moslem mosque or Protestant chapel. Men have got what they
> wanted through another kind of structure—the dam at Assuan.

"The shift from religious to scientific methods for achieving human aims" was an
undisputable consequence of twentieth-century triumphs. Like the Egyptians
who abandoned their ancient faith for the scientific altar, Fosdick noted the dwindling authority society vested in American religion. Fosdick did not suggest that
science was killing religion, but, like the Lynds in Muncie, he noted that the majority of Americans had ever less practical use for religion as a societal institution.[78]

Intellectuals, academics, and religious leaders sensed in the late 1920s and
1930s that they stood at the threshold of a new and uncertain order wrought by
science. Fundamentalism, though not defeated by the fiasco in Tennessee,

retreated from the public consciousness. Walter Lippmann's "acids of modernity" replaced the ancestral order of religious certainty with an age of shifting doubt. Churchmen and intellectuals now recognized religion itself as an evolving rather than constant institution.[79] One philosophy professor at Columbia wryly noted in 1929 that "you cannot live with machines, pull levers and turn switches, and retain your naïve trust in prayer or magic." H. L. Mencken used stronger language to articulate the changing role of religion. "Civilized man," he wrote, "has become his own god."[80]

Washington, DC, provided a final stage upon which the colossus of straw captured national attention, first with the growth of the federal state and later with the execution of the most terrible war in world history. Though it dwarfed both Muncie and Dayton, Washington in the early 1930s was a whelp compared to other world capitals like London, Paris, or Moscow. It was no national lodestone of culture or finance but instead a place devoted almost entirely to the affairs of state. Washington had known the fire of war, the shame of slavery, and the doldrums of a weak federal government. By the early years of the twentieth century, though, it was experiencing a renaissance of appearance and purpose. Urban designers gave it the National Mall, a growing bureaucracy gave it a host of new marble buildings, and an unprecedented economic crisis gave it powers and responsibilities once considered either unwarranted or simply unwise. Most important, it was there that the government emerged as protector and moral custodian of society—a role once reserved for religious institutions.

If by Thanksgiving Day of 1931 Washingtonians could not foresee the full scale of the Great Depression, they were nonetheless aware that something catastrophic loomed. The disease plaguing the nation's ramshackle financial structure spread from rural and isolated banks to the heart of American finance. By 1932, one in four Americans was unemployed. Gross national product plummeted 47 percent, and stock values lost three-fourths of their 1929 value. Marriages, divorces, and the birthrate plunged. Americans internalized societal failure, blaming themselves for the hardship that enveloped their families.[81] Despite all the gloom and pessimism that seemed to permeate the American psyche, the Episcopalian bishop of Washington was surprisingly sanguine. He ascended his pulpit and delivered his annual Thanksgiving address on November 26, 1931, before a nationwide radio audience. To him, the Depression, though malignant, presented American religion with an essential opportunity. It challenged the widely held belief that "the relaxing of religious practices can tend to advance our condition and to insure to us a larger freedom and greater security." A society that relegated religion to the backseat now needed a "deep, penetrating, character-forming revival of religion." Revival could pull a troubled people from spiritual, social, and psychological stagnation.[82]

Others joined the bishop in speculating that religion was a solution to the economic misery afflicting believers and nonbelievers alike. Religious leaders contended that religion was the first casualty of unprecedented prosperity and materialism. As one Los Angeles rabbi noted, "Religion . . . became the victim of this crude and materialistic outlook of life." When Americans found their wealth gone, religious leaders believed they would return in droves to churches and synagogues. The pastor of New York's Union Methodist Church chided Americans for thinking they could "corner prosperity." A colleague agreed, arguing that "a marked revival is imminent now; because of this time of poverty and unemployment when a certain emotionalism and feeling dwells in the minds of the people . . . they turn to the church for help." One religious leader summed up these sentiments best when he commented: "If we do get relief from this economic depression without a spiritual revival it will be a tragedy."[83]

As the Depression's stranglehold on society tightened, though, Americans did not flock to the churches and synagogues. By the early 1930s, Washington was no stranger to evolving relationships between religion and society, having already witnessed the urgent dreams and unyielding bluster of the Progressive Era.[84] So it was not surprising that Americans in the Great Depression turned the state for comfort, relief, and reform.

Franklin D. Roosevelt did not ignore the power of American religion. In fact, he drew more often on religious teachings and allusions than perhaps any other president. In his first inaugural address, Roosevelt assured his countrymen that they were "stricken by no plague of locusts," and he observed that the "money changers have fled from their high seats in the temple of our civilization." He eagerly spoke before many of the nation's major religious conferences, continuously assuring religious leaders that they were still relevant. As war clouds gathered on the European continent toward the end of the decade, the president declared a national day of prayer and supported the creation of "loyalty days," when Americans were encouraged to pray for peace and brotherhood. On one occasion, he went so far as to announce that any political, economic, or social problem could "find full solution in the fire of a religious awakening."[85]

Roosevelt's rhetoric fit well under the category of civil religion—the use of sacred vocabulary, imagery, and prophecy to bolster the legitimacy of the secular institutions.[86] The president used the Bible to explain his reforms in terms he thought most Americans could understand and to reassure his flock that his positions were not radical. One of his favorite examples was the Sermon on the Mount, and he urged Americans to be their brother's keeper.[87] Such biblical teachings seemed perfectly suited for the New Deal's communalist outlook, a connection not lost on A. A. Berle, Sr., whose son was a crucial member of Roosevelt's Brain Trust. "Christianity," Berle noted, "like the New Deal, is a form of collectivism." Other religious leaders lined up in support. The general secretary of the Federal Council of the Churches argued that the New Deal reflected Christian principles of economics like the "significance of daily bread, shelter, and security." Perhaps no churchman supported Roosevelt's civil religion more than Fosdick. He urged Americans to sacrifice self-interest for the good of whole society and warned that a rejection of the New Deal would pave the way towards fascism.[88]

Some of Roosevelt's key lieutenants also realized that sacred imagery could augment a secular movement. Secretary of the Interior Harold Ickes called upon national Presbyterian leaders to follow Christ's example and support the New Deal. Here was an opportunity, Ickes insisted, for religious Americans to support a new social and economic order in line with Christian teachings. "Christ wanted men and women to . . . be good neighbors," the secretary exclaimed. "He hated injustice with a righteous hatred. His whole life was a fight against oppression. This was the man who drove out the money changers from the temple." New York mayor and close Roosevelt ally Fiorello La Guardia also employed Christian teachings to show that New Deal policies were not as radical as some believed. "Can any economist," he asked, "improve on the law found in Deuteronomy?"[89]

No image resonated with Americans more than Roosevelt's discussion of money changers. Citizens flooded the White House with letters through the dark days of 1933 commending the president for his stand against greed. Many followed Roosevelt's lead and viewed the struggle with economic depression in Biblical terms. Exodus seemed a particularly well-suited analogy. "We are the children of Israel and our heavenly father has sent us a real leader to deliver us from the bondage of the Pharao[h]s of today," wrote a Detroit housewife. An Episcopalian minister noted that Roosevelt "believes that if he can win the faith and cooperation of the American people, the day of miracles is not past."[90]

But the New Deal was not premised upon sacralization. It was bureaucratized, methodical, and decidedly pragmatic. Harry Hopkins, the chain-smoking, gambling bureaucrat who headed the Federal Emergency Relief Association, would never be mistaken for the pious Progressive Walter Rauschenbusch.[91] Roosevelt's vision rested upon the conviction that reforms could create a society where no citizen was denied a basic standard of living. He sought to inject at least a modicum of security into the American social and economic system, not to shape the nation's religious culture.

With the New Deal, the state entered the lives of Americans in ways once thought impossible, and its role within society grew exponentially. This was the essence of secularization. The state took on many roles once the province of religion. It reassured Americans, succored the poor, and castigated the immoral. It taxed workers to provide the elderly with social security, planted new forests, patronized the arts, brought basic utilities to millions, and provided children with a hot lunch at school. Most profoundly, it offered hope and a vision of future progress.

Like a minister, Roosevelt reassured his flock and visited them weekly in his fireside chats. Like a saint he was often an object of adoration. Americans hung portraits of their president in their homes and businesses. In one southern textile town, a government worker told Harry Hopkins of the remarkable role Roosevelt played to average Americans. "He is at once God and their intimate friend," she reported. "He knows them all by name, knows their little town and mill, their little lives and problems. And though everything else fails, he is there, and will not let them down."[92]

Not all of America's religious leaders cheered the new social order. They worried that their followers were worshipping a false idol, and they realized that the New Deal was fundamentally changing the place of religion within society for the worse. An official within the Protestant Episcopal Church warned that "all over the country today thousands of men are building their hopes of the future on their faith in the personality of one man."[93] In Chicago, the Catholic hierarchy feared that Hopkin's Federal Emergency Relief Association would undermine immigrants' long-standing dependence on the church for relief. The archbishop called upon his government connections in Washington to have the Church's St. Vincent de Paul Societies categorized as an official distributor of federal relief funds, thus counteracting what he feared was New Deal secularization.[94] Perhaps Norman Vincent Peale, pastor of New York's Marble Collegiate Reformed Church, summed up the fears of his fellow religious leaders best. "In the old days people flocked to the church to pray to God that the evidences of his displeasure might pass," he grieved. "Today they pray to the government to write another code."[95]

Roosevelt understood that the power of American religion could be harnessed for support, but he also knew that the place of religion within society was changing. As an official town historian of Hyde Park, New York, the president mused that religion was once a "community affair," but over time competition and enmity stripped the town's religions of their potential.[96] Sitting at the Thanksgiving table in Warm Springs, Georgia, several years later, Roosevelt again noted the monumental changes in religion. Fifty years earlier, the president remembered, "there were a lot of very good religious people ... all over the United States who, when somebody in the family got infantile paralysis . . . would say it was an act of God, and they would do nothing more about it." But by the 1930s people demanded action and sought answers from the realm of science. "In other words," Roosevelt noted, "I think our attitude toward religion ... has changed."[97]

There were other signs, some of them highly impressionistic, that the Great Depression and New Deal altered the relationship between religion and society.

When the journalist Morris Markey packed up his Ford and set out across the nation in the early days of the crisis, he wanted to "talk to as many Americans as possible." He interviewed hundreds of Americans, "from coal miners who were hungry to bankers and business men and shopgirls and housewives." Within this large pool of diverse interviewees, "only one man said that his church, his God, was a prop to him." On the contrary, he observed, "Everywhere did I encounter skepticism, distrust, or amusement at the beliefs of our fathers." After his exhaustive road trip, Markey concluded that "Christianity is hardly to be considered at all as a force in American life, in directing its current or its desires."[98]

The same U.S. Census of Religious Bodies that revealed tremendous gains in American religion from 1906 to 1926 registered a significant decline in religious growth during the late 1920s and early 1930s. Church membership nationwide grew 19 percent from 1906 to 1916 and an astounding 30 percent over the next ten years. But from 1926 to 1936 nationwide church membership increased by a meager 2 percent. In that same decade some of America's largest denominations experienced significant losses, led by the Southern Baptist and Methodists Episcopal churches, which lost 23 percent and 14 percent respectively.[99]

More detailed observations and studies gave finer contours to the broad picture painted by census data. When the Lynds returned to Muncie in 1935, they were astonished to observe dramatic declines in church attendance from the already low 1924 levels. The Lynds noted that the erosion of Sabbath rituals continued amid the rise of a plethora of competing pursuits like golf, swimming in public pools, and road trips to nearby towns. More crucially, Muncie's citizens looked elsewhere for support during the darkest days of the Great Depression.[100]

In America's large cities like Chicago the exigencies of depression challenged the Catholic Church's authority. Though denominational controversies during the early twentieth century predominantly affected Protestants, America's Catholic hierarchy also faced issues of authority. Often these challenges stemmed from the Church's peculiar role as America's leading immigrant religion. Bishops regularly found themselves at odds with the immigrant laity, who held steadfast to ethnically segregated parishes and believed that they should have the power to make parish-level decisions.[101] When the Depression overwhelmed the diocesan system of relief, Chicago's Catholics grew embittered. Catholic Charities and the city's St. Vincent de Paul Societies were unable to cope with the flood of applications from Catholics seeking aid, while parishioners found the Church inadequate at their time of greatest need. Catholics began protesting Church fees for religious rites like marriage, baptism, and funerals. Catholic burials in Chicago declined during the Depression, and parishioners openly slandered neighborhood priests for their avarice.[102]

Even the rural South, a place often characterized as immune to secularization, felt the transforming impact of depression on American religion. A community study of southwestern Tennessee suggested that parents there passed fewer habits like prayer and Bible reading on to their children. Like the Lynds, the study noted the changing religious conceptions of the middle class. Sixty-four percent of all land owners no longer attended church, compared to 49 percent of tenant farmers.[103] James West's detailed examination of Plainville, a pseudonym given to a Missouri farming community, made similar observations. "There are many nonbelievers in Plainville," West noted. "Perhaps a fourth to a third of the people have been so permeated by rational ideas from the outside world that they no longer believe the received tenets of fundamentalist Protestant theology."[104]

Washington witnessed not only the effects of the New Deal but those of world war as well. If ever there was a conflict with the potential to become a holy war for Americans that realigned the relationship between religion and society, it was World War II. Global, vicious, and existential, it produced acts of staggering malevolence and public pledges of a crusade-like quality. It appeared to be a conflict in which church leaders could easily claim the side of good against evil. Such religious dimensions did not entirely escape President Franklin D. Roosevelt. When he unveiled his "four essential human freedoms" in January 1941, he included the freedom of religion. In the following year's State of the Union address, he portrayed the Axis powers as enemies of free worship and cautioned that "the world is too small to provide adequate 'living room' for both Hitler and God." Later that year, while accepting an award from a religious magazine, Roosevelt warned that the "spiritual liberties of mankind are in jeopardy."[105] He also considered religion a psychological salve. In his Christmas address to the nation in 1940, the president urged the citizenry to use the holiday's warmth to "set our hearts against fear." On Christmas Eve of the following year, with Winston Churchill standing beside him, Roosevelt reassured Americans that they could take a day off to celebrate with family despite the debilitating anxiety that marred the otherwise happy religious holiday.[106]

But World War II did not feel like a holy war to most Americans. Polling reveals that three in four believed it was not a religious struggle. On its eve, 50 percent of Americans thought that religion was losing influence within society, compared to only 25 percent who thought religion had enlarged its authority. Similarly, one in two admitted to attending religious functions less often than their parents, while fewer than one in five professed more frequent attendance. A mere 13 percent of Americans reported going to church more frequently because of the war, and 57 percent observed no increased religious interest within their communities. The trend became more apparent when Americans were asked whether greater economic security or increased religiosity was the best solution for world problems. Most chose temporal answers over spiritual remedies.[107]

There are several explanations for why World War II did not produce a spiritual-industrial complex like the Cold War. One is that the response from religious leaders was less intense than in America's two previous wars. When the USS *Maine* exploded in Havana Harbor in 1898, American religious leaders surged to the front of the pro-war movement. For Protestants, the war was a final act of the "imperialism of righteousness." For Catholics, war against a Catholic nation provided a priceless opportunity to prove their loyalty to the United States. Nineteen years later, during World War I, the National Catholic War Council and Protestant General War-Time Commission rallied the faithful to battle, while George Creel's Committee on Public Information spoon-fed religious leaders prewritten propagandistic sermons. From a religious perspective, war was cathartic. From a government perspective, in a society with an underdeveloped central state, religion was an important instrument.[108]

Yet during World War II many religious leaders stood somewhat detached. Pacifists comprised a significant bloc within American Protestantism. As Europe crumbled under the weight of the Nazi onslaught, American religious institutions seemed divided and disillusioned.[109] "We are asked to turn to the church for our enlightenment, but when we do so we find that the voice of the church is not inspired," bemoaned a 1940 editorial in *Fortune*. "The voice of the church, we find, is the echo of our own voices." One year earlier, the president of the Federal Council of Churches called upon the nation's religious leaders to remain neutral in the coming conflict, "because we know that war is futile and because we are eager through reconciliation to build a kindlier world." The dearth of religious fervor among America's clergymen surprised the editors of *Time*. "No bellicose drum-beating marks their attitude now," the magazine declared in 1941. By taking a more passive stand in the war, American religious leaders were only reflecting the wishes of the American people. Fifty-five percent of all Americans believed that preachers and priests had no business discussing the war from the pulpit.[110]

After the U.S. declared war on the Axis powers, some religious leaders glumly observed that the war inflamed secular feelings of patriotism but failed to intensify religious interests. "I see nothing whatever to indicate that the general tone has been raised," bemoaned a church-federation secretary in Ohio, "The secularism which characterizes our age is continuing at an unabated pace."[111] One study of church services in Kansas City on July 4, 1942, revealed that only one in five sermons addressed the war.[112]

A stronger explanation for this secular dimension was the Roosevelt administration's calculated decision not to frame World War II in essentially religious terms. This judgment was no doubt shaped by the strange bedfellows the politics of the conflict produced. Stalin and Roosevelt both knew that the well-publicized hostility of the Soviet regime toward religion was an obstacle to an alliance with the United States. If FDR employed pulpit and pew in his struggle against the Axis, he would expose himself to charges of blindness, expediency, and hypocrisy from those religious Americans—particularly Catholics—who considered Communism a far greater affront to God than Nazism.[113] Shortly after Germany invaded the USSR, Roosevelt wrote Pope Pius XII, asking him to instruct American Catholics to support an alliance with the Soviet Union. "In so far as I am informed," Roosevelt wrote coyly, "churches in Russia are open. I believe that there is a real possibility that Russia will as a result of the present conflict recognize freedom of religion." He knew that this was a gross exaggeration, and so did Pius XII.[114] After failing to obtain the pope's blessing, FDR began molding American public opinion on his own. In his press conference on September 30, 1941, he suggested the media read Article 124 of the Soviet Constitution, which guaranteed freedom of religion.[115]

Americans prayed during World War II. They attended their respective places of worship. Their leaders knew that faith would be a salve and comforting force for good. But victory could be achieved on the factory floor and through the bombsight. Understanding this illuminates not only the secular character of World War II but also makes the religious solutions proposed during the Cold War appear more improbable and astonishing. Being a colossus was not good enough. Power without faith was a delicate arrangement. When Toynbee arrived for his 1947 tour, he was already preaching to the converted. Signs, ill read or not, abounded that religion was no longer an indispensable gear in the machine of American societal progress. Go to a school, pick up a newspaper, ask a scientist, or observe the apotheosis of the state: Americans knew this much.

But before the bloodied fields and seas fell silent, a new conflict was already rising like a phoenix from the ashes of Berlin and Tokyo. As with the deadly call of the sirens, Communism presented a special kind of threat. And in this new struggle against the hammer, Americans grabbed not only the sword, but also the cross.

Enemy

"When a time revolts against eternity, the only thing to set against it is
genuine eternity itself."

—Nicholas Berdyaev, 1932

For those searching for the reasons why Americans framed Communism in such
distinctly religious terms, a good place to start would be at midnight in Long
Island's Sand Hill graveyard on New Year's Eve 1926. With the sounds of distant
whistles and firecrackers announcing the changing calendar, a young writer
named Whittaker Chambers made the first of two religious conversions that
would forever change his life. Standing in the snow beside the headstone of his
dead brother, he composed a poem. "Help me, God . . . To serve . . . The outrage
and hope of the world."

That night Chambers did not switch from one Protestant denomination to
another. Nor did he transform into a Catholic, a Muslim, or a Buddhist. Chambers converted to Communism. He was already a member of the Communist
Party. He had read its literature and contemplated its dreams. But until then he
had not given himself over to the movement spiritually. "I now first became a
Communist," he remembered. "I became irreconcilable." Thanks in part to Chambers, many Americans in the 1940s and 1950s considered Communism not only
a philosophy but also a religious system. And that is why the Cold War took on
the sense of religious urgency that World War II lacked. Political movements—
even those with some obvious religious facets like Nazism—could be dispatched
through military means. But religious movements required something more.

As for his second conversion, Chambers could not point to a single epiphany.
It happened in stages that began in 1937. When he started to break with Communism, he began a personal search for God. He started to pray, at first awk-
wardly. He noticed the intrinsic beauty and complexity of the world around him,
realizing that it was too perfect for the clumsy hand of random creation. He saw

fortunate occurrences as works of providence rather than mere coincidence. In small steps the spiritual force of conversion grew. "There tore through me a transformation with the force of a river, which, dammed up and diverted for a lifetime bursts its way back to its true channel," he recalled. "What I had been fell from me like dirty rags."[1]

Ailing and nearly destitute, Whittaker Chambers penned one of America's strangest yet most celebrated conversion narratives in 1952. He was a topic of dinner table conversations long before his book was published. An editor and writer for *Time* magazine, Chambers had gained notoriety for his accusation—lurid and stunning—that former U.S. diplomat Alger Hiss had been a Communist during his federal service. The trial that followed captivated the nation, divided Harry S. Truman and J. Edgar Hoover, and elevated to prominence a young California congressman named Richard Nixon. Reeling from hefty legal fees and his sullied honor, Chambers retreated to a Maryland farm and wrote his autobiography. Simply entitled *Witness*, the book was a sensation. Americans vicariously entered the realm of the Communist underworld—a place of clandestine movements, front organizations, and sinister designs. Yet at its heart, *Witness* was a story about faith. Like generations of born-again Christians before him, he described the tortured sins of the flesh, the follies of man, and the

In 1948 Whittaker Chambers testified before HUAC, setting into motion a series of events that would culminate in the publication of *Witness*, his best-selling conversion narrative. (Courtesy of the *New York World-Telegram and Sun* Newspaper Photograph Collection, Library of Congress.)

"screams of a soul in agony." His was a tale of good and evil. At long last he perceived the spiritually fatal ends of his former creed and the "fortifying power
of faith" in God's grace. After stumbling in the darkness for years, he finally saw
the light.

Chambers viewed the postwar period as a battle between two great irreconcilable faiths: freedom and Communism. It would end only with the destruction
of one and triumph of the other. He stripped Communism of its pithy mantras,
distilling its message into a single statement from Marx: "Philosophers have
explained the world; it is necessary to change the world." "It is not new," Chambers wrote:

> It is, in fact, man's second oldest faith. Its promise was whispered in the
> first days of the Creation under the Tree of the Knowledge of Good and
> Evil: "Ye shall be as gods." It is the great alternative faith of mankind.
> Like all great faiths, its force derives from a simple vision. . . . It is the
> vision of man's mind displacing God as the creative intelligence of the
> world.[2]

The driving force behind the Communist faith was dialectical materialism, a
conviction that humans alone could order the chaotic universe and achieve perfection. Though this belief was not original, Chambers argued that by combining
the faith of materialism with a major political movement, Communism presented a grave threat. The danger rested not in radical political or economic
changes but rather in its spiritual temptation. Its revolutionary drive captured
the working classes. Its vision hypnotized the educated. Most dangerously, as
Chambers observed, Communism provided "two certainties for which the mind
of man tirelessly seeks: a reason to live and a reason to die."[3]

At its core, the thrust of American secularization between 1900 and 1945 was
strikingly materialistic in Chamber's sense of the word. Progressivism attacked the
social, cultural, and religious fatalism prevalent in nineteenth-century American
thought. Not content to wait patiently for the assured progress the American
creed supposed, Progressives like Walter Lippmann sought "mastery" over the
"drift" of society.[4] As the century unfolded, the meteoric rise of science promised solutions to societal ills once thought incurable, and Roosevelt's New Deal
urged Americans to pave their own road to the Promised Land with the help of
an increasingly bureaucratic state apparatus. Consumption, invention, and full
bellies: these were America's new values, and they worried Chambers. It is little
wonder, then, that he enthusiastically managed the promotion of Arnold
J. Toynbee's *A Study of History* from his office in Time, Inc.'s Manhattan tower.

For Chambers, the simple notion of freedom as liberty of action or expression
was woefully inadequate. Freedom required a spiritual component to combat

Communism, and that special ingredient was the firm belief in God. "In the end," Chambers noted, "the only memorable stories . . . are religious and moral. They give men the heart to suffer the ordeal of a life that perpetually rends them between beauty and terror." He bemoaned the secularization of twentieth-century America, and called on his countrymen to recognize that religion and politics were symbiotic. The great battle between Communism and freedom was actually a "conflict between two great camps of men—those who reject and those who worship God."[5] In this rigid construction, sacred beliefs became a litmus test for secular action. The religious could not be Communists, but even more important, the irreligious could not be true Americans.

He belonged to a subset within the broad category of Cold War converts—those people who traded in the underground cell for the church aisle and the hammer for the cross, star, or crescent. Members of this select group were separated by age, nationality, gender, and temperament, but they shared several important traits. They were those to whom society had given much, whether education, intelligence, or wealth. They considered themselves intellectuals and spent untold time in quiet meditation on the crises and inequalities rattling the world around them. They were idealists who believed that these problems were not beyond solution. But most important, they spent their youth in search of faith, and not the religious faith of their parents, for that seemed an impossible acquiescence in an age of intellectual secularization. In their almost frantic groping for a faith system to make sense of an incomprehensible world, they found a powerful religion in Communism. "A faith is not acquired by reasoning," wrote novelist and Communist convert Arthur Koestler; "it grows like a tree. Its crown points to the sky; its roots grow downward into the past and are nourished by the dark sap of the ancestral humus."[6]

When the "dark sap" of Communism no longer sustained them, they abandoned it, and like most intellectuals they found the urge to write about the experience irresistible. Their private quests became public journeys. In making his own journey public, Chambers's road to Damascus came not only with a map but tour guides as well. On October 10, 1945, in a hushed chapel of New York's St. Patrick's Cathedral, Louis F. Budenz, the editor of the Communist newspaper *The Daily Worker*, knelt with his family before Monsignor Fulton Sheen and made his profession of faith to Roman Catholicism. As one of the Church's foremost anti-Communists, Sheen had been a victim of Budenz's acid pen during the 1930s. The monsignor responded with pleas that Budenz return to the Catholic faith. Disillusioned with the Communist creed and its irreconcilable relationship with Catholicism, the wayward editor began a course of religious instruction under Sheen's direction. After a conversion publicized in all of America's major newspapers, Budenz started a second career as an informant, professor of journalism at Catholic universities, and anti-Communist activist. He wrote of his conversion to Communism and subsequent return to Christianity, publishing the autobiography, *This Is My Story*, in 1947. It told of the spiritual crisis that brought him into the Communist fold and the spiritual bankruptcy that returned him to what he called "the faith of my fathers."[7]

The Budenz conversion was a public-relations coup for anti-Communists in general and for Sheen and the Catholic Church in particular. Sheen became the era's preeminent Communist converter. More sensational yet was the conversion of the Communist "spy queen" Elizabeth Bentley. Bentley offered up a story ready made for the tabloid press, with rumors of alcoholism and a long list of lovers. After officially turning on both the Communist Party and those she claimed had spied for her in 1945, Bentley sought spiritual refuge under Sheen's aegis. Her biographer considered the move "motivated more by opportunism than by ideology." Nonetheless, the press reported that on November 5, 1948, Sheen baptized Bentley in a Washington, DC, church. Louis Budenz and his wife, Margaret, served as her godparents.[8]

Other converted Communists joined Sheen's acolytes with the release of *The God That Failed* in 1949. Edited by the British politician Richard Crossman, it featured six essays by either former Communists or former Communist sympathizers—most notably British writer Arthur Koestler and American novelist

Self-styled "spy queen" Elizabeth Bentley converted from Communism to Catholicism in 1948 under the tutelage of Fulton Sheen. (Courtesy of the *New York World-Telegram and Sun* Newspaper Photograph Collection, Library of Congress.)

Richard Wright. Crossman's introduction described the work as a sort of collab-orative conversion narrative, in which each contributor "discovered the gap between his own vision of God and the reality of the Communist State." Koes-tler's confession came closest to depicting the journey Crossman had in mind, or at least its initial stage. "I became converted [to Communism]," he wrote, "because I was ripe for it and lived in a disintegrating society thirsting for faith." But if Koestler and his company succeeded in describing their youthful thirsting for a comprehensive system of faith, they failed to show how traditional faith systems had eventually slaked their spiritual thirst. In other words, *The God That Failed* was long on disillusionment but short on culmination. The coterie of intellectuals had set the stage and rendered the first two acts, but it was up to Chambers to perform the finale.[9]

Well-informed Americans everywhere knew about *Witness*. After winning a bidding war against *Time*, the *Saturday Evening Post* began serializing excerpts in February 1952. The following night Chambers read the book's foreword, the hauntingly simple "Letter to My Children," on NBC radio. He did it again the next day on television. Random House spent an unprecedented $30,000 that spring on publicity. Journalists and critics at newspapers and magazines jostled for the privilege of reviewing it. Not only did every major newspaper offer a review, little hometown papers did too. Many write-ups featured prominently on the front pages of arts, literature, and lifestyle sections. *Saturday Review* devoted nine pages to exploring its intricacies.[10] More important than reaching bestseller status, *Witness* pervaded the public consciousness and was discussed by those who never bothered to open it. Even Chambers's detractors agreed that he had produced not only a memoir but a work of literature.[11]

The salience Chambers afforded to religious faith became a dominant point of discussion among the reviewers. The host of NBC's radio show *A Citizen Views the News* announced that "Whittaker Chambers lost his soul to Commu-nism, then regained it through a strong new faith in freedom, sustained by an unwavering belief in the people." "The real issue is between God and atheism," opined the *Kansas City Star*. Anti-Communist columnist George E. Sokolsky called *Witness* the "hair shirt" of Chambers's conversion. The religious press was even more ebullient. "Every Christian ought to be that kind of witness, for his Lord," wrote the *Church Herald*. *Christian Century* noted that "for [Chambers] the world is a battlefield on which just one issue is being fought out—the issue between God and those who would destroy him." A contributing editor to the *Catholic World* called *Witness* "a study in religion." The book's undeniable reli-gious pulse forced even its harshest critics to fight on ground of Chambers's choosing. "From 'Witness' an unsympathetic reader might, in fact, conclude that God spent the past several years as a special aid to the House Committee on Un-American Activities," the *Nation* sneered. The *Weekly People*, the official organ of the Socialist Labor Party, accused Chambers of converting not to the God of the Bible but instead to the "great god of Capital."[12]

Just as Toynbee's writings came to embody the early fears with which the spiritual-industrial complex justified itself, Chambers's book epitomized the second source of its validation—a fear that Communism was not only an economic ideology with antireligious elements but was itself a sinister religion. The atheistic component of Communism did not constitute the absence of belief; it was an article of faith, the prerequisite for conclusions that humanity could become its own god. Communists were not simply nonbelievers. They worshipped at a different altar.[13]

The construction of Communism as a rival faith to Judeo-Christianity did not readily leap off the pages of Karl Marx or Vladimir Lenin. Rather, the conclusion developed in stages based on close inspection of both Communist writings and observations of Communism in practice within Soviet Russia. Marx's famous formulation of religion as an opiate was indelible, but firsthand accounts of religious persecution in Russia lent substance to these philosophical assertions. Beginning in the late 1920s, Americans studying Communism took this one step further. They began to argue that the movement took on characteristics of a religious faith, complete with prophets, zealous adherents, and a unique cosmology. Throughout the 1930s and 1940s this idea flourished, which led in turn to a powerful conclusion: if Communism was a dangerous religion, then a powerful weapon in the anti-Communist arsenal was genuine religious faith.

Few had the time, ability, and interest to read the ever-expanding corpus of Communist treatises, so the task of defining Communism for public and political consumption in the United States fell to a relatively small group of scholars, journalists, religious leaders, politicians, and Communists themselves. Beginning shortly after the Russian Revolution, this cadre of self-appointed experts produced a stream of speeches, editorials, articles, books, and pamphlets that laid an important groundwork for Cold War interpretations of the Communist threat and the subsequent sacralization of American society.

Most Americans knew little of Communism before Lenin's Bolsheviks stormed Petrograd's Winter Palace in November 1917. At first the Soviet experiment captivated the imaginations of American radicals, as well as many liberals. But after the Soviets struck a separate peace accord with Germany at Brest-Litovsk, thus freeing up German resources for battles against the Western allies, American opinion of the new Bolshevik state began to sour.[14]

The violence of Bolshevik leaders toward organized religion soon became the primary focus of American criticism. The nation's first direct exposure to the worsening religious conditions in Russia came in July 1919 during the height of the Red Scare.[15] Worried that the Bolshevik government would exterminate all religion in Russia, Patriarch Tikhon, head of the Russian Orthodox Church, dispatched an archbishop to New York. During his publicized visit, the archbishop fed the media stories of unbaptized children, murdered priests, and desecrated relics. Throughout the 1920s, secular and religious newspapers kept Americans informed of the deteriorating state of religion in Russia. Most accounts depicted a browbeaten nation of peasants struggling to retain their faith in a tempest of brutal religious repression. Reports and editorials carefully separated the pious Russian people from the sacrilegious Soviet state, a distinction that would blur considerably during the early Cold War. The Russian Orthodox Church survived into the 1930s, but it was a "starved specter that still drags on," noted the *New York Times*.[16]

Soviet attacks on the Orthodox Church were severe enough to garner widespread media attention, but the task of explaining the deep-seated impetus for this hostility fell to experts on Communism who analyzed the Soviet mind. Among them was Harold J. Laski, a professor at the University of London who became one of the most prominent political theorists of the twentieth century after spending some of his formative years in the United States writing for liberal journals. Laski's 1927 book *Communism* was a concise, well-written portal for any American entering the realm of Marxist theory, and though he became a Communist in 1931, he continued to exert significant influence on Communist and anti-Communist thought in America throughout the late 1920s and 1930s.[17]

Laski argued that the incompatibility of Communism and religion was a central pillar of Marxism for two chief reasons. The religious emphasis on supernatural forces governing the fate of humanity directly contradicted Marxist interpretations of history, which insisted that the material conditions of life drive all change. Beyond this conflict, however, was the even more troubling "incompatibility between the commands of most religions and the tactics of communism." Laski believed that religion treated submission to authority as an essential virtue. Victory over the bourgeoisie required the proletariat to cast off its chains and rise in revolutionary indignation. Thus the church was a significant obstacle to realization of a Communist world. Though Laski argued that Communism could not coexist with religion, he believed that Communists preferred a strategy of erosion rather than quick annihilation when confronting religion. Schools, he thought, would play a key role in accomplishing this task by teaching children to cast off the superstition of their parents.[18]

Early reports from the Soviet Union during the interwar years had followed this pattern. Despite the destruction of the czarist government, the Russian Orthodox Church was still a powerful institution, and the Bolsheviks approached it cautiously, favoring a slow process of state sponsored secularization. The government sponsored antireligious lectures, expelled church leaders from the military, and removed all spiritual curricula from state schools.[19] But in 1922, after five years of restraint, the Soviet state struck quickly. Infant baptisms ceased, the government removed the Bible from all schools and libraries, and the state ordered the confiscation of church wealth. Religious leaders who resisted were imprisoned or executed. That same year, Soviet agents forced Patriarch Tikhon to abdicate. Russia's church was crippled. In March 1923 Soviet officials committed one of their most publicized and shocking acts by trying and executing Monsignor Konstanty Budkiewicz, vicar general of the Roman Catholic Church in Russia. Newspaper front pages across America reported how the defiant clergyman was led into a cellar, forced to kneel facing his executioner, and shot in the head. He was denied Christian burial.[20]

By 1925, some observers believed that the conflict between the Soviets and religion had sparked the greatest religious conflagration in modern history. "So diabolical is this hostility," observed one Catholic writer, "so sharp is the antithesis between Christ's Gospel of charity and Lenin's gospel of hate, between the noble individualism of the Christian . . . and the degrading, materialistic, herd-like communism of the Marxist, that one is sometimes tempted to identify in Bolshevism the veritable anti-Christ of Revelation." Another essayist echoed Laski's arguments, noting that the Communists in Russia "seek to kill the spirit of religion, rather than the body."[21]

In the 1930s a new crop of exposés shed light on the conflict between religion and Communism. A frequent visitor to the USSR noted that "the dogmatic atheism required of all members of the communist party continues to be the implacable foe of every form of religion." On a more ominous note, he reported that an older generation of Russians who venerated the church was dying off, while the Soviets had "captured the youth of Russia almost solidly for communism and atheism."[22]

Anti-Communists held no monopoly on explaining Communist incompatibility with religion. Communists themselves did little to hide their contempt. Aside from Marx's infamous "opiate" remark, Lenin's *Religion* became the chief lightning rod for both criticism and acclaim. "Religion teaches those who toil in poverty all their lives to be resigned and patient in this world," Lenin wrote, "and consoles them with the hope of reward in heaven." He argued that religion was a "spiritual intoxicant" that numbed the pain of the workers' miserable existence. Equally important, religious notions of charity allowed the bourgeoisie to purchase their domination for the cut-rate price of sporadic donations to the less fortunate.[23]

Notable American Communists also criticized religion, and of all the faces of American Marxism that entered the public eye, few drew more attention than Earl Browder. The Kansas-born Browder became a socialist in his early teenage years and was a Marxist by the age of twenty. After working for a Communist front organization in Shanghai, he returned to the United States and became general secretary of the Communist Party USA after its leader William Z. Foster suffered a heart attack. Browder brought a new attitude to American Communism. Slender, tanned, and good looking, he stood in sharp contrast to the popular Communist stereotype of a swarthy foreign radical. More importantly, Browder was proud to be an American. He argued that Communism and patriotism were not mutually exclusive, and under his guidance Communism as a political and social force within American society reached its zenith in the 1930s, when the economic catastrophe of depression, New Deal protection of labor, and the menace of fascism provided Communists with wider appeal and a temporary shield against heavy-handed rebuke.[24]

Browder did not shy away from discussing the relationship between Communism and religion. In 1935 he held a forum in New York with Union Theological Seminary students. Parroting a line from Lenin, Browder announced, "We communists try to do the opposite of what religion does. We try to awaken the masses to a realization of the miserable conditions under which they live . . . to change these conditions of life now; not to wait for any supposed reward in heaven, but to create a heaven on earth."[25] The following year he expanded on this notion, attacking the submissive virtues exalted by religious institutions. Communism, on the other hand, sought to "rouse the masses from passivity."[26]

But Browder consciously avoided the blatant hostility of Lenin and tempered his criticism of religion in America. Though he felt that religion was an inescapably capitalist institution, he assured his fellow countrymen that faith was a personal matter immune from state-sponsored destruction. In 1938, Browder wrote an open to letter to American Catholics, assuring them that "Communists scrupulously respect all religious beliefs." Sensing that the American commitment to religious freedom was too deeply ingrained to assault, other Communists made similar arguments in the 1930s. In a letter to a Catholic prelate, William Z. Foster assured the Church that Communists in America stood "four square for full freedom of worship."[27] The same year that Browder held his discussion with students on religion, Harry F. Ward, a professor at Union Theological Seminary, contributed an article to *Christian Century* arguing that Communists in the West were not necessarily antireligious.[28]

Despite the best efforts of Browder and others to downplay the hostility of Communism to religion, the sheer momentum of anti-Communist writings to the contrary, coupled with unquestionable observations from the USSR, were too great to offset. Congress added considerable weight to the anti-Communist movement when in 1938 it convened a committee to investigate the "extent, character, and objects of un-American propaganda activities in the United States."[29] Chaired by Martin Dies, a Democratic congressman from Texas, the Dies Committee Hearings, which later became known as the House Committee on Un-American Activities (HUAC), shattered any lingering American doubts on Communism and religion. HUAC officially existed to investigate both Nazi and Communist propaganda activities, but the latter comprised the bulk of testimony and attention. Notable targets in its infancy included John Lewis's Congress of Industrial Organizations, the Works Progress Administration's Federal Theater Project, and the American Youth Congress.[30]

Not only did HUAC testimony shed light on purported Communist activities in the United States, its witnesses publicly elucidated a Communist worldview. Not surprisingly, they focused on Communist enmity toward religion. John P. Frey, president of the Metal Trades Department of the American Federation of Labor and an heir to Samuel Gompers's antiradical tradition, asked Dies if he could discuss the Communist hatred of religion. After receiving permission, he introduced a series of posters from the USSR. The first depicted the Red Army saving the world from the Roman Catholic Church, Mary and baby Jesus hypnotized by the allure of capitalism, and a comrade breaking an Easter egg. Another portrayed the Soviet industrial machine sweeping away God to create a heaven on Earth. Frey followed his shocking visuals by reading the dismayed

Martin Dies (seated, center) presided over one of the most criticized congressional committees in history, providing a platform for witnesses to explore the religious dimensions of Communism. (Courtesy of the Harris and Ewing Collection, Library of Congress.)

committee a series of quotations from Lenin, Stalin, and Browder. He had clearly established the antireligious aspect of Communism, but Frey contended that the opposite was also true. Communists could not be religious, and truly religious people could not be Communists.[31]

Later witnesses eagerly reinforced Frey's religiously motivated assault. Some alternated between truthful claims about purportedly atheistic organizations in the United States, many of which were secular rather than outright atheistic, and examples of Communist assaults on religion. By using this crude transitive property, witnesses followed Frey in defining Communism as antireligious while simultaneously lumping together all other antireligious American groups with the Red Menace. "This degraded, imported, anti-God theory and activity in the United States," the leader of one patriotic organization warned, "is breaking down the moral fiber of the people and at the same time destroying their patriotism and respect for government, law, and order." Likewise, the American Legion used the hearings as a publicity platform, announcing its commitment to rooting out all alien "isms" from American soil. Here Communism and atheism walked hand in hand down the road of treachery. A year earlier, the Legion's National Americanism Committee had published a book discussing the menace of Communism, which argued that Communists sought to "abolish Sunday."[32]

In 1940 Martin Dies published *The Trojan Horse in America*, a detailed and at times eloquent warning against Communism geared toward average citizens. Like the witnesses called before his committee, Dies discussed in depth the Communist hostility toward religion, noting that in the USSR "there is no room for God." But Dies went a step beyond merely cataloging the reasons for Communist incompatibility with religion. He argued that Communism was a powerful religion itself.

Dies began his book by recalling the siege of Troy, an allusion popular with Communists. In 1935, at the Seventh World Congress in Moscow, Comintern secretary Georgi Dimitrov called upon his comrades to adopt a strategy akin to that of the Greeks. Rather than employing force, Communists would use cunning and subtlety to achieve victory. Dies too recognized the Trojan Horse as the ultimate symbol of Communism, but he took the metaphor one step further. Dies recalled that not only was the horse considered a gift, but the Trojans were convinced it "was an object worthy of their religious veneration—an excellent substitute for the image of their goddess Pallas." "It is appropriate to recall at this point," Dies asserted, "that communism works to make its philosophy of dialectical materialism a substitute for religion." Not through arms or force but through insidious psychological invasion would the Communists bore their way into the soul of America, accomplishing what armies could not.[33]

Given this construction of Communism, Dies's conclusion was inescapable and significant: Americans had to fight faith with faith. By displacing God as the center of morality, Communism threatened to reinstate a "jungle code" of ethics, with men as the masters of their own destinies. For Dies, Judeo-Christianity offered the best possible counter to the "grotesque illusion" of Communism, since it rested on four essential moral propositions: God as the granter of freedom and sustenance, a respect for individuals because they are created in God's image, God as the only basis for a just and peaceful society, and a belief in spiritual rather than material forces. That same year, in a series of articles on HUAC, Dies was blunter and less inclusive of other faiths. "The real answer," he wrote, "lies in the restoration of Christian influence in America. . . . The irreconcilable conflict between the teachings of Christ and Marx is the issue upon which the future of Western civilization is staked."[34]

Dies's argument that Communism transcended mere hostility to other religions by acting as a faith itself was powerful but not novel. Beginning in the 1920s, journalists, scholars, and religious leaders had begun articulating similar views. This line of thought spread with arguments on the hostility of Communism to religion, but its conclusions were far more potent. What began with observations from the USSR on the similarities between Communism and religious devotion developed into theoretical forays into the thickets of the Marxist worldview.

In late 1924, the *Saturday Evening Post*, then the nation's top circulating periodical, ran a series of detailed articles by a reporter who spent several months in the USSR. The final installment examined the relationship between Communism and religion. In it the writer observed that Marxism was becoming the creed and gospel of Soviet Russia. "The man himself [Lenin] has been deified to a degree that cannot be appreciated until you witness the performance itself," he reported. "The bible of Bolshevism is embodied in the speeches and writings of the arch intriguer whose bier has become, like the tomb of Mohammed, the goal of innumerable pilgrimages." But one short anecdote was no doubt most shocking to the millions of *Post* readers. When visiting Moscow's largest orphanage, the reporter asked a young child, "Who is God?" Without hesitation the child pointed to a portrait hanging on the wall and answered "Lenin."[35]

These early musing on the religious aspects of Communism were little more than observations of Communists in action. But what creed drove Communists to religious fanaticism? One of the earliest and most complete examinations of Communism as a religion came from Reinhold Niebuhr. By the start of the Cold War Niebuhr had become perhaps America's most influential theologian since Jonathan Edwards. He was also staunchly anti-Communist. But during his early years at Union Theological Seminary, Niebuhr was devoted to achieving sweeping social change, and though he was intrigued by Communism, he never crossed the Marxist threshold.[36]

In April 1931 Niebuhr examined Communism from a religious viewpoint. On the surface, he admitted, it appeared to be nothing more than a "highly scientific and irreligious social philosophy," but upon deeper examination, he realized it was a new religious movement. He looked to the history of Western society for examples of similar movements and settled on the Enlightenment, which he believed was also a form of religious expression built around a dogmatic faith. Yet Communism appeared strikingly more realistic than its eighteenth-century cousin. Whereas the apostles of the Enlightenment trusted that progress was assured and automatic, converts to Communism believed that the world was drifting toward disaster rather than a preordained millennium. Niebuhr peeled back the layers of accumulated Communist theory and realized that the Marxist belief in historical materialism was the true heart of Communist faith. Though Marx's interpretation of history was complicated and multifaceted, Niebuhr condensed historical materialism into a single basic concept: that history is driven by material rather than spiritual forces. "Far from believing that history is proceeding automatically toward a millennium," he wrote, Communism "holds that history is drifting toward disaster. The saving faith is that somehow the new world will spring out of the disaster. The deus ex machina which it trusts is not the God of religious devotion, but a law imbedded in the processes of history."[37]

To Niebuhr, Marx's works were the Communist bible, and the writings of Lenin achieved "a dogmatic significance for [Communism] comparable to that which the thought of Thomas Aquinas had for the medieval church." Having established a doctrinaire faith, Communists could expect a sea of converts. "The world is still looking for workable combinations of the certainty which encourages action," Niebuhr wrote. He believed that Communism required primitive zeal, a pure and simplistic faith, to grow. Though such a faith would be little tolerated in the West, he thought it could grow mightily in Asia where the certainty Communism offered could conspire with the instinct for irrational action. In this respect, secularized and religiously moderate America would be at a severe disadvantage. "Those who fear too much the fanaticism which is the inevitable by-product of religiously created energy," he warned, "are consigned to social impotence by the multitude of their scruples." Here again the colossus-of-straw fear emerged. The fully secularized and smugly sophisticated West had lost touch with the primitive but more potent religious energies needed to engage Communism in the developing world.[38]

The following year Russian philosopher Nikolai Berdyaev offered an interpretation of Communist religion that supported many of Niebuhr's arguments. Like Niebuhr, Berdyaev rooted Communism in the Russian psyche. He also emphasized the Communist belief that mankind stood upon the edge of apocalypse from which all of humanity would be redeemed. But Berdyaev's insight was more penetrating, delving into the psychology of the human soul. "Communism should have a very special significance for Christians," he noted, "for it is a reminder and denouncement of an unfulfilled duty, of the fact that the Christian ideal has not been achieved." He dismissed the economic and political facets of Communism. It did not capture the hearts and souls of followers by emphasizing class consciousness; it seduced the masses by tapping into religious and even mythological themes. All humans, Berdyaev argued, were enchanted by the promise of utopia. Such was the dream of great philosophers like Plato, Jesus, and Thomas More. Like Christianity, Communism built itself around the concept of original sin—the sin of exploitation at the hands of an evolving economic system—but Communists offered redemption through worldwide catastrophe and the reordering of society that must follow. For Berdyaev, mankind had no hope in fighting Communism with political or economic weapons. Instead, Christianity, recommitted to its original ideals, offered the only possible answer. "When a time revolts against eternity, the only thing to set against it is genuine eternity itself," he exclaimed, "It is no use opposing Communism with ideas; it can only be done with religious realities."[39]

Throughout the 1930s a string of analyses of Communism, written mostly by theologians, followed in Niebuhr and Berdyaev's wake. After spending several months in an American Communist labor school, one observer was struck by the psychological similarities between zealous Christians and converted Communists. Communists had their missionaries, theologians, and even doubters. They wrote and sang their own songs, developing a hymnology akin to mainline faiths. Most important, the Communists he met shared the unflinching belief that theirs was the one and true faith. An English theologian followed, arguing that Communism was actually an offshoot of Calvinism since its followers believed in a predetermined and inevitable historical process. "Marxism is, in fact, Calvinism secularised," he argued, "for submission to a process may have something of the mystic quality of submission to the will of God." Other theologians disagreed, contending that "the vital principle in Marx's system is that man is sufficient for himself," a principle with implications, since if humans were entirely self-sufficient, they would have no need for God.[40]

Abba Gordin, the writer, philosopher, and dedicated anarchist, took this conclusion one step further, arguing that "Marxianity" not only contended that God was unnecessary, it replaced the divine with "class messianic faith." Whereas Christianity looked to Jesus as its savior and redeemer, Communism recruited an entire labor class, the proletariat, to bring about the "last days." Its eschatology relied not on a divine hand directing the apocalypse; it depended on a conscious act of mankind. Gordin believed that the "Collective Messiah" was an alluring concept. "The instinctive messianic spark glimmering in the heart of the laborer," he wrote, "the masters fan into a blaze which devours his hard-won common sense, his healthy realistic look on life, and he forgets himself and becomes an easy victim of fantasms." Like the serpent in the Garden of Eden, Communism offered laborers the knowledge and power of God.[41]

During the interwar years, assessments of Communism from liberal Protestants often ranged from ambivalence to admiration. The aims of the Soviet experiment were, at least on paper, consanguineous with the larger objectives of the Social Gospel movement—namely the application of spiritual energy to the disquieting problems of modern society. Harry F. Ward had by 1934 become the most visible expounder of such ideas through the publication of *In Place of Profit*, his most sweeping endorsement of the Soviet system. Later he would observe that Communism shared several key characteristics with other religious systems. "It has an iron moral discipline in matters of personal conduct, it generates unselfish and even sacrificial service, which can no more be dismissed as mere intelligent selfishness then the same aspect of evangelicalism," Ward glowingly wrote. "It has shibboleths and dogmas, and the same hard fanaticism that marks passionate missionary movements."[42] Ward was not alone. Indeed, in the words of one historian, "A trip to Russia became almost a *rite de passage* for left and liberal Protestant clergy in the 1920s and 1930s who wished to advertise their friendliness to social change in America."[43]

Other Protestant theologians were far less charitable. Matthew Spinka of the Chicago Theological Seminary produced the most complete and comprehensible examination of Communism as a religious system during the 1930s. Drawing on the insights of Niebuhr, Spinka defined Communism as "atheistic humanism," a religion that emphasized the agency of mankind in achieving redemption and a perfect world. Communism established itself as the only true object of adoration and reality. Like Christian premillennialism it argued that the Kingdom of God was at hand, but looked to a collective messiah rather than an individual savior. It had prophets like Lenin, heretics like Leon Trotsky, missionaries who spread the faith, and a class of theologians who interpreted its creed and issued dogmatic rulings. Like Catholicism, it was exceptionally hierarchical. But Spinka contended that Communism could not possibly serve the important functions of Christianity within Western society since it could neither solve the cosmic mysteries that captivated the human soul nor minister to its enduring spiritual needs. Most crucially, the Communist system of ethics was wholly insufficient. Christianity emphasized individual accountability and won "men from their merely selfish pursuits to the spiritual ideals of the Kingdom of God." But Communism shifted the burden of morality onto entire classes and justified any means, no matter how brutal, so long as they achieved revolutionary ends.[44]

These inquiries into the religious dimension of Communism seem like a trickle compared to the torrent of inquests created by the Catholic Church and its adherents. Unlike Protestant intellectuals who sometimes produced ostensibly objective or even flattering examinations of Communism, Catholics positioned themselves as its foremost enemy. The Church took a stand against Communism when hardly any Americans had even heard of Karl Marx. In 1846 Pope Pius IX issued an encyclical addressing "that infamous doctrine of so-called Communism which is absolutely contrary to the natural law itself," and Pope Leo XIII referred to Communism as a "fatal plague" in 1878.[45]

In America, Catholic attention began to focus intently on Communism following the Budkiewicz execution in 1923. The National Catholic Welfare Conference (NCWC), formed in 1919 to coordinate America's bishops, lent its weight to anti-Communist activities in the 1920s and 1930s. The NCWC advised Representative Hamilton Fish during his failed anti-Communist hearings of 1930 and worked closely with Martin Dies, the American Legion, Veterans of Foreign Wars, and the American Alliance. The organization also gathered intelligence from dioceses across America on Communist activities, requiring periodic reports from its bishops.[46]

While examinations of Communism by Protestant theologians offered a wide range of conclusions, Catholic thought, shaped in part by the NCWC, was more monolithic. Catholics argued that Communism was a unique faith, sinister in design since it threatened to upset both divine and earthly authority. They examined not just Communism but also the conditions allowing the movement to grow, assailing economic liberalism and the secularization it wrought. Not surprisingly, they argued that the Roman Catholic Church was the institution best equipped to fight the Communist menace. By leading the fight against something so essentially un-American, Catholics had a powerful defense against those questioning their allegiance or patriotism. This decision paid dividends. Catholics could point to the praise of Protestants like William Randolph Hearst, who used his publishing empire to applaud the Church's efforts. "I am an Episcopalian," Hearst wrote in 1935, "but I honor the magnificent courage, the inspiring crusading spirit . . . with which the Catholic Church has met this sinister Communistic menace."[47]

American Catholics in the 1920s and 1930s looked beyond the economic and political facets of Communism and readily saw a "social convulsion," "an awful disease," and a "false messianic idea." They considered Communism a mass religious neurosis. How else could one explain conversions by men and women with the most to lose in a Communist political or economic system? "If it were merely political or economic," wrote one contributor to *Commonweal*, "its appeal to individuals living in a state of comparative liberty and security would be inexplicable; but it is really the . . . arch-heresy of our age." The need for religion rested deep within the soul of all humans. Communism tapped and perverted this spiritual root.[48] It offered something that no other religion could: the promise of earthly perfection. "A new world is rising," observed a monsignor in 1937, "a mechanical world peopled by soulless machines. The God-man, shall be replaced by the Man-god."[49] Communists proposed their own millennium, but took the initiative rather than waiting for divine intervention.

Creating a heaven on Earth is a messy business, and Catholics consistently decried the social and economic disorder that would result. Communism stood for chaos and the Church for authority. On this front American Catholics took transatlantic cues. In 1937 two important Catholic statements from Europe addressed the role of the Church as a great bulwark of authority. Pope Pius XI released the encyclical *Divini Redemptoris*, which assailed Communism for upsetting the social order and threatening the foundations of Christian civilization. Earlier that year, the Catholic hierarchy in Germany composed an open letter published in newspapers across America pledging support for Hitler against the growing Communist menace. "Here, respect for authority," the clergy wrote, "there, constant rebellion against all authority, the collapse of all family life, contempt for love and loyalty, and poverty-stricken, uncared for children." Private property was the bedrock of ordered social life, and the German Catholics vowed to protect it. American Catholics followed their European counterparts. They argued that Catholicism was a faith grounded in social realism, a creed acknowledging the impracticality of utopianism. No social system could exist absent authority, one writer acknowledged; "Otherwise there is chaos."[50]

Catholics saw Communism as the progeny of larger trends, identifying two primary culprits: the growth of economic liberalism and the spiritual attenuation wrought by secularization. In *Divini Redemptoris*, Pius XI wrote, "If we would explain the blind acceptance of Communism by so many thousands of workmen, we must remember that the way had been prepared for it by the religious and moral destitution in which wage-earners had been left by liberal economics." Ironically, the Church agreed with Marx on this point. Liberal economics, considered synonymous with laissez-faire policy for most of the nineteenth and early twentieth centuries, had created such inequity and greed that workers yearned for change. In some critical ways, the Catholic Church competed with Communism for the same adherents—the poor and working class who regarded the industrial revolution through a veil of tears. Shortly after the pope's declaration, a Boston radio station broadcast a series of lectures by a local professor of theology on Catholicism and social revolutions. Like Pius XI, he argued that the "economic anarchy" produced by unfettered industrialization so denigrated mankind's material and spiritual essence that the sweet promises of Communism were attractive to hungry souls.[51]

Secularization and the colossus of straw it spawned gave the Communist advance more fuel. Edmund A. Walsh and Fulton Sheen, two of the American Church's dominant intellectuals, grounded their critiques of Communism in this and, in doing so, fused the two streams of thought that would justify the spiritual-industrial complex. A professor of international politics and Russian history, Walsh worked his way up the ladder at Georgetown University, helping to found its famed School of Foreign Service in 1919. He was rabidly anti-Communist, vigorously protesting official recognition of the USSR in the early 1930s.[52]

In 1935 Walsh delivered a verbally lyrical but intellectually brusque address before the American Academy of Political and Social Science. Standing before the acolytes of secularization, he announced that American society had made tremendous material progress in the first decades of the twentieth century at the expense of spiritual growth. America had become "so overdeveloped on its physical side that the spiritual and moral factors of life remain dwarfed and stunted through undernourishment." "We worshiped at the shrine of discredited gods," he continued, "whose high priests chanted a proud refrain: 'only inform, enlighten, sharpen, widen, and liberate the human intellect.'" A soulless society emerged from the costly process of secularization—a society that allowed its spiritual weapons to grow dull and rusted.[53]

Fulton Sheen also tied the Communist menace to secularization. Born in tiny El Paso, Illinois, Sheen studied in Europe and earned his PhD in philosophy from the Catholic University of Leuven in Belgium. He digested the complete works of Marx, Lenin, and Stalin, and, like Walsh, was an academic of sharp intellect. Sheen excelled in reducing even the most challenging intellectual issues to simple concepts that working-class American Catholics could grasp. His rare homilies at St. Patrick's Cathedral in New York became popular community events attended by local and foreign dignitaries. Beginning in 1930 he hosted a weekly Catholic radio show broadcast across America on Sunday nights. Like his wildly popular television program *Life Is Worth Living*, two decades later, *The Catholic Hour* often situated theology in the context of current affairs. Communism was a favorite target, and Sheen served as adviser to Martin Dies, though he declined an invitation to testify before HUAC.[54]

Sheen noted that Karl Marx was an atheist before he became a Communist, a significant observation since it inverted traditional conceptions of Communism and religion. Most religious intellectuals in the 1920s and 1930s observed that Communism bred an undying hostility to religion in the minds of its followers, but Sheen argued that Communism merely invaded spiritually weak hosts. The enticements of Marx would fail to penetrate the psyche of religiously grounded men and women. Yet he thought that America's increasingly liberal, materialistic, and secularized culture lowered resistance to Communist infection. In a

Fulton Sheen studied Communism from an early age and was one of the Catholic
Church's most popular and influential radio and television personalities from the 1930s
through the 1950s. His programs routinely discussed the religious aspects of
Communism and the spiritual means by which Americans could resist its seductive
promises. (Courtesy of the Harris and Ewing Collection, Library of Congress.)

1936 sermon at St. Patrick's Cathedral, Sheen informed parishioners that Communism was born of wretched times. "Because God is passing out of the world
we are having a new slavery," he exclaimed, "This new slavery takes possession
not only of the body, the labor and the private property of man but also of his
very soul." Several years later he quipped that "many of the ideas which our
bourgeois civilization has sold at retail, communism sells at wholesale."[55]

Later in 1943, as battles raged in Europe and across the Pacific, Sheen
devoted eighteen consecutive weekly broadcasts to the growing crisis within
Christianity. A master of analogy, he conjured the image of a ship laden with
barnacles. As the barnacles piled up, the ship slowed. So too was a normally
healthy society unbalanced by the accumulated weight of secularization, which
offered "superstition of progress." Material progress without commensurate
moral growth created a dangerously lopsided society. Like a ship in dry dock
having its barnacles scraped away, American society needed to rejuvenate its
failing spiritual health.[56]

If the problem of Communism crystallized during the 1930s in the minds of American Catholics, so too did its solution. One did not bring earthly weapons to a holy war. The answers were often rooted in specific Catholic traits like antimodernism and the protection of authority. In *Divini Redemptoris* Pope Pius XI portrayed Rome as the great bulwark against Communism. Catholic pamphlets in the late 1930s often assured American parishioners that the single best way to fight Communism was to live a good Catholic life. In 1935 Fulton Sheen called for the creation of a "Catholic proletariat." He nearly got his wish when, three months later, four thousand Catholic employees from the New York Department of Sanitation rallied at the Astor Hotel, proclaiming that faith had inoculated them against Communist infiltration. Later that year 43,000 Catholic laymen attended an anti-Communist rally in Cleveland headlined by former presidential candidate Alfred E. Smith, who touted the catechism as society's great weapon against Red promises. Some clergy went so far as to suggest that Communism was a truer faith than Protestantism. "You should tell your Protestant friends that only communism and Catholicism present an ordered way of life for the future," a New York pastor told his parishioners.[57]

Other Catholic leaders believed that the challenge demanded a greater solution than any one faith could offer. In their view, Communism was the antithesis of all Judeo-Christianity, and its defeat would require the entire American religious system. Liberal Catholic leader John La Farge, best known for his tireless advocacy of racial justice, argued that a nationwide recommitment to faith was the first step in combating Marxist ideology. "I believe that Protestants and Catholics can unite in such an affirmation," he wrote in 1936. "I believe it is imperative they do so, if they wish to stem this devastating evil in our midst." Many Protestants agreed. In August 1936 La Farge attended the Asheville Conference of Clergymen and Laymen in North Carolina, an interfaith effort organized by the America Forward Movement and committed to fostering "national righteousness." A month later Bishop John Francis Noll of Fort Wayne, Indiana, united with Robert Gault, a Protestant leader in the America Forward Movement, to lead a nationwide anti-Communist crusade. For a brief time, Noll and Gault even managed to enlist support from some of the nation's political leaders in their quest to erect a gigantic statue of Christ in Washington, DC, and at the second annual Loyalty Days observance in October 1936, Protestant, Catholic, and Jewish leaders adopted an anti-Communist platform, declaring that the Communist menace threatened all religions equally.[58]

Interfaith cooperation against Communism was significant given the long history of enmity between Catholics, Protestants, and Jews in America, but these conferences were harbingers of an equally significant trend. Though they themselves disagreed theologically, religious leaders cooperated for the sake of American loyalty and national virtue. They were arming the faithful with spiritual weapons, and the soldiers of righteousness prepared to fight for their country and its culture.

The rumblings of anti-Communism in the 1930s seemed to fall silent when the Axis powers rained war upon Europe in 1939. In the lead-up to Pearl Harbor, fascism replaced Communism as the nation's greatest perceived threat. A wave of "brown smearing" ensued that accused conservatives, many of whom were also anti-Communists, of harboring fascist sympathies. Groups like William Allen White's Committee to Defend America by Aiding the Allies claimed that anti-Communist groups had evolved into a fifth column, a Nazi underground. A far more powerful blow to anti-Communism fell in June 1941, when millions of German soldiers poured into the Soviet Union, making de facto allies of America and the Soviet Union.[59]

World War II significantly altered American opinions of the Soviet Union and Communism. Before the outbreak of war, a narrow margin of Americans considered Communism a greater threat than fascism, but less than a third believed that a war against the Soviet Union was probable in the next twenty-five years. Public opinion shifted significantly following the German attack on the Soviet Union, when less than 4 percent of all Americans sided with the invaders. After only two months of fighting on the Eastern Front, half of the country favored lending war materials to the Soviets, and three times as many Americans believed they would rather live under a Communist regime than a fascist one. By early 1943, a wide margin believed that the USSR would cooperate with the West following the war. When pollsters disaggregated their data into religious and income groupings, they found that low-income Catholics stood alone in their distrust of Communist cooperation throughout the war.[60] For most Americans, however, the clergy-executing, atheistic Soviet regime and its spiritual creed became the lesser of two evils.

Anti-Communist stalwarts refused to be swayed in this new era of good feelings. The American Catholic press generally continued to lambaste Communism and the USSR despite the best efforts of Roosevelt. An article in *Commonweal* reminded readers that "Russia as an ally presents Americans with major political, economic and religious problems." In Baltimore, a group of influential Catholic clergy and laymen took out a full page advertisement in the *Catholic Review*, declaring, "We do not, we will not, we cannot grasp the crimson-stained hand of Josef Stalin in his present plight." Non-Catholics like Martin Dies could be equally harsh in their anti-Soviet arguments. "In the name of thousands of voiceless Christian martyrs who have been murdered by the Soviets," Dies thundered, "I . . . protest against any effort to . . . dress the Soviet wolf in the sheep's clothing of the 'Four Freedoms.'"[61]

Favorable public opinion toward the Soviet Union reached a high tide in late 1943 but began to recede as early as 1944 when anti-Western campaigns in Soviet papers, coupled with the realization that the USSR was poised to conquer much of Eastern Europe, began creeping into the public, political, and religious consciousness. The decline intensified in early 1945 when Americans began worrying that the Soviets would fail to fulfill the promises made at the Yalta Conference.

As tensions between the United States and Soviet Union intensified throughout 1946, Americans girded themselves for a special kind of battle. The nation faced not only a despotic and irrational Soviet Union, but a powerful ideology as well. In grand arenas and small chapels, in street marches and the halls of power in Washington, Americans concluded that success in the postwar period could not be achieved with arms or material wealth alone. Many of the anti-Communist religious leaders whose cries were muffled by the strategic necessities of World War II reemerged in postwar America as spiritual Cold Warriors. In the 1930s they had honed their rhetoric, but historical circumstances remained aligned against the widespread public absorption of anti-Communist ideas. After World War II, however, the Soviet Union and its Communist creed emerged as the foremost threat to American peace and prosperity. Americans who had paid little attention to Earl Browder, the Dies Committee, or Communism in general throughout the Depression and war were soon saturated with anti-Communist arguments.

Catholics first ushered in their own self-professed time for choosing between God and man. In April 1945, Baltimore priest John Cronin completed a study for the NCWC, concluding that Communism was a serious threat to both the Church and U.S. welfare.[62] The Cronin report detailed Communist infiltration in labor, government, and racial organizations. It assailed American liberalism and outlined Communist methods for the indoctrination of youth. Cronin stopped short of predicting Communist takeover, but he concluded that domestic Communists could present a significant threat to society and religion when they worked in conjunction with Soviet political moves. Aside from vigilance, Cronin believed that the solution lay in a nationwide reeducation of Catholic laymen and clergy to the dangers of Communism and the power of the Church to combat it.[63]

International events, however, were the primary engines of Catholic anti-Communism in the immediate postwar period. In the 1940s Catholicism was still an immigrant religion whose adherents paid close attention to events in the old country. In America, spiritual warfare against Communism remained largely abstract, but Pope Pius XII and the Catholic Church faced a true holy war in the Eastern Bloc. As they had after the October Revolution in 1917, the Soviets and their allies wasted little time before bringing the hammer down upon the cross.

Pius XII began receiving reports of religious persecution from Church officials in Eastern European countries under Soviet control shortly after Germany's surrender. In September 1945, Poland's puppet government abrogated
the 1925 treaty that governed relations between the Vatican and eastern
Europe's most Catholic nation. Arrests and deportations followed. In many
nations now behind the Iron Curtain, the Church was the strongest, and in
some cases the only, institution with the resources to oppose newly installed
Communist governments. Realizing this, the pope held an extraordinary con-
sistory in February 1946. There he named thirty-two new cardinals, often promoting the most vehement anti-Communists. They would become his
generals in the coming war, men who, in the pope's words, were "in the front
lines of the church's life." Among those elevated to cardinal were Francis
Spellman of New York and the Polish bishop Adam Sapieha, who would join
with other anti-Communist heavyweights like Archbishop Aloysius Stepinac
of Yugoslavia and Joseph Cardinal Mindszenty of Hungary in leading the
Church's crusade.[64]

Francis Cardinal Spellman (third from left) greeting political officials including
New York Governor Thomas E. Dewey (right). With a chancery nicknamed "the
Powerhouse," Spellman made his home at the nexus of politics and religion, becoming a
fierce advocate for religious awakening in the name of national security. (Courtesy of the
Truman Library.)

Between 1946 and 1949, three conflicts of escalating intensity pitted Catholic prelates against Communist governments in their respective countries: the Polish crisis, the Stepinac arrest, and the Mindszenty trial. Each garnered widespread American public, political, and religious attention. The American media paid closer attention to the religious storm raging in Europe than it had to the Bolshevik persecutions two decades earlier. In newspapers, political debates, and relentless sermons, news of the crises reminded Americans of Communist hostility to religion, but more importantly they fueled the formulation of Cold War Americanism.

Poland had long been the Catholic crown jewel of eastern Europe, so when Soviet armies began their occupation in the final year of World War II, both Rome and millions of Polish-Americans began a nervous vigil. The Yalta Conference allowed for the creation of a provisional Polish government, and, not surprisingly, Soviet-backed Communists won the upper hand. America's Polish Catholics strongly opposed U.S. recognition of the new Polish government in the summer of 1945. Determined not to let Communists drive the Church out of Poland, Pius XII called upon Adam Stefan Sapieha, a folk hero who helped lead underground resistance to the Nazi occupation, to withstand the onslaught as cardinal of Krakow. The Communist government at first relied on antireligious propaganda, and when that failed, it removed religious instruction from schools, banned Catholic literature, and even resorted to occasional executions. The Polish bishops resisted, releasing their most defiant letter on Easter 1946. After criticizing Communist philosophy, they boldly declared that Poland "must remain Catholic." Yet Catholic Poland did not suffer the same fate as Orthodox Russia three decades earlier. Direct attacks on the Church failed to weaken public devotion. Realizing this, the Communist premier moderated his actions, and a period of religious détente began.[65]

American Catholics did not wait for Yalta before raising a political fracas. Many could see the writing on the wall after the formation of the Provisional Government of the Republic of Poland on New Year's Eve, 1944. On January 8, 1945, Catholics in Illinois formed the Polish-American Congress to protest the Communist takeover. A month later in Springfield, Massachusetts, the Association of Roman Catholic Priests of Polish Descent ratified a resolution calling upon the Church to oppose the new Polish government. Soon the cries of Polish Catholics grew to encompass the entire Church. Bishop John Francis Noll, editor of the popular weekly *Our Sunday Visitor*, accused Roosevelt of betraying his own Four Freedoms by allowing an antireligious government to gain power in Poland. Throughout 1945 bishops dedicated somber masses to the survival of Polish religion, and lay organizations like the Catholic Daughters of America and Knights of Columbus kept the issue in the forefront of Catholic consciousness. But despite the litany of protests, concern with Poland remained a distinctly Catholic issue in America.[66]

It was hardly surprising but nonetheless shocking when Communist police arrested Archbishop Aloysius Stepinac for treason on September 18, 1946. The move signaled Communist willingness to push tactics to the edge of respectability and reason. Josip Tito's regime charged Stepinac with assisting the Ustaše, a puppet government established by the Axis during World War II. Catholic leaders claimed the arrest coincided with a wave of religious persecution throughout the Balkans, and they pleaded for international intervention. On October 11, loudspeakers in village squares throughout Yugoslavia announced the predictable outcome. A court in Belgrade found the archbishop guilty and sentenced him to sixteen years of prison. Two days later the Vatican excommunicated Tito and every Yugoslavian involved in the case, including the jurors.[67]

The Stepinac case was front-page news across the United States, and Francis Cardinal Spellman, archbishop of New York, wasted little time before acting. Spellman saw in Stepinac a glimpse of himself—a Catholic leader who fought for both religion and nation against the gravest threat the Church had faced in centuries. Speaking before a convention of military chaplains, New York's archbishop bemoaned his counterpart's imprisonment "by men themselves imprisoned and enslaved by atheistic communism." He urged the chaplains to serve as a frontline defense against "the brutal bludgeon" of the hammer and sickle. He also raised money for and built Archbishop Stepinac High School in White Plains, New York. In rallies around the Northeast, Spellman claimed that the Stepinac crisis proved America's involvement in a battle for its very soul against "satanic Soviet sycophants." In New Jersey an estimated 140,000 Catholics staged a mass march, nearly two thousand high school girls formed a living rosary on the New York polo grounds, and the Archdiocese of Omaha collected over forty thousand signatures in a petition asking Truman to intervene.[68]

Widespread media attention and the magnitude of American Catholic protest demanded some political response. Speaking hours after news of the verdict reached Washington, Under Secretary of State Dean Acheson expressed concern over the state of civil and religious liberties in Yugoslavia. He stopped far short, though, of lodging a formal diplomatic protest, and Truman remained silent, to the chagrin of his Catholic constituency. Senator Robert F. Wagner of New York publicly lambasted the verdict, arguing that he and his colleagues "must exercise our moral leadership in this vital instance of religious persecution." Catholic congressmen attempted unsuccessfully to pass a resolution demanding that the State Department make a formal complaint. While Stepinac afforded American Catholics a strong unity of purpose, his trial still failed to marshal Protestant America.[69]

It took the martyrdom of a Hungarian Cardinal to turn the religious war behind the Iron Curtain into a full-fledged interfaith issue in early Cold War America. On July 7, 1947 József Cardinal Mindszenty sat in St. Patrick's Cathedral, feted by Spellman for his vociferous opposition to Hungary's Communist government. Of Pius XII's Eastern Bloc generals, Mindszenty was the most visible, most outspoken, and arguably the most dangerous to Communist designs. When the Hungarian state announced a plan to nationalize all schools, the cardinal mounted a crusade to protect the Church's educational influence, excommunicating every Catholic involved in the plan. Two days after Christmas 1948, police arrived at Mindszenty's residence to arrest him for treason.[70]

Between the Stepinac arrest in 1946 and Mindszenty's trial in February 1949, American Catholic anti-Communism exploded. Bishop Noll traveled the country urging the Catholic laity to become as fearless and zealous as their Communist enemies. Lay organizations like the Knights of Columbus, Catholic War Veterans, and the Catholic Daughters of America sponsored anti-Communist rallies in parishes throughout the nation.[71] Fulton Sheen once again emerged as the face of Catholic anti-Communism, repeatedly castigating the Truman administration for its friendship toward the Soviet Union. From January 26 to April 6, 1947, Sheen used his radio program, *The Catholic Hour*, to deliver a series of eleven addresses on the scourge of Communism. His lectures reached more than four million Americans each Sunday evening through 334 radio stations.[72]

Political rallies were an important aspect of the Church's anti-Communist program, but Catholic devotionalism was also significant. In their search for spiritual ammunition, American Catholics in the early Cold War found prophetic justification in the story of three peasant children who saw visions of the Virgin Mary near Fátima, Portugal. Between May and October 1917, the children claimed several instances of direct communication with Mary, who gave them sacred instructions. The Church accepted these "secrets of Fátima" in 1930, but few Americans paid much attention to the purported miracles until after World War II, when the visions seemed prophetic, prescriptive, and perfectly tailored to the Cold War. The Marian apparitions purportedly predicted the rise of the atheistic Soviet Union, but more important, Mary instructed the children that in exchange for Catholic devotion to her "immaculate heart," Russians would convert, and a period of world peace would follow.[73]

Beginning in 1947, Catholics across America spent each May Day in churches praying for the conversion of the Soviet Union. A year later 20,000 filled the Hollywood Bowl to pray en masse for a Russian religious revival. Fulton Sheen helped spread the Fátima story through his radio show and publications. Fátima provided Americans with a valuable Cold War lesson, he told his listeners: "the basic troubles of the world are not in politics or economics but in our hearts and souls." As the Cold War deepened, Catholic interest in the prophesies intensified, spawning a major motion picture, a Catholic lay organization devoted to propagating Marian devotion, and the hit song "Our Lady of Fatima."[74]

On February 7, 1949 a Hungarian court found Mindszenty guilty of treason and sentenced him to life in prison. Spellman was outraged, as were millions of American Catholics. In a rare sermon from the pulpit of St. Patrick's Cathedral on the day of the sentence, the cardinal rallied his flock to spiritual battle:

> A new god has come to you, my people. His fiery eyes do not flash through clouds of incense or from altar candles. They do not gleam from gold-framed darkened pictures of saints. . . . This is the red god. The Seine shudders at his impact and tries to break its banks. Westminster trembles before him like Jericho, and across the green ocean his shadow falls on the walls of the White House. Hosanna! New god.[75]

Spellman wrote letters of protest to Truman, organized rallies in New York, contributed articles to popular magazines, and established Cardinal Mindszenty Day, on which Catholics were to pray and protest. Speaking in Havana, the cardinal compared Mindszenty to Ignatius of Antioch, an early Christian martyr thrown to lions in the Roman Colosseum. Both men suffered at the hands of "sin-loving, God-hating men." As in Roman times, Spellman argued, "Followers of Christ are faced with equally vicious persecution as they refuse to do the bidding of malicious, cruel, anti-Christian tyrants." On June 28, Pius XII took what was perhaps the Church's most reactionary stance in the early Cold War when he released a decree excommunicating all Communists.[76]

Protestant leaders agreed that the events in Hungary underscored the incompatibility of Communism and religion. But some pastors could not bring themselves into a working alliance with the Catholic hierarchy without first tempering their stances. Consider the slew of sermons by New York ministers. The pastor of the Fifth Avenue Presbyterian Church reminded churchgoers that while he objected to Mindszenty's treatment, "no branch of the Christian Church has the right to demand the intervention of the United States government." The pastor of Irving Square Presbyterian Church went a step further by noting that "the Catholic Church itself does not advocate universal religious freedom." In a letter to Truman one Baptist professor of religion summed up the feelings of many Protestants toward Mindszenty by suggesting that he simply was not worth the start of a holy war.[77]

Mainline Protestant leaders may have been loath to join Catholics unreservedly, but they were beginning argue more intently that the threat of Communism affected all American religions. On Sunday, May 27, 1946, overflow crowds congregated at New York's Riverside Church to hear Harry Emerson Fosdick deliver his final sermon as pastor. On this special occasion, Fosdick could have addressed any one of the societal issues that occupied his career—racism, fundamentalism, injustice, or the progress of humankind—but he focused instead on Communism. "I pray that politically we may somehow succeed in getting on happily with Russia," he told the packed sanctuary, "but out of Russia has come an atheistic philosophy passionately believed in . . . which the Christian Church in these coming years will confront in head-on collision."[78]

Gone was the ambivalence and air of objectivity that some Protestant theologians assumed during the 1930s when examining Communism, replaced instead with the unequivocal hostility that Catholics had long since expressed. In late 1946 an influential Unitarian minister argued that Communism was nothing short of a full revolt against God since it recognized that every person held "the seed of a titanic, God-defying pride." As the Cold War hardened in 1947, the president of the Lutheran Augustana Synod warned two thousand delegates at a youth conference that "the powers of good and evil, of God and Satan, are fighting for the souls of men." In December, at the General Assembly of the Presbyterian Church in the United States of America, moderator Wilbur La Roe argued that the world was divided along ideological battle lines as Christianity faced Communism. The rhetoric trickled down to the foot soldiers as well. When a Presbyterian Church burned down in Milwaukee, the pastor blamed the disaster on "an extreme atheistic communistic group."[79]

Like Catholics, Protestant leaders believed that the rise of Communism coincided with the march of secularization. After Paul Hutchinson, editor of *Christian Century*, toured the world in early 1947, he sadly reported that churches had lost the confidence of the masses. "One of the reasons for the gains of communism," explained the pastor of Plymouth Congregational Church in New York, "is the weakening of the church and the weakening of the hold of spiritual strength on the lives of people." La Roe agreed. "We talk and sing about being good Christian soldiers," he worried, "but in actual practice we treat our religion so casually that our battle-line does not look to the world like a battle-line at all." Religion may have failed to harness the enthusiasm of its followers, but Communism had no such problem. A Los Angeles Evangelical pastor railed that "the Communist dupes give to their wicked work all the evangelistic zeal of the early Christian Church." In his estimation, the time had come for Christians to wield the "sword of God."[80]

The solution was simple. Religious revival would deprive Communists of their monopoly on zeal and passion. In 1947 the American Council of Christian Churches adopted a resolution declaring that "America's need is a reemphasis of Christ centered gospel preaching . . . which puts man into proper relationship

with God . . . rather than to flounder in man centered, God rejecting communism." The larger and more powerful Federal Council of Churches of Christ was
slow to adopt a similar stand, but its former president G. Bromley Oxnam
became one of the most prominent Protestant anti-Communists of the late
1940s. A liberal Methodist bishop, Oxnam became famous for his battle against
HUAC in the 1950s and his strident stand against official recognition of the Vatican. Early in the Cold War he toured America touting the line that bayonets
were useless in a holy war. "The massing of force . . . can, if we are successful,
defeat the masses who fight for Russia," he told a crowd of twelve thousand in
Cleveland in October 1946, "but it cannot eradicate materialistic philosophy.
That can be beaten only by a superior world view, a dynamic faith in Christ." Two
years later, Oxnam used the occasion of the quadrennial General Conference of
the Methodist Church to advocate the merger of all American Protestant faiths
into a single religion best equipped to combat the Communist scourge. A month
after his speech, opinion polls revealed that for the first time since polling began
Americans were split on the issue.[81]

Sidestepping the hyperbole and hysteria of many of his contemporaries,
Reinhold Niebuhr also recognized the religious dimensions of the new
struggle. In October 1947, at the New York Herald Tribune's annual forum, he
declared, "Our business is to make our cause more deserving of defense." "This
is particularly true," he argued, "in facing a nation which has become a holy
land of a secular religion." Six months later, in a piece for *Christian Century*, he
forcefully contended that Christianity was a key for both understanding and
combating Communism. In the Cold War, Christianity represented "the only
possibility of performing our duty without the alternate distractions of illusion
and despair."[82]

Christian success in the Cold War world required unity of purpose. Such
was the goal of one hundred American Protestant leaders who boarded the
Queen Elizabeth in 1948 to join 1,450 other delegates from forty-two nations in
Amsterdam for a spiritual gathering of forces without precedent. The World
Council of Churches signaled the continued desire for postwar ecumenicalism,
a movement that sought to accomplish in the spiritual realm what international organizations like the United Nations promised in the secular—namely,
the guarantee of world peace. The conference theme, "Man's Disorder and
God's Design," recognized the growing chasm separating secular action from
sacred intention.[83]

The churchmen spoke in generalities, but the specter of Communism cast a
long shadow over the proceedings. John Foster Dulles, future secretary of state
and Presbyterian layman, addressed that specter on August 24 during an
address to the entire assembly when he identified Communism as the prime
political and spiritual obstacle to greater world peace. He lamented the trend of

twentieth-century secularization that divorced political action from its religious underpinnings. "Once the connection is broken between faith and practices," Dulles warned, "practices . . . lose their moral significance and seem to be matters of expediency. As such they are vulnerable to attack by those who inject strong belief into different practices." If the religious foundation of Western society disintegrated, the spiritually formidable and perilous Communist philosophy might fill the moral vacuum. The Council appointed a committee led by Niebuhr to draft an official statement on Communism. Niebuhr's report synthesized two decade's worth of religious anti-Communist arguments into a succinct indictment: Communism falsely promised the redemption of mankind, it abrogated an individual's relationship with God, and it demanded a level loyalty and devotion that should be reserved only for the Almighty.[84]

Jewish anti-Communism was often drowned out by louder and more numerous Christian voices, but some Jewish leaders regarded the Mindszenty trial as a unique opportunity to unite America's faiths in common indignation. Several rabbis, believing that spiritual conflict with Communism was unavoidable, sought alliance with Catholics and Protestants. "It will not do," declared a rabbi from New York's Temple Emanu-El, "if Catholics, Protestants and Jews eagerly petition the support of all men of faith when their own are touched, and remain silent and aloof, when others walk in the valley of the shadow."[85] Though Catholic and Protestant leaders often framed the religious threat of Communism in Christian terms, they welcomed Jewish cooperation at anti-Communist rallies at Madison Square Garden and the Hollywood Bowl. J. Edgar Hoover was careful not to exclude Jews from his anti-Communist crusade, using the phrase "Judeo-Christian" to describe America's religious heritage.

But Jews were the major faith most reluctant to enlist in holy war. Throughout the "Red Decade" of the 1930s, American Jews were as a whole the religious group most tolerant of Communism. The career of Rabbi Benjamin Schultz demonstrated this reticence. Schultz would become America's most visible Jewish anti-Communist, but when he began using his position as spiritual leader of Temple Emanu-El in Yonkers to rally his flock to battle, his uncomfortable followers forced his resignation. Undeterred, the unemployed rabbi continued to call Communism a threat to America and Judaism.[86]

Schultz's misfortune was more attributable to bad timing than an errant message. As with Catholics, international affairs were the initial vehicles for Jewish mobilization. In March 1948, the director of European operations for the American Jewish Committee reported severe cases of Communist anti-Semitism, and he urged America's Jews to fight the religious persecution then underway. Three days after the committee's report, Schultz founded the American Jewish League Against Communism. He failed to reach consensus with all America's Jewish leaders, but he did win support from rabbis, businessmen, labor leaders, and well-known anti-Communists Eugene Lyons and George Sokolsky. The league underscored the incompatibility of Judaism and Communism and reached out to Christian leaders who shared its cause.[87] Schultz toured the nation telling tales of Jewish persecution in the USSR and the Soviet Bloc. He reported widespread instances of religious discrimination, including the planned deportation of 400,000 Russian Jews to the wastes of Siberia.

By 1949, Jewish leaders turned their attention to domestic issues. The former adviser of Jewish affairs to the U.S. military in Germany used the opportunity of the National Jewish Congress convention to declare that "Communism was hostile to the fundamental precepts of Judaism." Several influential rabbis from New York's Jewish community reached similar conclusions, railing against the "priests of the red doctrine" and proclaiming that religion was the key to Cold War victory. Schultz regularly joined Catholic and Protestant churchmen at rallies, spoke in Christian churches, and won an American Legion award in the summer of 1949.[88]

During the summer of 1945 few could have reasonably predicted that American society stood on the threshold of a period of revival and sacralization. If the dual crises of depression and world war could not arrest the trend of secularization, then the postwar world offered little chance of new direction. Of course this was nothing new. Religious leaders had long called for revival in times of trial and triumph. What made the early Cold War different was the degree to which other, secular institutions had reached the same conclusion.

If religious leaders wondered whether their secular counterparts would answer the call to endow religion with new national meaning, they did not wait long for an answer when Clare G. Fenerty strode to the podium of Madison Square Garden in the fall of 1946. He stood before a sea of twenty-two thousand who put aside their religious and political differences to unite against a powerful enemy at an anti-Communist rally. Fenerty began by declaring that the struggle confronting mankind transcended mere nations and political systems. Americans stood on the brink of holy war. He spoke of dark gods and Communist animalism—of vile creeds and spiritual redemption. Fenerty was not a theologian, pastor, or preacher, but a judge from Philadelphia—in some ways the very embodiment of secular America. But he blended well the sacred and secular, Americanism and religion. He stood on the dais as an American whose religion was inseparable from his citizenship. After fanning the flames of spiritual passion, he ended his rousing speech with a poem:

Jew and Protestant and Catholic,
Grasp the battle axe and spear,
Drive the hosts of hell before you

Like a herd of frightened deer;
Burst their ranks like bolts from heaven,
Down upon the traitorous crew
For the glory of the Crucified!—
And Jewish glory too![89]

America's spiritual-industrial complex had its justification.

PART TWO

MOBILIZATION

3

Political Institutions

"Communism cannot dominate unless it has the power to remake the
life of the people. It cannot ignore religion and do that."
—House Committee on Un-American Activities, 1949

"What sense is there in talking about separation of Church and State in the
United States, where the sessions of Congress are opened with a prayer . . . and
where some states forbid public office to atheists?" A Soviet official offered the
sharp riposte, but it did little to dampen the optimism of his interrogator, Con-
stantin de Grunwald. Grunwald had been fascinated by the Communist policy
toward religion, discussing it with different sorts of people in the Soviet Union—
from candid taxi drivers to fellow intellectuals and, of course, defensive public
servants. Born in St. Petersburg, Grunwald had fled his native land for France
when the Bolsheviks gained power. But in the summer of 1960 he returned and
set out on a journey of observation across the vast nation. The published record
of his travels, *God and the Soviets*, showed that Soviets had returned the favor by
paying attention to the place of religion in American life as well. No where was
this more apparent than in the words and deeds of its politicians.

American political leaders and the institutions they guided constituted an
indispensable element of the spiritual-industrial complex. As highly visible figures, they wielded great influence, especially when they joined together across
the ideological spectrum in promulgating similar arguments. They literally wrote
religious beliefs and practices into the nation's laws with their public-policy
decisions. Politicians and government officials in the early Cold War knew
something that their predecessors had long understood: Americans preferred
emotional crusades to mere expeditions. Elected officials have rarely if ever summoned the cold candor needed to justify war solely by economic or geopolitical
interest. McKinley wrapped the war with Spain in the cloak of human rights,
Wilson armed the doughboys in the Argonne Forest with his Fourteen Points

speech, and Roosevelt's Atlantic Charter and subsequent Four Freedoms lent moral purpose to the bloodiest conflict in world history. The Cold War was no different. Political leaders built upon decades of observations and analyses to reinforce popular conceptions of Communism as an evil religion whose defeat required more than material strength.

An English military historian once quipped that the Cold War pitted the Soviet idea against the American dollar.[1] But American politicians did not fight with riches alone. As in earlier conflicts with autocracy and totalitarianism, they fought with ideas to preserve their way of life, laboring to develop America's counterideology. It would be what Communism was not. It would turn shades of grey into black and white. Where the Communists stood for totalitarianism, Americans stood for freedom; where Communists supported collectivism, Americans supported free enterprise; and where Communists believed that humans were their own gods, Americans drew upon their faith in a higher power. Like Communism, Americanism comprised more than a political and economic creed. Its spiritual component was equally significant. Rather than serving as an institution protected by a Constitutional guarantee, religion became a protective shield, slashing sword, and the bedrock upon which American freedom drew its justification and strength. Simply put, religion became part of the Cold War solution for America's public servants.

President Harry S. Truman proved that it did not take an overtly religious man to grasp the value of religion in the Cold War. Throughout his life he remained a proud Baptist—quietly confident in his salvation and pleased with the democratic, nonhierarchical structure his denomination offered. As a U.S. senator, he occasionally dressed his speeches in biblical allusion, and as president he maintained a sizable collection of Bibles.[2] But he was often loath to wear the Baptist faith on his sleeve, and he rarely attended church. While working the counter at Clinton's Drugstore in Independence, Missouri, young Harry bristled at the hypocrisy of religious temperance advocates who stopped in for a ten-cent dram of whiskey each morning after breakfast. His skepticism of "amen-corner-praying churchmen" never wore off.[3] After his first meeting with a young Billy Graham in 1950, he was so disgusted by the evangelical preacher's over-the-top antics that he rebuffed Graham for the next seventeen years.[4]

Truman's ideological journey into the spiritual Cold War took time. When Yugoslavian authorities seized Archbishop Aloysius Stepinac in 1946, the president avoided comment. Two years later, when Hungarian police arrested Cardinal Mindszenty, the president and his cabinet were not so demure. The under secretary of state did not hesitate to call Mindszenty's arrest a "sickening sham" based on "patently false" charges, and Truman concurred wholeheartedly. Truman addressed the verdict against Mindszenty in detail two days later, calling it an "infamous" act that would forever haunt Hungarian history. While ruling out a complete diplomatic break with Hungary, he announced that the State Department would investigate whether or not the arrest broke a 1947 treaty pledging respect for personal and religious freedom.[5]

Truman's apparent change of heart was hardly astounding. In the two years since Cardinal Stepinac's arrest, the once fuzzy divisions of the incipient Cold War had sharpened into Manichean clarity. On March 12, 1947, he outlined what became known as the Truman Doctrine in a speech announcing U.S. aid for Greece and Turkey. Ten days later he issued Executive Order 9835, which implemented an anti-Communist loyalty program for the executive branch. That July, George F. Kennan created a public sensation by publishing an influential article in *Foreign Affairs*. American popular opinion hardened as well.[6] By early 1948, 73 percent of Americans believed that Russia would start a war to achieve its desired ends. Nearly three in four thought America was too soft in dealing with the Soviets, and half viewed war as inevitable.[7] Worry shifted from the states already under Soviet control in the east to the economic and political fragility of Western Europe. In April 1948 all eyes turned to the Italian elections, where for a time it appeared that the pope's own nation stood poised to embrace Communism. The tenor had not yet reached the alarming, and at times hyperbolic, level that the surprising events of 1949 would bring, but the seemingly inescapable realization that Americans were now in a serious, protracted struggle lent great weight to events in Hungary.

During this interlude Truman had reached the important conclusion that religion had a part to play in the unfolding standoff. After announcing the implementation of his eponymous doctrine, he started considering the conflict's religious dimensions. And where better to start than with an organization well versed in declarations of holy war—the Catholic Church. American diplomatic relations with the Holy See were historically poor, and for long periods nonexistent. In 1940 Roosevelt had dispatched Myron C. Taylor to Rome to establish closer ties with the pope during World War II. There Taylor, an Episcopalian, facilitated Roosevelt's pleas for Pius XII to soften the Church's stance on Communism. Truman sent Taylor back to Rome following World War II, much to the consternation of some Protestant leaders, this time given the task of inflaming religious tensions between Moscow and the Vatican.[8]

In the summer of 1947 Truman penned an extraordinary letter to the Vatican. "Your Holiness, this is a Christian Nation," he announced, proposing an alliance of moral and religious forces—a crusade by men of good will across the world against the evil encroachments of Communism. "I believe that the greatest need of the world today," he wrote, "is a renewal of faith. I believe with heartfelt conviction that those who do not recognize their responsibility to Almighty God cannot meet their full duty toward their fellow men." On August 26 Pius wrote back: "The foundations, we know, of such a peace . . . can be secure only if they rest on bedrock faith in the one true God, the Creator of all men." "Certainly," Pius asserted, "Your Excellency and all defenders of the rights of the human person will find wholehearted cooperation from God's Church."[9]

In the spring of 1948, the president began a new round of correspondence with the pope, his language peppered with biblical allusion and prophetic imagery, writing on March 26 that "this nation holds out the hand of fellowship to all who seek world unity under God, the Lord and Father of us all." Truman pledged America to the cause of bringing about the kingdom of God on Earth, a divine reformulation of the Communist equation he battled. He argued that basic acceptance of Christ underlay all of secular society, from schools and marketplaces to town halls and world parliaments. Pius was skeptical for understandable reasons. In the 1890s, the Catholic hierarchy had denounced the spread of Americanism, and the United States could not conceal a long history of anti-Catholic action. When the pope tactfully expressed his doubts to Truman, the president assured him of how often he reminded Americans that theirs was a Christian republic.[10]

In the end, America's alliance with the Vatican remained in spirit only, but the episode was meaningful for two reasons. First, it revealed the religious prism through which Truman viewed the fledgling Cold War. More important, the White House publicized the letters to Pius, giving all Americans a whiff of Truman's religious convictions. Some Protestants objected to their president's sudden chumminess with Rome, yet few could take offense at his larger message.[11]

Truman may have been pandering to the pope, but his claims were not exaggerated. Americans, led by their political leaders, were indeed beginning to believe once again what George Washington had proclaimed 150 years earlier: that the success of any nation was tied intimately to a moral culture, incubated and guarded by religion. Truman carefully cultivated this belief. He began his 1948 State of the Union address with a reformulation of Americanism. "The elements of our strength are many," the president declared. "They include our democratic government, our economic system, our great natural resources." But Truman called these "partial explanations. "The basic source of our strength is spiritual," he continued:

> For we are a people with a faith. We believe in the dignity of man. We believe that he was created in the image of the Father of us all. We do not believe that men exist merely to strengthen the state or to be cogs in the economic machine. . . . The faith of our people has particular meaning at this time in history because of the unsettled and changing state of the world.[12]

Thus, the essence of Americanism could not be found in the fruits of secularization or even in the miracle of democracy. In his attempt to paint Cold War ideology in black and white, Truman grasped for the one thing that unyieldingly divided both camps. During his correspondence with the president, Pius XII argued that Western institutions drew their strength from divine sovereignty, and here Truman seemed to agree. Marxist doctrine held that the economic means of production formed the base on which a superstructure of ideas and institutions grew. Truman accepted this metaphor, but in place of Marx's economic base he substituted a sacred foundation.[13]

The president amplified this message over the next five years. In October 1949, on the nationally broadcast radio program *Religion in American Life*, Truman told his countrymen that the "United States has been a deeply religious nation from its earliest beginnings." He exhorted Americans to actively practice their religious faiths. "Religion is like freedom," he explained. "We cannot take it for granted. . . . Unless men live by their faith, and practice that faith in their daily lives, religion cannot be a living force in the world today."[14] Nor was religion merely a negative right, as it had been formulated in Roosevelt's Four Freedoms.[15] Truman transformed a proscriptive entitlement into a prescriptive obligation, declaring that "each of us has a duty to participate—*actively*—in the religious life of his community and to support generously his own religious institutions."[16]

On Christmas Eve 1950, 1,200 citizens gathered in the twilight shadow of the White House to hear the president speak. Millions more heard him on the radio. "Never before in our lives has a Christmas seemed so important," Truman stated. The American Christmas had become in some sense a celebration of materialism. Urging his countrymen to look beyond "turkey dinners and stacks of gifts," he asked them to join him in rededication to spiritual faith. "I call upon all of you to enlist in this common cause," he beckoned. "We are all joined in the fight against communism. Communism is godless." He reminded Americans of the important role religion played in protecting the nation: "Democracy's most powerful weapon is not a gun, a tank, or a bomb. It is faith—faith in the brotherhood and dignity of man under God."[17]

Truman recognized the same moral lessons in the story of four World War II chaplains, a tale that would permeate America's Cold War consciousness. When German torpedoes ripped into the transport ship *Dorchester* in February 1943, nine hundred men plunged into the icy North Atlantic water. Only 230 survived, but those who did recalled the heroic actions of four Army chaplains who walked around the sinking ship to calm the troops. When lifejackets ran short, the chaplains removed theirs and sank into the black depths. Even more fitting, they represented the diversity of American religion—Methodist, Dutch Reformed, Catholic, and Jewish. On February 3, 1951, Truman dedicated a memorial to the

Honoring the ✝ OF ISSUE

FOUR CHAPLAINS

✡ A PRIEST, A RABBI ᴀɴᴅ TWO MINISTERS
WHO GAVE THEIR LIVES THAT OTHERS
MIGHT LIVE

ARMY TRANSPORT DORCHESTER TORPEDOED
BY SUBMARINE, FEBRUARY 3, 1943

Truman took the World War II story of the "Four Chaplains" and reworked it into a Cold War metaphor for interfaith cooperation and God-inspired freedom. (Courtesy of the New York World-Telegram and Sun Newspaper Photograph Collection, Library of Congress.)

chaplains in Philadelphia, spinning a World War II tragedy into a Cold War lesson. The chapel represented more than an act of selfless courage; it commemorated instead "a great act of faith in God." "The unity of our country is a unity under God," he said. "It is a unity in freedom, for the service of God is perfect freedom." If Americans returned to the faith of their forefathers, their president assured them they "need have no fear of the future."[18]

The definition of freedom Truman provided at the chapel dedication was an integral piece of spiritual-industrial-complex rhetoric. The Cold War was a multifaceted conflict, with its particularities often subsumed under the simple dichotomy of freedom versus slavery—the "Free World" against the shacklers of humanity. During his March 1947 speech introducing the Truman Doctrine, the president used the words "free" or "freedom" twenty-four times. But by calling service to God the "perfect freedom," he borrowed an idea once used by Puritans and soon to be employed by social conservatives. Both groups conceived of freedom not as the right to do whatever one wanted, but instead as the right to do what was morally righteous. This view differed from Roosevelt's popular vision of American freedom as personal security guaranteed by the government.[19] Truman may not have been fully aware of the implications of his redefinition, but his rhetoric wove religious practice into the fabric of the Cold War.

Those who shared Truman's vision, that freedom lay at the heart of the Cold War, gathered at the White House on May 22, 1947: CEOs, media moguls, and leaders of America's best known voluntary organizations. Answering the Justice Department's call, they adopted the title of the American Heritage Foundation and approved an ambitious plan.[20] They imagined a Freedom Train—a traveling exhibition of America's founding documents. From city to city it would reinforce American conceptions of freedom and highlight the difference between American liberty and Communist slavery. Its execution required unprecedented civic and business cooperation. The U.S. government lent the foundation one hundred original documents, the nation's railroads provided free transportation, corporations footed the bill, and the Advertising Council conducted a publicity blitz before the train arrived in each city. The train began its twelve-month tour in September 1947 and was a rousing success, viewed by three and a half million Americans in three hundred communities.[21] It was also among the spiritual-industrial complex's first ventures.

The Freedom Train was designed and forged as a Cold War weapon, ironically bearing eerie similarities to the Lenin Train of 1918 that distributed Soviet propaganda to rural Russia. The American Heritage Foundation eagerly highlighted the religious dimensions of the struggle. The train itself housed a special exhibit of important American religious documents, including the Mayflower Compact, Roger Williams's *Bloody Tenet of Persecution*, and the *Bay Psalm Book*.[22] Prior to its arrival, organizers instructed each host community to hold a "community rededication week," of which an "Inter-faith Day" was an important component. On this day, communities invited local religious leaders to deliver speeches on the religious foundations of American democracy and freedom. Rededication weeks culminated with mass recitations of an oath developed by the American Heritage Foundation. "The Freedom Pledge" began:

> I am an American. A free American.
> Free to speak—without fear,
> Free to worship God in my own way,
> Free to stand for what I think is right,
> Free to oppose what I believe is wrong.

Americans at the dawn of the Cold War eagerly accepted this affirmation of Americanism. In the New Orleans Sugar Bowl alone, 75,000 people recited the Freedom Pledge in unison.[23] They were affirming a particular brand of freedom— freedom to stand for what was morally right. This freedom emanated from a belief in God, the true north of all moral compasses.

The train was the brainchild of Attorney General Tom C. Clark, who hoped it would "be the springboard of a great crusade for reawakening faith in America." Clark could clearly see that religious conflict was inseparable from the Cold War, and in 1946 and 1947 he was the Truman administration's chief proponent for American sacralization. With his genial demeanor, customary bowtie, and

In 1947 Attorney General Tom C. Clark helped organize the Freedom Train and delivered a series of speeches across the nation calling upon citizens to recognize the need for spiritual mobilization. (Courtesy of the Truman Library.)

slicked-back hair, Clark fit the familiar image of a Southern country lawyer. Born in Dallas, he made a fortune litigating against a large landholder in the east Texas oilfields. Upon becoming financially secure, the thirty-eight-year-old took an entry-level job in the Justice Department in 1937, and within six years he had advanced to the position of assistant attorney general. In Washington he befriended Senator Truman and supported him over Henry Wallace for vice president in 1944. Truman returned the favor by appointing Clark attorney general, making the Texan the first person to climb to the top of the Justice Department ladder from its lowest rungs. As attorney general he oversaw Truman's loyalty program, fought the problem of juvenile delinquency, and guided the Justice Department through a period rife with fears of internal subversion. In August 1949, Truman rewarded Clark once again by appointing him to the Supreme Court.[24]

Like Truman, Clark eagerly enlisted the service of religion to achieve Cold War victory. In 1947, the attorney general embarked on a nationwide anti-Communist speaking tour reminiscent of the itinerant preachers and circuit riders who fomented the Second Great Awakening. Like Cardinal Spellman, Bishop Oxnam, and other religious leaders, Clark used his position to advocate a strand of Americanism premised upon religion. He understood America faced not just hostile nations but "violent foreign ideologies." Clark, a convert to Presbyterianism, viewed Communism as a hostile religious faith that drew strength from a "black Bible." Likewise, he believed that America's Cold War response should not concentrate on increasing material strength alone.[25] In one instance, he publicly wondered if St. Paul's admonition of the Corinthians was also a warning to Americans in 1947 that strength was possible only through spiritual unity. During a speech celebrating the 215th anniversary of George Washington's birth, he assured the crowd, "Our nation has grown in power and splendor under God." If Americans tended to both their physical and spiritual needs, he reassured his audiences, no foreign ideology could ever poison the country.[26]

Clark believed that the church could still inculcate moral attitudes indispensable to a vibrant, free society. "It is imperative that our people and our children return to God and walk in His ways," Clark told a Catholic group in Cleveland. Children raised in religious homes would be immune to the self-empowering promises of Communism. They would not turn to "false prophets" if they knew real ones. He took a page from Catholic intellectual Edmund Walsh by arguing that America's spiritual progress did not keep pace with scientific advances. Medicine and technology meant little unless the "spiritual values of life [were] burned into the hearts and souls of youths everywhere."[27]

His one-man crusade peaked in a crowded, sweltering Des Moines convention hall on July 25, 1947. The five thousand delegates to the twenty-first annual International Sunday School convention had worked for months to secure Clark as their keynote speaker. At 8:30 p.m. he took the podium and electrified the perspiring multitude. The world was changing, Clark warned. Everywhere a violent Communist ideology spread, forcing upon each soul a monumental decision. "Never in the annals of time has the matter been reduced to such terrifying simplicity," he thundered. "It is a choice between God and Mammon." He recalled the biblical parable of a man who built his house upon a solid rock foundation, so that when the floods came it would stand fast. Americans had to do same. "We must accept and practice the teachings of the Nazarene—or else," he warned.[28]

That night Clark laid out a divine model for human history, one that sharply contradicted both the Communist concept of economic determinism and the predominant American model of secular progress. "We must remember," the attorney general insisted, "that every step in human progress . . . received its ideological impetus from religion." His best evidence for so strong an assertion was America itself, since each great document in the nation's illustrious history flowed from the wellspring of divine inspiration. Clark told the approving crowd that Christianity and democracy were synonymous, that it was impossible to separate religious teachings from the American form of government, and that true loyalty and patriotism received power and endurance from God. Returning to the parable that opened his sermon, Clark ended with an audacious prescription for any secular official: "Let us build for the future on the rock of religion."[29] The thunderous applause that followed carried well beyond the Des Moines hall. Associated Press reporters attended the conference, and major newspapers, including the *New York Times*, publicized Clark's address.

Clark could have satisfied his audience without making such a bold case. Yet he was not interested in a tepid expression of political expediency. Convinced that Americans faced a fundamentally religious enemy, Clark called for a fundamentally religious solution. More important, he placed America's past and future in a sacred context. If true Americans throughout history had rooted their patriotism in God, then Cold War citizens could do no less. Clark's religiously inspired speeches against Communism faded toward the end of 1947.[30] Whether he was warned to tone down the rhetoric or simply believed he had successfully communicated his message, the attorney general helped prepare the ground for sacralization early in the Cold War.

Clark was by no means America's most respected authority on Communism. That honor belonged to his associate and friend J. Edgar Hoover. Few Americans brooded more about the dangers of domestic Communism, and fewer benefited more from the fears they helped create. After earning a law degree in 1917, Hoover entered the Justice Department as a clerk. His rise through the ranks was unprecedented, sparked by his leadership during the Red Scare of 1919. During this crisis Hoover managed the Palmer Raids with a boldness and efficiency that stunned both supporters and opponents, staging the largest mass arrest in U.S. history and sending 249 radicals on a one-way trip to the Soviet Union. He grew comfortable testifying before Congress and producing alarmist reports for public consumption. His actions also made him popular with the public and with government leaders. In 1924 he took over the Federal Bureau of Investigation (then known as the Bureau of Investigation) and headed it until his death in 1972.[31]

When World War II ended, Hoover was fifty years old and had already spent more than half his life obsessed with the Communist threat to America. He remained fixated on Communists rather than Nazis even during the darkest days of the war, and as Americans braced for ideological conflict with Communism after 1945, his mania began to look more like vigilance. Hoover's intelligence networks, he believed, revealed a reinforced domestic Communist presence poised to destroy the American way of life. This assessment was not entirely paranoid. Convinced that the battle would turn on public opinion, he used the FBI to fight a war of information. The Bureau trained its field agents to cultivate a nationwide anti-Communist consensus by working with local media groups. It leaked intelligence estimates to anti-Communist allies like HUAC and established liaisons with Hollywood studios, who subsequently reintroduced the image of the heroic, anti-Communist G-man to American moviegoers.[32]

The FBI's best tool in shaping public opinion was Hoover himself. A prolific writer and public speaker, he traveled the nation offering both a severe assessment of the Communist threat and a clear-cut solution. Construing Communism as a fundamentally spiritual peril, he gave religion a prominent role in his proposed plan for its defeat. Although a lifelong Presbyterian, he recognized an indispensable ally in the Catholic Church and Cardinal Spellman, its most virulently anti-Communist leader. Hoover and Spellman shared information and participated in a joint operation to fight Communist infiltration in labor unions. Both men were religious and patriotic, and both believed that love of country was inseparable from love of God. In 1946 they issued a joint pamphlet on the dangers of Communism. In it Spellman was reserved, but Hoover called for a full religious revival. He bemoaned the impact of secularization, which in his mind had destroyed religious influence in America. "Americanism finds its most lofty expression in terms of spiritual development," he proclaimed. "The Ten Commandments cannot be improved upon, nor can the Sermon on the Mount be surpassed as a guide for ethical conduct."[33]

On March 26, 1947, Hoover delivered a risky address before HUAC. Upset by what he perceived as Truman's unwillingness to take the Communist threat seriously, Hoover decided to appear before some of the president's archenemies in Congress. He knew that Truman, already under assault from Republicans for being too soft on Communism, would not risk the political fallout accompanying any attempt to remove him as director of the FBI. The testimony proved well timed and influential, forming a blueprint that other anti-Communists followed well into the 1950s—a concise explanation of the Communist menace and its weaknesses. The members of HUAC thanked Hoover profusely, offered him compliments, and gushed over his insight. His presence lent substance and legitimacy to their enterprise; their forum gave him a platform to wax philosophical about the aims and means of the Red menace. Communism, he informed them, was a psychic and spiritual disease capable of quick transmission. Like a virus, it would infiltrate the American host and destroy it from the inside.[34]

He had diagnosed the problem, and like any good physician he offered a cure. The best way to fight Communism was "vigorous, intelligent, old-fashioned Americanism." But here he meant something more than the celebration of democracy, apple pie, and baseball. His definition of Americanism included the active worship of God, and he filled his testimony with religious references: Communists worshipped Lenin as a god, and his writings were their bible. Men and women who turned toward Communism were "converts" who espoused "a cause that is alien to the religion of Christ and Judaism." If left unchecked, Hoover warned, Communism would destroy the sanctity of the home and undermine America's faith in God. At a minimum, concerned Americans should go to church or synagogue.[35] Hoover wanted publicity, and his appearance before HUAC paid off. In June his pug-like face and pinpoint eyes appeared on the cover of *Newsweek*, along with a cover story he wrote entitled "How to Fight Communism." As with his testimony before HUAC, he again ended the article on a religious note, construing democracy and religion as two sides of the same coin. "We should never forget," Hoover pleaded, "that Communism begins with the group; democracy and Christianity begin with the individual."[36]

Hoover provided U.S. legislators with the mandate and ammunition to fire the opening shots in their own holy war against Communism. The members of HUAC released a collection of pamphlets in 1948 designed for use in churches, schools, and homes. The 100 Things You Should Know About Communism in the U.S.A. series comprised individual tracts on education, labor, government, and religion. Each posed a sequence of loaded questions with carefully manipulated answers. In *100 Things You Should Know about Communism and Religion*, HUAC offered a Congressional imprimatur for the arguments religious leaders had been making since the 1930s. The committee delivered a litany of horror stories—warnings of padlocked churches, imprisoned pastors, unbaptized children, charred Bibles, and Christmas holidays spent toiling in a managed economy. They also labeled Communism a religion itself. But HUAC argued that American religion was more than an institution in need of protection; it was the keystone of the nation's Cold War success. "The faith your pastor teaches is Communism's deadliest enemy," the Congressmen proclaimed:

> Communism cannot dominate family life, for example, until it has first fought its way past the influence of religion upon the family. Communism cannot force its own brand of moral code upon a person without first destroying his moral code rooted in religion. Communism cannot make education a weapon in its hands so long as religion is secure in its own right to teach and educate. Communism cannot dominate unless it has the power to remake the life of the people. It cannot ignore religion and do that.[37]

Religion was thus America's ideological armor. Allowing it to rust would open a host of national institutions to direct attack. Reforging it, as HUAC advocated, would provide an impenetrable defense.

Calls for a spiritual crusade did not stop at the doors of the HUAC hearing room. Some members of Congress found a religious solution to Communism too tempting a political issue. Beginning in 1946, a handful of representatives began the Congressional process of sacralization that would culminate eight years later with a series of resolutions that inserted God into currency, the national motto, and the Pledge of Allegiance. Some introduced antireligious documents like the "Communist Ten Commandments" into the *Congressional Record* to underscore the antipathy between spiritual and material faith.[38] Karl E. Mundt of South Dakota, a self-professed Communist expert, proposed legislation that declared Communism was "not a political policy, but . . . an international conspiracy and an atheistic and an antireligious ideology."[39] Others emphasized the spiritual foundations upon which American democracy and freedom rested. A Congressman from Mississippi even claimed that the same Communists threatening America in the 1940s had hounded Jesus Christ in Roman times. "It is the same old gang that composed the fifth column of the crucifixion," he argued on the House floor.[40]

Perhaps Rep. Noah M. Mason of Illinois best articulated the main difficulty in fighting Communism. "Mr. Speaker," he bellowed from the floor of the House, "Communists do not walk around carrying signs lettered, 'Look! I am a Communist!' Communists can best serve the party by masquerading as orthodox, loyal Americans." What was needed, then, was an ideological inoculation, some form of conditioning that could not only identify the true Americans, but also ensure immunity from Communist infiltration. Judeo-Christianity served this end. On August 5, 1949, Rep. George E. Christopher reinforced Mason's message when he stood in the House chamber and worried that the Western World was "returning to the Dark Ages." But he did not fear for himself or his constituents in Missouri, simple folk who had long cherished their religion. With a love of God tested and triumphant through the trials of prosperity and depression, they could not succumb. Recalling his childhood in a God-fearing household, Christopher announced, "The training I received in my early youth made me so immune to communism by the time I was 12 years old that all the minions of Hell from Herod to Joe Stalin could not have changed me." Central to his preparation was the Bible, which sat on the center table at his parents' home. "Atheism is the handmaiden of communism," he reasoned. If Americans wanted a Communist-free society, they needed to find God.[41]

The Senate was more restrained. Still, conservative figurehead Robert A. Taft of Ohio warned his constituents that "the Communists have made their beliefs into a crusading religion." Senator Alexander Wiley of Wisconsin declared that religious faith was the central issue in the unfolding Cold War. Speaking in 1949 from the Senate floor, he laid out a divine model of American history. Christopher Columbus, the Pilgrims, the Founding Fathers, and Abraham Lincoln all "looked for the guidance of Almighty God in what they were trying to do." Wiley urged his colleagues, then debating ratification of the NATO treaty, to pass a resolution declaring that the West stood united by an underlying faith in God. Meanwhile, the Senate's own chaplain played down the criticism that Americans rooting out domestic Communism were on a witch hunt. "It's a Judas Iscariot hunt," he reasoned.[42]

At first glance it seems perplexing that the senator who lent his name to an era of anti-Communist combat was so reluctant to anchor a campaign to religious justifications. Joe McCarthy might have been an ideal high priest for national spiritual revival. A graduate of Jesuit-run Marquette University, he was a lifelong, devout Catholic. While critics and allies alike agreed that McCarthy was a man of deep religious conviction, he seemed never to have absorbed fully the Church's teachings on Communism and was reluctant to make his mission a holy crusade. Prominent Catholic anti-Communist John Cronin tried and failed to mold him into a formidable religious force. His strident and unflinching anti-Communist posture made him a natural ally of powerful Catholics like Cardinal Spellman, but liberal Catholics considered McCarthy a grave liability. To be sure, McCarthy could not altogether avoid religious expression in his undertaking. He warned Americans that they faced not just Communism but "atheistic Communism." In May 1950 he publicly wondered if Americans stood at "that final Armageddon foretold in the Bible—that struggle between light and darkness, between good and evil, between life and death." Still, by choosing not to emphasize religion, McCarthy rendered a great service to the spiritual-industrial complex. Had he wrapped his divisive campaign in a spiritual mantle, it may have divided the early Cold War religious consensus.[43]

Savvy citizens understood full well the credibility Congress afforded spiritual inoculations against Communism. When, for instance, historian Daniel
J. Boorstin testified before HUAC in 1953, the University of Chicago professor recalled his former attraction to Communism. When one interrogator
asked him to prove his current opposition to Communism, Boorstin almost
instinctively reported his religious activities. Not only did he tell the committee about his active participation in religious groups like Hillel, he also
spoke of his efforts to develop a religious awareness in his students by showing
them the connections between spiritual faith and American historical traditions. Boorstin invoked the words of Jefferson: "Can the liberties of a people
be thought secure if they have lost their only firm basis—the belief that those
liberties are the gift of God?" HUAC was satisfied.[44]

A witness of a decidedly higher profile used the spiritual inoculation defense
that year as well. On July 21 Methodist bishop G. Bromley Oxnam appeared
before HUAC in an attempt to clear his own name. Though he had spent the last
several years calling for a religious solution to Communism, Oxnam, like other
figures of the Protestant left, had been far more sympathetic to the Soviet Union
before World War II. As HUAC began probing possible Communist infiltration
into the nation's churches, Oxnam became a popular target—accused of saying
the right things but thinking the wrong ones. After sitting through the official
opening of the committee and the routine snapshots of eager photographers, the
bishop began his testimony by making the argument that his faith made Communist sympathy impossible:

> When I declare, "I believe in God, the Father Almighty," I affirm the
> theistic faith and strike at the fundamental fallacy of communism,
> which is atheism. I thereby reaffirm the basic conviction upon which
> this Republic rests. . . . When I declare, "I believe in Jesus Christ, His ·
> only Son, our Lord," I am affirming faith in a spiritual view of life. By
> doing so I repudiate the philosophy of materialism upon which com-
> munism is based.[45]

Throughout the proceedings, a crowd of over five hundred onlookers, many of
whom were clergymen, applauded Oxnam. The bishop was firm, but not humor-
less. Most important, he affirmed for HUAC, the crowd, and the nation the relationship between Americanism and religion. It was an alliance that permitted no
flirtations, spiritual or intellectual, with the Communist foe.[46]

This strategy of defense was not employed only on Capitol Hill. In 1956 the
New York Court of Appeals upheld a damages award given to two political
operatives who sued for libel after a local campaign advertisement called them
Communists. Over the objections of the defendants' attorneys, the district

judge allowed the plaintiffs to use their demonstrated religious belief in Roman Catholicism as proof that the charges could not have been true. The appeals court agreed, noting, "We are all in agreement that all churches in America affiliated with or belonging to recognized religious groups are opposed to communism. . . . No church may survive under it." As the original trial judge noted, the Red-baiting of demonstrably religious people was an act that warranted even steeper damage awards.[47]

The most visible, and unlikeliest, incarnation of spiritual inoculation was Congresswoman Clare Boothe Luce of Connecticut. A playwright, journalist, and onetime sex symbol for New York's literati, she had increased her influence substantially after marrying publishing mogul Henry R. Luce in 1935. Like many writers and intellectuals in the 1930s, she shunned organized religion and flirted with Communism only to reject Marx as the Red Decade waned. In 1942 a local political strategist convinced Luce to run for a Connecticut congressional seat. She won handily as a Republican and built her reputation on routine and sometimes entertaining assaults on Democratic foreign policy.[48]

Her immunization and subsequent crusade against Communism did not begin with international observations or the forceful warnings of J. Edgar Hoover. It flowed instead from personal tragedy. In January 1944, her daughter, Ann, died in a car accident during her senior year at Stanford University. At the time Luce was in San Francisco visiting Ann, and in her initial grief she spontaneously ran to a nearby Catholic church. Kneeling alone and spiritually broken, she began a two-year journey toward conversion, aided by Fulton Sheen. As he had done with Louis Budenz, Elizabeth Bentley, and other wayward souls, Sheen shepherded Luce away from the pitfalls of secularism and Communism into the welcoming arms of Catholicism. Luce had America's foremost anti-Communist teacher, but Sheen quickly realized the potential of his pupil. "She intuits," he wrote. "She sees things all at once."[49] In February 1946, Luce was confirmed at St. Patrick's Cathedral.

Following her conversion Luce decided not to seek reelection. Instead, she spent much of her final year in Congress advocating a religious solution to Communism. Separating genuine calls for sacralization from those born of political expediency was difficult in the Cold War, but few could doubt Luce's earnestness. Her rhetoric smoldered with zealous intensity. Following a long line of Catholic argument, she called Communism "the ultimate perfected religion of materialism." Widening her critique beyond card-carrying members of the Communist Party, she defined materialists as people who believed the "common man lives by bread alone." The New Deal had exalted the material over the spiritual. It had weakened America, Luce joked, by convincing men and women that "all will be good and happy when all have two cars in every garage, two chickens in every pot, and two pairs of nylons on every chicken." A citizenry of full bellies and empty souls was already halfway down the path to Communist conversion.[50]

She continued the fight after leaving Congress in magazine articles and convention speeches. In a contest with Communism, Truman acknowledged, religion was part of the solution, but for Luce a Christian revival was the sine qua non of any victory. In her worldview faith was a constant—a requisite need for belief in something beyond reason that all humans shared. Against a burning faith, whether false or true, lukewarm opinions had little chance. "The yawning agnostics," she warned, "the sneering finger-drumming atheists, the drooling, sentimental, misty-eyed humanitarians ... will not save us from the fiery sons of Marx." Only men and women who burned with an intense faith could withstand the challenge of Communism.[51]

By 1952 the manifestations of a renewed religious agenda in Washington were unmistakable. In February, Billy Graham preached from the steps of the U.S. Capitol, warning that corruption and sin threatened to destroy the marble city.[52] In April, Truman signed into law a Congressional resolution establishing an annual National Day of Prayer. In May hundreds of religious leaders arrived in the chilly capital for the Washington Pilgrimage. Like worshippers at the hajj a half world away, they would visit monuments and shrines and listen to speeches by government officials on the inseparable bond between government and God.[53] That same month, J. Edgar Hoover warned, "Strong moral character is the chief need of 1952. The young person who dedicates his life to spiritual principles will always be on the true path—a path which the Communists can never cross."[54] America's political parties trod the path Hoover described. *New York Times* writer James Reston likened Eisenhower's campaign appearances that summer to William Jennings Bryan's barnstorming campaigns on behalf of the old-time religion. At their nominating convention in July, the Republicans asserted in their platform, "There are no Communists in the Republican Party. We have always recognized Communism to be a world conspiracy against freedom and religion." The Democrats refused to be outfaithed when they released their platform two weeks later, beginning and ending the document with appeals to God and including an ode to the Ten Commandments.[55]

Although Eisenhower's election ostensibly offered a change of course from the twenty years of Democratic presidential rule, the international struggle against Communism wore on, and in critical ways the new administration would continue down paths well traveled by Truman and his deputies. Eisenhower would not abandon Truman's holy war; he would intensify it.

The victors lunched in the dignified South Room of the Hotel Commodore in New York on January 12, 1953—"eight millionaires and a plumber," as one journalist dubbed Eisenhower's cabinet appointees. Half a world away, the war in

Korea had reached a frustrating stalemate. Soviet power and influence continued to expand. While the cabinet was no doubt eager to rush headlong into these weighty issues of geopolitical strategy, they first had an inauguration to plan.[56]

How in 1953 would the new president use this occasion inspire, unite, and prepare a prosperous populace twice victorious over depression and world war for the trials that surely lay ahead? Religion played more than an incidental role. Eisenhower's inaugural ceremony brimmed with religious rhetoric—not the biblical allusions and symbols FDR found helpful in explaining the New Deal, but a commitment to religion for its own sake. He would not use the sacred to legitimize the secular, as Roosevelt had, but rather the secular to legitimize the sacred. The first step was creating the Inaugural Committee on Religious Observance. Even before the ceremony, the group began grooming the nation. They encouraged churches and synagogues across America to pray on the weekend before the event, and they organized a preinaugural service for Dwight and Mamie Eisenhower at the National Presbyterian Church the morning of January 20. Edward L. R. Elson, an old friend and future spiritual guide, conducted the twenty-minute program, delivering an appropriate blessing for any leader of holy war: "Make him a channel of Thy Grace and an instrument of Thy Power upon this earth, that righteousness and truth, justice and honor may be promoted and upheld among men and nations of this world."[57]

Public worship on the eve of inaugurations was common, but carefully crafted religious messages in the inaugural parade were not. Under a cloudless blue sky, "God's Float" led the procession down Pennsylvania Avenue. It featured an edifice crowned with a golden dome. A rod topped the dome, so that, as the procession's chairman wrote, "those viewing the parade will be unable to tell whether there's a cross or a beam of light at the tip of the rod." Paintings of devout throngs at diverse houses of worship decorated the float's base: Catholics gathered outside of St. Patrick's Cathedral, Princeton undergraduates exiting a campus chapel, Jews praying in a synagogue, South Korean soldiers worshipping an ocean away, a New England church stood in quiet winter repose, and the Massachusetts Avenue mosque appeared, then still under construction. Embossed at the front and rear of the float were the words "In God We Trust."[58] Garish, unsubtle, and bold, it may have stirred the memories of those old-timers who remembered the *Saturday Evening Post*'s accounts of Bolshevik parades with banners proclaiming "Communism is the Natural Enemy of Religion."[59] Just as Lenin had tried to secularize Soviet society, thirty years later Eisenhower would use state occasions to sacralize America.

The most memorable religious expression at Eisenhower's inauguration was not the church service or even the parade. After taking the oath of office, the president asked the masses arrayed before the Capitol to bow their heads in prayer:

"God's Float" led Eisenhower's 1953 inaugural parade, displaying the words that would soon become the national motto and signaling the importance of spiritual mobilization in the new president's Cold War strategy. (Courtesy of the National Park Service.)

> Almighty God, as we stand here at this moment my future associates in the Executive Branch of Government join me in beseeching that Thou will make full and complete our dedication to the service of the people in this throng, and their fellow citizens everywhere. Give us, we pray, the power to discern clearly right from wrong, and allow all our words and actions to be governed thereby, and by the laws of this land.

Eisenhower looked to "eternal moral and natural laws." The ability to determine right from wrong was a divine virtue and not the product of government guidance. He argued that progress was "imperiled by the very genius that has made it possible." "Faith" was the key word of his inaugural—not faith in progress, but faith in those "gifts of the Creator" that undergirded the American way. And Eisenhower did not stop with a clear delineation of the American creed. He characterized the faith of America's enemies as well, those whose fidelity "knew no god but force, no devotion but its use." By interpreting the world crisis in terms of rival faiths, he warned Americans that "nothing lies safely beyond the reach of this struggle." Religion and spirituality were not ornaments of a secular ritual. Eisenhower wove them into America's national creed and tied them to the fate of mankind.[60]

Eisenhower's public-relations team notified the press that the president had composed the prayer hastily before the ceremony.[61] Perhaps they felt that a measure of spontaneity would enhance public reverence. Or maybe they tried to emulate the legendary story of Lincoln's words after the battle of Gettysburg. The prayer, widely reported as a new precedent in inaugural addresses, was neither impulsive nor an expression of cynical political piety. Eight days earlier, in New York, Eisenhower and his cabinet had discussed the inaugural address in depth. After the waiters cleared the dishes at the Commodore, John Foster Dulles, Presbyterian layman and appointee as secretary of state, complained that the original speech draft was far too focused on material strength.

"You talked about interdependence," he protested to Eisenhower, "with the emphasis entirely on the material aspect of the matter, that we need places for our surplus and getting our raw materials. I suggest bringing in the cultural and spiritual values."

"But we must remember also today that unless we can put things into the hands of people who are starving to death we can never lick Communism," the president-elect responded.

"In Indiana today," Dulles retorted, "the great peril of Communism comes from intellectual centers."

"I had the feeling, too, that the place to tie everybody together is on your faith," interjected Harold Stassen, Eisenhower's former Republican opponent.

"This is what I had at one time," the president replied. "Again, I don't want to deliver a sermon. It is not my place. I am not an ordained minister. But I firmly believe that our government . . . is deeply embedded in a religious faith."[62]

Dulles won the argument. The inaugural address did at times sound like a sermon. Press accounts called it "solemn" and "reverent."[63] Eisenhower repeatedly asked for God's guidance. He spoke of "man's long pilgrimage from darkness toward the light" and called for "conscious renewal of faith in our country." He told Americans and the world that material strength was empty if not guided by a corresponding spiritual force.[64] The meeting at the Commodore set the tone for the years of battle against Communism that would define Eisenhower's presidency. While the president and his advisors knew that the Cold War divided along economic and political faults, they would take every opportunity to cast it in spiritual terms.

Like Truman, Eisenhower grew up in a small town in America's heartland. He and his five brothers under the watchful eyes of strict religious parents, members of the Anabaptist River Brethren sect and converts to a faith that would become known as Jehovah's Witnesses. Twice a day the family read from the Bible and prayed.[65] All manner of vice, from tobacco to gambling, was sternly discouraged.

Young Ike may have learned the habit of appealing to the Almighty from his religious upbringing, but the specific teachings of his family faith failed to take hold. His lifelong love of poker no doubt raised eyebrows, and his decision to become a career soldier was even more radical, since pacifism was a nonnegotiable tenet of his childhood creed. Independent for the first time in the stone barracks of West Point, he was rarely found in the chapel. Gauging the general's faith during World War II is difficult, since some of his religious actions may have been more myth than fact. In his message to U.S. troops before the D-day invasion, Eisenhower certainly asked for the "blessing of Almighty God," but tales from a year earlier that he prayed alone on a Maltese mountaintop before the landings on Sicily seemed oddly similar to Parson Weems's account of Washington at Valley Forge.[66]

Eisenhower did not attend church regularly again until after his election to the presidency, a fact that critics charged was motivated by political calculation. One journalist called the Eisenhower years a period of "piety on the Potomac," implying a sense of counterfeit or cynical revival.[67] Indeed, by the 1952 elections, the country was approaching the high point of its postwar religious renewal, and the new president would have been foolish to swim against the tide. But an examination of Eisenhower's religious statements and actions in the years preceding his election, as well as those during the campaign itself, weakens this critique considerably.

Before announcing his candidacy, Eisenhower had been busily building his spiritual bona fides. After his appointment as president of Columbia University in the spring of 1948, a skeptical reporter asked him for a statement of personal faith. "I am one of the most deeply religious men I know," Eisenhower retorted. "I do not believe that democracy can exist without religion, and I do believe in democracy."[68] That same year he began work on the National Education Association's Educational Policies Commission, which released the landmark Cold War report *Moral and Spiritual Values in Public Schools* in 1951. Unlike Truman, Eisenhower developed a warm relationship with evangelical prodigy Billy Graham, who once told the general that the fate of America and the world could hinge upon his decision to run for president. According to Graham, the two met for several hours in Paris in 1952 while Eisenhower was the supreme commander of NATO. There Eisenhower bemoaned the descent of American religion into "politics and other things it had no business delving into." "The American people will have to get back to Biblical Christianity," Graham recalled the general proclaiming, "and I must lead them."[69]

Though the contours of Eisenhower's personal religion were unclear in the years before his election, he developed a crucial conception of the value of religion in the Cold War premised upon three central ideas: that American democracy depended on religion, that Communism was at its heart a dangerous religious creed, and that successful nations balanced both material and spiritual strength. Eisenhower would escalate the holy war Truman had started, preside over the most indelible codifications of American religious heritage, and become the political figure most identifiable with the spiritual-industrial complex. With the possible exception of Abraham Lincoln, no president tied religion and societal conflict together more effectively. The parallel is instructive, for, like Lincoln, Eisenhower came to office as a member of no religious group. Rather than weakening his religious authority, this circumstance may have aided it greatly. Eisenhower was a living embodiment of the nonsectarian ideal—religious but churchless. When he spoke of the Almighty, Americans did not wonder if he was referring to the Baptist god, the Catholic god, or the Jewish god. It seemed as though he was referring to the same god as the Declaration of Independence.

In August 1953 Eisenhower's special assistant Robert Cutler informed United States Information Agency chief Theodore G. Streibert that the president would welcome a blueprint for spiritual mobilization.[70] Following what was by then a well-established pattern, the United States Information Agency formed a committee led by individuals representing an array of major institutions: a former ambassador to the United Kingdom, the National Commander of the American Legion, and officials affiliated with the American Federation of Labor, Boy Scouts, National Education Association, and the Advertising Council. Fifteen months later the committee presented Eisenhower with its findings in the *Interim Report on Our Moral and Spiritual Resources for Brotherhood*. Also known by the punchier title "One Nation Under God," it stressed the need to weld religion to democracy. The two comprised the "basic spiritual foundations of our American heritage," and the committee called for public comparisons between the Bible and America's most revered national documents, since together they epitomized "the moral and spiritual resources in our heritage in a way that no historical summary can approximate."[71] The report was more a rubber stamp than a call for new direction. The president had been following the blueprint since his initial campaign for office.

For Eisenhower, perhaps the single greatest justification for sacralization was that the miracle of America would have been impossible without religious belief. He sometimes reflected upon the privilege of growing up in a religious home. "The history of our country is inseparable from the history of such God-fearing families," he explained on the campaign trail.[72] In stump speeches he argued that American traditions and values could be summarized by the simple phrase "In God We Trust," four words that were later codified as the national motto.[73] As president he continually asserted the primacy of religious belief in American government and life. It was the angle of observation through which the American experience could be understood. "I happen to be the Chief Executive of a nation of which the government is merely a translation in the political field of a deeply-felt religious faith," Eisenhower announced in 1953. Two years later he supplied the American Legion valuable ammunition in its Back to God campaign by declaring that "without God, there could be no American form of government, nor an American way of life. Recognition of the Supreme Being is the first—the most basic—expression of Americanism."[74] Even the American Revolution, largely understood as either an economically or ideologically motivated event, symbolized for Eisenhower a spiritual conflict. In this retrofitted construction, Patrick Henry's famous speech was actually a religious call to arms, and the Founding Fathers "well understood that they were fighting for spiritual values."[75]

If Eisenhower reduced Americanism to religious belief, he could do no less to Communism. Truman had called Communism godless, but Eisenhower spent almost as much energy emphasizing the religiousness of the Marxist creed as he did its American counterpart. With a rhetoric at times approaching the pitch of a sermon on Armageddon, he fashioned his presidential campaign into an anti-Communist religious crusade. "What is our battle against Communism if it is not a fight between anti-God and a belief in the almighty," a campaign statement asked. He called upon supporters to realize "the great spiritual differences between our country and that of the Soviet Union," bidding them to repeat Rudyard Kipling's lines: "Lord God of Hosts be with us yet, lest we forget, lest we forget."[76]

His most forceful and extraordinary description of the Communist faith during the campaign came on its last day, in Boston. Eisenhower used the eve of the election to deepen Americans' understanding of the Cold War as a spiritual contest. He called the impending election a "troubled and decisive moment in the history of man's long march from darkness to light." He spoke of "night and of day," of the "evil" Americans faced and the "goodness" they treasured. America was in a struggle not only for survival but also for salvation, and Eisenhower believed that more was needed in such a battle than diplomacy or calculation. "You can pay ransom for the body," he pleaded, "but never for the soul." As the crowd cheered, he delved deeper into the heart of the Communist faith—deeper than any president had in the past or would in the future. Communism was an evil faith because it denied dignity to mankind. It posited that mankind was an "organic accident" akin to the "forces that rust iron and ripen corn." In short, Marx and those who expanded on his philosophies robbed people of spiritual meaning and destiny. Eisenhower assured Americans that Communism was no reincarnation of old czarist ambition—no mere "fig leaf" for irrationality by an older name, as George F. Kennan had suggested. It stoked an old fire in a new way, and that made it dangerous. But this strength could be turned into a weakness if Americans recommitted to their own faith, and here Eisenhower had more in mind than democracy, equality, or freedom. The "life-giving fire of faith" he prescribed taught the divine origins of humanity and the "sublime meaning of our brotherhood under His fatherhood."[77]

Yet to Eisenhower Communism did not pose the only spiritual threat to America. His countrymen held the seeds of their own destruction in the form of wealth, technology, automobiles, and new appliances. He believed that healthy nations were both material and spiritual entities. A religious but materially poor nation risked irrelevance, whereas a "people of plenty" without religious grounding risked recklessness, and this is what Eisenhower most feared. The only appropriate action was to make spiritual growth commensurate with material increase, thus laying to rest the colossus of straw.

The first step was convincing Americans that national spiritual growth was out of alignment to begin with. During the last weeks of the general election campaign, vice-presidential nominee Richard Nixon announced that the "greatest service that can be rendered in public life today is to help in the revitalization and rebuilding of spiritual and moral strength in America."[78] Eisenhower frequently told his fellow citizens that they too often thought of power in terms of "broad acres" or "great factories."[79] This was dangerous, he informed cadets at the Naval Academy, because "material things pass."[80] There was peril in Americans and the world associating the United States with the "speed of our automobiles" or "the wonderful gadgets that we use in our homes." Eisenhower argued that America was great long before appliances and television sets. "Throughout its history," he contended, "America's greatness has been based upon a spiritual quality."[81]

Where better to underscore America's neglected spiritual dimension than in the celebration of its physical might. Early in his presidency Eisenhower used the dedication of North Dakota's Garrison Dam for such a purpose. The dam itself was an ode to America's power—the ability not only to construct in five years the fifth largest earthen dam in the world but also to reshape the earth's surface and flood abandoned towns on a biblical scale. Behind its 210 foot embankment rested the world's second largest reservoir. Forty congressmen and ten thousand people traveled to the site for Eisenhower's dedication in June 1953.[82] The president could not help but marvel at the achievement, but he tempered his exuberance. Marxists, as he would later explain, were the worshippers of "machines and numbers."[83] Americans would not pray at that altar. Eisenhower's words resounded across the North Dakota prairie: "The nation, like each of us, is both a material and a spiritual thing."

> To remain free [other nations] must be both spiritually and materially strong just as must we.... That is what will keep our spirit and our strength able to say to all others, "Do not attack us except at your peril because we are going to live under God as a free, secure and peaceful people."[84]

He later explained that America was a "spiritual organism."[85] While president of Columbia University, Eisenhower had once informed IBM executives that individuals were more than bundles of animalistic impulse.[86] Now for him the same was true of the United States. Nations were more than the spiritual sum of their individual parts; they possessed souls themselves.

Winning a holy war required actions as well as words. Eisenhower knew that he would have to lead by example. The most pressing action was choosing a church. Some of his advisors worried that their leader's lack of an official religious affiliation could reflect poorly, and if letters from the public were any guide, the president's handlers were not alone in this fear.[87] More important, Eisenhower could not urge Americans to attend religious services while choosing himself to ignore the Sabbath. The question was not *if* the new president would join a church, but rather *which* one he would choose. In the end, Eisenhower selected the National Presbyterian Church led by Edward L. R. Elson. His wife, Mamie, was already a baptized Presbyterian, the congregation had ministered to a host of former presidents from Andrew Jackson to Woodrow Wilson, and the current church membership boasted religious cold warriors J. Edgar Hoover and Tom C. Clark.

One of the National Presbyterian Church's strongest selling points was Pastor Elson. An Army chaplain during World War II, he had been appointed special envoy to the German Protestant Church by Eisenhower during the early postwar period. As pastor in Washington, he was friends with Truman, who on occasion attended his services. But his spiritual relationship with Eisenhower gave Elson a new level of authority as one of America's leaders in a holy war. In 1954 the pastor dedicated his popular book *America's Spiritual Recovery* to his new presidential disciple, "who by personal example and public utterance is giving testimony to the reality of America's spiritual foundations." The book was a warning, battle cry, and prescription. Elson worried that the nation was teetering on the brink of spiritual collapse. The predicament's cause was internal, in that Americans were too materialistic, and external, since Communism had become the "new evangelism."[88]

Dwight and Mamie Eisenhower arrived at the N Street Chapel of the National Presbyterian Church at 8:30 a.m. on February 1, 1953, for the first and only presidential baptism in American history. The president insisted on undergoing the rite like any other convert. Standing before a group of church elders, Elson asked Eisenhower if he promised to live a Christian life. "I do," replied the president before kneeling. Elson consecrated the water, dipped his right hand into it, and then placed his palm upon the president's forehead. "Dwight David, I baptize thee in the name of the Father and of the Son and of the Holy Spirit, and may the Lord defend you With His Grace," pronounced Elson. Eisenhower rose and shook hands with the elders before signing the church's membership book and baptismal record. Then he and Mamie walked to the main sanctuary and took their places in the sixth pew. Neither the church nor the White House alerted the media of that morning's baptism, but they hardly kept it a secret. Reporters from the Associated Press, *New York Times*, and *Washington Post* had camped out in the back pews, and the story made the front pages of broadsheets across America the next day.[89]

In the coming years, Elson believed he had baptized the nation's greatest religious leader. He recalled how Jesus had wept for Jerusalem—that cauldron of faith, politics, and power in Roman times. Just as the Messiah cried for the pitiful capital of ancient Israel, Elson envisioned him looking down on Washington with sadness after World War II. It was a divided, secular, and spiritually bankrupt city. But surely, thought the pastor, in Eisenhower's first term Jesus's disappointment would be replaced with beaming approbation. Washington, DC, was "all aglow today with a creative spirituality," and one "committed layman" deserved the most credit.[90]

Possessing at last the religious credibility baptism afforded, Eisenhower began leading his crusade by example, and prayer seemed a good place to start. A week before the inauguration, Elson sent the president-elect a letter suggesting he begin each cabinet meeting with a prayer, particularly since he embodied in the pastor's mind the spiritual battle against Communism and moral indifference. Three weeks later, Eisenhower informed his cabinet that all meetings would begin with a few moments of silent prayer.[91] Nor did prayer stop at the cabinet doors. Eisenhower's first term became synonymous with public entreaties to God. Not all were the administration's idea. By June, Fulton Sheen's flock had flooded the White House with more than fifty thousand requests for a national day of prayer. Technically, the pleas were redundant, since Congress had passed a resolution calling for a National Day of Prayer a year earlier, but such a spiritual outpouring could only have strengthened the president's convictions. Eisenhower used his National Day of Prayer proclamations to assert the importance of religion in the nation's founding, arguing that in their moment of peril, Americans could do no worse than emulate the Founding Fathers.[92] When in 1953 Senator Frank Carlson of Kansas invited Eisenhower to join in a Congressional prayer breakfast, the president readily accepted. Calling in a favor from hotel magnate Conrad Hilton, Eisenhower secured the ballroom of Washington's Mayflower Hotel. Two hundred fifty guests were expected, but over four hundred arrived. Hilton absorbed all the costs. Within a few years, three thousand people were regularly attending the annual affair.[93]

But Eisenhower understood that prayer transcended national boundaries, and he was mindful of how it might resonate in Cold War battlegrounds around the globe. At the suggestion of California senator William F. Knowland, Eisenhower called upon the world to join America on September 22, 1954, in the Day of Prayer for Peace.[94] As part of the Day of Prayer for Peace, Americans were encouraged to visit their respective places of worship.[95] Eisenhower had little control over citizens' actions on the appointed day, but the federal bureaucracy was well within his religious gravitational pull. Secretary of agriculture and future president of the Church of Jesus Christ of Latter-Day Saints Ezra Taft Benson instructed his employees to clear all appointments between 11:30 and 11:45 so they could sit and pray together in their offices. "God rules in the affairs of men and nations," Benson informed his department heads, "and it is well for us to join together in rekindling our faith and determination that freedom shall yet bless all mankind."[96] This would not be the last time government workers and Americans were called upon to pray for victory in Eisenhower's crusade. More days of prescribed prayer would follow—some prearranged and some ad hoc.

This emphasis on common faith in the face of a foreign creed catalyzed the most significant period of legislative sacralization in American history. From 1954 to 1956, Congress engaged in a concerted and bipartisan effort to legislate faith. The products of this effort remain intact today both as monuments to Cold War sacralization and testaments, often cited by religious interests, to America's important sacred heritage.

With Eisenhower setting a decidedly religious tone, the first phase of the campaign transpired in a rather unlikely place: the U.S. Post Office. By April 1953, Postmaster General Arthur E. Summerfield found his office buried beneath an avalanche letters and telegrams from citizens demanding the words "In God We Trust" appear on new stamps. Nor was the deluge indiscriminate. Michigan senator Charles E. Potter had already introduced a bill requiring all U.S. stamps to bear that phrase after June 30. In the House, Rep. Louis C. Rabaut, also of Michigan, proposed another resolution compelling the Postal Service to print that same motto upon all cancelled letters.[97] "In God We Trust" had appeared once before on a 1928 stamp, which celebrated the sesquicentennial of the Valley Forge encampment with an image—quite familiar to cold warriors—of Washington kneeling in prayer.[98] The bills never made it out of their respective postal committees, but Summerfield could not ignore the momentum behind such resolutions. A year later, the Postal Service unveiled a new eight-cent stamp bearing the motto in a red arch over an image of the Statue of Liberty.

The decision to use the motto on an eight-cent stamp was strategic, since that was the standard rate for international postage. Over 200 million "In God We Trust" stamps would carry letters around the world each year, a "beacon of hope and opportunity to oppressed peoples everywhere," as Summerfield put it. Stamp-dedication ceremonies were often command performances attended by second or third tier dignitaries, but Eisenhower, Dulles, and Cardinal Spellman all graced Summerfield's launch of the new stamp. The secretary of state believed the stamp would affirm America's determination "to stay free and to stand firm with those who are like-minded." Spellman called the motto a "God-saving message" that would "inspire enshackled peoples everywhere." The president hoped it would bring a message to all corners of the world that America stood for more than gadgets and material gain. For him, the stamp captured the spiritual quality on which American success had been based.[99]

By the time of the stamp dedication, Congress was debating a change to the Pledge of Allegiance. In fact, little in the way of actual disagreement developed over the merits of such an alteration. If anything, the only debate in the Capitol's chambers came from those vying to make their reasons for the amendment seem the most sincere. While the simple addition of the words "under God" to the pledge was merely one act in a larger process of Cold War government sacralization, it would serve through the coming decades as the poster child of America's holy crusade—encapsulating for some a time when the government took religion seriously and summing up for others the irrational anti-Communist frenzy of the 1950s.

It is ironic, then, that the Pledge of Allegiance was originally written by a Christian socialist. Francis Bellamy, a pastor turned journalist who spent his earlier career delivering sermons in Boston with titles like "Jesus the Socialist," penned the pledge to coincide with the four hundredth anniversary of Columbus's first expedition to America.[100] It first appeared inside the September 8, 1892, edition of the popular magazine *The Youth's Companion*. This earliest incarnation read:

> I pledge allegiance to my Flag,
> And the Republic for which it stands:
> One Nation indivisible,
> With Liberty and Justice for all.

Bellamy worked in concert with the National Education Association as part of the Columbian Public School Celebration. With further backing from President Benjamin Harrison and Congress, more than twelve million school children recited the new Pledge on Columbus Day the following month. The original pledge also called for children to raise their right arms to the flag, a gesture later dropped for its disturbing similarity to the Nazi salute. Though its birth had been a success, the pledge did not become an established patriotic expression until the American Legion and Daughters of the American Revolution sponsored the first National Flag Conference in 1923. Within a year the words "my flag" were officially changed to "the flag of the United States of America." By World War II thirty states had passed laws requiring the flag salute in public schools.[101] It had become a staple of classroom rituals and patriotic events across the nation, notwithstanding a successful challenge to mandatory recital by Jehovah's Witnesses in 1943.[102]

As the nation's most visible and most popular patriotic affirmation, the pledge was an ideal project for the spiritual-industrial complex. The Knights of Columbus, America's largest Catholic fraternal organization, acted first. Its board of directors decided in April 1951 that all chapter meetings would begin with a pledge that included the words "under God." At their annual meeting in August 1952, the Knights adopted a resolution calling upon Congress to do the same. By early the following year, other civic and religious organizations like the 800,000 member New York Fraternal Congress joined the movement. Democratic congressman Louis C. Rabaut became the first national lawmaker to act on this recommendation when he introduced House Joint Resolution 243 in April 1953. He prickled at the pledge's secular message, which for him represented a cold prayer to an institution "evolved out of the human mind and established and maintained by human hands alone." America's oath was a form of state idolatry similar to that practiced by the Hitler Youth or Communist children. "Our country was born under God," he argued, "and only under God will it live as a citadel of freedom."[103]

The words "under God" conveyed an important history. Their most renowned usage came in Lincoln's Gettysburg Address during the height of another national crisis. It was only fitting, then, that Eisenhower sat in the Great Emancipator's old pew at the New York Avenue Presbyterian Church in celebration of Lincoln Sunday on February 7, 1954. With so influential a captive audience, the Reverend George M. Docherty refused to let the historical parallels speak for themselves. That Sabbath he delivered one of the most influential sermons of the early Cold War.

Docherty meditated on the meaning of Americanism. In soaring and beautiful prose he catalogued those disparate elements that formed the core of American identity: fireworks on Independence Day, pumpkin pie cooling on a windowsill, eating popcorn at a ballgame, rocking on the porch in a wicker chair on a Sunday afternoon. But underneath this inventory of pleasant images coursed the true essence of Americanism: fundamental belief in God's law. Lincoln understood that notion. Docherty argued his message at Gettysburg was "the text of our day and generation also."

> We face, today, a theological war. It is not basically a conflict between two political philosophies—Thomas Jefferson's political democracy over against Lenin's communistic state. Nor is it a conflict fundamentally between two economic systems—between, shall we say, Adam Smith's "Wealth of Nations" and Karl Marx's "Das Capital." . . . It is the view of

man as it comes down to us from the Judao-Christian [*sic*] civilization in mortal combat against modern, secularized, godless humanity."[104]

A Scotsman by birth, Docherty told of his revelation upon hearing his children recite the Pledge of Allegiance. It struck him that something important was missing. Aside from its mention of the United States, the reverend concluded that it could have been the oath of any nation. "In fact," Docherty preached, "I could hear little Muscovites repeat a similar pledge to their hammer and sickle flag in Moscow with equal solemnity."[105] This logic would prove the most frequently cited congressional justification for amending the pledge.[106]

Docherty took the rhetoric one step further, expressing in sharp words what many thought but few admitted publicly. Perhaps anticipating the opposition his plan might generate, he ended the sermon with a discussion of nonreligious Americans. He explained that an atheistic American was a "contradiction in terms." Secular Americans were "spiritual parasites" who lived on the "accumulated Spiritual Capital of Judaio-Christian [*sic*]" labor. It was a crude logic. Americans could not deny Judeo-Christian teachings and at the same time live by the Judeo-Christian ethic. Those who lived without this ethic fell "short of the American ideal of life." In short, they really were not Americans at all.[107]

After the service, Eisenhower told Docherty that he agreed wholeheartedly.[108] Reports of the sermon and full-length copies began to circulate in the capital.[109] Michigan senator Homer Ferguson introduced Joint Resolution 126 three days after Docherty's sermon, which he credited in a Senate report as the most important catalyst for the legislation that followed. "The spiritual bankruptcy of the Communists is one of our strongest weapons in the struggle for men's minds," Ferguson wrote, "and this resolution gives us a new means of using that weapon."[110] Members of the House introduced sixteen additional resolutions demanding the addition of "under God," nine by Republicans and seven by Democrats. Of the eighteen total resolutions, Catholic legislators submitted ten. Though the South had long been associated with religious fervency, none of the resolutions came from southern congressman. Few, in fact, came from districts outside the northeast.[111]

The Senate passed Ferguson's Pledge of Allegiance resolution quickly and without debate on May 11. The House took up the resolution on June 7. Some representatives like Rabaut and Oregon's Homer D. Angell argued that the Cold War "would ultimately . . . be won by the system of government which is founded on true and lasting principles." "Bombs and guns have been tried and failed," argued Angell.[112] Others emphasized the worldwide message such a resolution would send. Oliver P. Bolton of Ohio believed that by adding "under God" to the pledge, Americans would give hope to those parts of the world resisting Communist infiltration. It would remind them that humans were not "mere cogs in a machine." A colleague from Louisiana concurred: "Communism with its siren voice of false appeal is heard round the world and many peoples and many nations fall prey to these false headlights on the shores of time." New Jersey's Peter Rodino, Jr., who like Rabaut, Angell, and Bolton had introduced his own resolution, skipped over the corporeal debate entirely, quoting from the Psalm 91: "He that dwelleth in the aid of the Most High, shall abide under the protection of the God of Heaven. . . . Thou shalt not be afraid of the terror of the night."[113] The resolution carried unanimously.

That Congress passed the Pledge of Allegiance resolution is hardly surprising. By the spring of 1954, the national momentum behind the change was indisputable. A Gallup poll showed that 70 percent of Americans favored addition of "under God." Countless constituent letters demanding action inundated Congressional offices.[114] In May 1954, the Massachusetts legislature passed its own resolution in favor of amending the pledge, noting that "spiritual values are every bit as important to the defense and safety of our nation as are military and economic values."[115] The *New York Journal-American*, whose editorial board had been shaped by Hearst, opined, "It seems to us in times like these when godless Communism is the greatest peril this nation faces, it becomes more necessary than ever to avow our faith in God."[116]

While public consensus overwhelmingly backed change to the pledge, the same Gallup poll revealed than 20 percent of Americans opposed it. The Unitarian Ministers Association, for example, went on record in opposition.[117] Newspapers received concerned warnings from secular citizens.[118] So too did Eisenhower.[119] The fact that the Pledge of Allegiance resolution emerged unscathed from Congress, without so much as a whispered objection, signaled both the extent to which religious conceptualizations of the Cold War had become accepted, irrefutable fact as well as congressional awareness of the dangerous threat Communism posed. But the unanimity with which Congress acted evinced something even more significant: opposition to sacralization was considered tantamount to disloyalty and indefensible un-Americanism. For those legislators with qualms—and there must have been some—the proposed change probably seemed like an acceptable compromise compared to other proposals then being floated by colleagues. Vermont senator Ralph E. Flanders's resolution amending the Constitution to include the phrase "This Nation devoutly recognizes the authority and law of Jesus Christ" no doubt made a nonsectarian revision of the pledge seem more palatable. It was no time for profiles in secular courage.

On Flag Day, June 14, 1954, the president signed the bill into law. "In this way we are reaffirming the transcendence of religious faith in America's heritage and future," he wrote in a signing statement; "in this way we shall constantly strengthen those spiritual weapons which forever will be our country's most powerful resource in peace or in war." Senator Ferguson and Congressman Rabaut presided over a flag ceremony on the Capitol's steps in which they led the Congress in recitation of the new pledge.[120] Pleased with it actions, Congress authorized the printing of 681,000 copies of the updated pledge for distribution to the public. By July, school boards in the suburbs of Washington, DC, had approved plans for the new pledge's recitation during the coming school year. The New York Board of Regents did the same in September. Within a year, the amended oath even had its own official song, composed by Irving Caesar, whose previous hits included "Tea for Two" and "Is It True What They Say about Dixie?"[121]

Bellamy's potential reaction to the amended pledge is, of course, impossible to know, but in a culture obsessed with centuries-old, original intent, it is an illustrative endeavor.[122] As a committed Christian leader, Bellamy afforded God an important place in his notion of Americanism. The true significance was not Bellamy's omission of reference to God but rather his apparent conclusion that no such mention was needed. For him the relationship between the nation and the Almighty was implicit and assumed.[123] Thus, this legislative action in the Cold War was in some ways a testament more to the corrosive effect of twentieth-century secularization than to the exigency of Communist aggression.

Bellamy would have agreed with Eisenhower's frequent diatribe against materialism, but for an entirely different reason. As a Baptist preacher, he deplored the rapacious pursuit of American gain made possible by the sweat of the lower classes. "Capitalism must pass into the kingdom of love," he argued. He bridled as "the atoms on top of the sand heap" pressed down "harder and harder [upon] the atoms below."[124] Bellamy believed that the best check on materialism was not necessarily a spiritual one but instead a recommitment to American ideals like justice and liberty. Had he preached these notions during the early Cold War, he might have found himself hauled before HUAC or tarred by J. Edgar Hoover, so complete was the religious fault separating Communists from anti-Communists by 1954.

Congressional sacralization did not end with changes to the pledge. Not content with religious expressions on paper alone, the nation's legislature decided to make its own surroundings more in keeping with the religious renewal then underway. While the Pledge of Allegiance bill was moving through both houses, Congress also passed Concurrent Resolution 60, directing the Capitol architect to construct a religious chamber. The Congressional Prayer Room opened in 1955. Accessed through the rotunda, it was decorated in blue and focused upon an open Bible sitting on a white oak altar. The spiritual refuge had kneeling benches, seating for ten, and a stained glass window depicting Washington kneeling in prayer. The words "Preserve me, O God, for in thee do I put my trust" encircled the president. Above him hung Lincoln's phrase "This

Nation Under God." Now, in the sacred confrontation against Communism, legislators could seek divine guidance before making important decisions. Perhaps they could rest easy in the knowledge that no similar chamber existed in the Kremlin—at least not one in current use. After all, the Chudov Monastery and Ascension Convent had been dismantled in 1917 to make room for Communist Party offices.[125]

Over the next two years, political discussion shifted from "under God" to "In God We Trust." Like "under God," those four words could trace their origin in the American lexicon to the Civil War, when the director of the U.S. Mint drew upon the fourth stanza of "The Star-Spangled Banner":

> Then conquer we must, when our cause it is just,
> And this be our motto: "In God is our Trust."

In 1865 Congress passed a bill permitting inscription of "In God We Trust" on seven popular coin denominations.[126]

"In God We Trust" reigned unchallenged as the unofficial motto of American coinage until Theodore Roosevelt's second term as president. Convinced that the United States needed currency that matched its growing power in measures of artistry and symbolism, Roosevelt tasked a favored sculptor with redesigning the nation's coins in 1905, and the artist promptly dropped the motto.[127] A determined coalition of religious leaders, patriotic organizations, and politicians rose in opposition. Though the president argued that such statements printed on currency only cheapened religion, calls of "sacrilege" and "infidel" made Roosevelt's position too tenuous for even the bully pulpit to overcome. Roosevelt decided against spending any more political capital on a seemingly insignificant issue, and in 1908 Congress overwhelmingly passed a new law making the Civil War–era inscription mandatory.[128]

When Congress resurrected the issue of God and currency in 1955, it hardly reopened an old wound. Rep. Charles E. Bennett of Florida credited the president of the Florida Bar Association with giving him the idea to complete the process of monetary sacralization begun during the Civil War. He introduced House Resolution 619, which mandated that "In God We Trust" be inscribed on all U.S. money, including, for the first time, paper currency. The timing of Bennett's bill may have seemed almost providential, since the U.S. Mint was about to upgrade its printing machines. The under secretary of monetary affairs informed Bennett that Eisenhower would look favorably upon the change. Congress used tested and true justifications for the bill, tying the legislation to the spiritual threat of Communism and the need to strengthen American freedom under God. Soon the world's foremost currency would announce with every transaction America's clear position on the religious question central to the Cold War.

Bennett's bill quickly passed both houses of Congress in June and was signed into law by Eisenhower on July 11, 1955.[129]

In its final major act of legislative sacralization during Eisenhower's first term, Congress turned its attention to establishing a national motto in 1956. At the time America had no official slogan, though the phrase "E Pluribus Unum" came closest to serving this end. Latin for "one out of many," it was incorporated into the Great Seal of the United States by an act of Congress in 1782 and inscribed on U.S. coins beginning in 1795.[130] But by the mid 1950s, legislative opinion favored a different adage. A House report considered "In God We Trust" "superior" to "E Pluribus Unum." It would be "of great spiritual and psychological value to our country to have a clearly designated national motto of inspirational quality in plain, popularly accepted English," the report concluded.[131] House Joint Resolution 396, a four-line bill adopting "In God We Trust" as the national motto, passed through Congress without floor debate, and Eisenhower signed Public Law 851 on July 30, 1956 as he cruised to a landslide reelection victory.[132] As with the currency law the previous summer, few Americans objected.[133]

Perhaps the dearth of media coverage was one indicator of growing fatigue with sacralization. Still, the legislative edicts were significant, both for the shifting perspectives they substantiated and for the cultural residue that would remain for future generations. Mottos encapsulate in a few words the motivations and intentions of social groups, organizations, or even nations. Both "E Pluribus Unum" and "In God We Trust" spoke to the dilemmas of national unity, but it is telling that lawmakers in the Cold War decided that faith in God, rather than faith in the nation's ability to weld together disparate interests, was "superior." Public Law 851 faded quickly into memory. As the years passed, the new national motto, like the new pledge and the political rhetoric accompanying it, seemed less a Cold War construction and more an eternal American truth— passed down, perhaps, from the lips and quills of the founders themselves.

4

Security Institutions

"Our over-all objective in seeking the use of religion as a cold war instrumentality should be the furtherance of world spiritual . . . health; for the Communist threat could not exist in a spiritually healthy world."
—Psychological Strategy Board, "Inventory of Instrumentalities," 1951

Acting simultaneously with the exhortations and legislations of politicians, America's national-security institutions implemented their own series of policies premised upon the conclusion that faith could be a weapon in the Cold War. Security analysts explored the ways that spirituality could strengthen the nation's psychological character, and they speculated on the disadvantages of a spiritually enervated population. Military leaders experimented with programs designed to create a new generation of religiously grounded soldiers. A reenergized propaganda establishment tinkered with a host of schemes and programs contrived to contrast America's God-centeredness with the Communist rejection of the supernatural.

The year 1946 was a watershed for American security analysts. In that deep breath before the Cold War's full onset, they recognized that Soviet power was conspiring with Communist ideology to produce a new conflict of political, economic, and spiritual dimensions. By January policy analysts were beginning to conclude that relations with the Soviet Union would be different from anything the United States had known before. Edward F. Willett, in his top-secret January 14 report "Dialectical Communism and Russian Objectives," noted that there was little ostensible reason why a bitter struggle between the world's superpowers should develop. But beneath the everyday machinations of state interest, Willett saw that the Communist philosophy of life would make conflict nearly unavoidable. After discussing the economic and political elements of the Communist worldview, he turned to religion and morality. "Any relaxation in Communist opposition to religion," he wrote, "should probably be regarded more properly as a temporary departure to allay opposition rather than as a change in basic philosophy." He believed that Communist enmity to religion was animated by a deeper moral impetus, which justified any action, no matter how violent or evil, if it brought about the ideal Communist society.[1]

Like Reinhold Niebuhr and Martin Dies before him, Willett recognized that Communism was more than a political or merely antireligious movement. When this viewpoint was applied to American national security, the full ramifications of the Communist faith crystallized. "It should be clear at the outset that under these circumstances the United States is laboring under a severe disadvantage," he warned. "Russia is a nation with the Messianic goal, the driving force around which a crusading spirit can be built up. Our driving force is only the somewhat passive concept of self-defense."[2] America would be severely disadvantaged in a battle of asymmetric zeal—a battle in which the fanatical war cries of Communist faith drowned out the American chants of state interest. A counterfaith, then, was desperately needed, something to arouse American fervor in the impending conflict.

Five weeks after Willett released his report, George F. Kennan, then serving in the Soviet Union, transmitted his famous "Long Telegram" from Moscow to the State Department. It would form the ideological and strategic frame around which the nation's foreign policy was later constructed. Kennan argued that previous American approaches to the Soviet Union were dangerously flawed. The Soviets could not be tamed by sycophantic gestures or bribed into compliance. The prophetic certainties of Marxism found refuge in the traditional insecurities of the Russian soul, producing a nation that combined irrational hostility with deadly capability. The USSR was driven by an illogical internal engine, and external forces like foreign diplomacy could not shape Soviet action. Kennan believed that the Soviet Union was "impervious to the logic of reason" but "sensitive to the logic of force." When confronted directly, the Soviets usually backed down. Kennan's conclusions immediately found enthusiastic reception in Washington. The Containment Doctrine was born.[3]

Kennan was applauded for his sensible approach to the Soviets, emphasizing the traits they shared with a long line of totalitarian predecessors, but he could not avoid noting the ideological and ultimately psychological facets of any confrontation with Russia.[4] He viewed Communism as a seductive philosophy. Like Catholic commentators, he used the analogy of disease to explain the Communist menace. Diseases rarely struck perfectly healthy bodies, he argued. They fed instead on weakened tissue. "Much depends on [the] health and vigor of our own society," Kennan explained. "This is [the] point at which domestic and foreign policies meet. Every courageous and incisive measure to solve internal problems of our own people is a diplomatic victory over Moscow worth a thousand diplomatic notes and joint communiqués." Like Willett a month earlier, Kennan believed that victory in the mounting Soviet conflict depended on internal vitality. Militarily, the Soviets were weak. In the fight against this new enemy, national self-confidence and the preservation of the American way counted.[5]

In early 1946 few Americans had heard of Kennan or the embryonic strategy of containment. But when Winston Churchill strode to the podium of tiny Westminster College in Fulton, Missouri, on March 5, the nation listened.[6] Churchill's expressed purpose was to convince America that postwar alliance with Britain was necessary. The phrase "special relationship," coined by the former prime minister to describe transatlantic friendship, immediately entered American parlance. So too did Churchill's "iron curtain" metaphor. In many respects he articulated Kennan's basic sentiments to a far wider audience. The Soviet Union was an irrational, tyrannical state that should be treated as a threat rather than a friend. More importantly, he echoed Kennan's assumption that the USSR knew no logic but force. But he also understood that this new conflict transcended the realm of foreign policy. Communism wormed its way into the domestic sphere, poisoning nations from within. Only materially and morally strong societies could withstand this "growing challenge and peril to Christian civilization." Churchill framed the contest as a battle between ideologies as well as armies, dashing hopes for a peaceful and cooperative USSR. One week after his "Sinews of Peace" speech, American popular opinion of Russia plummeted.[7]

Three months later, John Foster Dulles published a two-part article in *Life* called "Thoughts on Soviet Policy and What to do About It" that placed religion at the center of Cold War strategy. The grandson and nephew of secretaries of state and son of a Presbyterian minister, Dulles situated a belief in the efficacy of moral force within a foreign-policy framework. He also accepted the narrative of secularization, noting that the twentieth century had led to a "steady exhaustion of our spiritual springs." Like other analysts he believed that national security abroad rested in part upon domestic vitality. But Dulles went a step further in tying American survival to sacralization.[8]

Dulles understood the unfolding Cold War as an "impact of the dynamic upon the static." A spiritually stagnant American society "equipped only with the material products of past greatness" would be unable to "resist the penetration of alien faiths." The Cold War would be a battle of competing definitions, since the Soviets too laid claim to the mantle of freedom and democracy. They characterized themselves as the world's true agents of change. America had to reclaim this distinction in the eyes of other nations, and Dulles believed that U.S. foreign policy needed to reunite faith and practice. The answer was spiritual containment. "Soviet leaders," Dulles wrote, "would know that their project is impracticable against a people who believe that their freedoms flow from their Creator and who also use those freedoms with the restraint which is enjoined by divine commandment." Rather than meeting Soviet aggression with military power, as Kennan suggested, Dulles advocated the application of moral and spiritual force.[9]

Though security analysts offered differing viewpoints, they shared three basic assumptions: conflict with the Soviets would be unlike anything the U.S. had faced; ideology, psychology, and spirituality would play an important role in any victory; and America's domestic vitality would directly influence its ability to achieve international victories. As American political leaders reached consensus on the religious means by which Communism could be combated, so too did the nation's warriors.

It had long been popular to assert there were no atheists in foxholes, but the U.S. military tried to ensure there would be none in the training barracks either. The armed forces provided an opportunity for the conclusions of security analysts to be fashioned into specific policy reforms. The catalyst was Truman's decision to enact a new system of universal military training (UMT). Rather than relying on a selective service or a volunteer fighting force, he proposed a year of mandatory military training for every young American man upon graduation from high school. Men between the ages of eighteen and twenty would be required to enter a six-month program, after which they could choose to either enlist or train for another half year. The military estimated that one million men would receive training annually. Truman appointed a special commission to study the feasibility of UMT, and his administration began a concentrated publicity blitz in 1947 designed to assuage deep-seated American fears of "Prussianization."[10]

The plan bore great security potential, but it also carried significant risk. America's fighting force in World War II had been older, more mature, and better educated than the eighteen- and nineteen-year-olds that would enter the UMT program. By 1948, minors would make up half the total armed forces and account for 70 percent of all new enlistments.[11] Military leaders and the American public worried that these new recruits were too naïve, impressionable, and prone to vice. The military would have to coddle, serving them in a sense as surrogate parents and educators. And here American leaders recognized a critical opportunity. Army chief of staff George C. Marshall held fast to the belief that spirituality was the linchpin of morale. He believed that this type of confidence could "only come out of the religious nature of a soldier who knows God and who had the spirit of religious fervor in his soul."[12] Military leaders could engineer a generation of patriotic, virtuous Cold Warriors.[13] But at the same time, they realized that the plan risked creation of a Frankenstein's monster—a large, unruly standing military devoid of virtue. The plan needed a failsafe. In the final analysis military leaders decided the best option was not to pull the plug on their monster but to give it a soul, and to this end religion became indispensable.

Brigadier General John M. Devine arrived at the rolling, wooded hills of Fort Knox, Kentucky, on November 8, 1946. He had served under Patton in the hedgerows of Normandy and later commanded the Eighth Armored Division. But this time the Pentagon entrusted Devine with an entirely different assignment. He would oversee one of the most revolutionary experiments in American military history—a plan to morally and spiritually engineer the U.S. Army.[14] Truman and the military needed proof that UMT would not simply Prussianize or corrupt America's impressionable youth. They also recognized a priceless opportunity to create a perfect soldier who could ground lethal capability in a religious framework. And so the Fort Knox experiment began.

The first training cycle began with the arrival of 664 volunteers at Fort Knox in early 1947. With an average age of seventeen and a half years old, they were still boys, and Devine refused to put them through a trial by fire. A Father Flannigan in fatigues, his domain sometimes looked less like a fort than a boarding school with guns. He housed recruits in comfortable, dormitory-style quarters, fed them family-style, and instructed his officers and staff sergeants to act like father figures. Instructors did not teach recruits to hate their enemies. They did not yell at the young men or embarrass them publicly after a mistake. The general believed that all young men were essentially "good" at heart. But these

Weekly religious services were mandatory for these trainees at Fort Knox in May 1947. Soldiers who refused to attend had to meet for one hour with one of the base's chaplains instead. Even when religious attendance was no longer mandatory, 90 percent of recruits continued attending church or synagogue. (©1947 by *The Courier-Journal.*)

reforms paled in comparison to the new role that Devine afforded religion in his little utopia. Religious instruction and guidance was the thread holding the Fort Knox experiment together. So important was religion to Devine's program that the army regulars on the base called it "Father Devine's Heaven."[15]

The key to Devine's religious project was an overhaul of the military chaplaincy. The U.S. military had long called upon the nation's religious groups to supply chaplains during times of war and peace, but the chaplaincy was informal, disorganized, and altogether erratic. Chaplains needed to be ordained, but aside from this qualification the armed forces had no universal system of training. Nor did chaplains have an official code of conduct. They ran religious services, prayed before battle, proselytized, and offered informal counseling. The first hints of change to this system arrived in World War II, when the army began standardizing the chaplaincy. Regulations required one chaplain for every 1,200 soldiers. The army built thousands of wooden chapels with rotating altars that could easily be switched for varying religious services. The navy began constructing permanent chapels on its bases, signaling a greater commitment to military spirituality. But Devine envisioned something far greater. He wanted a highly organized chaplaincy integrated into the army command structure. In his experimental unit, he recruited two chaplains, one Protestant and one Catholic, and gave them highly visible offices in the camp headquarters. While army trainers worked on the recruits' physical prowess, the chaplains would develop their souls. Their duties went far beyond a weekly church service or a prayer before battle. The Fort Knox chaplains were teachers, missionaries, and counselors.[16]

Shortly after arrival, each recruit met individually with one of the chaplains. Devine believed strongly in "breaking down the barrier that so often exists between the chaplain and the soldier." The chaplains compiled a "religious profile" of each trainee for his permanent record. These profiles went beyond a simple accounting of denominational preference, probing not only a recruit's religious beliefs but his attitude towards religion as well. Devine declared it a "revelation." "It proved at once," the general reflected, "that our original assumption that the average 18-year-old is not a cynic on matters of religion was true." As a result of these early interviews, 160 Protestants and thirty-nine Catholics agreed to an intensive program of religious instruction with the chaplains. Before the end of basic training, the Catholic chaplain confirmed twenty-six recruits and baptized twelve. Not to be outdone, his Protestant colleague converted 102.[17]

As a cohort, the recruits were 76 percent Protestant, 22 percent Catholic, and 2 percent Jewish. A minority reported attending religious services before arriving at Fort Knox. Regardless of their church-going habits, Devine made Sunday attendance of religious services mandatory for the first four weeks of training. If recruits felt strongly about not attending religious services, they had to meet individually with a chaplain for one hour in lieu of public worship. Devine formed a committee of local civilian religious leaders that kept in constant contact with recruits throughout the training period. After the initial four weeks of mandatory on-base religious worship, the committee encouraged the men to join local congregations on Sundays and invited them into their homes for religious holidays. Nor were the chaplains' duties limited to the Sabbath. On weekdays they conducted mandatory classes and lectures. The first lecture's subject fit in perfectly with the larger theme of sacralization then being touted by Truman, Congress, and the business elite: "How our country, with its many liberties, privileges, and opportunities, is founded on moral and religious principles." Future topics varied from applications of everyday morals to religiously focused sex education.[18]

Devine not only charged his chaplains with religious instruction, he made them moral police and emphasized a program of "Christian manners." Obscene language in the experimental unit was strictly forbidden and could lead to disciplinary action. Recruits were served no alcohol on base, and Devine convinced local bartenders to refuse them service when off duty. Chaplains banned any "suggestive" literature, replacing it with works from their approved library. Recruits could not decorate their barracks with pinups, and condoms were confiscated, since they violated the camp's emphasis on abstinence. These men bore little resemblance to the American GIs that British citizens jokingly described as "overpaid, oversexed, and over here" during World War II. A 1947 article from the *Army Information Digest* assured concerned military commanders and the public that Devine was not emasculating the new universal soldier. "There is no lack of virility . . . in the cadre or the trainees; no prissiness," it stated. "Barrack talk is seldom about women." In a photograph labeled "Trainees Off Duty," the *Digest* avoided stereotypical depictions of recruits playing cards or baseball. Instead, the editors published a picture of a young soldier praying in a community church.[19]

The Fort Knox experiment was a rousing success. The U.S. Army demonstrated on a small scale the means for creating a force of holy warriors ostensibly immune to vice and imbued with religious zeal. Only 37 percent of all recruits attended religious services regularly upon entry into the unit, but after initial training, 90 percent reported attending church or synagogue the previous week. Nine in ten enjoyed the regular chaplain lectures, and only four percent anticipated not attending church once religious participation became optional.[20] At the same time Devine was training his new recruits, Truman's Advisory Commission on Universal Training was compiling the Compton Report, a detailed recommendation for nationwide adoption of UMT that built on the arguments of security analysts like Willet and Kennan. Predictably, the report praised the Fort Knox experiment for making available to soldiers of little or no religious faith the "fundamental principles from which all moral values stem."[21] Armed with a rec-ommendation backed by tangible results, Truman moved the proposal forward.

Rarely in political history does an issue achieve the degree of public consen-sus that UMT enjoyed. Nearly 80 percent of all Americans favored universal service. The entire military establishment, including wartime heroes Dwight D. Eisenhower and Douglas MacArthur, stood behind it, as did major veterans' organizations like the American Legion and Veterans of Foreign Wars. The nation's largest newspapers endorsed the plan, and the *New York Times* noted that the proposal was "not an issue that required selling to the American public." Truman made the enactment of UMT a primary goal, casting it publicly as the highest realization of true democracy. Many Republicans agreed.[22]

Although it seemed so succesful, Devine's program was a startling exercise in social control, and a dedicated minority of Americans opposed its adoption. Labor unions like the CIO feared militarization. Teachers and professors cringed at the prospect of the military taking over the education of high school gradu-ates, and the Association of American Colleges voted 219 to 69 against UMT. Surprisingly, some of the stiffest opposition came from religious leaders. Though universal training would give religion a greater voice in the military, they worried that the plan would make war inevitable. The New York Conference of the Meth-odist Church, led by Bishop G. Bromley Oxnam, approved a statement against UMT, as did the General Assembly of the Presbyterian Church. In the summer of 1947, 652 religious leaders signed a petition calling mandatory service an un-American form of indoctrination.[23]

Determined though they were, these opponents would not have been able to derail UMT. That power belonged to a small group of Republican conservatives led by Ohio senator Robert A. Taft. As chairman of the Senate Majority Policy Committee, he determined the order and importance of legislation considered, and Senate Republicans were weary of challenging him. Taft had two major ob-jections to UMT. As a fierce opponent of the New Deal, he criticized the plan for its cost. The yearly expense for UMT would be at least $2 billion, a figure more than the entire annual military budget prior to World War II. But his opposition went deeper than dollars. "The Army wants boys for twelve months consecu-tively," Taft claimed, "because it wants to change their habits of thought, to make them soldiers . . . for the rest of their lives." He argued that UMT would subject "American youth to the complete domination of the Government during their most formative period." This level of social control was incompatible with the long American tradition of free thought, and Taft called it un-American. Despite widespread public rebuke and dissension within his own party, he stood firm, repeating the old arguments that once guided American military policy. In the end, he waited Truman out and won.[24]

Though UMT had been scuttled, the lessons of Fort Knox lived on. Young recruits were not the only soldiers Devine had been training during the experiment. No fewer than eighteen generals attended workshops at the base to learn Devine's program. In addition, eighty company-grade officers and as many non-commissioned officers arrived at Fort Knox every two weeks for abbreviated courses on teaching and leadership techniques. Six new chaplains rolled in each month for similar training starting in July 1947. Army leaders, newly schooled in the "Knox Methods," soon implemented them at other bases like Fort Dix, where chaplains' lectures on religion became mandatory and church attendance nearly doubled.[25]

Devine's training provided a blueprint for establishing the new role of religion in the Cold War military, and Truman wanted to expand on the general's vision. On October 27, 1948, he created the President's Committee on Religion and Welfare in the Armed Forces, also known as the Weil Committee after its chairman, Frank L. Weil, of the Jewish Welfare Board. The committee was composed of civic leaders, educators, social service administrators, and the religious leaders Weil, Edmund A. Walsh, and Daniel A. Poling, whose son was one of the four World War II chaplains who drowned on the *Dorchester*. Together they were a fitting microcosm of the diverse sectors of society that made sacralization possible.[26] Officially, Truman charged the Weil Committee with "encouraging and promoting the religious, moral, and recreational welfare and character guidance of persons in the armed forces and thereby enhancing the military preparedness and security of the nation." It was a bold statement, writing religion into national security, but the Cold War threat seemed unprecedented as well.[27]

Truman joined the Weil Committee for its first official meeting in December. "You know," the president began, "it is alarming ... to find out how little some of our young people understand what we mean by a moral code and ethics of living. That is the reason we can't get peace in this world. We have one power to deal with that does not believe in moral codes and continues to break them." The committee summed up the problem more crisply: "How can the values of democracy be preserved and extended in an unavoidable armed economy of possible long duration?" The goal was to return soldiers to civilian life as better citizens than they were when they enlisted. This inverted a centuries-old paradigm. Rather than being a threat to the values of democracy and virtuous citizenship, a standing military could be their guardian. The Weil Committee knew that religion was the paramount factor in this new equation, and the members decided on a three-point program. They would establish links between military bases and surrounding communities, raise public awareness of the peacetime serviceman's spiritual needs, and conduct a thorough appraisal of military policies regarding religion.[28]

The Weil Committee released an initial set of recommendations in March 1949 geared toward communities near military bases. "The fabric of our society for generations to come will . . . be affected by the influence of military training upon so many future community leaders," the report noted. "We owe it to ourselves, we owe it to our children, and we owe it to the memories of those who gave us our freedom to guarantee the religious and moral welfare of our peacetime servicemen and women." The committee urged communities to encourage service personnel to attend local religious services each weekend and to include them in positions of leadership. The report recommended that local churches and synagogues begin religious education classes and maintain reading rooms for soldiers, sailors, and airmen who had little or no faith. To reach even more potential personnel, the Weil Committee called for chaplain exchange programs in which local religious leaders would come onto bases and teach while chaplains worked in the community. Lastly, to reinforce the religious gains made during military service, the committee suggested church members write letters to the parents of young men they had met. This would reassure concerned parents that their sons and daughters "will be better when they come out of the service than when they went in."[29] Communities across America responded to the Weil Committee's recommendations. Many established GI hospitality centers that blended religious instruction with recreation. Others opened their churches to social activities and parties.[30]

Before making any further recommendations, the committee members decided to canvass American military, religious, and government leaders. In May 1949 the Weil Committee held the National Conference on Community Responsibility to Our Peacetime Servicemen and Women in Washington, DC. In speeches and discussions, the participants argued that the U.S. military faced two unprecedented enemies. Some, like the American representative to the UN Atomic Energy Commission, believed that the gravest threat came from Communism itself. He argued that all previous civilizations shared a common religious background. "Now, for the first time in history," he warned, "a group of men who control . . . the bodies, and, to a large extent, the minds of from 10 to 25 percent of the world's peoples deny these beliefs." Others, like the U.S. Social Security commissioner, acknowledged the threat of Communism but believed that the greatest threat to the American way of life came from the militarization needed to defeat the Soviets. Religious leaders thought the danger of both militarism and Communism was attributable to secularization and the sense of despair that had fallen over America's youth. Still, they took the opportunity to celebrate what was in their eyes an even more extraordinary historical development: for the first time religion was at the core of a presidential committee.[31]

Though it emphasized the importance of community religious involvement, the Weil Committee left its most indelible imprint on the military chaplaincy, which made Devine's vision a reality for all branches of the armed forces. In July 1949, the secretary of defense established the Armed Forces Chaplains Board, charged with advising the military brass and developing uniform religious policies. The following year the Weil Committee released a report entitled *The Military Chaplaincy*, which placed religion in the military at the center of national security. Like so many other leaders in American society, the members of the Weil Committee defined the Cold War in religious terms. "Because of the world's unprecedented awareness of the need for spiritual vitality," the committee wrote, "the importance of the work of the chaplaincy has reached an unparalleled peak." It mailed copies of this report to the governors of all forty-eight states, who lauded its recommendations. Many incorporated parts of the report into their Thanksgiving Day proclamations. "Torn away from their families and loved ones," the governor of North Carolina declared, "our men and women in uniform need the armor of religion and an inner spiritual security."[32]

Weil himself proved the most fervent and articulate messenger on this point. In a 1950 speech before military chaplains in Washington, he called the Cold War an "unparalleled struggle for the minds, the hearts, and the imagination of men around the world." Like so many other Cold War leaders, he believed that differing conceptions of religion defined the conflict:

> If our churches, temples, and synagogues were to be destroyed, or if organized religion were to become decadent and lifeless, our freedom which we cherish would have lost its first, its greatest, its final bulwark of defense. In fact, our democratic heritage is so completely a child of religion that it may be reasonably doubted that our American version of Democracy can survive if religion becomes desiccated and sterile.[33]

Military leaders agreed wholeheartedly. General C. T. Lanham observed, "No longer are we content to regard the religious and moral welfare of our men with indifference." General Lucius D. Clay called for a "spiritual airlift" in Berlin. What began with Devine in 1947 blossomed into a period of full-fledged military sacralization.

In 1949, the Freedoms Foundation, a nonsectarian civic group founded by two Los Angeles admen, enshrined the connection between national defense and religion by building a chapel at Valley Forge. There General Washington had kept his forlorn army intact through a gnawing winter. According to early Washington biographer Parson Weems, one day a Pennsylvanian Quaker came upon Washington praying alone on his knees in the snowy woods. So moved was the Loyalist by the general's conviction and faith that he reconsidered his opposition to the revolution. "Thee knows that I always thought the sword and the gospel utterly inconsistent; and that no man could be a soldier and a Christian at the

Washington kneeling in prayer at Valley Forge. Though no evidence exists that this scene took place, it became a prominent symbol for groups like the Freedoms Foundation in the early Cold War. (Engraving by John C. McRae, 1866. Courtesy of the Library of Congress.)

same time," he informed his wife, "but George Washington has this day convinced me of my mistake."[34] Weems made the entire story up, but Cold War Americans hardly seemed to care. Washington provided a superlative template for the military's new emphasis on religion—a man whose faith sustained him through the anxiety and travail of war.

The Freedoms Foundation benefited from a close connection to the military. Supported by Eisenhower, it worked in conjunction with both the Office of Armed Forces Information and Education and the Armed Forces Radio and Television Service. The foundation encouraged all school children to make a "pilgrimage" to the historic site. It began giving out cash awards for good citizenship and reserved the highest honors for Americans who served as living embodiments of true freedom. These awards went to the leaders of sacralization, men like Fulton Sheen, Billy Graham, and Eisenhower.[35]

In 1950 the Freedoms Foundation bestowed its highest honor on Omar Bradley. A superior athlete and scholar, Bradley was planning on a career in the military until a Sunday-school teacher suggested he apply to West Point. Like Devine, he served with Patton during World War II before being promoted to commander of the First Army in northern France. After the war he headed the Veteran's Administration until his appointment as army chief of staff in 1948.

That year in Boston on Armistice Day, Bradley offered his own version of the colossus-of-straw formulation:

> With the monstrous weapons man already has, humanity is in danger of being trapped in this world by its moral adolescents [*sic*]. . . . We have grasped the mystery of the atom and rejected the Sermon on the Mount. Man is stumbling through a spiritual darkness with the precarious secrets of life and death. The world has achieved brilliance without wisdom, power without conscience. Ours is a world of nuclear giants and ethical infants.[36]

In 1949 Bradley was made the first chairman of the Joint Chiefs of Staff. He brought his concern for the proper exercise of unprecedented power to Valley Forge two years later when he came to accept the Freedoms Foundation's highest honor. "If we seek to protect the freedom which we hold in trust, we must provide more than material things," Bradley reflected. "Divine Providence gives us another, and greater strength which has never surrendered to any threat or peril."[37]

With a presidential committee and key military leaders calling for a renewed commitment to religion in the armed forces, reforms in the army and air force followed almost immediately. Shortly after the start of the Fort Knox experiment, the army instituted a revamped program of mandatory religious instruction called the Chaplain's Hour, which it renamed Character Guidance in 1948. In the first twelve weeks of training, new recruits attended a minimum of six hour-long lectures given by chaplains, whose topics included the Ten Commandments, the sanctity of marriage, the relationship between democracy and religion, and the dangerous faith of Communism. All other personnel had to attend similar lectures monthly. The policy continued, largely unchallenged, until the early 1960s.[38]

The crux of the Character Guidance courses was the belief that people were moral beings whose sense of right and wrong stemmed from religion. Recruits read in their Character Guidance workbooks that "the Moral Law has to do with our attitude towards God and toward our fellow men. The first part of the Moral Law is concerned with matters of worship, adoration, and reverence toward God in life and speech." The army held that good character combined both personal and civic virtues, and religion underwrote both. Personal virtues like faith, hope, and love were "specifically encouraged and given an opportunity to go to work in attendance at Sunday School, at religious services, as well as at prayer meetings and devotions." Civic virtues came from the relationship between a nation and God.[39]

This curriculum seemed tame compared to that of the newly independent Air Force. There the U.S. Air Force chief of staff gave the head of the air force chaplaincy, Major General Charles I. Carpenter, free rein to institute his own character-guidance program. Carpenter had a bachelor's degree in divinity and began his career in the armed forces as a Methodist chaplain. Assigned to the army air force in World War II, he seemed an ideal candidate to carry out Truman's mandate for sacralization in the air force after being named chief of the air force chaplains in 1948.

Carpenter created lay retreats for air force personnel. He opened up air bases to preaching missions by nonmilitary religious leaders and organized a conference on spiritual life for airmen. Like Devine, Carpenter made his chaplains moral police. They reported incidents of moral laxity, approved all on-base entertainment, monitored all troop literature, removed questionable materials from base libraries, and confiscated obscene materials. The chaplains also coordinated with the local religious community to ensure airmen could integrate into nearby congregations. But Carpenter believed that his chaplains could do more. Religion could solve the personal problems of air force personnel. In one case cited by a U.S. Air Force report, an officer had "embarrassed the military by neglecting to adequately provide for the needs of his family." After meeting with a chaplain and attending church regularly, however, he "stated that the sermons heard in the chapel gave him new courage and also helped him to realize that he had a responsibility to his family, to society, and also to God." In another case, an air force surgeon diagnosed an airman with neurosis that stemmed from religious confusion. He prescribed a session with the chaplain, who set up a "systematic plan" of religious treatment.[40]

Carpenter's character-guidance program was a well-organized vehicle for religious propaganda. In late 1948 he met with representatives from the Moody Institute of Science (MIS), an evangelical organization devoted to repairing the damage done by the Darwinian revolution in general and the Scopes trial in particular. Based in Hollywood, MIS began producing a series of films that, by observing the wonders of science and nature, emphasized the plausibility of God's purposeful design over scientific randomness. Each film manipulated scientific observations into evidence for biblical literalism. Rather than destroying spirituality, they held, science could reinforce it. Carpenter thought the MIS films would be suitable teaching aids in his new character-guidance program. He agreed to distribute the films *God of Creation*, *God of the Atom*, *Voice of the Deep*, and *Dust or Destiny* to airbases in America and around the world. The air force provided a MIS representative with a fully crewed B-25 that traveled from base to base preaching the evangelical message. By 1951, nearly 200,000 airmen were watching the films each year, and the air force claimed that as a result church attendance among service personnel had increased by 17 percent.[41] Troops reported high levels of satisfaction with the reorganized chaplaincy, and Carpenter's curriculum was popular with those outside the military as well. When, in 1954, the Government Printing Office published his character-guidance program, secular and religious educators eagerly laid down $1.80 to purchase the textbooks.[42]

When Truman disbanded the President's Committee on Religion and Welfare in the Armed Forces in February 1951, he considered it a success. Weil and his colleagues, together with military leaders, believed they had solved a long-standing problem. America could maintain a large standing military without compromising those virtues the republic depended upon. The army and air force character-guidance programs were both in place on June 25, 1950, when Northern Korean troops stormed across the 38th parallel. Between June 1950 and the summer of 1952, well over two million new recruits entered the armed forces. In the first full year of the Korean War, army chaplains alone conducted over 200,000 religious services and held 78,000 classes on religious instruction.[43] Over the next decade, millions more would complete the religiously centered training programs in the U.S. military. Many would attend religious services

American soldiers celebrating Catholic mass during the Korean War in 1950. That year alone, Army chaplains conducted more than 200,000 religious services. (Courtesy of the Truman Library.)

for the first time. They would return to civilian life with a greater knowledge of religion and its crucial role in American society.

U.S. security analysts understood that the Cold War would rage in minds and souls of non-Americans, especially those in the ideological battlegrounds of Europe and the developing world. Winning a holy war required changes in both domestic practice and international perception. The Soviet Union offered sweeping change at a time when the status quo seemed unbearable. They fed the mind and body. American Cold Warriors, on the other hand, concentrated at first on feeding the body, but this did not satisfy those psychological needs Soviet propagandists had long appreciated. Realizing that they labored under a serious disadvantage, American policymakers waged a worldwide war of ideas aimed at mitigating the Communists' psychological advantage. Not surprisingly, U.S. propagandists threw everything they could at Communism—freedom, democracy, material wealth, respect for the individual—but in the early Cold War, religion proved a particularly sharp instrumentality. In covert discussions and public action, religion became part of America's program of psychological warfare. Now Americans would bring the cross down upon the hammer.

Cold Warriors did not invent the use of propaganda in wartime but they perfected it. The twentieth century's great ideological struggle coincided with a technological and professional communications revolution. Radio and television could disseminate information more quickly and more widely than print. At the same time, scholars, journalists, and business leaders were developing the nascent field of public opinion. During World War II, propaganda fell under the larger heading of psychological warfare, which encapsulated those actions that weakened the enemy without the use of military force. General Eisenhower established a Psychological Warfare Branch composed of skilled British and American propagandists, and he credited it with obtaining enemy surrenders in the North African and Italian campaigns. MacArthur created his own psychological corps in the Pacific, dropping some 400 million leaflets before Japan's surrender. Victories over the mind made victories over the body easier or even unnecessary. Perception became more important than truth.[44]

The directors of American psychological warfare may have experienced success in World War II, but at first they looked like amateurs compared to the Soviets. Predictably, in the immediate aftermath of World War II, Soviet propagandists prepared for psychological warfare across a weakened Europe. Yet their American competitors dismantled the U.S. propaganda apparatus. The Office of War Information closed in 1945, and what remained of its psychological-warfare capabilities was folded clumsily into the State Department. During this ideological demobilization, security analysts in early 1946 began warning policymakers that success in any conflict against Communism would depend on a massive psychological-warfare program.[45]

By December 1947, Truman's newly created National Security Council decided that America was losing the battle of information and ideas. NSC-4, a report by the National Security Council, declared that the Soviets were "employing psychological, political and economic measures designed to undermine non-Communist elements in all countries." The U.S. psychological response, on the other hand, was uncoordinated and in many cases nonexistent. "The present world situation," the report concluded, "requires the immediate strengthening and coordination of all foreign information measures of the U.S. government designed to influence attitudes in foreign countries in a direction favorable to attainment of its objectives."[46] NSC-4 was top secret, but U.S. congressmen who traveled to Western Europe in 1948 returned home and publicly lamented the psychological lashing America was then taking at the hands of the Communist propaganda machine. They resolved to supply U.S. psychological-warfare operations with the resources needed to turn the tide.[47]

In early 1948, Congress passed the U.S. Information and Educational Exchange Act, which gave American psychological operations legal cover and funding. In June, NSC-10/2 established the Office of Policy Coordination within the CIA to handle covert nonmilitary action against the Communist Eastern Bloc, including propaganda, economic warfare, sabotage, and assistance to "underground resistance movements." Flush with money and support, a highly independent CIA would score some of its most celebrated—and notorious—victories in the next few years, from Tehran to Guatemala to Radio Free Europe. Meanwhile, the State Department supervised overt psychological operations, particularly through the use of international education and cultural programs. News of China's fall to Mao's Communists and Soviet detonation of an atomic weapon in 1949 lent greater urgency to this effort.

NSC-68 arrived in the summer of 1950 and forever altered the way American security experts conceptualized and fought the Cold War. When Kennan articulated his containment policy, he acknowledged the place of psychology and ideology in the developing conflict against the Soviets, but an economy of force remained central. He argued that Americans should only defend certain economic and strategic strongpoints against Soviet encroachment. But his successor in the State Department's Policy Planning department, Paul Nitze, who authored NSC-68, advocated a perimeter defense that would check enemy expansion anywhere. This increased the field of potential battle from Western Europe and a smattering of other critical regions to the whole of the developing world. The directive also cast the Cold War as a fundamental conflict of values, ideas, and morals. At times NSC-68 resembled less a security document than a philosophical and moral treatise. The Soviets were "animated by a fanatical faith."

They found existential meaning only by "serving the ends of the system." In this "perverted faith," Nitze wrote, Communist society "becomes God, and submission to the will of God becomes submission to the will of the system." Likewise, Americans drew strength from the "contagious" concept of freedom, thought by many military and political leaders in 1950 to flow from religion. Nitze summed up America's fundamental purpose with a quote from the Declaration of Independence: "With a firm reliance on the protection of Divine Providence, we mutually pledge to each other our lives, our Fortunes, and our sacred honor." And so the logic of force was joined with the logic of faith.[48]

NSC-68 reaffirmed previous mandates for psychological operations, and one year later, in April 1951, Truman created the Psychological Strategy Board (PSB). Composed of the CIA, Departments of State and Defense, and the Joint Chiefs of Staff, the PSB would coordinate all American psychological operations. The new agency fell under the directorship of Gordon Gray, a Yale-trained lawyer and former secretary of the army. Afforded a broad mission, Gray and the PSB wasted little time before investigating the potential role of religion in psychological warfare. In its first few months of existence, the PSB compiled an "Inventory of Instrumentalities" that cataloged all possible avenues of psychological attack against the Soviets. Religion had a central role:

> The potentialities of religion as an instrument for combating Communism are universally tremendous. Religion is an established basic force which calls forth men's strongest emotions. Because of the immoral and un-Christian nature of Communism and its avowed opposition to and persecution of religions, most of the world's principal religious organizations are already allied with the cause of the free nations. Our over-all objective in seeking the use of religion as a cold war instrumentality should be the furtherance of world spiritual health; for the Communist threat could not exist in a spiritually healthy world.[49]

The notion that America should, or even could, become a guardian of worldwide spirituality evinced a shocking optimism, but it also revealed the remarkable emphasis security experts placed on the special function of religion in the early Cold War.

The PSB released two major reports in May 1952—one estimating the efficacy of psychological operations and the other establishing a future strategic framework. Both underscored the important role religion could play in achieving American strategic goals. Religion was one of few values uniting the world that the Soviets could not co-opt. If the United States could define the global conflict as a holy war between traditional religious faiths and Communism rather than an economic and political struggle between the oppressed and the powerful, the

Soviets would be severely disadvantaged. "The United States can retain its allies," the PSB concluded, "only by persuading them that the U.S. position is to their best interests and comes within the framework of their moral and spiritual beliefs as well as the interests and moral and spiritual beliefs of the United States." Future psychological operations would portray U.S. policy as a "truly Christian approach ... characteristic of the American people." In a holy war, simply lauding one's own beliefs was never enough. The PSB suggested a direct attack on the Soviet faith. It called for psychological operations to refute the teachings of prophets like Lenin and Stalin that would cast doubt on their "deification" and expose their creed as dangerous and detrimental.[50]

The PSB vision of religion owed much to an earlier report by a State Department advisory panel working within the United States Information and Educational Exchange (USIE). An overt psychological program authorized by Congress in 1948, USIE worked to cultivate a favorable image of America worldwide. In 1951 the agency established a three-person council of religious leaders charged with investigating the "moral and religious factors" of psychological warfare.[51] That summer the panel released a report whose assumptions and recommendations influenced psychological operations for the next few years. It concluded that American national security depended on a balance between material might and spiritual conviction:

> To build this "balance of spirit," three things are necessary: (a) we must convince others of our own moral and spiritual stamina and dependability, (b) we must arouse others to the defense of their own right to moral and spiritual freedom, and (c) we must use the interest which we share with others in the preservation of moral and spiritual values to cement friendship and understanding among all peoples who cherish those values.

America could cement its role as not only the leader of the free world, but also the world's great champion of religion. Although the Soviet Union was America's chief rival at the time, the panel did not think that Communism was the greatest obstacle to bolstering America's religious reputation worldwide. Rather, they identified secularism as the chief impediment. "Care must be exercised," the panel concluded, "to make clear that this separation of church and state does not in any way imply incompatibility or hostility of either toward the other, nor prevent cooperation between the government and religious institutions." In a spiritual crusade, the longstanding tradition of secularism was a necessary casualty.[52]

The panel's recommendations were no doubt self-serving. It is hardly surprising that religious leaders would select a religious solution. But the panel's plan was well within the parameters of acceptable psychological operations. Some of their specific proposals were already being implemented, though these were intended for domestic and not international audiences. The report proposed that public leaders emphasize the historic and continuing influence of religion on American society, the spiritual roots of U.S. institutions, and the religious component of major holidays. By 1951 these efforts were well under way. The panel also suggested that politicians demonstrate the importance of religion in their personal lives. Here Truman had some room for improvement, although his religious rhetoric had intensified after 1947. Yet the USIE report argued that these steps were only half the battle. "A balanced projection of the U.S., or even the development of a full understanding of American life and institutions including its moral and spiritual aspect, is not enough," the report concluded. "If the threat of Communism is to be met effectively, a moral and spiritual offensive is necessary."[53]

The State Department took arguments like these seriously. It operated 165 "information centers" around the world—special libraries where foreigners could obtain books, newspapers, and pamphlets. Beginning in 1952, the USIE ensured that each information center contained "balanced collections of U.S. publications which portray America's spiritual heritage and religious values in true perspective." Ample copies of the Bible began arriving, along with religious periodicals like *Christian Century, Commonweal,* and *Commentary.* The State Department also sent periodic religious news dispatches to its embassies complete with analyses of the event's implication to Communism. The Voice of America enlisted American religious leaders to broadcast messages into nations under Communist control. Cardinal Spellman recorded a special Easter message in 1950. The archbishop of Baltimore addressed the Eastern Bloc in a 1951 Christmas message. "These feasts have special meaning for everyone throughout the Christian world, but they have special meaning for you, dear friends in Hungary and Czechoslovakia who languish under a tyrant's rule," he said. "Take courage from the example of St. Stephen, who gave his life in its very prime rather than deny Christ."[54]

Roger Lyons, Voice of America's director of religious programming, oversaw the spiritual offensive. Assisted by a panel of religious advisers, he used his programming to impart two messages. The first highlighted the importance of religious freedom and attacked the Communist animus toward religion directly. The second emphasized the importance of religion in American society. "Spiritual and moral factors enter into every phase of our output, and not just into specifically religious services," he reported in 1952. "They permeate all our programs whether we are trying to give a picture of the life of a farmer in the mid-West, covering a meeting of the American Foreign Policy Association, or a village church service." Lyons went beyond merely combating the colossus-of-straw image; he created in the minds of foreigners an image of a righteous American state driven by religious zealotry. In this ideation the United States seemed the perfect foil for Communist designs—a nation ready to martyr itself so that others could worship God.[55]

While Voice of America fed its religious propaganda to the masses, the PSB decided to target the Communist elite. In 1952 the agency initiated the U.S. Doctrinal Program to "create confusion, doubts and loss of confidence in the accepted thought patterns of convinced Communists, captive careerists . . . and others under Communist influence susceptible to doctrinal appeals." Rather than broadly assaulting Communism with generalities, the Doctrinal Program would dismantle the intellectual apparatus holding Communist ideology together. It did not take long for analysts to realize that the Communist intolerance of religion and rejection of individual morality were major Soviet vulnerabilities. They drew up detailed plans for doctrinal warfare and charged various government agencies with carrying them out.[56]

But if security advisers had hoped the PSB would effectively coordinate and implement their doctrinal recommendations, they were in for great disappointment. Gordon Gray and his small staff were lost in the mutating postwar bureaucracy. At times the infant agency faced open hostility from officials in the State Department, who would not yield authority. Truman did not intervene on the PSB's behalf in these intergovernmental struggles, and the agency was all but dead by the end of 1952. Though there was no denying the PSB's shortcomings, the agency managed to build an important consensus regarding the role of religion in psychological operations—a collection of abstract proposals the next generation of security agencies would make real.[57]

The Eisenhower administration provided psychological operations with a much-needed second wind designed in part to define the Cold War in religious terms. By emphasizing prayer and religious belief, Eisenhower hoped to cast the division between Cold War nations as both spiritual and economic. This would require faith in the psychological operations Truman had initiated and subsequently starved. Eisenhower's national security advisor Robert Cutler had broached the topic back in January 1953 at the Hotel Commodore. He had served as Gordon Gray's assistant in the PSB, and with a measure of influence his old boss never enjoyed, he would give psychological operations the teeth they lacked under Truman. Eisenhower and the cabinet listened as Cutler argued that Cold War strategy was essentially "psychological." He explained that American security experts excelled at developing strategies, but unless these messages were disseminated properly to Americans and foreigners, they were worthless. "You can make the best Chevrolet in the world," Cutler reasoned, "but if the public does not understand it they might go out and buy a Hudson." The president-elect agreed.[58]

Eisenhower created two new agencies to coordinate and implement psychological strategies. In August 1953, he established the United States Information Agency (USIA), which pulled propaganda operations out from underneath the State Department's complex bureaucracy.[59] Though its functions were many, the

USIA attempted to shape worldwide perceptions of Americans, their values, and their mission rather than allowing the Soviets to do the same. A month later the president also replaced the Psychological Strategy Board with the Operations Coordinating Board (OCB). The OCB would work as an adjunct to the National Security Council, adding needed specificity to that committee's general plans and coordinating with other government agencies to implement approved psychological operations. At last Eisenhower had put into place a psychological and propaganda apparatus worthy of the Cold War.[60]

The USIA and the OCB cooperated closely on psychological operations, and on religious matters both continued the work of their predecessor agencies. NSC 162/2, which laid out Eisenhower's initial security plan, cited the need for "mobilizing the spiritual and material resources necessary to meet the Soviet threat."[61] In response, the OCB created the Ideological Subcommittee on the Religious Factor and charged it with developing a "spiritual factor" in Cold War national security. They did not wait long to act.[62]

In August 1954, the World Council of Churches held its second assembly in Evanston, Illinois. Sixteen hundred delegates from forty-eight countries descended upon the Chicago suburb. They came from many corners of the world, bearing tales of Communist enmity toward their faith. A West German churchman warned of antireligious crackdowns across the eastern border. The Lebanese ambassador to the United States observed that, absent a religious offensive, Communists would win ideological battles in Africa and the Middle East. A Presbyterian missionary who served in China told of a "bamboo curtain" impenetrable to all ideologies except religion. The first World Council of Churches in 1948 had condemned Communism, but many of its delegates favored tepid, even conciliatory, expressions of disapproval. In 1954 their denunciations left less room for ambiguity. And this time U.S. propagandists were there to capture it all.[63]

On Sunday, August 15, the gates of Soldier Field opened to the public at 5:00 p.m. Two hours later a throng of 125,000 people filled the football stadium. They came for the "Festival of Faith," a well-publicized and brassy kickoff to the second World Council. As a cool southeast breeze blew from Lake Michigan, the council delegates marched into the arena like a Roman legion back from battle against the barbarian hordes. And in a way they were—for many served on the front lines of the Cold War against a hostile faith. Clad in robes and carrying banners, they took their positions, and the assembled masses sang the hymn "Faith of Our Fathers," whose third stanza reads:

> Faith of our fathers! We will strive to win all nations unto thee,
> And thru the truth that comes from God
> Mankind shall then indeed be free.
> Faith of our fathers! Holy Faith, we will be true to thee till death.

Backed by a chorus 2,500 strong, actors pantomimed the story of creation and other "works of God through time." A string of short speeches and prayers by prominent church leaders followed.[64]

From a propagandist's point of view, the event was ideal. For three years national security analysts had pointed to religion as a potential U.S. strength and Soviet weakness. Now, in the heart of America and with much of the world watching, the United States could showcase its deep religious commitment and polish its credentials as the spiritual leader of the Free World. The OCB knew that success depended on Eisenhower, and the president did not disappoint. On August 19, he arrived at Northwestern University and addressed the World Council, striving to permanently dispel the colossus-of-straw myth that had long worried political and military leaders. Claiming to speak for all Americans, Eisenhower acknowledged that many world religious leaders thought the United States placed its trust in "material values." Indeed, the president admitted that Americans did emphasize "those scientific, material, and military means that ensure or enhance our safety, and discourage aggression against us or our friends." "But," he continued, "we know that there is no true and lasting cure for world tensions in guns and bombs." Drawing on the fruits of eight years of sacralization, Eisenhower told the delegates that Americans were an "essentially religious people" who could "see the value of religion as a practical force" in their affairs. He pointed to dramatic increases in church membership and Bible sales as proof that religion in America was not merely "traditional" or "theoretical." He accentuated the diverse but deep religious beliefs of the Congress. Smiling coyly at the archbishop of Canterbury, Eisenhower cited the mentions of God in the Declaration of Independence, as if to offer some evidence that America's religious commitment was not born of geopolitical expediency. Finally, at the urging of the OCB's ideological subcommittee, the president called upon people in all nations to join him in periodic prayers for world peace.[65]

The World Council of Churches, and Eisenhower's speech in particular, was a masterstroke for the USIA. The agency emphasized America's role as a religious nation and spiritual leader, the "heroic efforts" of churches behind the Iron Curtain "in the face of heavy and cruel government pressures," and the "absence of American illusion concerning the materialistic Communist philosophy, which is fundamentally hostile to religious faiths." During each day of the two-week conference, USIA propagandists produced three or four stories for transmission around the world. Voice of America covered the event closely, and the agency's motion-picture service edited the highlights into a newsreel for distribution overseas. A three-thousand word abridgement of Eisenhower's speech was copied and distributed to State Department information centers. To enhance the contrast, the USIA often followed reports from the Evanston meeting with news of Communist crackdowns on religion.[66]

Reports from the World Council were part of a larger USIA psychological offensive built around religion that was underway by 1954. Early that year, the agency named D. Elton Trueblood, a former Stanford professor of philosophy and a Quaker, chief of religious information. Trueblood ensured that U.S. propaganda emphasized record rates of American church membership and contrasted these reports with discussions of the falsities of the Communist faith. Voice of America developed the radio program *A Nation at Worship*, which rebroadcast sermons by U.S. religious leaders. In 1954 it added the program *The Life We Prize*, a radio show with weekly scripts depicting the democratic aspects of American religious life. Hungarians could listen to the report "Christianity and Communism Confront Each Other." New Zealanders could open their newspapers and read the American dispatch "Religion: The Strongest Ideology." Muslims in the Middle East could flip through the pamphlet *Red Star over Islam*, and Buddhists in Southeast Asia could do the same with *Buddhism under the Soviet Yoke*. The radio service developed a series of lectures on the compatibility of science and religion to counter Soviet claims that the two were mutually exclusive. Meanwhile, the USIA flooded its overseas information centers, frequented by over 54 million visitors in 1953 alone, with more books and articles describing American religious convictions and arguing that religion and Communism were contradictory.[67]

One of the most illustrative battlegrounds for U.S. psychological operations was in Southeast Asia, where, in 1931, Reinhold Niebuhr had predicted the religious aspects of Communism would find their deepest appeal. More than two decades later, he could once again wear the prophet's mantle. In the spring of 1954, the French military sustained a surprising and ruinous defeat in the battle of Dien Bien Phu at the hands of Communist-backed resistance fighters deep in the jungle-covered hills of Vietnam. The French defeat bore troubling similarities to Britain's 1946 decision to cut back support for Greece and Turkey. Where once old imperial powers had fended off Communists, the United States would commit its treasure and, in the case of Southeast Asia, its blood as well.[68] But before American troops arrived in Vietnam, American leaders would authorize a religious offensive.

U.S. support for a Catholic leader in a nation that was 90 percent Buddhist may have seemed unexpected were it not for the American conception of the Cold War as a religious conflict. Even before the French defeat, Eisenhower and the National Security Council decided to exploit the "religious issue" in Vietnam. The president noted that during the Hundred Years War Joan of Arc had galvanized the French populace, and Dulles reminded his colleagues that Vietnam was home to well over a million Catholics. The search began for a modern-day incarnation of Joan of Arc who could unite the peasants and summon them to religious action. Ngo Dinh Diem cast himself in this role, and his ascent to the position of prime minister of Vietnam in July 1954 can be largely attributed to his Catholic, anti-Communist credentials. Prior to a triumphant return to his native homeland, Diem had spent three years living in one of Cardinal Spellman's New Jersey seminaries. During his stay in the U.S., he cultivated important relationships with American political and religious leaders. One all-Catholic luncheon held in May 1953 at the Supreme Court Building proved particularly instrumental. Justice William O. Douglas invited Diem, Cardinal Spellman, senators John F. Kennedy and Mike Mansfield, a State Department representative, and future chairman of the House Foreign Affairs Committee Clement Zablocki. The group formed a nucleus of support for Diem, helping to push him to the front of the State Department's list of potential leaders for Vietnam. American intelligence estimates had concluded that many of Vietnam's other religious groups were infiltrated by Communists. Catholics were the surest source of anti-Communism in Indochina.[69]

In September 1954, two weeks after Eisenhower addressed the World Council of Churches, Vice President Richard M. Nixon forwarded the OCB a proposal from Edward Elson's Foundation for Religious Action, a "private" organization devoted to uniting "all believers in God in the struggle between the free world and atheistic communism." With a governing board that included USIA religious chief Trueblood and Eisenhower's personal pastor, it was in fact an unofficial arm of the U.S. religious offensive.[70] The foundation's plan called for "the utilization of the religious factor to intensify local anti-communism" in Southeast Asia. Before the U.S. sent official military consultants to Indochina, the American psychological-warfare community dispatched religious advisers to the region. The Foundation for Religious Action called its strategy a "religious crusade against communism, but with positive proposals for a new order of independence and prosperity in Southeast Asia." "It seems to me that there is a great value in an operation of this type," Nixon wrote in his endorsement.[71]

The foundation sent an envoy to South Vietnam, along with a Catholic agent selected by the archbishop of Washington. Cardinal Spellman visited Saigon the following summer with a $100,000 aid check in hand, denying criticism that this was an anti-Communist bribe. Meanwhile, the USIA upheld its end of the bargain by saturating the airwaves with Voice of America messages and tailoring its printed propaganda specifically to Southeast Asia's religions. In "A Primer on Communism," the USIA devoted a section to Soviet and Chinese enmity towards Buddhism. The pamphlet accused Stalin of eliminating 200,000 Buddhists in Central Asia, claimed that Chinese troops were using monasteries as military camps, and warned that Buddhist priests were forced to attend lectures by "illiterate, atheistic Communist propagandists." Keeping with its strategy of highlighting America's spiritual heritage, the Voice of America broadcasted a special program describing America's Thanksgiving holiday in 1954. "If Thanksgiving Day means anything at all, it means that we give thanks for being creature of the Almighty God who, in the beginning created

Heaven and Earth," the broadcast explained. "It implies that we came from the hand of God—not from the beasts of the jungle."[72]

American psychological operations spilled over the Vietnam border. The OCB sent a Buddhist adviser to Cambodia to inform the nation's monarch "that his faith requires him to do battle against the Vietminh and the Chinese communists." American agents also cultivated a religious alliance against Communism with a Thai police general who founded the Society for the Promotion of Buddhism in July 1954. Soon "instruction teams" funded with American dollars were traveling through villages in Thailand—colorful bands of dancers, comedians, puppeteers, and soldiers who taught peasants "The Seven Bad Things about Communism." First on this list was that Communism would destroy religion. By May of 1956, an estimated three million Thais had witnessed these presentations. That same spring the OCB formed the Committee on Buddhism to coordinate its religious offensive into 1957.[73]

Eisenhower followed up his World Council of Churches appearance with a religious appeal to the Soviet Union and its satellites. Under the president's direction, Congress passed a resolution declaring September 22, 1954, a National Day of Prayer for Peace. On its eve, Eisenhower entered the Voice of America studios and recorded a special religious message. At the OCB's urging, the president continued his religious appeals, asking the world to pray the following summer before the Geneva Summit.[74]

America's religious propaganda offensive in 1954 had been perfectly timed. In July the Soviet Party Central Committee initiated a brutal crackdown on religion. The USIA could not have hoped for a better contrast to their pro-religious propaganda. For reasons that still remain unclear, Nikita Khrushchev ordered an immediate halt to the campaign in November. In the interim, Americans thought they had undermined the Soviets in the eyes and ears of religious people throughout the world. For the next six years, Soviet leaders would leave religion largely untouched.[75] Perhaps they realized what U.S. psychological strategists had already concluded: that religion was an American strength and a decided Soviet weakness.

Or perhaps the Soviets opened a history book and discovered the true origin of the word "propaganda." It was not coined by an intelligence operative or Bolshevik pamphleteer. The word came from Rome and the Catholic Church, who, early in another holy war—the Thirty Years War—issued the *Congregatio de Propaganda Fide*, or *Sacred Congregation for the Spreading of the Faith*. As it turned out, the Soviets too were relative newcomers to the field of psychological operations. Grasping propaganda's religious core, Americans summoned an older force than Communism to win hearts and minds throughout the world. American strength had spiritual guidance, or at least that was what everyone thought.

Societal Institutions

"Almighty God, we acknowledge our dependence upon Thee, and we
beg Thy blessings upon us, our parents, our teachers and our country."
—Regent's Prayer, New York Public Schools, 1951

On May Day 1950, Mosinee, Wisconsin, became the only American town to fall under Communist rule during the Cold War. In the early morning hours, secret police entered the homes of prominent citizens, arresting them in their pajamas. The mayor surrendered the sleepy paper-mill town of 1,400 to the invading Communists at 10:15 a.m., a pistol pointed at his back. Hundreds of citizens gathered in the city park—renamed "Red Square"—with children sporting Communist Youth armbands. Down the street, at Immanuel Evangelical Lutheran Church, agents arrested the reverend in the middle of his morning religious service, announcing "We are confiscating this church as an institution against the working class."[1]

It was a well-publicized charade. Local members of the American Legion designed the stunt to simulate life under Communism, and by sunset life in Mosinee was back to normal. But for its citizens who lived through a day under Communist rule and the many millions more who read about it, the threat from Communism appeared all too real. The next day they could return to city hall or pray in their preferred house of worship. Their town and nation were safe, at least for the moment.

The Mosinee exercise vividly demonstrated the effect that Communist takeover would have on the most visible institutions in American society. As might be expected, political and religious institutions were the first to be targeted. But the event's organizers also commandeered the town's schools, forcing children to wear red armbands. They assumed control of the *Mosinee Times*, using its presses to print a four-page propaganda tract. The "new" leaders placed placards in the windows of Mosinee's businesses and industries, announcing that such enterprises had been nationalized. They abolished all voluntary associations. Downtown, at the Mosinee Theater, the Communists even banned the recently released film *Guilty of Treason*, a dramatization of the Cardinal Mindszenty story, for its positive portrayal of Christianity.[2]

These institutions—educational, media, business, voluntary associations, and entertainment—contributed to the process of secularization in the early twentieth century. In places like Muncie and Mosinee, they increasingly assumed societal roles and functions once dominated by religion. Yet in the early Cold War, these same institutions worked to make religious belief not only central to the Cold War but to the proper functioning of American society as well. Just as leaders in government and the security establishment acted upon fears that the United States was in external danger from Soviet Communism and internally imperiled by spiritual bankruptcy, the heads of America's schools, newspapers, corporations, citizen groups, and movie studios would try to lead society toward a revitalized understanding of religion's potential.

If the Cold War was indeed a battle of ideas, as American leaders claimed, then classrooms would be the front line.[3] Indeed, the conflict opened a new chapter in the debate over the relationship between religion and public education. The professionalization of education in the late nineteenth and early twentieth centuries had pushed religious instruction out of the classroom and contributed to the process of secularization. But the conflict with Communism demanded a reevaluation of this precedent. Americans had long viewed the public school as an inculcator of the virtues and values necessary to maintain democratic society. Never one to downplay the Cold War threat, Attorney General Tom C. Clark warned that "the Communists have started a campaign to recruit our children to their ideology. . . . [They] know that if they get the children today, they will have the nation tomorrow."[4]

The federal commissioner of education, John W. Studebaker, agreed. Speaking in November 1947 before 1,300 educators, he urged his audience to "make clear by contrast the threat involved in the Communist ideology with its overt and covert effort to undermine and to subvert our western democratic civilization."[5] Two months later the U.S. Office of Education initiated the Zeal for American Democracy program, in which school districts across the nation began implementing curricula designed to give students an understanding of the American Way of Life. Twelfth-graders in Des Moines studied the philosophical differences between Communism and democracy. Elementary students in Quincy, Massachusetts, read special comic books exploring the advantages of life in America. In Tulsa administrators added a unit called "The American Dream" to history courses.[6] Studebaker envisioned the Zeal for American Democracy program as a reaffirmation of the nation's "democratic faith," a seemingly secular conception, were it not for the religiously grounded definitions of democracy then in vogue. Not surprisingly, he thought the program should "give [students] an understanding and appreciation of the ethical and spiritual values, as well as the material benefits, of the American way of life."[7]

Religious leaders were already promulgating the view that democracy grew like fruit on a sacred limb. Writing in 1946, evangelical author Verne Paul Kaub did not construe the Cold War simply as a battle between Christianity and Communism. Like most American political leaders, he labeled it a conflict between Communism and the American way of life. But Kaub argued that Christianity undergirded American society. Free enterprise, belief in free will, republican government, and the sanctity of individuals were all Christian doctrines. In short, as he insisted, "the rock upon which America was founded is the Christian faith." Even the American conceptualization of history implied progress through providence, Kaub wrote, whereas Communists believed in economic determinism. "These two philosophies, Christianity and Communism, cannot logically exist in one heart and mind," he reasoned. "Either one or the other can be accepted, or both rejected, but both cannot consistently be accepted." Since Christianity was America's foundation, Kaub's logic led to an even weightier conclusion: to be an American, one had to accept some basic religious premises.[8]

Kaub credited American Catholic leaders for developing similar arguments, and rightly so. For Francis Cardinal Spellman, Communism was "un-American" because the ship of Americanism was lashed to spiritual moorings. True Americans needed to do more than celebrate democracy; they needed religious faith. In November 1946, a group of influential American bishops, including Spellman, issued a statement reflecting on the precarious position of individuals in the postwar period. They welded Americanism to spiritual conviction by proclaiming the Declaration of Independence "the basic tradition of Christian civilization." Their message soon filtered down through the hierarchy, bringing Communism, religion, and freedom into the same conversation. "The frantic fear of Religion on the part of Red Fascist Tyrants," railed a Catholic pamphlet in 1947, "arises from the fact that true democracy is based finally on Religion."[9]

Educators could probably have ignored Kaub or Spellman had their positions not been repeatedly reinforced by political leaders. Truman, Clark, Hoover, Congress, and the military vigorously emphasized the inseparability of democracy and freedom of religion. Toynbee went a step further. By arguing that the decline of civilizations began with spiritual bankruptcy, he leveled a challenge against one of the educational system's primary functions within society—the maintenance of virtue.

The British professor's warning resonated with the National Education Association (NEA) when it gathered for its annual meeting in Cleveland in the summer of 1948. With nearly half a million members, the NEA was America's largest and most influential educational organization. On July 7, 1948, Vera M. Butler, a professor of education, rose before the general assembly and delivered a speech entitled "Now Is the Hour." She began with Revelations 3:2: "Be watchful, and strengthen the things which remain, that are ready to die: for I have not found thy works perfect before God." Echoing Toynbee's findings, Butler attributed the ultimate destruction of Athenian democracy and the fall of Rome to their internal spiritual weakness. Yet according to Butler, Rome could have been saved had it found the "Golden Mean of Christianity." Likewise, America could stave off its looming decline by looking to the "Golden Mean of Democracy."[10]

A day after Butler's speech, a committee at the NEA convention presented the report *The Role of the Public Schools in the Development of Moral and Spiritual Values*. It recommended that schools across America include "recognition of the greatest force in life—the power of God" in moral curriculum. "We submit," the report stated, "that the principles of American democracy are rooted in Christian belief; that the perpetuation of American democracy is contingent on the moral and spiritual values held by the individual." The representative assembly agreed, tasking the NEA's Education Policies Commission with further study of the importance of moral and spiritual values.[11]

The NEA Educational Policies Commission had to tread delicately. Though the legislative and executive branches of the federal government had forged a consensus on the need for sacralization, the Supreme Court remained skeptical. In 1945, Vashti McCollum, an atheist, had sued the Champaign, Illinois, board of education for its religious education program. The school district had instituted a "released time" program in 1940. Once a week for half an hour, students whose parents signed a waiver received religious instruction inside the classroom from local Protestant and Catholic leaders. Students whose parents did not sign the waiver left the classroom for a study hall.[12] By the end of 1948, the NEA estimated that 27 percent of all public school districts had released-time programs serving an estimated 700,000 students.[13] Released time seemed like a mutually beneficial arrangement for educators, religious interests, and society. By sacrificing an hour or two each week, districts gave themselves cover from accusations that public schools were becoming too secular.

So it was with shock and outrage that Americans absorbed the news out of Washington on March 8, 1948. Though McCollum met defeat in the Illinois state courts, she won a December 1947 hearing in the U.S. Supreme Court. In an 8 to 1 decision, the Supreme Court ruled against the Champaign board of education, striking down the released-time program. "This is beyond all question a utilization of the tax-established and tax-supported public schools system to aid religious groups to spread their faith," wrote Justice Hugo Black in the majority opinion. It was far shorter and tamer than the concurring opinion delivered by

Felix Frankfurter and supported by Robert H. Jackson, Wiley B. Rutledge, and Harold H. Burton. Frankfurter gave a brief history of American education, from Puritan common schools to the modern day. Admitting that public schools began as religious agencies, he drew on the sentiments of James Madison and Horace Mann to argue that public schools were the single "most powerful agency for promoting cohesion among a heterogeneous democratic people." Public education had become secular over time, and the justices were content to maintain that practice. Stanley Forman Reed was the lone voice of dissent. In his view, the court could not be certain that the framers' original intention for the Establishment Clause was only to prevent the creation of a state church rather than to erect a wall of separation between state and church.[14]

The McCollum decision was surprising given the *Everson v. Board of Education* ruling a year earlier, in which the Supreme Court upheld the use of public money to fund transportation of students to and from religious private schools in a 5 to 4 decision.[15] Though dismayed, school districts, parents, and religious leaders did not abandon released time or their Cold War efforts to instill American youth with the moral and spiritual values necessary to triumph in the conflict against Communism's countervailing religious pull. Months later, at the NEA's national convention in Boston, the delegates adopted a ban on Communist teachers. An NEA report released in support of the ban tied Communism to morality and religion, noting that "Communism is more than a political party.... Freedom of religion and conscience go out the window when Communism comes in. Any means, no matter how it outrages human personality, is moral under the Communist code."[16]

The momentum for spiritual and moral education continued to build. A year later former "spy queen" and converted Catholic Elizabeth T. Bentley testified that the secular education she had received as an undergraduate at Vassar College ensured that she was a spiritual "pushover" when she began dabbling in Communism. In 1951 the Educational Policies Commission, a twenty-member board including Eisenhower and Harvard's reform-minded president, James B. Conant, issued *Moral and Spiritual Values in the Public Schools*, which built on the NEA's initial 1948 report. They presented their detailed findings at the general meeting in an atmosphere already rife with fears of continued secularization. There a PTA representative from Idaho called upon the general assembly to acknowledge that every child "has a right to a secure faith in God" and that the American Way was "nurtured by the firm belief that all who live possess the spirit of God." Frank K. Weil, former head of Truman's Committee on Religion and Welfare in the Armed Forces, followed, informing the 14,000 educators assembled in Atlantic City that the single greatest contrast between Communism and American democracy was the American shared "belief in a supernatural power beyond any on this Earth." To him, moral and spiritual values were "a bulwark of our national strength."[17]

The widely publicized and disseminated *Moral and Spiritual Values in the Public Schools* was descriptive, prescriptive, philosophical, and at times purposefully vague. It reaffirmed the public school's primary role in providing succeeding generations with the moral development required for the maintenance of any free, democratic society. But the commission left little doubt as to why moral and spiritual education was so timely a topic:

> As the Commission has pointed out elsewhere, the nations of the world are deeply divided. The hard core of this division is a moral issue—a profound and probably irreconcilable difference of viewpoint concerning standards of human behavior.... To be sure, the defense of freedom in the modern world has become in part a problem in military strength and strategy.... But it is also, as in the last analysis it always has been, a problem in moral and spiritual development.[18]

The report reduced the global spiritual conflict to an individual level, calling for the development of "inner moral restraints" in American students that could strengthen the nation against the threat of totalitarianism. According to the report, individualism was a religious value. "The inherent worth of every human being," wrote the commission, "is basic in the teachings of Christianity and many other great religions."[19]

The Educational Policies Commission knew that the NEA could not endorse blatant proselytizing within the public schools, but it advised teachers not to avoid religious discussions in the classroom. In the NEA's program, students would be encouraged to discuss their own religious beliefs, and teachers were encouraged to demonstrate their approval of students' participation in religious activities. Furthermore, the NEA encouraged its members to discuss religious beliefs, emphasizing "the important part they played in establishing the moral and spiritual values of American life." Most significantly, the Educational Policies Commission vowed to prevent a dedicated minority from derailing their program. "Avowed atheists" and "opinionated bigots" would not be allowed to "cripple this important aspect of American public education." After all, reasoned the commission, "though a few children may come from the homes of communist or other totalitarian opinion, the public schools teach the principles of democracy."[20]

If concerned Americans were waiting for a sign from above, they received it in June 1952. Though not an endorsement from the Almighty, the Supreme Court's decision in *Zorach v. Clauson* was perhaps the next best thing. Few school districts scrapped their released-time programs in the wake of the McCollum decision, and this triggered a slew of lawsuits. The one that eventually reached the Supreme Court began in New York with atheist leader Joseph

Lewis, president of the Freethinkers of America. It targeted the New York City board of education, which had operated a released-time program protected by state law since 1940. Worried that his atheist credentials would sour the petition, Lewis dropped his suit in favor of another filed by Brooklyn parents Tessim Zorach and Esta Gluck. After losing in the New York Court of Appeals, they appealed to the Supreme Court.

In a 6 to 3 decision, the Supreme Court ruled that the New York released-time program did not violate the Constitution, because religious instruction took place outside the schools. William O. Douglas wrote the majority opinion, explaining that the state and religion need not be "aliens to each other—hostile, suspicious, and even unfriendly." Douglas took the argument one step further in an oft-quoted paragraph that began: "We are a religious people whose institutions presuppose a Supreme Being." The court worried that by striking down the New York program, the state would be favoring irreligion over religion. "When the state encourages religious instruction or cooperates with religious authorities by adjusting the schedule or public events to sectarian needs," Douglas argued, "it follows the best of our traditions."[21]

Douglas's immaterial declaration of America's religious heritage signaled for many the court's endorsement of sacralization.[22] The makeup of the court had changed since McCollum as well. Truman appointed two new associate justices in 1949, former Indiana senator Sherman Minton and former attorney general Tom C. Clark, only two years after his fiery anti-Communist sermon in Des Moines. Their votes made the difference. Shortly after their confirmations, Minton and Clark had joined Chief Justice Vinson and several senators for a prayer breakfast. After finishing his toast and eggs, Vinson spoke. "I am not a preacher or even the son of a preacher," he declared, "but I know we must adhere to ideals of Christianity before we can have a lasting peace." Borrowing from Toynbee, the chief justice warned that, absent such unity, American civilization would crumble from within. Not surprisingly, Clark agreed. "No country or civilization can last unless it is founded on Christian values," he said.[23] It seems at least possible that, when deciding the Zorach case, the justices understood that their case was not only about classrooms in Brooklyn but also about the need for the spiritual mobilization then under way across America.

The Supreme Court's decision set off another round of in the sacralization of public education. In San Diego, the public schools adopted a new spiritual curriculum in 1952 that drew on the Ten Commandments and the Psalms. Further up the coast, the Los Angeles public schools hired a supervisor for the district's expanding moral and spiritual values program.[24] A survey of middle and high school teachers in California revealed that more than 90 percent believed that students needed to be taught faith in a higher power.[25] The New York Board of Regents, in consultation with religious leaders, approved the following prayer

for use in the state's public schools: "Almighty God, we acknowledge our dependence upon Thee, and we beg Thy blessings upon us, our parents, our teachers
and our country." The board justified the prayer by referencing "concentrated
attacks by an atheistic way of life upon our world."[26] Some of New York's largest
school districts, including Syracuse and Rochester, made the prayer mandatory.[27]
The New York City school board mandated that school children begin each day
by singing the fourth stanza of the patriotic hymn "America," which read:

> Our fathers' God to Thee,
> Author of Liberty,
> To Thee we Sing:
> Long may our land be bright
> With freedom's holy light;
> Protect us by Thy might,
> Great God, our King.[28]

The NEA was also emboldened by the Zorach decision. At the 1952 general
meeting, the assembly heard Charles P. Taft, younger brother of conservative
standard bearer Robert A. Taft, as he demanded that the nation's public schools
hire only teachers who had a personal religion. The organization did more than
politely listen to Taft's suggestion; soon the NEA established the Committee on
Teacher Education in Religion. The new committee, assisted by a generous private grant, began pilot programs in religious education at schools of education to
help teachers encourage students to "explore the resources of religion as a basis
for durable convictions."[29]

The confluence of classroom, anti-Communism, and religion found its purest
expression in the story of Bella Dodd. Born in Italy, she immigrated to the United
States as a child, worked her way through college, and ascended the leadership
ranks of a New York teachers union. Like Whittaker Chambers, she became a
Communist, admitting as much in 1944. And, as with that fellow traveler, she
marked her breakup with Communism by finding God. Dodd wrote of the
ordeal in her 1954 autobiography, *School of Darkness*. She made the decision in
1950, and, not surprisingly, Fulton Sheen was the instrument of her metamor-
phosis. Upon first meeting with the Catholic leader, Dodd recalled kneeling
with him in prayer before a statue of Mary. "I don't remember praying," she
wrote several years later, "but I do remember that the battle within me ceased,
my tears were dried, and I was conscious of stillness and peace." On April 7,
1952, with *Witness* about to be released, Sheen baptized Dodd at the font of St.
Patrick's Cathedral, as he had with Louis Budenz. Just as the revelations from
other former Communists had sounded the warning of Communist infiltration
in government, Dodd's revelations confirmed the movement's interest in the

American education system. But *School of Darkness* was not without a glimmer of hope. "New armies of men are rising," its final paragraph began, "and these are sustained not by the Communist creed but by the credo of Christianity."[30]

This trend of sacralization in education enjoyed wide but far from unanimous support in American society. The reemphasis on spiritual and moral values forced a peculiar alliance between secularists and some religious leaders. Understanding why secularists opposed curricular changes is easy. A century-long process of decreasing religious salience in American public education was reversing. The trend was enough to make the *Washington Post*, usually supportive of national religious renewal, a little queasy. "Grave difficulties arrive," wrote its editors in 1952, "when any religious group attempts to prescribe a remedy that rests upon the public schools."[31]

Often the strongest and most surprising critiques of moral and spiritual education came from those Cold Warriors most dedicated to religious revival. Their animosity toward the new trend in education seems counterintuitive until one examines the true nature of curricular changes. America's holy warriors saw in the public-school reforms a cynical tactic designed to allay anti-Communist concerns while ceding little actual ground to religion. Schools were not returning to the nonsectarian but religiously infused model of the mid-nineteenth century, they argued. Instead, educators paid lip service to a vague and religiously bankrupt concept of "moral and spiritual values." Indeed, by the NEA's own definition, moral and spiritual values were "those values which, when applied in human behavior, exalt and refine life and bring it into accord with the standards of conduct that are approved in our democratic culture." The San Diego public schools considered spiritual values to be beliefs "which contribute to the dignity and worth of human personality."[32]

The National Catholic Welfare Conference looked suspiciously at the NEA's 1951 report on moral and spiritual values, wondering whether the NEA proposal was actually a Trojan horse designed to appease those societal forces demanding sacralization in public education. The Catholic Church called the NEA's vague definition of moral and spiritual values "totally unacceptable." Still, Catholic leaders grudgingly acknowledged that the report did mark some progress, no matter how slight or ill conceived, in the sacralization of public education.[33] Nor was disappointment at the NEA's seemingly tepid reforms limited to the Catholic Church. Publishing baron Henry R. Luce, an ardent Presbyterian anti-Communist, openly wondered in October 1951 whether the sacralization of public education was doing more harm than good. "A principal effort of the National Education Association in the last few years has been to equip itself with an ample, up-to-date stream-lined larder of spiritual and moral values," he once observed at a university address. "Perhaps they will soon have them quick-frozen to keep that fresh, tender, juicy, ethical flavor."[34]

Though these criticisms were not without merit, they often reflected a failure to grasp the significance of new policies adopted by the NEA and school districts across America. Religion was afforded a new, albeit restricted, place in classrooms. School children who had for years begun each day with the simple Pledge of Allegiance—before the insertion of the words "under God"—now followed the ritual with a nonsectarian prayer. Teachers who had been taught to avoid religious discussions in the classroom were now encouraged to lead them. As with the military's character-guidance programs, moral and spiritual education would remain in force throughout the 1950s until a new examination of the Communist threat and a different interpretation by the Supreme Court arrested the process of sacralization in public schools.

In the decades before World War II, the media had also been agents of secularization. Then journalists devoted far less attention to religion, and when they did write about religious topics, their articles were often negative.[35] But scarcely twenty years after the acerbic editorials surrounding the Scopes trial, circumstances had changed. The media recast religion as a bulwark against Communism and a guarantor of freedom.

Newspapers and magazines seized early on Communist atrocities against religion in Russia. Writers dispatched horrific tales of executed priests, despoiled relics, and unchurched masses. In a detailed 1946 exposé, the New York Times's Moscow correspondent picked up the thread from the prewar era of observations on the religious aspects of Communism. He worried that the Soviet reliance on this dogmatic faith would make rapprochement with the West impossible. "When the Soviet representatives meet ours at the conference table," he wrote, "they are in fact meeting the last tottering princes of original sin; and they cannot give way to us without yielding divine principle."[36]

The postwar situation altered the media's basic message on Communism. What before had been a deplorable but distant problem pitting religion and Communism inside the Soviet Union transformed into an international conflict involving America. In 1946 the Memphis Commercial Appeal became one of the first secular American newspapers to frame the inchoate Cold War in religious terms. In a series of editorials, the paper argued that Christianity could not coexist with Communism. "The choice is between God and these United States," the editors wrote, "or communism and social and economic enslavement by the forces of the antichrist." The nation's largest and most respected newspapers followed. Anne O'Hare McCormick, a longtime New York Times correspondent, called the conflict a "war on the side of angels." The Times editors labeled it a "struggle for men's souls;" the Washington Post declared the Cold War a battle against "pseudo-religion;" and the staunchly conservative Chicago Daily Tribune wrote of "the godless religion's new crusade." The Wall Street Journal opined that though Americans "customarily think of democracy as the implacable foe of Communism, it is the Christian framework which is." In his search for comparison, Walter Lippmann looked a millennium earlier to the battle between Christianity and Islam.[37] Newspapers not only cast the conflict in spiritual terms, they also publicized religious observances and helped launch the careers of new religious leaders. While attending a young Billy Graham's 1949 Los Angeles revival, devout Christian anti-Communist William Randolph Hearst cabled his newspaper editors a two-word order: "Puff Graham." Soon the evangelical preacher was a household name.[38]

By the late 1940s Hearst had been surpassed as America's preeminent press lord by Henry R. Luce, whose magazines reached approximately one in five Americans weekly. Luce redefined American journalism by launching *Time* magazine with a former Yale classmate in 1923. They believed that newspapers and magazines inundated middle-class American readers with unnecessary information and bored them with cumbersome syntax. *Time* synthesized and analyzed the news each week, affording busy readers a lively yet intelligent take on current events. Whereas rival magazines published pieces from a large and relatively diverse pool of contributors, most of *Time*'s articles came from staff writers and offered no byline. This gave the magazine a strong sense of stylistic uniformity and afforded Luce a level of ideological cohesion found only, if at all, on the editorial pages of competing periodicals. Following his business partner's unexpected death in 1929, Luce took sole control of Time, Inc., subsequently founding *Fortune* and revamping the ailing *Life*.[39]

In a 1941 editorial in *Life*, Luce proclaimed the dawn of the "American Century," a period in which American power, coupled with moral righteousness, would bring peace to the world.[40] Critics considered him the worst kind of neo-imperialist, but his dreams accorded with the visions of future policymakers like John Foster Dulles who welded religious morality to the framework of foreign policy. Well before the end of World War II, Luce had presciently concluded that America was poised to exercise unprecedented economic and military power. He worried, though, that his countrymen were dangerously unprepared for the task of steering and maintaining such a nation. They were living in what Luce called a state of "outer tragedy and inner chaos." Here he reformulated the basic conclusion that his friend and mentor Walter Lippmann reached two decades earlier. Materialism was empty and even dangerous without the guidance of spirituality.[41]

As the Axis threat waned and Americans looked with hope and apprehension to the postwar era, Luce reached two significant conclusions: that Communism would become the greatest obstacle to the American century, and that secularization would make American victory impossible. Unlike J. Edgar Hoover and Fulton Sheen, Luce was not as well versed in Marx. His position was instead influenced by personal experience and conversations with friends and advisers. Luce maintained a lifelong interest in China. In 1940, his father completed one of the first English works on Chinese Communism. During World War II, when few Americans had even heard of Mao Tse-tung, Luce was receiving routine dispatches from his foreign correspondents highlighting the weakness and brutality of Chiang Kai-shek's American-backed regime.

Two advisers significantly shaped Luce's understanding of Communism's designs and weaknesses. The first was his wife, Clare Boothe Luce, for whom Communism was an evil religion that could only be met with the fiery zeal of a Christian nation. The second was Whittaker Chambers, the Communist turned Christian warrior. Chambers slowly climbed through the ranks of Time, Inc. and had entered the inner circle of advisers that Luce depended on for business and editorial decisions. In 1944 Luce made Chambers the head of Time's Foreign News. Predictably, Chambers molded Time into an anti-Communist mouthpiece. Though Luce's other publications strived to maintain greater neutrality, in time they too came into the same ideological orbit.[42]

To Luce, Communism posed the greatest ideological threat to American political and moral hegemony. He called it the most "dynamic, ideational force in our world." When in February 1945 Rep. Karl E. Mundt requested Time, Inc.'s endorsement for a permanent HUAC, Luce readily acceded.[43] While he counted anti-Communists like Mundt, Cardinal Spellman, and Chambers as allies, he viewed the Communist threat differently. In his view, it was a symptom and not a disease. Like his wife, Clare, he understood faith as a psychological imperative sought by all people. If religious faith waned, other dogmas would take its place. The success of Communism, then, was not attributable to its message but rather to the fact that it offered people the spiritual certainty they no longer found in Christianity. All the shocking anti-Communist propaganda and shopworn tributes to democracy that America could muster would fail to arrest the Marxian surge. But if Americans filled the spiritual vacuum, if they made religious faith commensurate with military and economic power, then Communism would dissipate.[44]

Though his knowledge of Communism may have been underdeveloped, Luce spoke on religious matters with justified authority. Employees considered Luce's insistence upon riding alone in the elevator the thirty-six floors to his penthouse each morning a sign of elitism, but he actually took that time to pray.[45] Luce was the son of Christian missionaries to China, and his father, a professor of theology, endowed him with a level of religious knowledge uncommon in businessmen of the age. Luce delighted in speaking before religious groups and fancied himself an amateur theologian. He was active in the Federal Council of Churches and the National Conference of Christians and Jews, and he sat on the board of directors of Union Theological Seminary.[46]

Henry R. Luce, shown with his wife, Clare Boothe Luce, in 1954, was America's preeminent publishing baron in the early Cold War. He also contributed to the spiritual-industrial complex by sitting on numerous boards of directors and allowing his prominent magazines to promote a religious understanding of Communism. (Courtesy of the *New York World-Telegram and Sun* Newspaper Photograph Collection, Library of Congress.)

Luce's understanding of American history guided his prescriptions. He laid this out emphatically during a 1946 address to the Duke Divinity School. "A hundred years ago this land of ours was pervaded with a profound sense of optimism," he began.

> There was in every town and hamlet, an earnest faith in God. Men and women prayed every day. There was a strong moral sense. It seemed as if there had occurred one of those rare moments in human history when the spirit of Promethean achievement and Homeric adventure was matched by a religious sense of duty and of the moral purpose in the universe.[47]

Religious faith had once made America and its people great. Whereas the historian Frederick Jackson Turner lauded the frontier as the wellspring of American exceptionalism, stability, and innovation, Luce tied these qualities to American religious devotion—a faith that made democracy, freedom, and the pursuit of social justice possible. He recognized that secularization had sundered the relationship between religion and society in modern America. The frontier may have passed permanently into wistful memory, but Luce refused to believe that secularization had taken society past the point of no return.[48]

Of course Luce could make the greatest contribution to sacralization through use of his media empire. Time, Inc. was too large an operation to exert constant control over. He rarely involved himself in the day-to-day editorial decisions of his magazines, leaving this to a trusted cadre of hand-picked editors. Still, few avowedly secular magazines took religion as seriously as *Time* and *Life*. Luce had a talent for finding spiritual diamonds in the rough, none more glittering than a certain English professor of history. "Ten years ago," Luce recalled in 1952 during a dinner for his editors, "I was initiated into a little cult of those who had discovered Arnold Toynbee." Though he had been impressed with Toynbee since their first meeting in 1942, Luce's decision to let Chambers fashion *A Study of History* into a Cold War religious lesson was a critical step in building the consensus upon which the spiritual-industrial complex depended.[49]

The visages of many religious anti-Communist leaders graced the cover of *Time* in the early Cold War, among them Spellman, Niebuhr, Oxnam, Sheen, Pius XII, and Graham. Under the influence of Chambers in the early postwar period, *Time's* many articles on Communism often highlighted the creed's religious components. The magazine eagerly published a version of *New York Times* foreign correspondent Brooks Atkinson's observations on the religion of Communism, and Chambers certainly had a hand in shaping the 1948 cover story that marked the centennial of the *Communist Manifesto*. Marx himself appeared on the cover of that issue, his fiery eyes making him look more like a demon than a man. The piece predictably construed Marx's creed as profoundly religious and labeled its leader an "evangelical atheist."[50]

Luce exerted greater influence on *Life*, and one influential 1947 editorial laid out a religious vision remarkably similar to his own. "The Road to Religion" emphasized those properties that separated religion from other institutions. It argued that religion meant more than the brotherhood of man or a code of ethics. These were the fruits of religious experience, handed down by generations more pious than postwar Americans. True religion was revolutionary, otherworldly, and radical. It possessed qualities that no secular institution could claim. But Americans had grown spiritually complacent. The editors compared this apathy to fourth-century Alexandria where, under a "soft doctrine," its citizens had come to believe the dictum that "truth is reason, not mystery." Into this state of ancient secularization stepped St. Anthony, who restored the mystery and wonder of religious belief. And if America was indeed a modern day Alexandria, it needed a St. Anthony.[51]

Although Luce believed religious revival was a revolution from the bottom up—once remarking that there was no formula to manufacture Christianity—he was often first in line to endow and manage a plethora of large-scale religious projects aimed at sacralizing society in the name of anti-Communism. Luce traveled the nation delivering speeches before religious and secular groups on the necessity of spiritual revival. As he remarked at Union Theological Seminary, "No nation . . . was so obviously destined for some special phase of God's eternal purpose."[52]

Luce was not only a journalist but a businessman as well, and American business was indispensable to the process of sacralization. It provided much-needed money, offered its talents for organization and advertising, and advocated stances that an officially secular government could not. A period of spiritual corporatism followed. Business leaders wielded influence over their employees and the public at large. When World War I–ace and Eastern Airlines president Edward V. Rickenbacker called for a "crusade against the Red Anti-Christ," Americans listened. When a General Motors consultant implored the Rotary Club to join him in forging a united spiritual front beginning with the reintroduction of religion into public schools, they applauded. When the chairmen of Standard Oil, General Electric, Bell Telephone, and U.S. Steel funded the Freedom Train, they flocked to it in the millions. Gone and forgotten was the spiritual hubris of industrial titans like Henry Ford, who proclaimed machinery America's "new Messiah" and believed that corporations alone could inculcate morality. These visions now smacked of Communism. After Henry Ford II took over the family business, he proudly displayed his religious orthodoxy, even joining Luce on the national advisory council of the Foundation for Religious Action.[53]

Writing in the immediate postwar period, historian David Potter searched for the one characteristic that set Americans apart from their counterparts across the world, and he settled on the profound implications of abundance, dubbing Americans a "people of plenty." But to be a great force, abundance required a corresponding institution, and Potter believed that advertising filled this role. What began with tiny notices tucked away in the back pages of nineteenth-century newspapers and magazines transformed into bloated, glossy, and prescriptive announcements in the postwar period. Advertisers changed strategies from simply targeting segments of existing demand to manufacturing demand that did not exist before.[54] These techniques of modern advertising, when applied to religion during the early Cold War, formed a major component of the spiritual-industrial complex. Business leaders were not interested in swaying Catholics toward Protestantism or vice versa. They sought instead to create new demand for religion. In this way the tools of materialism would fuel a revival of spiritualism.

In 1949 American business leaders began an advertising campaign without precedent. For three weeks beginning November 1, they saturated radio, print, television, and billboards with messages urging Americans to mobilize spiritually. Led by General Electric's president, Charles E. Wilson, the Religion in American Life (RIAL) campaign was made possible through the cooperation of corporations, religious leaders, and the government. The Advertising Council, a business enterprise formed in 1942 to marshal the newfound powers of marketing to the war effort, served as the coordinating organization. America's most prominent corporations donated money and the creative energies of their employees. The J. Walter Thompson Company, credited with inventing modern American advertising, developed the ads. American periodicals, radio networks, and budding television stations donated valuable space and time. Added up, these contributions exceeded $3 million over the initial three-week campaign.[55]

As with most successful ad campaigns, RIAL used celebrity endorsements to convince Americans that religious participation was a normative act. Jackie Robinson, Norman Rockwell, the image of Betty Crocker, and J. Edgar Hoover appeared in print discussing the importance of religion. The evening before the campaign began, President Truman endorsed RIAL in a live address. "Each one of us can do his part by a renewed devotion to his religion," he spoke. "If there is any danger to the religious life of our Nation, it lies in our taking our religious heritage too much for granted."[56] Some ads featured celebrities discussing their personal faith. Others focused on lonely people, those worried about the future, or children searching for security and meaning. Yet the specter of Communism hung over the enterprise, providing a sense of urgency. One print ad, entitled "Democracy Starts Here," depicted a group of children singing in a choir, their cherubic faces illuminated by a light from above. The text followed:

> The way I see it, when you're a father you're automatically a founding father too. . . . Totalitarian countries do a top-flight job of founding their philosophies, their nations, in the hearts of their youngsters. I think what they give them is faith—faith in false gods . . . a burning, positive, dynamic faith which permeates their lives. Some folks think we can challenge that faith simply by being against it. But that's like scolding an atom bomb. The only force which can conquer faith is a greater and deeper faith.[57]

The idea of Communism as a faith—forged in the 1920s and 1930s by theologians and intellectuals who concluded that Communism was a faith, rescued from oblivion by religious leaders after World War II, fanned by politicians as they contemplated the Red menace—was distilled by RIAL's execs into a terse, simple statement. The following year, as RIAL geared up for another campaign, Wilson called the program an effort toward "spiritual rearmament." Truman once again endorsed the plan, noting, "These are times that demand the vision and fortitude of men of faith such as never before in the history of the world."[58]

The RIAL campaign ran for ten consecutive years, from 1949 to 1958, and reached millions of Americans. In its first year, more than two thousand communities participated by holding grassroots religious mobilization campaigns. Three thousand towns and cities joined in 1950. The Outdoor Advertising Agency donated 5,200 billboards across America, and 1,800 daily newspapers published editorials supporting the program or carried RIAL advertisements. By 1956, more than three hundred television programs aired the calls for religious mobilization. If stacked on one another, the RIAL posters alone would extend twelve miles into the sky. Impressed by RIAL's success, Truman tapped "Electric Charlie," as Wilson was known, to head the Office of Defense Mobilization. After all, if he could muster American spirituality, mobilizing its material resources would be straightforward by comparison.[59]

In sheer scale, RIAL was nonpareil, but it shared a common objective with other efforts toward spiritual mobilization, each enlisting Americans in the Cold War religious struggle. When, for instance, church bells rang across America on July 4, 1951, it was no spontaneous outpouring of religious patriotism, but rather the culmination of another carefully orchestrated plan. Like RIAL, the Committee to Proclaim Liberty (CPL) was made up of America's business, religious, and political elite. But rather than attempting to foment a religious revival, the CPL strived to convince Americans that God was the guarantor of true freedom. Independence Day seemed the perfect opportunity. It was the most secular of American holidays—a time of fireworks, parades, flags, and picnics—when Americans celebrated the achievement of men rather than the workings of the Almighty. But the CPL envisioned each July 4 as a day of solemn religious observation when church leaders would expound upon the connection between religion and Americanism. James C. Ingebretsen, the committee's coordinator, contended that "it is not only proper to give prayerful thanks to God for liberty on the 175th anniversary of the Declaration of Independence, but that it is only in this spiritual understanding of the true source of our liberty that our country will be able to survive."[60]

CPL boasted the backing of fifty-six overseers, a figure chosen to mirror the number of men who signed the Declaration of Independence. These were to be America's new founding fathers, men who would be remembered not for chartering the nation but instead for returning it to its spiritual foundations. The list included entertainment industry celebrities like Bing Crosby, Ronald Reagan, Cecil B. DeMille, and Walt Disney. Joining them were titans of business such as J. C. Penney, Fred Maytag II, and Conrad Hilton. Religious leaders Norman Vincent Peale and G. Bromley Oxnam contributed, as did national politicians and the presidents of Brown University and the University of California. With

In a sign of how some efforts of the spiritual-industrial complex worked to reinforce others, the Freedoms Foundation awarded the Committee to Proclaim Liberty with one of its medals in 1951. (Courtesy of University of Oregon Special Collections.)

these names sparkling on the letterhead, CPL distributed over 150,000 missives to other institutional leaders across America.[61]

CPL's vision would have withered without a well-crafted publicity campaign. Here, as with RIAL, its well-connected board members made the difference. Major American newspapers such as the *Los Angeles Times* and *Chicago Sun-Times* carried editorials lauding the proposal. Thirty-one governors signed declarations instructing their electorates to use Independence Day for religious reflection. "The question which must be determined is whether we and the other people of the free world, through faith in God and belief in the dignity of man, can match in fervor the fanaticism of atheistic and totalitarian communism," California governor Earl Warren proclaimed. "The fate of the world is in the balance until this conflict is resolved." One of CPL's backers was the president of the U.S. Chamber of Commerce, and businesses across the country were encouraged to provide the effort with free promotion. Customers of San Diego Gas & Electric, Detroit Edison, and Utah Power and Light received CPL flyers inserted into their monthly bills. Gates Rubber Company in Illinois devoted most of its monthly company magazine to the CPL's "Freedom Under God" theme. The entire effort culminated at 9:30 p.m. on Sunday, July 1, when CBS broadcast the "Freedom Under God" program. Jimmy Stewart, Bing Crosby, and Gloria Swanson spoke during the eclectic half-hour event, which featured a blend of church choirs and military speeches. They instructed all patriotic Americans to attend their places of worship on "Independence Sabbath" and to reread the Declaration of Independence as the church bells rang on July 4. General Matthew B. Ridgway provided the keynote address from his office in Tokyo. "However well equipped with the finest arms that science and loyal people can provide," he said, "no army will long succeed without those spiritual values." CPL repeated its efforts from 1952 to 1957.[62]

A Los Angeles pastor and CPL member announced that "firecrackers won't save freedom." His simple statement encapsulated in four words the fundamental beliefs shared by fellow contributors. "We must have faith in Him to be able to stand firm against the forces of atheism and barbarism throughout the world," Ingebretsen declared. "We must look to God for the courage and wisdom to reestablish our freedom and security here in America." Tying this sentiment back to Independence Day, one CPL advertisement announced that "state despotism is no respecter of persons or of places. It can and does raise its ugly, un-Godly standard over the traditionally free soil of England with the same brash assurance that characterizes its sway in Communist Russia." Rewriting the Revolutionary War as a religious crusade was a historical stretch, but urgency left little room for accuracy. If freedom was indeed at risk, then the topic of debate turned to the best method for protecting it. By choosing to emphasize July 4, the CPL sent the unmistakable message that civic conceptions of freedom were wholly inadequate in the Cold War. Simply calling oneself an American was not enough. "As a good American," one pamphlet read, "you believe that God is the Creator of all men . . . your rights, and the rights of your fellow-men, are God-given . . . [and that] as a personal creature of God, each of us is equal in the sight of God."[63]

The committee members argued that Independence Day began as a religious holiday, only to become another casualty of secularization. On this point they were mistaken. After all, in the eighteenth century, even Christmas was not considered a major religious holiday. The Fourth of July in the early republic was a time of parades, military musters, drinking, and civic speeches that were scarcely the embodiment of religious observation.[64] If by chance the holiday fell on a Sunday, Americans put off their celebrations until Monday, a clear sign that they considered Independence Day a secular occasion.[65] American religious leaders had given Fourth of July orations, most notably during times of war, but these were often patriotic pronouncements in which religion cast its lot with the state. Yet on July 4, 1951, the opposite rang true, literally. Rather than serving as one of many props to the state, religious groups asserted the preeminence of the sacred over the secular.

The cadre of business leaders who made RIAL and CPL possible also turned their attention to international affairs. The religious dimensions of the Cold War remained troubling but nonetheless distant for most Americans. In Europe, however, the spiritual abstract had become all too tangible. General Lucius D. Clay, the American military governor of Germany during the Berlin Airlift, worried that the Soviets were winning the ideological battle in Europe. In 1950 he conceived a plan to rally Americans behind their European allies. The United States had saved West Berlin from starvation by flying in crucial supplies, but Clay envisioned a "spiritual airlift." This was the birth of the Crusade for Freedom, with a national board of directors that included twelve U.S. senators, publishers like Henry R. Luce, religious leaders like Reinhold Niebuhr, the heads of Hollywood's largest studios, and business executives.[66]

The crusade had a simple aim. Each American was asked to donate one dollar and sign a Freedom Scroll. The donations would pay for the construction of a ninety-eight-inch, ten-ton bronze "Freedom Bell" to be installed in West Berlin. Any leftover funds would be applied to the fledgling Radio Free Europe, a privately funded series of stations launched in July 1950 to combat Communist propaganda.[67] Around its circumference, the Freedom Bell displayed figures representing the five races of humanity passing the torch of freedom. Etched beneath was the inscription: "That this world under God shall have a new birth of freedom." By signing the Freedom Scroll, Americans made the following pledge: "I believe in the sacredness and dignity of the individual. I believe that all men derive the right to freedom equally from God. I pledge to resist aggression and tyranny wherever they appear on earth."[68] The Crusade for Freedom enlisted thousands of volunteers across America to operate signature-collection centers. In Washington, DC, citizens could sign outside the District Building. In New York City, they could contribute at their local firehouse.[69] To generate publicity, organizers sent the Freedom Bell on a twenty-one city tour, and the *New York Times*, *Washington Post*, and *Los Angeles Times* widely covered the crusade and supported it in editorials. On the evening of September 4, Eisenhower delivered an address supporting the cause that was carried by all four of America's major radio networks. He spoke of Communist "godless depravity in government" and asked Americans to declare their faith in freedom and in God. They responded in the millions.[70]

The crusade explained its mission in a straightforward statement: "The soul of the world is sick, and the peoples of the world are looking to the United States for leadership." It beckoned Americans to light the lamps of spiritual guidance. And so they did. Twenty-five million signed the Freedom Scroll, raising $3.5 million for Radio Free Europe. Millions more observed "Freedom Sunday" on October 8. Crusade for Freedom wrote to over 80,000 religious leaders requesting they prepare sermons emphasizing "the truth that all human rights are derived from God." New York's acting mayor Vincent Impellitteri urged residents to spend the day offering "thanksgiving to the Almighty for safeguarding our way of life against the evil forces who would destroy it and by begging God to give hope and courage to the enslaved peoples of the world seeking to regain freedom and self-government."[71]

RIAL, CPL, and Crusade for Freedom grew in the same climate, tended by the same men, and for the same purpose. They sold religion to Americans, using celebrity endorsements, modern advertising techniques, and Cold War urgency. Each ideological "purchase" fueled the process of sacralization. But Americans also joined these campaigns because the cost of participation was cheap. For a

dollar and a sermon, they received the self-assurance of having done their patriotic duty and the warm satisfaction of pummeling the Reds. Some who waited in
Washington, DC, for their chance to sign the Freedom Scroll believed that with
a stroke of the pen they could hurtle a dart at the heart of Communism. "There's
nothing complicated [about] why I'm signing," explained a government clerk.
"Belief in freedom is the answer." A twenty-year-old electrician joined the crusade to end the Cold War. "I am enlisting in the Navy in the next few days. I want
to get this mess over," he said. Others were signing the scroll to "bring the boys
home" or so that their husbands could be peacetime soldiers.[72] Conventional
wars were decided on the battlefield and in factories rather than civilian queues.
Whether out of naiveté, optimism, or induced belief, Americans held fast to the
notion that they each had a part to play in the unfolding battle. This time they
would not collect scrap metal or plant victory gardens. Their task was simpler
but more abstract.

Meanwhile, voluntary associations, which experienced highs in membership
and influence in the early Cold War years, committed themselves to a similar
mission.[73] The Daughters of the American Revolution awarded a medal to a
Brooklyn educator who advocated the teaching of religious beliefs in public
schools. The Rotary Club published a recommendation touting the recent
release of a book examining Communism's spiritual duplicity, and the Fraternal
Order of Eagles installed Decalogue monuments in city parks and public buildings. In 1952 a Los Angeles chapter of the Kiwanis Club sponsored the printing
of 20,000 booklets detailing the spiritual perils of Communism. Delivered to
area homes by the Boy Scouts, the tracts argued that Communism inspired the
sort of fanatical actions that "only a religion can inspire."[74]

The American Legion made perhaps the best organized and most consis-
tent contributions to the spiritual-industrial complex of any voluntary association. Its interest in Cold War sacralization was unsurprising. The Legion's
constitutional preamble, written by early anti-Communist congressman Hamilton Fish III, began with the simple phrase "For God and Country." But in the
effort to bond religion to American civic life, the Legion's commanders knew
that actions spoke louder than words. The organization had long been a
Red-baiting powerhouse, committing itself to "100 percent Americanism" and
eagerly testifying before the Dies Committee in the 1930s.[75] Flush with new
recruits in the aftermath of World War II, the Legion geared up for holy war. At
its national convention in 1949, the Legion's leaders heard Philadelphia mayor
Bernard Samuel warn, "We have seen and are seeing an attempt to spread irreligious ideology in our own nation." Two years later, in Miami, Notre Dame
law dean Clarence Manion suggested the Legion create a Cold War battle flag.
On one side would be an inscription reading "This nation is for God," and on

the other a second inscription: "The only chance for the survival of American self-government is the revival of personal self-respect for the Ten Commandments." It was hardly the kind of concise slogan well-suited for battle cries, but the message resonated.[76]

By August 1952, when it convened its annual convention in New York, the Legion claimed more than 2.7 million members in more than 17,000 posts. In June the organization had chartered the Committee on Religious Emphasis, which it charged with leading the Legion's new spiritual drive. The committee managed the Back to God program, a campaign conducted both from the national headquarters and at the grassroots by posts in every state. This campaign had three stated goals: family devotion, regular church attendance, and religious education of youth. Members were instructed to set aside a daily period for family prayer, to say a blessing before all meals, and to turn to the clergy regularly for spiritual counsel. The national commander directed all posts to advertise local churches and set aside ten minutes each meeting for prayer. February became "Legion Go to Church Month," and each post was charged with tending to the spiritual needs of local children. They sponsored free transportation to Sunday schools, conducted religious censuses, offered rewards to the most devout children, and created religious posters for schools.[77]

The media gushed. "Never in our country's history has there been a greater need for public acknowledgement of Deity," opined the *Miami Herald*. The *Charleston Gazette* considered Back to God a bold plan to wean the masses off their materialistic diets. In Maine, newspapers reprinted "My Legion Prayer," written by a local post commander and former World War II commando: "We pray, too, O God of justice, for the flag of our country. . . . Suffer not the Red to obliterate the white and blue, nor the hammer and sickle to replace the Stars and Stripes." The *Spokane Chronicle* mused that "shades of the Pilgrims who carried rifles with them to their church services must be hovering over a modern host who are seeking to lead America's fighting men back to faith in God."[78]

The Committee on Religious Emphasis inundated the public with brochures, pamphlets, and radio programs. Its members created the "Back to God kit," a packet consisting of a suggested ten-minute talk, editorial, and fifteen-minute radio script.[79] The highlight of the Back to God program was an annual television program held in February to kick off the Legion "Go to Church" month. The first program in 1952 received little free publicity from the media. This changed in 1953, when newly inaugurated Eisenhower and Vice President Nixon agreed to participate. Eisenhower delivered a written message, but Nixon made the journey to New York for a live appearance. "Moral decay from within has destroyed more nations from within than armed might without," he told the national audience.[80]

The following year Eisenhower delivered a live address for the Legion's February 7, 1954, telecast carried by CBS, the Armed Forces Radio Service, and

Voice of America. It resembled less a joint call for spiritual renewal than a carefully tailored history lesson. Popular author and pastor Norman Vincent Peale began with a prayer: "Ours is the first great nation in history to be established upon a definitely religious base. Our country will remain strong as long as we remain religious." Then came the silky words of Bishop Fulton Sheen, recounting the story of how the Founding Fathers determined the origins of American rights. According to Sheen, they considered the notion that rights came from the majority or the parliament but realized that such guarantees could be abrogated by popular or legislative whim. So the Founding Fathers settled upon the concept that rights came from God, who could make them inalienable. "It becomes as simple as this," Sheen explained with customary analogy; "if we are to keep our perfume, we must keep our flowers . . . and if we are to keep our rights and our liberties, then we must also keep our God." Eisenhower echoed Sheen's claims, concluding, "Whatever our individual church, whatever our personal creed, our common faith in God is a common bond between us."[81]

It was only a matter of time before the entertainment industry made its contribution to the spiritual-industrial complex. Its leadership absorbed the political and religious discussions then under way, while idea men fashioned them into patriotic, but nonetheless marketable, products. It was an excellent fusion of information dissemination and old-fashioned money making.

Religious institutions, particularly the Catholic Church, recognized the potential of entertainment media. Comic books were among the first products used to reinforce Cold War religious messages. For instance, in 1947's *To Make You Think*, a Protestant minister is one of the few citizens to defy the Communist organization plotting to take over America. After enduring constant harassment and a church bombing, he was taken by Communist agents to a backcountry road and executed. In a later frame, two Communist leaders, looking suspiciously like liberal college professors, discussed their war against religion. "How long are we going to fight the churches?" the first asked his comrade. "We'll never stop," the second replied. "It's either the church or us. . . . The churches teach the importance of the individual. Therefore, all religions must go!" During the height of the Mindszenty crisis in Hungary, another comic book depicted the beleaguered cardinal as a superhero of sorts, deftly outwitting swarthy, mustached, and altogether sinister-looking Hungarian Communists. In the end it took eighty armed guards to arrest the graying cleric.[82]

Fulton Sheen excelled at using radio actors to dramatize the need for spiritual mobilization. His weekly radio program, *The Catholic Hour*, devoted the entire month of September 1950 to a four-part theatrical miniseries on the history and danger of Communism. By then Sheen was attracting an ever-increasing audience. So popular was *The Catholic Hour* that when Sheen switched to television two years later, his ratings nearly eclipsed programs featuring Milton Berle and Frank Sinatra.[83]

The final installment of the National Council of Catholic Men's four-part dramatization of the Communist menace, entitled "Awake or Perish," begins with an American family sitting around the dinner table. Danny, the eldest son, is preparing to leave for the Korean War. Upset, his father exclaims: "The only way to stop these Communists is to drop a few atomic bombs on them. That'll show them." At this moment a narrator breaks in—an omniscient voice from above.

"Is that the only way?" the narrator asks. "Bombs kill people, not ideas, and Communism is a deadly idea."

"One of my teachers says that the *only* way to stop Communism is to make democracy work," interjects Danny's younger sister, Jeanie.

"That is a dangerous and very popular argument," the narrator states. "Notice that word 'only,' . . . the 'only' way. Putting in the 'only' means we *either* have to improve democracy *or* accept Communism."

Then a chorus of voices begins chanting.

> "A Communist is *not* a Protestant."
> "A Communist is *not* a Jew."
> "A Communist is *not* a Catholic."

The narrator returns, warning, "In the long run all of us—Catholic, Jew, Protestant and those Americans who may acknowledge no formal religion—must rearm physically and be reborn spiritually."

"Let the Kremlin tremble at the spiritual and physical vigor of the United States of America!" the chorus shouts.

This short dramatization contains virtually every important facet of the argument for American sacralization: Communism is a spiritual threat that weapons alone could not defeat. Secular democracy will fail in defeating the Red scourge, but democracy grounded in a religious foundation will triumph. Religious Americans are immune from Communist infiltration and conversion. All major faiths need to unite against a common spiritual enemy. The Soviet Union's greatest fear is not American nuclear attack but American religious revival.[84]

But when it came to the sacralization of popular culture, no medium outshined the American film industry. In the early Cold War, America was a nation of moviegoers, and Hollywood a seat of concentrated power. In B-grade science fiction and biblical epics, in G-man thrillers and martyrs' biographies, Americans received an anti-Communist religious education as cinemas became Cold War classrooms. Sacralization through film was hardly surprising given the high levels of cooperation by studio executives, directors, and actors with organized attempts at spiritual mobilization. The vice president of Paramount Pictures joined Walt Disney, Bing Crosby, Ronald Reagan, and Cecil B. DeMille on the governing board of the Committee to Proclaim Liberty, and the president of 20th Century Fox sat on the board of directors of the Crusade for Freedom. Producer Walter Wanger headed the Los Angeles division of Crusade for Freedom, and the Motion Picture Alliance for the Preservation of American Ideals, then under the leadership of John Wayne, eagerly lent support. On the eve of the crusade's October 1950 campaign, film-industry leaders held mass meetings at studios throughout Hollywood asking their employees to join. Standing before a replica of the Freedom Bell, Louis B. Mayer, the boss of MGM Studios and arguably the most powerful man in American film, told his employees, "We must meet the big lie with the big truth."[85]

Mayer's words struck close to home. In 1950 Hollywood was still fighting what it considered a big lie, namely the popular image of the industry as a hotbed of Communism. In October 1947 HUAC took J. Edgar Hoover's advice and launched an investigation of Communism in Hollywood. Some witnesses called before HUAC, such as Ronald Reagan and Gary Cooper, cooperated. Others, like the screenwriters and directors known as the Hollywood Ten, refused to discuss their membership in Communist groups. Hollywood's film bosses knew they stood on the brink of a public relations fiasco. With the Cold War escalating, the taint of Communism threatened Hollywood's bottom line. On November 24, 1947, a group of influential producers held a war council at New York's Waldorf-Astoria Hotel. There they decided to blacklist the Hollywood Ten, along with anyone else who expressed Communist sympathy or refused to answer HUAC's questions.[86]

The film industry repeatedly sought to prove its anti-Communist, pro-American credentials. Starring Ingrid Bergman, *Joan of Arc* (1948) must have struck moviegoers as more than a little relevant—a warrior of God imprisoned, mistreated, and burned at the stake for her religious faith. *Guilty of Treason* (1950) lacked all subtlety, depicting the arrest and trial of Cardinal Mindszenty. Reviewers considered some of the torture scenes graphic but found Charles Bickford's performance convincing.[87] And then there was *Quo Vadis* (1951). Though based on a novel nearly fifty years old, MGM's epic told a familiar story of Christianity on trial in a pagan empire. The film brought to millions of Americans explicit scenes of Christians tortured at the hands of a foreign faith. This powerful symbolism was not lost on the *Los Angeles Times*'s reviewer, who noted: "In dealing with the cruelty and barbarism on the one side as opposed to the faith and determination of furtive, frightened believers of Christ and his teaching, the picture will carry a vital impact for thousands upon thousands of viewers."[88]

Hollywood's contribution to the spiritual-industrial complex was not entirely reactive. Cecil B. DeMille, America's foremost filmmaker, was an anti-Communist long before it was fashionable in Los Angeles. Together with Walt

Disney and Leo McCarey, he founded the Motion Picture Alliance for the Preservation of American Ideals in 1944, a stridently anti-Communist organization designed to organize a silent majority within Hollywood against "Communists, radicals, and crackpots." As the Cold War hardened, so too did DeMille's conviction that Americans faced an unprecedented struggle. "There are no noncombatants in this war for the minds of men," he argued on behalf of Crusade for Freedom. "Those chains, woven of lies, we must strike off by means of the sharp, piercing, shining sort of truth."[89]

A significant part of the truth DeMille had in mind was religious. The son of an Episcopal lay minister, he had a penchant for biblical epics. Not only did they make for dramatic and visual feasts, DeMille recognized their Cold War potential. He ascribed poor reviews of his 1949 film *Samson and Delilah* to Communists and their antireligious philosophy.[90] So when DeMille began work on his final masterpiece, he left nothing to the imagination of viewers. He labeled *The Ten Commandments* "the Greatest Event in Motion Picture History," and for a time it was. The film raked in more than $65 million in 1956 and remains one of the highest-grossing films of all time when adjusted for inflation. After the overture, DeMille appeared on-screen, emerging from behind a mammoth curtain, and took the extraordinary step of personally introducing his film to moviegoers. He called it "the story of the birth of freedom." "The theme of this picture," DeMille continued, "is whether man ought to be ruled by God's law or whether he ought to be ruled by the whims of a dictator like Ramesses. Are men the property of the state or are they free souls under God? This same battle continues throughout the world today." Before retreating behind the drapery, the director announced that he would donate all profits from the film to a religious and educational trust fund.

Americans were not simply watching a three-thousand-year-old biblical tale. They flocked by the millions, perhaps unknowingly, to a modern-day morality play. They were the inheritors of an ancient wisdom, handed from down from God to his surrogates. This God-given freedom could rescue modern-day slaves around the world from the thralldom of Communism as it had freed the Israelites from Egyptian servitude millennia ago. Armed with this sacred justification, the "free souls under God" were destined to triumph.

No film articulated the religious solution to the Cold War more effectively than Harry Horner's *Red Planet Mars*. Released in 1952, the United Artists production joined a growing list of science-fiction films that explored the miracle of scientific discovery and its capacity to cause great harm. The plot was simple but profound: scientist Chris Cronyn uses newfangled radio-transmitter technology developed by the Nazis to send messages to Mars. The Soviets, having captured the same technology, race the United States in an attempt to "seek the secrets of a wiser civilization." But Cronyn makes contact first and asks the Martians how they manage to live in peace without killing each other. They reply in a series of biblical messages, warning earthlings against worshipping false gods, ordering them to "love goodness and hate evil," and suggesting they follow in the footsteps of Christ. The pivotal moment comes in the Oval Office, where Cronyn, his wife, the president, and the secretary of defense debate whether or not to publicly release the messages. Cronyn, ever the proponent of scientific reasoning, counsels the president not to release them. But his wife, recognizing the power of the sacred over the secular, calls the messages "the Martian equivalent of the Sermon on the Mount." The secretary of defense sides with Cronyn. "This time Cronyn is right, Mr. President," he warns; "we can't hitch our wagon to *that* star." The president turns to his adviser. "We've switched stars, Mr. Secretary," he says, "Now we're following the Star of Bethlehem."

Release of the Martian messages has an immediate and revolutionary effect. In America citizens who once shunned religion turn off their radios, put down their magazines, and flock to churches. But as Voice of America broadcasts the Martian messages into the Eastern Bloc, something far greater occurs. Throughout the countryside peasants dig up holy relics long buried, while roving packs of soldiers fire indiscriminately at impromptu religious gatherings. These scenes of chaos fade to an austere Moscow war room, where the Soviet leadership panics and plans on killing millions in order to destroy the public's faith in a higher power. A Stalin look-alike calls in his puppet, the Russian patriarch, ordering him to cooperate. But throughout their meeting the sound of peasants singing religious hymns in the streets continues to grow. In the end, the people take up the cross against the hammer, dethrone the Communists and install the patriarch as their interim leader. He denounces Communism, frees Eastern Europe, and ends the Cold War. Satisfied, Mrs. Cronyn provides an unmistakable moral. "Prayers were given to us long before wires," she reminds the audience.

The message was clear. Science, bombs, and money could take Americans only so far. The protagonists managed to uncover wisdom that people had known all along. Aside from a few plot quirks, *Red Planet Mars* could have been written by Fulton Sheen, J. Edgar Hoover, Clare Boothe Luce, or any one of the many Cold Warriors who recognized the power of religious faith.

Ostensibly, the institutions that contributed to the spiritual-industrial complex shared a common purpose but operated independently. Politicians delivered speeches, generals reformed training procedures, and Hollywood produced a bevy of religious films. In reality, each of the spiritual-industrial complex's undertakings employed leadership and strategies drawn from multiple institutions.

These efforts benefited from the guidance of interlocking directorates. A small group of men, representing a host of different institutions, led the spiritual-industrial complex's signature programs. General Electric president Charles

E. Wilson directed the RIAL committee and also served on the boards of both the Freedom Train's American Heritage Foundation, the Crusade for Freedom, and the CPL. Reinhold Niebuhr and Barney Balaban, the president of Paramount Pictures, sat on the RIAL and Freedom Train boards, while Balaban's lieutenant helped oversee the CPL. Eisenhower served on the NEA panel that recommended a new spiritual-values curriculum, and he shepherded the Freedoms Foundation before becoming president. Such committees served as a training ground for the bolder policies he would support from the Oval Office. Henry R. Luce was busiest of all, lending his clout and advice to the Freedom Train, Crusade for Freedom, RIAL, and CPL. Religious conceptions of the Cold War formed in one committee spread over time to others. When planning for the sacralization of American society, it was a small world.

Beyond the boardroom, the spiritual-industrial complex's enterprises were mutually reinforcing, often drawing on the contributions of multiple institutions. Political leaders depended on a sympathetic media. Military reform boards like the Weil Committee enlisted the help of educators and business leaders. Psychological-warfare operations depended on the cooperation of American religious institutions. Endeavors like the CPL required the public endorsements of politicians, the free publicity of newspapers, and the collaboration of businesses who inserted promotional materials into customer's monthly bills. Likewise, the American Legion's Back to God campaign relied upon the generosity of television networks and the exhortations of public servants. When it came to making American society more religious, institutions never acted alone. Instead, they created a directorate that included leaders from other powerful institutions. This offered legitimacy, but, more important, it pooled political, economic, and cultural power.

Consider the Foundation for Religious Action in Social and Civil Order (FRASCO), cofounded in 1954 by Eisenhower's personal pastor, Edward L. R. Elson, and Episcopalian rector Charles W. Lowry. They created an interlocking directorate that included leaders from several important institutions. Billy Graham brought his religious celebrity to the table, Henry Ford II brought the backing of big business, Herbert Hoover brought the legitimacy and connections of a former president, George Meany brought the support of big labor, Gordon Gray and Elton Trueblood brought the experience of America's psychological warfare apparatus, and Henry R. Luce brought both the influence of a media magnate and the experience of having served on many of the spiritual-industrial complex's other committees. In fact, Luce's publications had already raised the profiles of both Elson and Lowry. The founders agreed on a mission statement that shared important similarities with peer organizations: "To unite all believers in God in the struggle between the free world and atheistic Communism which aims to destroy both religion and liberty." Next, FRASCO decided on a program of action that depended on the contributions of those institutions represented on its advisory council. In addition to its aforementioned covert missions to Southeast Asia, the foundation organized the First National Conference on the Spiritual Foundations of American Democracy, held November 8–10, 1954, in Washington. For funding it required the sponsorship of businesses. For authority it required the imprimatur of political institutions—Eisenhower attended, along with Missouri senator and former secretary of the air force Stuart Symington. For visibility it required the media, and reporters from major American newspapers reported from the convention floor. For impact beyond America it needed international reach, and cameras from the USIA rolled, displaying the religious underpinnings of democracy for all the world to see.[91]

During the 1950s FRASCO held three more such conferences, and these gatherings proved valuable opportunities to network with other institutions contributing to the spiritual-industrial complex. In conjunction with the Department of Defense, in 1956 FRASCO developed a program designed to emphasize the spiritual dimensions Armed Forces Day, normally celebrated annually on the third Saturday of May. So close was the relationship between the security establishment and FRASCO that Lowry delivered lectures like "Religion in the Current Struggle" at the National War College's National Strategy Seminar, and his organization collaborated with the Office of Armed Forces Information and Education to create a recommended book set that emphasized the spiritual basis of democracy. FRASCO also enlisted the cooperation of educational institutions after the creation of its Committee on American Education and Communism. Groups like the American Political Science Association joined the program to "energize our accepted institutions in the present, global war of ideas and spiritual powers."[92]

The spiritual-industrial complex, embodied by organizations like FRASCO, devoted money and, more importantly, the valuable time of its overseers to an impressive venture. But did it work? Did these notions—with all their dreams and dollars—percolate from the halls of power to the living rooms of the average American and make a difference? That depends on who one asks.

PART THREE

CONSEQUENCES

6

The Renewal, the Critics, and the Unraveling

"President Eisenhower, like many Americans, is a very fervent believer
in a very vague religion."

—William Lee Miller, 1953

Religious leaders in the early 1950s could scarcely contain their glee. "I've been here 17 years, and in the last eight months . . . we've registered the largest attendance I've ever seen," reported one New York pastor in 1952. "For the first time on various Sundays, we've had to put the 'completely filled' sign out on Fifth Avenue." Edward L. R. Elson declared that the nation was in the midst of "the greatest moral resurgence and spiritual awakening in the history of our land." Church donations increased sharply. Sales of Bibles were twice as high as in the previous decade, seminaries operated at full capacity, the rabbinate boasted record enrollments, Fulton Sheen was receiving four thousand letters per week, 20,000 Christians filled the Hollywood Bowl at 3:00 a.m. on Easter Sunday for a religious ceremony at dawn, and millions more woke up early to watch the service on television. Religious titles accounted at times for up to half of the national bestseller list, thanks to the success of works like Sheen's *Life Is Worth Living*, Billy Graham's *Peace with God*, and Fulton Oursler's *The Greatest Story Ever Told*. Norman Vincent Peale's *The Power of Positive Thinking* remained a bestseller from 1952 to 1955.[1]

Determined not to come down on the wrong side of the spiritual revival, some of Hollywood's stars shed their collective reputation for sin, divorce, and liquor-infused debauchery. Magazine cover girl Colleen Townsend abandoned her contract at 20th Century Fox to marry a theology student and proselytize with Billy Graham. Penny Edwards, show girl and sometime lover of leading men like Tyrone Power and Rory Calhoun, gave it all up for the Seventh-day

Adventists. June Haver briefly left the silver screen for a convent. Other stars like Roy Rogers, Dale Evans, and Jane Russell formed the Hollywood Christian Group to "reach the un-churched in the entertainment industry." Prominent Jewish entertainers like Eddie Cantor and Jack Benny worked visibly in their respective congregations and participated in national appeals for religious renewal.[2]

Public pronouncements of spiritual belief by prominent individuals became fashionable. Edward R. Murrow's radio program *This I Believe* gave famous Americans a forum for discussing their deepest convictions and the paths by which they had reached them. During the early 1950s *This I Believe* reached nearly forty million Americans twice weekly on 196 radio stations. It was translated into six languages and broadcast on a further 150 international stations by Voice of America. In print it appeared in eighty-five major American newspapers and ninety-seven foreign broadsheets. Americans and others around the globe listened as the military governor of Germany, Lucius D. Clay, asked Americans to pay back God by protecting freedom. They heard Justice Douglas of the Supreme Court urge a return to the "faith of our fathers . . . that dedicates us to something bigger and more important than ourselves or our possessions." Herbert Hoover argued, "Always growing societies record their faith in God; decaying societies lack faith and deny God." Charles Darwin's grandson risked ridicule by admitting that he was "perfectly content" to live without a "mystical sense of religion," but his view was buried by an avalanche of other religious testimonials by Adlai Stevenson, Toynbee, Truman, and Helen Keller.[3]

Signs of the renewal also appeared on American college campuses. In 1952 Harvard president James B. Conant announced a $5 million campaign to revamp the university's divinity school.[4] The initiative followed an earlier campaign designed to reemphasize the importance of religion at Yale, though this would prove insufficient for undergraduates like William F. Buckley, Jr. Campus observers noted that increased student interest did not result in chapel attendance but rather in the intellectual and spiritual search for answers. Religious-studies courses burgeoned. Students began studying anew and in earnest the works of St. Thomas Aquinas and John Calvin. "A shift is coming," Conant's successor Nathan M. Pusey predicted in 1956. "It was only yesterday that theology was simply 'tolerated' within universities. . . . Today it is almost universally acknowledged that the study of religion rightfully belongs."[5]

From the classroom to the living room, Americans prayed more visibly than ever before. During Eisenhower's first term, prayer became an exercise in social acceptance and public duty. The president prayed before cabinet meetings, athletes prayed before competitions, enthusiasts of Peale prayed for wealth, celebrities prayed for continued popularity, schoolchildren prayed for protection, and the obese prayed for weight loss. Popular magazines featured articles on proper prayer technique. Railroads printed grace on their dining-car menus. Prayer guides like *Pray Your Weight Away* and *Go with God* made their way to the best-sellers list.[6] Those too busy or uncreative to come up with their own entreaties to the Almighty could pick up the phone and call Dial-A-Prayer.[7] Public-opinion polling revealed the magnitude of the praying 1950s. Ninety-four percent of Americans believed in the power of prayer, and 82 percent reported praying often or occasionally.[8] Of those who prayed, most preferred to do so before bed each night. What were Americans praying for? Not for victory in the Cold War, as Eisenhower might have hoped. The most popular reason for prayer given by respondents was to ask God for personal favors, help, or guidance. Only 14 percent prayed to give thanks.[9]

Likewise, interest in the Ten Commandments experienced its own renaissance. The most conspicuous illustrations of this renewed interest were DeMille's epic film and the monument installations sponsored by the Eagles, but these were not the first attempts to dust off the old tablets during the early Cold War. In New York a humble stenographer used her hard-earned savings to place an advertisement celebrating the Decalogue on one of the city's subway cars. She was outdone by locals in North Carolina, who recreated the original tablets on the side of a mountain with concrete letters five feet high. Jewish leaders were especially keen to promote greater nationwide acceptance of the Ten Commandments, since they affirmed a Judeo-Christian bond. "The Ten Commandments," said one rabbi, "have come to stand for the same common heritage in American moral life as have the principles of democracy in our political life."[10]

Another inescapable sign of the religious renewal was the rise of religious leaders to a level of national fame that Jonathan Edwards, Charles Grandison Finney, or Dwight L. Moody never enjoyed. The eldest son of a careworn Methodist preacher, Norman Vincent Peale assumed the pastorate of New York's Marble Collegiate Church in 1932. Throughout the 1930s the bright and energetic Peale built his congregation with sweat, dedication to teaching the art of Christian living, and a well-publicized disdain for the New Deal. Peale first rose to national fame in 1945 with the founding of his popular magazine *Guideposts*, but he would become a full-blown sensation with the publication of *The Power of Positive Thinking* in 1952.[11]

Fortuitously released a month before Eisenhower's election, Peale's message combined religious teachings with a self-help message. "If you read this book thoughtfully," he informed readers in the introduction, "you can experience an amazing improvement within yourself." He wrote each chapter in the first person and organized it around a central lesson. Peale shared the concerns and problems of people he had met, making suggestions for how his readers could overcome similar obstacles. Sinfulness and the vengeful God of centuries past were noticeably absent in Peale's teachings. Snide journalists dubbed it "feel good theology."

Criticisms aside, the New York pastor became a sensation. By the mid-1950s his newspaper column boasted ten million weekly readers, and his weekly radio program attracted three million listeners. *Guideposts* enjoyed a circulation of half a million. *The Power of Positive Thinking* sold over a million copies.[12]

Arguably the only American religious leader more prominent than the positive-thinking pastor was Billy Graham. Graham became synonymous with resurgent evangelicalism in the 1950s. He preached the time-tested messages of sin and redemption, but blended them with a charismatic style and marketing technique that became the template for those who followed. The turning point came with 1949's Los Angeles revival. The two-month crusade attracted 200,000 to his preaching tent, including popular Hollywood stars like Jimmy Stewart and Spencer Tracy. Later that year, his rally at the Boston Garden attracted 16,000. From Boston he went to South Carolina and then to Washington, DC, drawing previously unimaginable crowds. In 1954 he crossed the Atlantic and set England alight with religious fire. But it was his 1957 revival in New York that cemented his status as America's most influential religious leader. A pilgrim in what many considered an unholy land, Graham captured the attention of New Yorkers, 100,000 of whom filled Yankee Stadium on the final night. The New York crusade was notable not only for the two million people who heard Graham speak, but also for Graham's invitation of Martin Luther King, Jr. to the pulpit. Like Peale, the evangelical prodigy made ample use of popular media to spread his message. Graham's *Hour of Decision* played on radios weekly, his newspaper columns appeared in print nationwide, and in 1956 he cofounded the influential magazine *Christianity Today*.[13]

Unlike previous religious renewals, America's spiritual turn in the 1950s can be measured statistically. In 1951, American religious groups claimed a total of 88 million members. By 1961, these same denominations and faiths claimed more than 116 million, an impressive increase of 31 percent, especially since the U.S. population grew only 19 percent during the decade. The percentage of Americans who belonged to a church or synagogue rose steadily, setting records throughout the decade, from 57 percent in 1952 to 60.3 percent in 1955. While Protestants grew a healthy 23 percent, Catholics could claim an explosive 46 percent increase.[14] Because such figures depended on the calculations and, in many cases, estimations of religious leaders, they are inexact. But one cannot deny that something statistically extraordinary occurred during the early Cold War.

Church attendance swelled as well. Beginning in the mid 1930s, Gallup pollsters routinely measured rates of attendance by asking Americans if they had attended religious services the previous week. Attendance sank slowly through the 1930s, reaching a nadir of 35 percent during World War II. By 1957, reported attendance had climbed steadily to approximately 50 percent.[15] Recent studies conducted by sociologists suggest that Americans tend to exaggerate rates of attendance in opinion polls, but whether or not church attendance actually increased substantially during the 1950s, the polls reflected the normative influence that religious participation exerted.[16] Another measure of this effect can be detected in the percentage of people professing belief in a higher power. Undoubtedly, an overwhelming majority of Americans have always believed in God. Ninety-four percent of respondents admitted as much in a 1947 survey. By early 1953, more than 99 percent professed a similar belief. It seems doubtful that nonbelievers disappeared altogether. Rather, during the height of Cold War sacralization, as religious belief became tantamount to patriotism, atheists and agnostics most likely chose to hide their doubts.[17] Indeed, in 1954, when researchers returned to Plainville, a pseudonym given to an anonymous Missouri farming community, they noticed that the nonbelievers had gone underground. During the first round of research from 1939 to 1941, social scientists detected a sizable group of agnostics, atheists, and irreligious inhabitants. In their follow-up thirteen years later, the researchers concluded that the number of nonbelievers in Plainville had probably remained constant, but that "many agnostics . . . do not declare their belief, and at the same time advocate support of local churches, arguing that they stand for moral right as opposed to wrong."[18]

The American public also perceived the shifting relationship between religion and society. During the period of societal secularization in the 1930s, only 29 percent of Americans believed that the influence of religion was increasing in their communities, and only 18 percent reported attending religious services more often than their parents. By the end of Eisenhower's first term, on the other hand, nearly 70 percent of Americans believed that the influence of religion on society was increasing. More impressively, four in five thought that religion could answer all or most of the problems facing their nation.[19] America was not only experiencing a renewal in religious interest but also a restoration of public faith in religious solutions. The scientific and other manmade achievements in which Americans had placed great trust before Hiroshima no longer had a monopoly on remedies and explanations in the postwar period.

Americans tended to downplay the significance of the Communist faith as a factor in the 1950s religious renewal. Nonetheless, polling revealed the degree to which the nation had recognized the antireligious component of the Marxist creed. Even in 1947, before the most widespread attempts at Cold War sacralization commenced, 70 percent of Americans believed Communists would destroy Christianity if given the chance. Two years later, only one in ten believed that a person could be both a Communist and a Christian.[20] When asked to explain the growing influence of religion in society, Americans offered up a plethora of answers. A plurality simply did not know how to explain it. Some credited publicity and advertising; more believed it was due to fear; and still others pointed to religious training U.S. troops had received—all components of the spiritual-industrial complex. Only 2 percent attributed the renewal to Eisenhower, and just 1 percent believed it had something to do with combating Communism. Still, when the president called upon Americans to go to church and pray the Sunday before the Geneva Summit, 11 percent of those who packed the pews on July 17, 1955, credited Eisenhower's plea as the cause of their attendance.[21]

These stories and statistics suggest that the spiritual-industrial complex was a success. Indeed, the revival of religious interest paralleled its efforts as faith became a significant topic of national conversation and the secularization of yesteryear a fading memory. But laying the surge at the complex's feet is far too simplistic. Other factors, such as prosperity, the baby boom, anxiety, the rise of dynamic new religious leaders, and new means by which these leaders could spread their messages, all contributed to an ecclesiastical "perfect storm." While it was impossible to prove that the spiritual-industrial complex drove America's renewal of religious interest in the early Cold War, this did not stop its contributors from taking credit. It did not stop the renewal's critics from leveling their most serious charges against the politicians and policies central to its efforts. Nor did it not stop everyday Americans from acknowledging that such efforts made a positive difference. The complex and the religious renewal were tied to one another. They grew together. And as one languished, so too did the other.

Obscured by the ebullience of spirituality and prayer in the 1950s were signs that America's religious renewal was slackening. By 1962 only 45 percent believed that religion was still expanding in influence. This percentage continued to fall, reaching a low of 33 percent in 1965.[22] Polling questions like these were value-neutral. They did not ask Americans whether or not they approved of religion's declining influence on society. Were that the case, most Americans would have deplored the return of secularization.[23] But the renewal began leveling off in other statistical measures as well. Between 1960 and 1962, for instance, the percentage of Americans who were members of religious groups fell slightly, as did the number of ordained clergy.[24]

A less quantitative sign of the receding crest of religiosity came from the West Coast. Once an upholder, if only for a passing moment, of sacralization through celluloid, Hollywood portended a greater societal shift with the 1960 release of *Elmer Gantry*, which adapted Sinclair Lewis's caustic portrayal of religious hypocrisy to the silver screen. Starring Burt Lancaster, who won an Academy Award for his portrayal of the title character, it was controversial enough for its producers to keep the script a secret until production began. The film's screenwriter, Richard Brooks, had tried to sell his script in Hollywood since 1954, but his timing was poor. "Now you listen to me," he recalled one producer telling him, "I'm a regular churchgoer, see? An' if you think I'm gonna

let 'Elmer Gantry' be made at this studio, you're outta your ever-lovin' mind."
Even as they spoke, Cecil B. DeMille was gearing up for *The Ten Commandments*. But by *Elmer Gantry*'s release, DeMille was dead, a passing that coincided
with Hollywood's experiment in piety.[25] That year at the Academy Awards,
Lancaster's competition for best actor included Spencer Tracy, nominated for
his portrayal of Clarence Darrow in *Inherit the Wind*, a fictionalized account of
the 1925 Scopes trial that drew on the themes of McCarthyism and ignorance.
The fact that in the same year the film industry dusted off two relicts from a time
of marked secularization was a coincidence, not a conscious decision. What
remains significant about their critically acclaimed runs in theaters across
America was the simple fact that neither would have had a chance of getting the
green light five or ten years earlier.

The changing role of religion in American society may have seemed like a
magical turn of events, shaped by crisis and anxiety. Indeed, sacralization was the
product of crisis. But it sprang from a particular kind of crisis—one in which
religion could serve as part of the effective solution. The usefulness of religion in
the Cold War was not self-evident to most Americans; they needed direction. So
too did sacralization require more than the words of religious leaders. Had effort
been the only requisite, they would have arrested the tide of secularization
decades earlier. Sacralization required consensus. And as that consensus began
to disintegrate, so too would its spiritual fruits.

America's spiritual-industrial complex provides its chroniclers with no obvious
end date. Some of its ventures, like the CPL, had faded by the mid 1950s. Others,
like the practice of using religious institutions to reinforce foreign-policy goals,
survived throughout the Cold War. Because no American leader announced an
official end to the holy war against Communism, it is necessary to search for a
cluster of symbolic actions—some obvious and others more subtle—that heralded a growing disinclination to construe the Cold War in religious terms.

Even at the height of the spiritual-industrial complex and the corresponding
period of religiosity in the 1950s, dissenters and doubters voiced their concerns.
The dissenters, consisting primarily of sardonic social commentators, lacked the
bravado of modern-day secularists. Most of them, in fact, were religious themselves. They focused their criticism not on religion itself but rather on what they
perceived to be its cynical employment. None of the other dissenters could
match in attention or criticism the furor caused by Senator Matthew Neely on
March 28, 1955. Speaking before United Autoworkers Convention in Cleveland, the eighty-year-old West Virginia Democrat launched a scornful assault on
Eisenhower's abilities and intentions. He likened him to Alice in Wonderland,
questioned his qualifications, and insulted his golf game. These affronts would
have been dismissed as the bitter ramblings of a cranky old man had he not also

questioned Eisenhower's use of religion. "Eisenhower never joined a church until after he became President," Neely observed. "Next Monday, I don't want to have to see in the papers a picture of the President and a story that he attended this or that church." And then the kicker: "Any man who tries to parade his religion that way before the public is ungodly."[26]

Neely had attacked the high priest of the spiritual-industrial complex, and the reaction was swift and unforgiving. Only weeks earlier, the Republican National Committee had approved a resolution declaring that the president "is not only the political leader but the spiritual leader of our times." Eisenhower's pastor, Edward L. R. Elson, leaped to the president's defense, calling his faith "transparently sincere." Senator Barry Goldwater of Arizona accused Neely of attacking not only a justifiably pious Eisenhower but also "the traditional and constitutional guarantee of religious freedom." The president's press secretary responded with the adage "What Peter says about Paul tells more about Peter than it does Paul." Republican congressmen called it "the foulest blow struck in politics," and Neely's Democratic colleagues refused to lend him their support. The *Chicago Tribune*'s editorial board called it "The Season's Low." The *Washington Post and Times-Herald* attacked Neely, declaring, "A man's faith has no place in the political arena."[27] The maxim might have applied equally to Eisenhower, but most interpreted the senator's comments as an attack on any president who demonstrated personal faith rather than as a rebuke of those who displayed their religion for political reasons.

Neely was not alone in his critique. William Lee Miller, a professor of religion and a writer and editor for *The Reporter* magazine, had been criticizing Eisenhower's moral and religious crusade from the outset—as a sanctimonious slurry he called "piety along the Potomac." Developing a theme that other critics would sharpen, Miller wrote that "President Eisenhower, like many Americans, is a very fervent believer in a very vague religion." He commented on the extraordinary arc of government sacralization that began with a National Day of Prayer in 1952 and culminated in the adoption of the National Motto "In God We Trust" in 1956. Something about these gestures disturbed Miller. "Since this is official religion in a land without an official religion it cannot be very deep," he wrote in 1954.[28]

Even more troubling for Miller was the exaltation of acts over beliefs. American leaders celebrated prayer without telling Americans what to pray for, they lauded church attendance without telling Americans which church to attend, and they invoked a generic God. This was perfectly logical from the perspective of Cold Warriors, since any religion positing a higher power could defeat Communism just as sure as it could help make American spiritual strength commensurate with material power. But by externalizing faith, the spiritual-industrial complex had made outward appearances of religiosity more important than inner, private belief. Miller detected this trend as early as Eisenhower's inauguration. "We worship our own worshipping," he lamented.[29]

Other dissenters focused their attention on the new phenomenon of suburban godliness. In addition to being a decade of religious renewal, the 1950s were also the age of suburbanization, and the confluence of piety and prefabricated homes proved too tempting a target for some.[30] Much of this critique grew out of the work of David Riesman, whose "lonely crowd" hypothesis mourned the breakdown of inner-directedness. Suburbia, with its perceived premium on conformity, looked like the place America's moral gyroscopes stopped spinning. *New York Times* religious news reporter Stanley Rowland, Jr., groused about how faith had become fashionable during the Eisenhower years in the nation's suburbs. "On weekdays one shops for food, on Saturday's one shops for recreations, and on Sundays one shops for the Holy Ghost," he wrote. Rowland believed that religion served its adherents best when it existed in tension with society. But the suburban church had become "a tame captive of its community."[31]

This notion of religious captivity in America's suburbs was first raised by Episcopalian reverend Gibson Winter. In a sharp *Christian Century* editorial that was republished in *Time*, Winter warned that the suburban cult of success had tainted the church as well. Pastors and churchgoers across the nation were obsessed with growth and financial statistics rather than the real work of salvation. The journalist and social commentator William H. Whyte added to these suspicions with the publication of his bestselling book *The Organization Man* in 1957. In his case study of Park Forest, a planned suburban community south of Chicago, Whyte noted several manifestations of the "very vague religion" Miller had been cataloguing since Eisenhower's inaugural. When surveyed on the most significant factors in choosing a church, Park Forest residents considered location more important than denomination.[32]

More significant than the dissenters were the doubters—religious scholars and leaders who did not necessarily object to the religious renewal but who regarded it a failure. They looked at the amassed statistical indicators of revival but took little joy or comfort in them. A Methodist pastor in Queens frowned upon the "revival by slogan and easy formula." A Presbyterian church official bemoaned the fact that "most people seem to want God as you want a hot water bottle in the night—to get you over a temporary discomfort." Seventh-day Adventists called it "juke box religion."[33] Others began wondering if the construction of the Cold War as a spiritual struggle—the "worship God so we can lick communism" effect, as Union Theological Seminary professor Robert McAfee described it—had produced side effects. A Unitarian minister from San Francisco worried if making "belief in God a test of proper hatred of communism" had in the end reduced notions of the Almighty "to the level of the fierce tribal deity of the early Old Testament."[34]

Such observations seemed like trifles compared to Will Herberg's *Protestant—Catholic—Jew*. Born in a Russian village to Jewish, though proudly atheistic, parents in 1901, Herberg followed the path of his parents' faith, or lack thereof, after the family settled in the United States. By his teenage years he was a dedicated Communist, and he contributed as a young man to the paper *Workers Age*. But his faith, like that of others who flirted with Communism, did not survive the 1930s. Herberg did not mark his apostasy by kneeling before Fulton Sheen at the altar or by ratting out his fellow travelers. He found hope and purpose in the works of Niebuhr, so much so, in fact, that upon their first meeting Herberg considered converting to Christianity. At Niebuhr's urging, he instead endeavored to explore the tenets of his own traditional faith. In Judaism he found a workable combination of activism and realism.[35]

Herberg's approach and conclusions in *Protestant—Catholic—Jew* were shaded by both the religious renewal then underway and the sociological renaissance in postwar America. Absent Eisenhower or Riesman, the work would have made considerably less sense. Herberg believed that the great mass of immigrants who began arriving in 1870 created not only an infinitely more diverse society but also a "new form of self-identification and social location" known as the ethnic group.[36] Ethnicity bred cohesion, but second-generation immigrants realized that it restrained their ascents to desired levels of respectability, assimilation, and advancement. Casting off their hyphens, they and their children simply became Americans. The third generation of immigrants, though, having achieved a level of incorporation into American society their grandparents could only have dreamed of, suffered from a new dilemma—the problem of "belonging" and "self-identification." Herberg argued that the third generation considered the resurrection of ethnicity unthinkable, but religion provided a Rosetta Stone for decoding their own identities and a category of belonging craved by America's expanding ranks of the "other-directed." Religious consciousness replaced ethnic consciousness. Herberg called this phenomenon the "triple melting pot."

Three pots of boiling religiosity might have made a perfect recipe for spiritual indigestion if not for the presence of a more powerful force—the American way of life. This Herberg described as a "common religion" that "constitutes a faith common to Americans and genuinely operative in their lives." He counted everything from secularized Puritanism to Coca-Cola to religious tolerance as tenets of America's religion.[37] The American way of life, a common religion then headed by Eisenhower, had become "the cult of culture and society." The nation had converted its "immense and undeniable moral superiority over Communist tyranny into pretensions to unqualified wisdom and virtue."[38] Americans knew less about their three great traditions of religious faith at a time when record numbers reported subscribing to them. As William Lee Miller had noticed, Americans placed their faith in faith, and for Herberg this was idolatrous.

The same year that Herberg released his best-seller, Reinhold Niebuhr began raising his own doubts. Five years earlier he had looked skeptically at the dawn of America's "revival," wondering if it would become a true awakening.[39] By 1955 he had answered his own question. He believed he was witnessing a revival of "interest in religion," as opposed to a revival of religious faith. Echoing Herberg's observations, Niebuhr identified a troubling aspect of 1950s spiritual renewal that succeeded in making both religious leaders and secularists equally apprehensive: the conflation of religion with Americanism. "We Americans have somehow combined good plumbing with religious faith in the 'American way of life,'" he observed. Predictably, Niebuhr objected to this development not only because it watered down religion but also because it constructed a view of human history that only emphasized good, thereby disavowing any doctrine of misery and evil. "Thus," he explained, "the official religion perpetuates the idea that democracy is possible only upon the basis of illusions about human nature." There was danger in this self-congratulatory form of state-sponsored faith. At least Billy Graham, Niebuhr thought, had built notions of sin and evil into his public theology.[40]

In the summer of 1955, *Commonweal*, the liberal Catholic weekly then under the influence of John Cogley, went to war against the *St. Louis Register*, another Catholic paper, over the appropriateness of the spiritual-industrial complex. *Commonweal* reminded its readers that a "good American may be a pagan, an agnostic, or an atheist," and a "saint may be an anarchist." In a series of counter editorials, the *Register* attacked *Commonweal* for believing that there could be no positive relationship between civil activity and religion. In a surprising rebuke that countered much of the Catholic Church's official stance on Eisenhower's use of religion, *Commonweal* let fly its criticisms. "Far too much loose talk about 'God and America' is heard these days," the editorial announced. "From the speeches of some politicians one gathers the impressions that religion . . . should be cultivated as a potent instrument in the cold war and that the Almighty has enlisted in the army of the 'free world' for the duration." In tying religion to contingent things—in making Americanism a "fifth mark of the Church"—the editors worried that combining faith with patriotism would destroy both.[41]

Christianity and Crisis, a liberal Protestant weekly magazine founded by Niebuhr, joined with *Commonweal* in denouncing what it deemed the "perpetual official moral diatribe against Communist countries," but for a different reason. Evincing the realist approach to foreign policy of its founder, the journal began its April 28, 1958, issue with a plea for a new approach to the Cold War. Rather than treating Communism as a social and spiritual disease, its chairman John C. Bennett called for American leaders to accept that "communism is here to stay." Bennett admitted that the anxiety from which the spiritual-industrial complex drew its justification had proven unfounded, and he celebrated the fact that "Communist ideology, with all the propaganda, education, terror and brainwashing that have gone with it, has not distorted the minds of people nearly as much as many of us once feared."[42]

Having had time to grasp the dissents and doubts of religious leaders, the young theologian Martin E. Marty afforded the pious 1950s a more definitive verdict in 1958. Though concerned primarily with the fate of Protestantism, his book *The New Shape of American Religion* united the critiques of Miller, Niebuhr, and Herberg into a joint indictment of what he called a "national religion." Whereas Herberg believed this national faith served as the fire heating his triple melting pots, Marty saw it as a separate faith—a fourth melting pot. This national religion endangered America's traditional faiths. Throughout most of the American history, its threat had been slight, thanks in part to the laissez-faire attitude of government toward religion. What made the 1950s different was the "institutional sanction" afforded to religious belief. Marty believed that the state had nationalized religion while still operating within the boundaries of constitutional constraints. The result was "religion-in-general," which rooted itself in no systematic theology. Rather, religion-in-general elevated "an attitude toward religion to religious ultimacy." "Democracy becomes the ultimate," Marty grumbled, "religion the handmaiden." As religion-in-general grew, it wore down the once distinct edges of traditional faiths, sapping the theological vitality and tradition of "religious voluntaryism that was America's outstanding institutional contribution to religious history."[43]

Marty went in search of the god of religion-in-general and found him "cuddled up right next to us." He discerned three basic traits of this god, and they were hardly the stuff of Old Testament forewarning. First, America's new god was "understandable and manageable." Second, he was "comforting," a pal in the sky Americans could turn to in times of despair. Lastly, he was a regular Joe, an "American jolly good fellow."[44] These attributes could have also been applied with equal validity to Eisenhower, the comforting father figure watching over the nation in its holy war against Communism. Nor was this image of God altogether different from the one the president routinely invoked.

In different words and phrases, the dissenters and doubters shared one inescapable conclusion: America's postwar "revival" was no revival at all. Whether they called it the worship of worshipping, the growth of faith in faith, or the exaltation of mere attitudes to ultimacy, they pointed to the same sad fact. The spiritual-industrial complex, that joint effort of government, business, educators, the media, and others, had privileged visible acts over internal beliefs. It had created a broad umbrella of religious acceptance under which Americans could shelter themselves without troubling themselves, and this sucked valuable oxygen from the fires of what might have been a true national awakening.

Whereas the military-industrial complex threatened liberty, the spiritual-industrial complex imperiled the vitality of American religiosity.

America's Cold War policy of revival demonstrated the consequences of interference in the nation's religious economy. Put simply, religion is most robust when it exists in tension with society and exacts a high cost of participation. When it comes to attracting and maintaining religious followers, one might think the blander and more accessible forms of religious expression enjoy a certain advantage, but sociologists of religion completed detailed explorations of sect growth and denominational decline to disprove this. In his groundbreaking and controversial 1972 work *Why Conservative Churches Are Growing*, Dean M. Kelley called the widely held belief that blander is better "a recipe for the failure of the religious enterprise." The more demanding religious groups—in this case those of the proliferating evangelical movement—were flourishing at the expense of the mainline denominations.[45]

The lessons learned from denominational growth and decline can also be applied to the spiritual-industrial complex. In its quest for the lowest common spiritual denominator—a religious system of belief guaranteed not to upset anyone but the most ardent atheists and secularists—the spiritual-industrial complex opened itself to criticisms that it had spawned only a vague and rather bland religiosity. Historians and sociologists may be tempted to use the term "civil religion," the use of the sacred to legitimize the secular, to describe this facet of the spiritual-industrial complex. But early Cold War leaders did the opposite. Rather than seeing religion as a means simply to buttress the state, they used the secular to legitimize the sacred, and in doing so they may have released much of what tension still remained between society and many religious institutions.[46]

The religious rejuvenation of the 1960s and 1970s, an age that saw the reemergence of evangelicalism as a social, political, and cultural force, arrived only after America's spiritual-industrial complex sputtered out. That breakdown may have been one of the greatest gifts ever given to religion by industry and the state. It was too late for some denominations of the old Protestant order, whose memberships would erode significantly in the following decades. But new sects would employ the fear of secularism as a rallying cry, pushing for further deregulation of the religious marketplace.

While critics and doubters questioned the efficacy of the spiritual-industrial complex and pointed to its unintended side effects, the nation's leaders began questioning one of its basic assumptions: that closing the gap in spiritual enthusiasm and power was crucial to Cold War victory. Portents of a new and decidedly more secular conception of the Cold War had started appearing by the mid 1950s. In June 1955, army intelligence released the ill-fated pamphlet "How to Spot a Communist," designed to give troops the tools of detection necessary to purge their ranks of Marxist traitors. Still in the heyday of its spiritually-centered character-guidance program, the army devoted one-third of the booklet to religion. "While it is generally believed that Communists are atheists as a result of their political indoctrination," it declared, "it appears likely that many find in Marxist philosophy a substitute for religion in which they had previously lost faith."[47] Arguments like these were common in years past, but influential newspapers like the *New York Times* began to lampoon the enterprise. "One doesn't know whether to laugh or cry at the contents of the pamphlet," wrote the paper's editorial board. The ACLU worried that it would encourage Americans to spy on each other, and rather than making a stand, the army confiscated and quickly destroyed most copies of the pamphlet.[48]

Several months later, America's psychological-warfare operations received a thorough reevaluation in a committee formed by Nelson A. Rockefeller, the newly appointed head of the OCB. Rockefeller assembled a panel of experts including Harvard professor Henry A. Kissinger to appraise U.S. propaganda strategy. Their cumulative report, "Psychological Aspects of United States Strategy," emphasized the need to promote a counter ideology to Communism, but the "religious factor" once of interest to the OCB had disappeared entirely. The new strategy rested on painting Communism as a radical, dogmatic, and irrational ideology while simultaneously depicting a far more subtle American political and economic system. Gone were fears that Americans were not zealous enough for a conflict with the fanatical Soviets. Now Communist fervor, once considered a Soviet strength, was deemed a decided advantage for the Free World.[49]

Next was the Killian Report, a top-secret document presented to the National Security Council in late 1955 and leaked in part to the media, which recommended that the United States devote new resources to the development of nuclear missiles. The Gaither Report, released in 1957, further weakened notions of American material superiority. In it, security experts concluded that Soviet GDP was growing at a significantly faster rate than America's, and that Soviet military technology and capabilities had achieved parity with the U.S.[50] In January 1958 the Rockefeller Fund rushed release of a report on Cold War military strength. Eighteen months in the making, it called for significant increases in military spending, a buildup of nuclear missiles, and reorganization of the U.S. military command structure.[51] Americans may have won the spiritual war of words, but they worried that the Soviets were winning the war of technology and military strength.

In his second term, Eisenhower demonstrated an ability to break free of the impulse to qualify discussions of material matters with a countervailing mention of spiritual values. Four years after Dulles persuaded him to emphasize spiritual ideals in his first inaugural address, the president delivered an oration from the Capitol's steps that was markedly different in tone. Eisenhower still declared

Communism an "evil" in the second inaugural. But he chose this occasion to underscore the "material wants common to all mankind." He believed that the world was beginning a search for a new freedom—"freedom from grinding poverty."[52] Still, he did not abandon his old standby altogether. His farewell address returned to the theme that informed his electoral campaign eight years earlier: that material growth came at a spiritual price. "We cannot mortgage the material assets of our grandchildren without risking also the loss of their political and spiritual heritage," he warned, calling upon all nations united "under God" to join the crusade for justice and freedom. Fittingly, Eisenhower ended his presidency the same way be began it—with a prayer.[53]

Eisenhower was able to downplay American material strength early in his presidency because the nation possessed so much of it. This changed when a Soviet rocket blasted the 183-pound satellite Sputnik 1 into orbit in 1957, undermining American assumptions of technological and material superiority. "The United States has hitherto bragged that it was the most powerful country on Earth," gloated a Chinese newspaper editorial, "but now it is lagging behind the Soviet Union to a growing extent."[54] Press accounts covered in rapt prose every beamed signal, every speculative guess at Sputnik's size or purpose, and every Soviet claim of scientific discovery gleaned from their tiny satellite. In an even more fitting gesture, the Soviets unveiled a postage stamp depicting Sputnik circling the globe.[55] It was an appropriate counter to America's "In God We Trust" stamp, signaling an achievement greater than the declarations of religiosity then emanating from Washington.

Nixon's mission to Moscow in July 1959 inadvertently offered another illustration of this unraveling consensus. The vice president, who had built his political career on a policy of zero tolerance toward Communism, tried his best on the plane ride to learn a few words of Russian—an olive-branch gesture James Reston called "just good enough to be understood and bad enough to be both amusing and disarming."[56] Nixon arrived to officially open the American National Exhibition in Moscow, a USIA propagandistic extravaganza designed to win the Cold War ideologically. The Soviets had opened a similar exhibition in New York, and Americans were eager to return the favor. It presented a priceless opportunity to "sell" Americanism to the Russian people, and U.S. technicians worked feverishly on completing the project in time for Nixon's arrival.[57]

The only irony more striking than Nixon laughing it up with Khrushchev in Moscow was the location of their most famous exchange. Surrounded by a mob of photographers, translators, body guards, and interested bystanders, the two cold warriors squared off not in some spartan war room but rather within a prefabricated American model kitchen built by a Florida property developer.[58] It was an absurd setting—tucked into the large indoor exhibition hall at Sokolniki Park—but even more bizarre was the conversation that followed.

"I want to show you this kitchen," Nixon told the premier. "It is like those of our houses in California." He called attention to a built-in, panel-controlled washing machine.

"We have such things," Khrushchev retorted.

Nixon went on to highlight the wonders of material abundance. He explained that Americans produced thousands of similar machines, ready-made for instal-lation in new homes across the nation to "make life easier for our housewives." He bragged that average American steelworkers could afford the same house in which the two leaders stood.

"Don't you have a machine that puts food into the mouth and pushes it down?" Khrushchev asked sarcastically. "Many things you've shown us are inter-esting but they are not needed in life. They have no useful purpose. They are merely gadgets." The banter continued for some time, drifting from politics back to washing machines and finally to the question of foreign military bases.[59]

Of course it would be too facile to assert that the Kitchen Debate represented some sort of instantaneous switch from a spiritual strategy to a material one. After all, the Sears Roebuck catalog had always proved itself a valuable Cold War weapon alongside the Bible. Still, the U.S. ambassador to the Soviet Union and Eisenhower's brother Milton, both of whom watched the spectacle in person,

Gadgets, not Bibles, were most prominent in the USIA's American National Exhibition in Moscow, site of the famous "Kitchen Debate" between Vice President Richard Nixon and Soviet premier Nikita Khrushchev. (Courtesy of *U.S. News and World Report* Photograph Collection, Library of Congress.)

were less than thrilled. Indeed, it seemed at the time to be an utter disaster from most diplomatic vantage points.[60] Rather than extolling the merits of democracy or faith, Nixon framed the debate in material terms—the precise understanding of American power Eisenhower and Dulles strove to deemphasize beginning with their meeting at the Hotel Commodore back in 1953. Technological innovation, household gadgets, industrial wealth—these were the things Eisenhower believed Americans had purchased at the expense of spiritual growth. If only the discussion could have occurred inside a model American church.

But Nixon was certainly on the same page as the exposition's coordinators. The event itself was an homage to materialism. Dozens of Russian workers could crowd into the Circlorama and experience the moving thrill of a San Francisco cable car on a 360-degree stereoscopic movie screen. Russian women in drab overalls could watch American models parade New York's latest styles in a fashion show while their brothers and husbands perused a collection of Detroit's newest automobiles. The Communist press tried to emphasize the dirty underbelly of capitalism, and worried party leaders organized a counter fair devoted to promoting the appeal of Soviet consumer goods. But the damage had been done. "Look," rejoiced one of the USIA's guides, "they are smashed."[61]

Perhaps when the torch passed "to a new generation of Americans," it signaled also the demise of those fears articulated by Bradley, Lanham, and Eisenhower—fears of understanding power in exclusively material terms. The first Catholic to win his party's nomination since Alfred E. Smith's landslide loss to Hoover in 1928, John F. Kennedy might have been the religious figurehead holy warriors were waiting for. He was not, and he evinced no desire to be one. If campaign rhetoric is any guide, Kennedy had reached a very different conclusion than Eisenhower eight years earlier. Whereas Eisenhower emphasized spiritual vigor, the young senator from Massachusetts had learned through the old general's errors that "neither smiles nor frowns, neither good intentions nor harsh words, are a substitute for strength."[62] By strength he meant not power in both spirit and body, but material strength in its coldest, most tangible expressions. He coined the term "missile gap," which specifically addressed American nuclear disadvantage but also symbolized the wider decline of U.S. power relative to the Soviet Union.

Material strength became the centerpiece of Kennedy's general-election campaign. There would be few firm delineations of the Communist faith—few cautionary tales of materialism gone sour—but rather a list of observed Soviet accomplishments and American failures. "Communist power has been, and is now, growing faster than is our own," he informed the attendees of the VFW's national convention, "and by Communist power I mean military power, economic power, scientific and educational power, and political power." He lamented the fact that the first satellite was called Sputnik rather than Vanguard or Explorer, that the first object to the reach moon was called Lunik, and that some of the first living creatures to orbit Earth were called Strelka and Belka rather than Rover or Fido.[63] When Kennedy discussed his "Pathways to Peace," he emphasized harmony through strength.

In his list of the five things that people around the world most respected, Kennedy afforded no place for moral stewardship. To him, the world admired strength, achievement, sincerity, peace, and prestige, in that order.[64] For Kennedy, poverty and hunger were Communism's greatest allies abroad. Rather than casting itself as the world's moral and spiritual guardian, as it had under Eisenhower and Dulles, America could fight Communism in the developing world by feeding, clothing, and educating the vulnerable masses.[65] "If Mr. Khrushchev had our food resources, he would be using them to spread the doctrine of communism," Kennedy stated. "I want to use them to spread the doctrine of freedom."[66] Like Truman and Eisenhower before him, Kennedy understood the Cold War policies abroad were intimately linked to policies at home. He agreed that Americans needed to set a powerful example, but in a different way. Eradicating domestic poverty, illiteracy, and disease would speak far louder than professions of faith.[67]

Nixon, notwithstanding debates in model kitchens, took a position against Communism contiguous with Eisenhower's. In August 1960 he released "The Meaning of Communism," a detailed position paper outlining the threats and challenges presented by the creed. The divergence from Kennedy's position was barefaced. Nixon argued that the struggle would not "be decided in the military, economic, or scientific areas," since "the test is one not so much of arms but of faith."[68] Speaking to the VFW national convention two days before Kennedy, the vice president made an argument similar to Eisenhower. "Too often we put our reliance solely on our military strength, our diplomatic policy, the productivity of our factories," he said, and then went on to plug spiritual and moral values.[69] To be sure, Nixon at times emphasized material strength exclusively, and Kennedy did not ignore religious conceptions of Communism entirely, but they offered different models of the Cold War.[70] The most fundamental difference was this: Nixon saw Communism as a font of evil, while Kennedy believed Communism fed off existing evil. The distinction was important. If one believed that Communism was evil itself, then the battle against it would be ideological, summoning those moral and religious forces for good in defense of freedom's citadel. But if one believed the enemy's creed exploited existing evils like hunger, poverty, and ignorance, then the fight would be material.[71]

This is not to say that Kennedy avoided talk of morality and religion. Those tropes were too ingrained in American political culture to ignore. His inaugural address acknowledged that "the rights of man come not from the generosity of the state but from the hand of God." He equated America's mission in the Cold

War with "God's work."[72] On Sundays he attended Mass in local parishes from Middleburg, Virginia, to Hyannis Port and Palm Beach. He wanted Americans to know that he prayed regularly, fasted during Lent, and believed that American democracy stood in part upon religious traditions. In reality, the depths of his religiosity may have been quite different. Ted Sorensen, Kennedy's indispensable advisor, recalled that the president rarely if ever spoke about his religious beliefs or prayed publicly.[73] In this sense, Kennedy bore a striking resemblance to Franklin Roosevelt, who often employed religious imagery in public speeches while keeping his personal faith shrouded from even his closest companions.[74]

The difference between Eisenhower and Kennedy's beliefs turned on the state's role in religious matters. Eisenhower was America's most powerful proponent of sacralization since Lincoln. He strove to harness government, business, educational, and media power to reendow religion with new meaning in a holy war. Kennedy abandoned this program for politically sound reasons. The Cold War, now fifteen years old, had not produced the sweeping domestic conversions to the Communist faith that had concerned J. Edgar Hoover, Tom C. Clark, or Claire Boothe Luce. The uncertainty and speculation once at the forefront of American consciousness had diminished. There were fits of anxiety still to come, but the kind of Communist infiltration depicted metaphorically in cinematic romps like *Invasion of the Body Snatchers* seemed an ever fainter possibility. Further, Kennedy had built his campaign around the promise of material and technological superiority. The spiritual toll of material strength would be an unavoidable risk in the shadow of Sputnik. Perhaps most critically, Kennedy was politically sensitized to the so-called religious issue. In his watershed address before the Greater Houston Ministerial Association in September 1960, he argued that there were "real issues which should decide this campaign. And they are not religious issues." He decried any president who would accept instructions on public policy from religious organizations and promised to make decisions based on his personal conscience rather than his religious convictions, in part to stave off public fears that he would take cues from the pope.[75]

Kennedy had another reason for distancing himself from the spiritual-industrial complex: the growing conclusion among liberal politicians and journalists that virulent anti-Communism was becoming a weapon of the American right. Worries about the fusion of anti-Communism, politics, and religion in the military intensified over the next several years and culminated in the summer of 1961 after Senator J. W. Fulbright, chairman of the Senate Foreign Relations Committee, wrote a widely publicized letter to President Kennedy and Secretary of Defense Robert McNamara. The twenty-two-page missive, which became known as the Fulbright Memorandum, charged that military education programs carried out under the aegis of anti-Communism were becoming platforms for "Radical Right-Wing" political propaganda. When the memo was leaked, conservative political leaders howled in protest, framing the issue in terms of both security and liberty. The Department of Defense immediately issued a directive that restrained officers from championing conservative policies during public duties and appearances.[76] The spiritual-industrial complex was the product of remarkable though tenuous consensus among the political powerbrokers of American society. When that widely held agreement grew strained under the weight of political debates, so too did the policy of religious revival.

The courts dealt the spiritual-industrial complex its coup de grâce. Whether by coincidence or design, the Kennedy years witnessed the swiftest and most surprising period of judicial secularism in American history. The Supreme Court, in its most contentious and publicized decisions since *Brown v. Board of Education* in 1954, ensured that many of society's institutions could no longer participate in the nation's holy war. Critics considered the rulings an assault upon religion, but, more accurately, they addressed the publicly sponsored program of sacralization in place since the late 1940s.

In 1951 the New York Board of Regents had approved a nondenominational prayer for use in the state's public schools. The implementation of the prayer trickled down to school districts throughout the state with little fanfare. This changed when Steven Engel visited his son's elementary school classroom in the fall of 1958. Joined by four other plaintiffs, Engel, with legal help from the New York Civil Liberties Union, sued the school board in January 1959. The parents claimed that teacher-led recitals of a prayer violated the establishment clause of the First Amendment and made their ten nonbelieving children social and spiritual pariahs. Though state courts ruled in favor of the school district, the Supreme Court agreed to hear *Engel v. Vitale* in April 1962.[77]

By the spring of 1962, a mere decade after Eisenhower started his religious crusade, the pursuit of moral and spiritual values lauded by educators and politicians was under attack. From Chelsea, Massachusetts, to White Plains, New York, and Camden, New Jersey, the battle over religion and public schools flared. Religious groups in Washington, DC, and its suburbs had filed lawsuits against recitation of Bible verses in classrooms. The Florida Supreme Court put forth its own compromise between secularists and proponents of sacralization, ruling that public schools could not officially celebrate Christmas or Easter but could continue to read from the Bible. The secular agenda divided America's major religious groups—Catholics generally in opposition, Jews generally in favor, and Protestants, in the words of one leader, "split right down the middle."[78]

The Supreme Court left little room for ambiguity when it ruled on *Engel v. Vitale*. In a six-to-one decision (Justices Frankfurter and White abstained) the court deemed recital of the Regents' Prayer unconstitutional. In his majority opinion, Hugo Black wrote that the Founders believed religion was "too personal,

too sacred, too holy, to permit its 'unhallowed perversion' by a civil magistrate."
It was a stinging rebuke not only of the school board but of the government's
efforts since the start of the Cold War. The lone dissent came from Eisenhower
appointee Potter Stewart, who would reprise that role numerous times during
the Warren Court's string of sea-changing decisions. Stewart argued that the
court was venturing down a slippery slope, since one could not draw distinct
lines between school prayer and other religious expressions embedded within
American political culture. Interestingly, he leaned heavily on recent examples
like the Pledge of Allegiance, the printing of "In God We Trust" on currency and
its adoption as the national motto, and William O. Douglas's religious declaration in *Zorach v. Clauson*.[79] Thus a tautology used by the opponents of secularism
in future decades developed: America employed these expressions because it
was religious, and America was religious because it employed these expressions.
Sacralization had become a self-justifying endeavor.

Predictably, the decision created a furor. Cardinal Spellman was "shocked and
frightened." The National Association of Evangelicals called the decision "regret-
table," and Billy Graham urged his countrymen to reverse the ruling with a constitutional amendment. Concerned, just as Eisenhower had been, with America's
religious image abroad, Graham called upon the country to prove to the world
that "we are a nation under God." The American Legion agreed wholeheartedly,
and sociologist Will Herberg predicted that the public would not allow the
decision to stand.[80] The media were divided. Hearst newspapers called it a "mis-
interpretation of the Constitution," and the *Baltimore Sun* wondered if "we are to
have new coinage inscribed 'in blank we trust?'" But most major newspapers,
including the *New York Times* and *Washington Post*, supported the court.[81] The
ruling divided the religious press as well, including the reliably liberal periodicals
Commonweal and *Christian Century*. The former concluded, politely and hesi-
tantly, that the court went too far, while *Christian Century* declared the decision
a victory for freedom of religion.[82]

Congress, which had passed measures like the Pledge of Allegiance amendment and national motto unanimously, was generally embittered. Senators and
representatives called *Engel v. Vitale* a "gross distortion," "most unfortunate," and
a "power grab" by "drunken men." Southerners proclaimed its similarity with
Brown v. Board of Education eight years earlier, since in both cases, they reasoned,
a renegade court had overturned centuries of tradition. In defending school
prayer, many of the court's congressional detractors followed Justice Stewart's
logic by citing the policies of 1950s sacralization as historical precedents. They
mentioned the recently completed Capitol prayer room, new national motto,
National Day of Prayer, and "In God We Trust" currency. As if these arguments
were insufficient, some congressmen played what they considered a trump
card—Communism. Senator Herman E. Talmadge of Georgia scoffed at a new

generation of Americans who worried that the U.S. was forty years behind the Soviet Union in some measures of social justice. "Did it strike the Senator's mind, as it did mine, that we are about forty years behind Russia in prohibiting the youth of our country from praying?" he asked sarcastically. A congressman from Mississippi declared that the only people celebrating the ruling were a handful of American atheists and "world communism under the leadership of Premier Khrushchev." A colleague from Florida agreed that "if the Supreme Court were openly in league with the cause of communism, they could scarcely advance it more than they are doing now." Only a day after the decision, Congress began considering a constitutional amendment to undo the damage.[83]

Tying *Engel v. Vitale* to the pressures and demands of America's holy war might have been an unbeatable tactic a decade earlier, but such rhetoric fell flat in 1962. Of all opinions in America, the most important was President Kennedy's, and he was surprisingly equanimous. When asked about the case during a press conference, the president noted that people were divided in their reactions, but that if they truly supported the Constitution, they would support the Supreme Court decisions "even when we may not agree with them." Then, making a savvy political pivot, he argued that by removing prayer from public schools, the court had given parents an opportunity to reinforce their children's religious development at home.[84] It was an argument for the reprivatization of spirituality.

A year later the other judicial shoe dropped, this time prohibiting Bible reading in public schools. With *Abington School District v. Schempp*, the Supreme Court, in an eight-to-one decision, invalidated a Pennsylvania statute requiring public schools to begin each day by reading at least ten Bible verses. By extension, the ruling also settled *Murray v. Curlett*, a case consolidated with *Abington* that challenged a Baltimore school-district policy of reading a chapter of the Bible each morning in public schools.[85] But this time the public, political, and religious reaction was far tamer. To be sure, South Carolina senator Strom Thurmond still appeared on the CBS evening news to say that the decision "drives another nail in the coffin being prepared for a free and God-fearing America by the secularists and Socialists of the world," and a colleague called the ruling "ungodly." But as Congress began debating a constitutional amendment, a broad coalition of religious groups including Lutherans, Baptists, Methodists, Episcopalians, and Jews backed the court. As many as 160 congressmen supported the amendment, but that fell far short of constitutional requirements.[86] The order in which the court considered these major cases no doubt played a role in the more muted reaction to *Abington v. Schempp*. After ruling against a nonsectarian and bland prayer, a decision banning Bible reading seemed temperate by comparison.

The most symbolic and least considered aspect of *Abington v. Schempp* was the judge who penned the majority opinion. This was Tom C. Clark—the same man who, as Truman's attorney general, conceived the Freedom Train as a means of "reawakening faith in America," the same man who wondered if St. Paul's spiritual warning to the Corinthians might also have been a caveat to Americans, the same man who in 1947 dazzled the Des Moines Sunday school convention by declaring it impossible to separate the state from religious teachings. Sixteen years later, Clark argued that the state was duty bound to a position of neutrality on religion. "We have come to recognize through bitter experience," he wrote, "that it is not within the power of government to invade that citadel, whether its purpose or effect be to aid or oppose, to advance or retard."[87] He repudiated the central tenet of the spiritual-industrial complex—the idea that in a time of holy war the state should sanction religious belief and practice.

The Supreme Court decisions in 1962 and 1963 could not have single-handedly ushered in a new period of secularization, but they at least halted the march down the road of sacralization. Public schools, once considered a major battle ground in America's holy war, were rendered spiritually neutral. And the trickle-down effect permanently altered other critical components of 1950s sacralization, not the least of which was the military's character-guidance program. U.S. army recruits began complaining about the religious nature of character guidance as early as 1960, but these concerns achieved a new level of standing in the wake of *Engel v. Vitale* when the director of the ACLU in Washington brought the grievances of "religious indoctrination" directly to Secretary of the Army Cyrus R. Vance. In March 1963, Vance acted, ordering his chaplains to create a new, secular version of character guidance removed from the chapels and absent the sermonizing once encouraged by the brass since the days of the Fort Knox experiment.[88]

By then, as educators purged their curricula of religious instruction, networks had stopped televising religious appeals by organizations like the American Legion. In fact, the Legion's Back to God campaign had folded several years earlier, petering out like so many other programs of the spiritual-industrial complex. The RIAL campaign was ended, though a tamer version would reappear in later years. Organized attempts to ring church bells on Independence Day were over. Fewer Americans were going to church, and fewer still believed that religion was maintaining its influence upon society. Even Toynbee seemed a stale relic.[89] The Baby Boomers—many of whom had worshipped with their parents in a time when America was godly, Communism was evil, and their nation was God's country—would challenge the decade of their childhood during the decade of their maturation.

Eisenhower lived long enough to see *Time* magazine raise the question "Is God Dead?" He saw troops pour into Vietnam, the stirrings of rebellion on the nation's university campuses, the growing realization that America would have to coexist with the Soviets, and, of course, the slow dissolution of the spiritual-industrial complex. In December 1968, as he lay dying in the Walter Reed Army Medical Center, the former president welcomed Billy Graham. So it went for the spiritual-industrial complex's major contributors. Dulles had died almost a decade before. Henry R. Luce had passed only months earlier. J. Edgar Hoover, who never gave up the spiritual fight, was in his final years. So was Niebuhr.

Graham recalled that winter meeting.

"Billy, you've told me how to be sure my sins are forgiven and that I'm going to heaven. Would you tell me again?" the former president pleaded.

Graham took out his Bible. The two discussed salvation for some time before praying together.

"Thank you," Eisenhower said. "I'm ready."[90]

The Remains

"There are but two ways for us to go. We can go on making a god of
government, or we can return again to the government of God."
—Kenneth W. Sollitt, Illinois pastor, 1951

"Thus Arcadia stands today on the verge of holy war."[1] Mayor Edward L.
Butterworth was living through any politician's worst nightmare. His city of
50,000, which had grown like a suburban weed from the soil of San Gabriel
Valley ranchlands, had been rocked to its spiritual, ideological, and political
core. And all because of a book.

Nikos Kazantzakis's *The Last Temptation of Christ* had been translated into
English two years earlier, quietly sitting shelved at Arcadia's public library. But in
the summer of 1962 its inclusion in the library's catalog sparked an unexpected
controversy that bitterly divided the churches, politicians, and citizens of the
Los Angeles suburb.

In *The Last Temptation*, Jesus does not accept his mission as eagerly as is traditionally portrayed. He doubts himself. He is reluctant. He struggles with
temptation. Though few of the library critics who emerged in the Southland
controversy read the novel, finding elements worthy of condemnation demanded
little effort. Kazantzakis transformed the son of God into a mere man—an
imperfect human with hopes, fears, and desires.[2] Not only did this tarnish the
image of the Messiah in the minds of concerned Arcadians, it symbolized the
sinister designs of powers bent on the destruction of the American way. Some-
where between the end of America's state-sanctioned religious revival and the
rise of the Christian Right, between the acme of liberal consensus and the ascendancy of political conservatism, between the pious 1950s and defiant 1960s,
there was Arcadia.

Arcadia's story is one footnote from one city, hardly generalizable or repro-
ducible in any social-scientific sense. But contained within its story is the

aftermath of early Cold War sacralization. The city's "holy war" did not pit Americans against Communists; it arrayed moderates against conservatives, secularists against sacralists, Americans against Americans. The unfolding battle cannot be appreciated in isolation from the efforts of the spiritual-industrial complex that preceded it. New movements appeared that year in Arcadia, incubated during the religious crusade against Communism, which would give modern American political and religious history a new shape in subsequent decades.[3]

The official start of the controversy came in the last days of August 1962 when two prominent Arcadia pastors lodged official complaints against *The Last Temptation of Christ* in separate letters to the library board. James M. Beasley, pastor of Arcadia Union Church, fired a familiar salvo: "Our nation was founded by Christian people, based on Christian principles and if we desire to continue our freedom and way of life we must do all we can to halt the attacks of the enemy upon our nation and way of life." He worried about "hidden and violent forces" dedicated to the downfall of the world's foremost Christian republic.[4] Four days later, J. Davis Barnard, pastor of the Arcadia Presbyterian Church, also wrote the library board. He sharpened Beasley's critique, forcefully employing the double-edged rhetoric of moral decay and historical religious precedent. He reminded the board that Arcadia was "part of an overwhelmingly Christian nation." Barnard argued that, as a public institution, the library should conform to moral standards, "the ethical precepts of our forebears," and "the sensibilities of Christian people."[5]

The library board ignored the pastors' recommendations, and the threat of open conflict seemed to fade over the following two months. But during September and October the Arcadia Americanism Committee, a hodgepodge of politically and religiously conservative individuals and interests, rallied citizens to the cause with a series of public mailings. The rights of the Christian majority, the committee members argued, should not be limited by those "who plan to destroy the Christian religion." Nor could freedom of conscience become the Trojan horse used to weaken the religious foundation of public morality. "Unless we are willing to fight this deadly conspiracy to the finish," one mailing proclaimed, "what right have we to remain in Churches, posing as Christians?" The irony was that the only real conspiracy involved conservatives rather than camouflaged Communists. After all, the Arcadia Americanism Committee, under the direction of John Birch Society members, had carefully selected the suburb as the site for the battle between politics, religion, and ideology.[6]

Letters to the library board advocating the removal of *The Last Temptation of Christ* trickled in during October and early November, but J. Davis Barnard officially threw down the gauntlet during a November 9 phone conversation with library director Homer Fletcher.[7] During the brief discussion, Barnard demanded the book's removal from the library's shelves, and he threatened that if Fletcher did not act, he would be removed himself. Angered by the director's tenacity, Barnard quickly ended the conversation.[8] He next turned to the Arcadia Council of Protestant Churches, where on November 15 he secured a fourteen-to-seven vote in favor of his agenda.[9] Two weeks later the council agreed during a closed door session to bring the full weight of Arcadia's conservative Christian base to bear upon the library board and city council.[10]

By the end of November, the full scope of conservative mobilization was laid bare. On November 30 the front page of a Pasadena newspaper carried the headline "Book Protests Rock Southland Libraries." Suburban grassroots movements in Monrovia, Alhambra, Downey, Long Beach, Fullerton, Santa Ana, Newport Beach, and Ontario were waging similar battles against *The Last Temptation of Christ* across greater Los Angeles.[11] Libraries and city councils in the San Gabriel Valley found themselves confronting an organized campaign that would test the rising power of Christian conservatism. With no citywide election in the near future, the Christian conservatives chose to proceed with a two-pronged attack. The recently formed Citizens Committee for Clean Books, as the new organizational face of the local conservative movement, coordinated an intensive letter-writing campaign. Realizing that this would not be enough, conservative leaders also began circulating petitions, with the goal of collecting five thousand signatures. The Citizens Committee for Clean Books operated signature-collection tables outside of church services, and petitions were reportedly even passed through the pews during Catholic Mass.[12]

The controversy grew. On December 16 a full page ad appeared in the *Arcadia Tribune* entitled "The Truth in the Library Issue." The ad, sponsored by the Citizens Committee, appealed to the dual identity of residents as Christians and taxpayers, asking: "Since taxpayers PAY for the library, PAY for the books selected and PAY for the librarian's salary, is it unreasonable for a large segment of the people to want the right of determination on ONE out of 10,000 books?"[13] While committees demonstrated resolve through petitions, flyers, and advertisements, concerned citizens contributed to a letter writing campaign. "It is an affront to all Christian people and could only have been written to destroy our Christian nation," wrote one resident to the library board. "This is a Christian country and I am sure you are as aware as I am that there are hidden and violent forces dedicated to making it otherwise," wrote another. "The printed word is one of their methods."[14] The most complete argument came from a husband and wife:

> As J. Edgar Hoover and other great students of Communism have attested, Christianity is one of Communism's greatest obstacles in taking over this country or any other country. The Communists are

working hard to get an anti-Christ, anti-God society established. . . .
In the future, let's not ask the people of this great city to purchase a
book supporting such a Communistic theory.[15]

Perhaps sensing the political delicacy of the situation, the Arcadia city council did not act for several months. To ease tensions, Fletcher placed the book on
a restricted shelf, unavailable to minors without parental consent, thus neutral-
izing a key element of the Christian conservative argument. But the controversy
continued to spread. In February the Citizens Committee presented the city
council with five thousand signatures demanding the removal of *The Last Temptation of Christ*, though close analysis later revealed that more than two thousand
of the signatures were invalid.[16] The petition was accompanied by a new wave of
letters urging censorship. Monsignor Gerald M. O'Keeffe, pastor of Holy Angels
Catholic Church, rooted his argument in the social duty of community leaders.[17]
"It is my position," wrote O'Keeffe on February 5, "that the placing of the book
in question, in our city library, was and is offensive to the public good, as well as
to the moral standards of a reputable segment of our citizenry."[18] In a letter
written the same day, H. Warren Anderson, chairman of the Arcadia Council of
Protestant Churches, supplied a sharper argument:

> A decision to retain this book in the library would indicate to many a
> gross failure of an organized community to regulate one of its public
> institutions, thereby granting that institution license to pollute and poi-
> son the mind and soul of a community. . . . Patriotism could be vilified,
> religious [sic] ridiculed, pornography glorified and socialism or com-
> munism encouraged.[19]

But the battle was not as one-sided as the conservatives had hoped. Though
the Arcadia Council of Protestant Churches and the Citizens Committee pro-
jected a sense of religious cohesion, Arcadia's spiritual community was divided
over the issue of censorship. J. Davis Barnard managed to procure a strong resolution from the council during its November 15 meeting, but ten churches
abstained, weakening Barnard's apparent mandate. Most of the censorship campaign was controlled by a spiritual triumvirate: Arcadia Presbyterian Church, led
by Barnard; Holy Angels Catholic Church, led by Monsignor O'Keeffe; and
Arcadia Union Church, led by James M. Beasley. Warren Anderson, chairman of
the council, and the Citizens Committee often served as their mouthpiece.
Nonetheless, disputes within the council and Arcadia's Christian community
were well known, as newspapers reported the internal dissension over the censorship crusade.[20] One could add the city's library director and his congregation to the growing coalition of anticensorship Christians. In a letter to Mayor

Butterworth, Arcadia Church of Christ's pastor lauded Fletcher as a devout Christian and able director of the church's vacation Bible school.[21]

Local newspapers also came to the defense of the beleaguered library. In early December the *Star-News* ran a Sunday editorial calling for citizen action, particularly by moderate Republicans: "If the rank and file of the citizenry does not speak up, city officials, library boards, and libraries may easily be swept aside by a wave of prejudice set in motion by a small but determined minority."[22] The editorial's importance was twofold. It succinctly stated the basic tenets of the anticensorship argument employed by Arcadia's liberals and moderate conservatives. The library's defense would rest on the long-established tradition of freedom of conscience. Second, it served as a call to arms, and many heeded its cry.

Letters began to pour in to the Arcadia Public Library and city hall in support of the library board and Homer Fletcher. The ACLU, American Library Association, and the International Freedom Committee all offered assistance. A Los Angeles man offered $5,000 to anyone in Arcadia who could show him conclusive proof that Jesus Christ was the son of God.[23] A letter of encouragement even came from an Episcopalian pastor in Iowa.[24]

The Citizens Committee presented the Arcadia City Council with its five thousand signatures on Tuesday, February 5, 1963. Faced for the first time with a rough measurement of community outrage, the five members decided finally to act.[25] The controversy that first began the previous summer came to a head in a tense city council meeting on March 19. After an invocation by a Catholic priest, Mayor Butterworth read a statement unanimously passed by the council that supported the library board's decision. "The City Council," declared Butterworth, "supports and endorses the principle that no governmental agency has the right to censor what the individual reads." After tentatively endorsing this general statement, council members qualified the mayor's remarks. One councilman cautioned that, "I am very definitely opposed to 'censorship' but by the same token I am as definitely in favor of very rigid and careful 'book evaluation and selection practices.'" Another went a step further, waxing moral on the council's statement. "It is an enigma to me," he said, "to comprehend, much less understand the ultimate impact of a trend which appears to slope downward into a dilution of moral integrity and moral responsibility." He continued: "I am unable to accept the concept that just because ideas are expressed in words and printed in ink upon paper and bound between covers of a book [they] are immune to accepted standards of conduct."[26]

Though the city council had officially supported the library board, three of the five councilmen tempered their apparent conservative Christian rebuke with a litany of qualifications. As one moderate Republican resident observed in a prepared statement before the council that night, the individual statements amounted to a de facto three-to-two vote of no confidence in the library board.[27]

The voice and power of thousands of citizens were certainly difficult for any politician to ignore, but as far as the Council of Churches and Citizens Committee
were concerned, the city council did not go far enough. Three days later the Citizens Committee ran another large advertisement in the local paper under the
headline "Over 5,000 Petitioners refused by Arcadia City Council."[28] The council tacitly supported the library board's decision not to remove *The Last Temptation of Christ*, but it also recommended establishing a special closed shelf where
certain books would be off limits to minors. In taking the middle road, the city
council left both sides of the censorship issue unsatisfied and irate.

Rather than ending the library controversy, the Arcadia city council perpetu-
ated the debate by asking the library board to establish the closed shelf. Tensions
ran high through the spring and early summer of 1963 before the board finally
took up the issue of the closed shelf. Despite heavy pressure from the city council to adopt the closed shelf, the board voted three to two against the proposal.[29]
Embarrassed and pressured by the conservative Christian coalition, the councilmen considered a change in the city charter that would give the city council
the power to veto any library board policies. The measure was defeated three to
two in a contentious meeting that October.[30]

The book retained its role as a wedge in Arcadia. Shortly after the city
council rejected a plan to strip the library board of its independence, Barnard
carefully eyed the upcoming municipal elections. In a newspaper interview,
he spoke of his conservative Christian coalition. "They feel they were badly
let down by certain city council members," Barnard began. "Their displeasure
will be reflected in their vote when these councilmen seek to be re-elected."[31]
Two sitting councilmen echoed Barnard's sentiments, calling for a reexami-
nation of the city-charter change that would place the library board under
direct council control.

The city councilmen who opposed the charter change were not the first politicians against whom Christian conservatives directed their ire. The race for
Arcadia school board in April 1963 became the most bitter in city history. Three
incumbents, endorsed by the John Birch Society, ran as a single slate. The library
controversy was the campaign's pivotal issue, and the greatest threat to the conservative slate's triumph was a moderate who supported the library board's
decision not to censor *The Last Temptation of Christ*. In a much-discussed political maneuver, the Citizens Committee for Clean Books mailed two anonymous
letters to voters the day before the election. The first was a personal attack on the
moderate incumbent, and the second rehashed the book-banning controversy.
A bipartisan group of moderate Arcadia lawyers led by Mayor Butterworth protested the mailing to the state attorney general, and the local press denounced
the Citizens Committee. Despite protests and shocked sensibilities, all three
incumbents were narrowly reelected.[32]

In many ways the city council election of 1964 mirrored the school board. Two of the eight candidates for the council, one a member of Barnard's congregation and the other from O'Keeffe's parish, ran as a ticket. Together they pushed a common conservative agenda, and both made the library issue the central issue. A joint campaign letter justified their candidacy on the values-voter grounds that would soon dominate Republic politics: "because they are the best qualified to keep Arcadia a good place to live and raise a family."[33] The candidates enjoyed support from conservative Christians and the Citizens Committee, who provided a spate of anonymous mailings that echoed the basic arguments made by the Arcadia Council of Protestant Churches one and a half years earlier.[34]

The city council elections officially ended the Arcadia library controversy. One of the two right-wing candidates was elected. *The Last Temptation of Christ* remained on the shelves of the Arcadia Public Library, and Arcadia's conservatives failed to achieve their narrow goals. The petition drive and letter campaign did not sway the city council or the library board. The library board president retired in the summer of 1963, and head librarian Homer Fletcher left Arcadia the next year for a better job far away. While the conservative coalition failed to achieve its specific objectives, the movement was a rousing success. It rallied thousands of conservative Christians across the San Gabriel Valley, demonstrating the effectiveness of single-issue, local grassroots campaigning. If the controversy had indeed been a test of the California liberal consensus, then the right-wing mobilization and rhetoric passed with flying colors. The small setbacks of the early 1960s laid the groundwork for the great victories of 1966 and 1980. Conservative rhetoric and strategies of mobilization were crafted and sharpened in hundreds of communities like Arcadia across California and the nation, learning the skills necessary for future triumph in the lessons of defeat.

A library board member ended a summary of the entire episode on an ominous note. "The storm in Arcadia has subsided," she concluded, "but the vicious elements that caused it have not dispersed. Without warning, they could again burst loose, but not only in our community—they just might rip into yours. Are you ready, I hope?"[35]

The Arcadia episode, and others like it, came as a surprise to liberal and moderate observers. But seen in its context at the tail end of the spiritual-industrial complex's efforts, there is nothing extreme or illogical about the talking points of those favoring the novel's removal. Belief that Communism was a religious doctrine best withstood by the propagation of a counter faith; assertions that American society depended on a religious base; assumptions that the nation's institutions were central to the maintenance of spiritual energy; claims that America's material power flowed from its capacity to maintain a cohesive moral order: these were not just right-wing talking points. The same logic had passed the lips of moderates like Truman and liberals like Niebuhr with regularity since the beginning of the Cold War. Arcadia's procensorship coalition did not introduce new arguments; they held fast to older arguments while much of society developed new ones.

On a local level Arcadia fits within broader trends. The library controversy united the suburb's conservative Christian community. Decades earlier such a coalition would not have been impossible, but it would have been rare—the kind of union held up as a model of the fellowship achievable at some future time. But by the 1950s, what mattered was that people had religion, not the specific religion to which they subscribed. Communism may have had a divisive impact on the peoples of the world, but it was a powerful, unifying force for American religious groups. The differences in doctrine that once spawned anti-Semitism, anti-Catholicism, and theological battles within Protestantism seemed slight in comparison to the jarring faith of the Communist. At least Protestant, Catholic, and Jew believed in a higher power, a moral code delineated from above, and the utter inability of mankind to perfect itself absent divine intervention.

Ironically, Kennedy's election was made possible in part by the very spiritual-industrial complex he tried to downplay. In 1937, nine years after what some perceived as the anti-Catholic electoral defeat of Democratic presidential candidate Al Smith, Gallup found that 30 percent of Americans would not vote for a well-qualified Catholic president. By the late 1950s, this number had fallen by a third.[36] Even more striking was the change in public attitude toward Jews. Over the same period of time, the percentage of Americans who claimed they would not vote for a well-qualified Jew fell from 47 percent to 22 percent.[37] This newfound tolerance of other faiths only extended to those who shared a belief in God. In 1958, three in four Americans declared that they would not vote for a competent and experienced candidate who happened to be an atheist.[38] To be sure, there were still Protestants like Paul Blanshard who warned against the growth of Catholic power in America. There were still Catholics who, like the Jesuit editors of the weekly journal *America*, warned their "Jewish friends" against appearing too gleeful after the *Engel v. Vitale* ruling.[39] But in a nation of jubilant dedications to the interfaith example of the "Four Chaplains"—in a society where Joe McCarthy feted anti-Communist rabbis at lavish testimonial dinners, Jews like Frank K. Weil headed presidential committees on religion, organizations like FRASCO recruited Jewish and Catholic leaders, and spiritual celebrities like Norman Vincent Peale reminded Protestants that "Catholic and Jewish groups too are vigilant"—warnings like these seemed increasingly anachronistic.[40]

The Arcadia crisis matters most because it reveals the emergence of popular social movements incubated and advanced by the religious battle against

Communism that would come to exert a powerful influence on American society. The first is modern political conservatism. The movement's revitalization has been considered inseparable from the growth of the New Deal order, and many forays into the pith of its ascendancy focus on the period after 1960, but it was no coincidence that the laying of modern conservatism's ideological and organizational foundations coincided with the growth and subsequent demise of the spiritual-industrial complex.[41] While no reputable history of conservatism overlooks its deep roots in anti-Communism, the movement also owed a great debt to the period of postwar sacralization. American conservatism was not monolithic. Rather, it was composed of ideological constituencies, overlapping at some points and mutually exclusive at others.[42] The true marvel of the movement has been conservatives' ability to maintain a sense of ideological cohesion. And though the many constituencies of modern conservatism evade simplistic categorization, it is possible to identify two main schools of thought. The first, libertarianism, which has roots in classical economics, is secular. The second, traditionalism, which posits at its core the order and conventions fashioned by God, grew fat on holy war.[43]

The richest and most influential description of traditional conservatism came from the learned Michigan State professor and political theorist Russell Kirk. *The Conservative Mind*, published in 1953, laid down in fluid prose the principles of a counter ideology to the triumphant liberalism touted by scholars, politicians, and cultural observers. Kirk's political system was no "pseudo-conservative revolt"—no channeled and irrational rage against social progress by the economically and intellectually dispossessed.[44] Instead, Kirk traced Anglo-American conservatism to the warnings of Edmund Burke, who recognized in the French Revolution the danger in the untethered cult of progress. Kirk looked on American liberalism with equal distaste and apprehension. It brought reform by committee, it loosed society from the bonds of long-established traditions, and it converted the state from a "divinely ordained moral essence" into an unwieldy, secular behemoth. Liberalism was the fanatic creed of people in love with change.[45]

How appropriate that Kirk collected his thoughts at Piety Hill, his ancestral home in the stump country of Michigan. Piety, or, more specifically, religious orientation, was the linchpin of the traditional conservative worldview he detailed. According to Kirk, the first canon of conservative thought was the "belief that a divine intent rules society as well as conscience." Conservatism was merely the political manifestation of a greater spiritualism. "Political problems," Kirk wrote, "at bottom, are religious and moral problems." So too did religious understanding inform his view of social change. Conservatives, Kirk believed, could not set themselves against all change, but radical change was more a "devouring conflagration" than a "torch of progress." How was it possible for

conservatives to distinguish between the two? For Kirk a single-word explanation sufficed: providence. "Providence is the proper instrument for change," he
contended, "and the test of a statesman is his cognizance of the real tendency of
Providential social forces."[46]

Kirk was not alone in harboring fears about societies that rejected divine
guidance. University of Chicago professor Richard Weaver had circulated similar fears in the slim volume *Ideas Have Consequences* in 1948. A history of philosophy, the work shared with Kirk a distrust of progress and optimism and with
Niebuhr a commitment to acknowledging the inherently sinful nature of humankind. Weaver believed that the quest for rationality begun in the Enlightenment
had resulted in a "long series of abdications": the attempt to solve all of nature's
sacred mysteries, the belief that people were shaped entirely by their environment, and the transformation of religion from an eternal instrument of divine
intent to an institution of "ambiguous dignity." This sorry state Weaver called
"abysmality." The more that people strove to establish themselves as the centers
of authority, the less authority they actually maintained. Theirs was a world of
"practice without theory," of "hysterical optimism" and the pursuit of ideals that
prevailing assumptions had made worthless. Weaver did not frame it as such, but
his work was a headlong attack on the process of secularization. He called it
"man's passage from religious or philosophical transcendence," and he attacked
the prevailing assumption that it was a story of progress. For Weaver, as with
Niebuhr, religion was not bereft of optimism. On the contrary, its promise of
salvation brimmed with hope. But religion, or at least the religion Weaver had in
mind, did not promise its followers perfection on earth, and it balanced accounts
of people's good with warnings of their capacity for great evil.[47]

Clarence Manion had also spent the late 1940s meditating on the dangers of
unrestrained optimism and the promise of religiously grounded conservatism.
As dean of law at Notre Dame University, he published in 1950 *The Key to Peace*,
a widely read accounting of conservatism and Americanism. In its accessibility,
crispness, and conviction, it was a forerunner to Barry Goldwater's *Conscience of
a Conservative*. Both contained calls for limited government, strict construc-
tionist intepretations of the Constitution, and dire warnings of Communism on
the world stage. But whereas the Arizona senator's manifesto was decidedly secular, Manion's statement of belief was thoroughly religious. The work began by
comparing the indulgent, godless, and materialistic French Revolution with its
humble, pious American counterpart. "Our American forefathers knew that
God must be in the government of any people in order to insure them against
despotism," Manion wrote. "This official conjunction of the laws of God with the
Constitutions and laws of the land is the basic and controlling ingredient of
Americanism." Manion did not call himself a conservative, for at the time it was
not a well-defined category of political belief. But after retiring from Notre Dame

and suffering from a highly publicized falling out with Eisenhower, he became an important figure of the emerging American Right. In 1954 he launched the *Manion Forum*, a syndicated radio program recorded from his home in South Bend, Indiana, which reminded his audience each week that both conservatism and Americanism shared a common link from above.[48]

Half a continent away, an undergraduate at Yale was fighting, and losing, the same battle. After two years service to the army, William F. Buckley, Jr., arrived at the college in 1946 and quickly established himself as an iconoclast extraordinaire. His editorials in the *Yale Daily News* became talking points for undergrads and professors alike. His unswerving faith in the free market and passionate defense of individual liberty made him a conspicuous figure. Buckley chafed under the auspices of professors who protected their opinions behind the unassailable barricade of academic freedom. Not content to limit his diatribes to the student newspaper, he wrote *God and Man at Yale* in 1951. Composed in the first person, it had all the characteristics of a catty tell-all from a disgruntled former student. But adherents to the the nascent conservative movement took notice, wondering if they had found their "young Saint Paul."[49] Yale took notice too, even commissioning a committee to investigate Buckley's charges.[50]

Though limited in scope to his experience at Yale, Buckley's debut book was substantial because it construed the battles between Communism and capitalism, individualism and collectivism, and Christianity and atheism as three facets of an identical confrontation. He came to Yale looking for "allies against secularism and collectivism." He found instead agents bent on subverting religion and individualism. "I myself believe that the duel between Christianity and atheism is the most important in the world," Buckley wrote. "I further believe that the struggle between individualism and collectivism is that same struggle reproduced on another level." He accused Yale's professors of indoctrination, not so much the plainly detestable exhortations of hardened atheists, though there were a few, but rather a steady drumbeat against the presence of "moral absolutes" and "intrinsic truths." Those teachers who did address Christian principles approached them so tepidly that all meaning was lost. "So long as what they profess can be subscribed to wholeheartedly by an atheist," Buckley warned, "we have not, really, got religion at all."[51]

Arguments like these set the jewel of faith in God foremost on the crown of traditional conservatism, but such ideas were hardly novel. This was the old colossus-of-straw fear, tweaked and politicized. Kirk, Weaver, Manion, and Buckley had taken up the pen at an ideal time. Their arguments fit well within the broader set of concerns guiding the efforts of the spiritual-industrial complex— less the trappings of thinkers well outside the mainstream and more an echo of the many politicians, educators, and business leaders then directing an experiment in societal sacralization.

Taking this logic one step further, conservatives applied the same critiques against Communism, secularism, and irreligion with equal brio to liberalism. If God guided and defined the slow change conservatives preferred, then by definition the "radical" change pursued by liberals was ungodly. Kirk accused liberalism of positing that education, legislation, and environmental improvements could produce "men like gods." Weaver charged it with changing people from protagonists with souls to mere "wealth-seeking and consuming" animals.[52]

For conservatives, "materialism" was the term used to link liberalism to Communism, and a versatile term it was. It implied the absence of any otherworldly force governing humanity's affairs, the belief that thoughts, feelings, and actions could be explained in terms of physical matter and natural phenomena, and the faith that progress was possible only through the tangible achievements of humanity. Yet materialism had a wider connotation as well: the conviction that earthly possessions and physical well-being constituted the greatest good in life. Conservatives knew that true Communists swallowed these propositions whole, but they were equally concerned with liberals nibbling around their edges. Buckley used the word "collectivist" rather than "Communist" in his criticism, since it easily accommodated the Keynesian managed economy. Fulton Sheen concluded that the products American society sold at retail the Soviets sold at wholesale. When Clare Boothe Luce said that "no Christian saint ever had more faith in the power of God's grace to transfigure his own nature than a Communist has in the power of State ownership of electricity and plumbing to transfigure all human nature," she and her audience no doubt had the Tennessee Valley Authority in mind as well. Chambers wrote that the crisis of civilization "exists to the degree in which the Western world actually shares Communism's materialist vision," and Manion reminded his readers that "government cannot make men good."[53]

The readers of Henry R. Luce's *Life* magazine may not have known it, but tucked into the February 2, 1948, issue was one of the sharpest expressions of this emerging conservative critique. In "The Devil," Whittaker Chambers imagined a conversation between himself and Lucifer in a Manhattan club on New Year's Eve. Satan pulls up a chair and, after exchanging some pleasantries, describes hell's "New Deal," a plan to "destroy man by seducing him through good." Rather than working actively to corrupt humanity, the Devil discovers that he can simply "move with the tide and leave the rest to rationalism, liberalism and universal compulsory education." The Devil chuckles, "Oh, how well I know the rationalist and liberal mind—the modern mind that still does not understand the nature of a commonplace like electricity but does not hesitate to question the existence of Heaven and Hell." Chambers is unimpressed. As the conversation continues, he succeeds in forcing the Devil to admit that there are obstacles, namely intellectuals like Niebuhr and Toynbee—both of whom had become heroes in Chambers's eyes. As the conversation nears its end, the Devil finally reveals his true motivation. "[I am] sterile," he says. "My greatest master-piece is never more than a perversion—an ingenious disordering of Another's grand design." The party around them dies down. "Happy New Year, young man," Satan says, before leaving.[54]

Life's readers were not eavesdropping on a conversation between Whit-taker Chambers and the Devil, of course. They were reading a conversation between Chambers and himself, or, more accurately, between Chambers in 1948 and Chambers in 1926. The Devil did not come to Chambers in his youth as an apparition or a demon in the desert; it came as quasi-religious faith called Communism. It preyed upon good intentions and promised to make gods of men. Chambers had been to hell and back again, and soon the whole country, and indeed the world, would read about it. Communism was, to be sure, a prob-lem, but its audacity limited its ascendancy. Liberalism, Chambers believed, suf-fered from no such handicap. It began with noble goals but paved the way for greater evils. In this sense, Communism was liberalism fully realized.

This dual belief, that conservatism was rooted in faith and that Communism was rooted in liberalism, became a blueprint for political action in the late 1950s, as grassroots political groups became increasingly influential. Ironically, these groups often borrowed from Communist techniques of organization—making ample use of cheaply produced tracts and small-group meetings, often held in the homes of members. Little wonder, since, like Communists in the 1930s, the conservatives of the 1950s possessed an intellectual corpus but were culturally disinherited.

Some early efforts of the spiritual-industrial complex served as incubators for the conservative mobilization that took liberals by surprise in the late 1950s. The Committee to Proclaim Liberty, for instance, served such a purpose. Its board of advisors was center-right, with leaders drawn from across the political spectrum, but CPL sprang from a right-wing organization called Spiritual Mobi-lization that was devoted to harnessing religious leaders toward the goal of a drastically enervated federal government. Clarence Manion sat on the CPL board, and he no doubt smiled after reading through some of the sermons that religious leaders delivered on Freedom Sunday in 1951. "Today America stands at a cross-roads," preached the pastor of the First Baptist Church in Menota, Illi-nois. "There are but two ways for us to go. We can go on making a god of govern-ment, or we can return again to the government of God."[55] The pastor, like other conservatives who participated in early Cold War's spiritual battle, recognized that each stone thrown by liberals at Communism had the potential to ricochet back at their own policies and ideologies.

In 1958, as the spiritual-industrial complex's consensus collapsed under the weight of new assumptions and unrealized warnings, two other important grassroots organizations came into existence. Both were conservative, both worried that America's leaders were no longer taking the spiritual threat of Communism seriously, and both were unabashedly religious to the core. The first, founded in St. Louis by Phyllis and Fred Schlafly, took for its name a reminder of Communist hostility toward religion. The Cardinal Mindszenty Foundation (CMF) worked to restoke the flagging fires of American Catholic anti-Communism. It published a monthly newspaper called the *Mindszenty Report*, designed an anti-Communist study program, organized a series of seminars across the United States, and produced a short radio program. After only several years of operation, the CMF boasted three thousand study groups across America. Ten years earlier the foundation would have fit within the contours of the spiritual-industrial complex—albeit on its fringes—but by the late 1950s, it was considered extreme and anachronistic. Even Reverend John Cronin, lauded in the late 1940s for his alarmist assessments of Communist infiltration, attacked the CMF under the auspices of the National Catholic Welfare Council for what he considered to be its vehemence and recklessness.[56]

The criticism the CMF drew was nothing compared to that garnered by the John Birch Society, an organization too conspiratorial for William F. Buckley, Jr. to stomach. Indeed, the "Birchers" came to symbolize the dangerous combination of status anxiety, anti-intellectualism, and acute paranoia.[57] While it may appear that the organization materialized out of nowhere, its formation makes a good deal more sense when situated within the broader sacralization of American society during the late 1940s and 1950s.

The John Birch Society was at its core the political expression of a religious conviction. Its founder, the former candy maker Robert Welch, was the son of poor fundamentalist Baptist parents. After an unsuccessful campaign for political office in Massachusetts, Welch spent much of the 1950s spreading conservative messages through speeches and tracts. On December 9, 1958, in Indianapolis, he and eleven other men founded the John Birch Society, after several days of intense discussions and lectures. The text of these lectures was compiled into the John Birch Society *Blue Book*, which became the organization's canonical text. Spiritual battle against Communism was the backdrop against which all of Welch's warnings of treason, political conspiracy, and rampaging government bureaucracy played out. As with so many other and more moderate cold warriors, Welch adopted the form of the modern jeremiad. The nation, he warned, was living in a "spiritual vacuum." He lamented the passing of an older, more religious age and argued that fundamentalists offered the best hope of restoring America to its God-loving roots. Spiritual decline was, of course, only half the problem. Not surprisingly, Welch conceptualized the battle against Communism as primarily religious. "This is a world-wide battle," he lectured, "the first in human history, between light and darkness; between freedom and slavery; between the spirit of Christianity and the spirit of anti-Christ for the souls and bodies of men."[58]

The name of the society itself conjured images of holy war. In 1954 Welch published a slim book describing the life and death of Captain John Birch, a Christian missionary who joined the U.S. military during World War II and died in August 1945 at the hands of Chinese Communists. Welch thought that Birch "personified everything that the Communists hate": he was deeply religious and patriotic. His martyrdom proved that true Christians "would not even stand passively on the sidelines and allow crimes against the code of Christian civilization to be perpetrated without protest and militant action." This murder, committed a mere ten days after Japan's surrender, was for him the opening shot of the Cold War. "With his death and in his death the battle lines were drawn," he concluded, "in a struggle from which either Communist or Christian-style civilization must emerge with one completely triumphant and the other completely destroyed."[59]

By the time of the Arcadia library crisis, the John Birch Society operated some one hundred bookstores around the country, and its membership numbered at least 40,000 people.[60] These members proved instrumental in organizing the campaign to remove *The Last Temptation of Christ* from the public library's shelves. With respect to the importance of religion in bolstering American society and combating Communism, their arguments held sway through much of the early Cold War. But as the Cold War conceptions of moderates and liberals shifted, conservatives found themselves increasingly isolated.

The climate could not have been better for traditional conservatives like Buckley, Chambers, and Kirk to reinvigorate a weakened political ideology whose central tenet supposed the eternal and moral order established by God. Kirk realized as much. "The celebrants of the Feast of Reason, could they see the Anglo-American civilization of 1952, would be astonished to find Christianity still enduring on either side of the Atlantic," he mused. Kirk saw in this spiritual kernel—resistant through the centuries to the slings and arrows of enlightenment, materialism, and neurotic optimism—the best hope of conservative renewal, and he identified spiritual and moral regeneration as the chief task of the modern conservative.[61] Moderates like Eisenhower made this a prime theme of their rhetoric in the 1950s, but though they called for religious renewal, they almost invariably buttressed the New Deal order. And while these calls faded as the 1960s dawned, traditional conservatives continued to bolster their ranks with religious Americans concerned as ever with moral decay and Communist subversion.

The rise of modern religious conservatism also benefited from the legacy of the spiritual-industrial complex. Signs were everywhere in Arcadia's bookshops and neighborhoods in the early 1960s that the locus of anti-Communist religious

energy was moving away from the mainline. Religious conservatism found organization and expression in the city's churches. The same trend occurred nationwide, particularly among the growing number of Americans who considered
themselves evangelical.

While historical explorations of modern political conservatism have become
a thriving cottage industry, analyses of the Religious Right are a factory enterprise, commanding the attentions and talents of journalists, sociologists, historians, and independent writers. This movement is large and visible enough to
subsume much of recent American religious history into its ever-expanding
aggregation of investigations, films, and articles. The interest is entirely understandable. After all, religious conservatives, and evangelicals in particular, are
living proof that religion continues to exert a measurable influence upon the
ideas, actions, and culture of a large swath of American society. Nowhere has
this been truer than in the connection between white Protestant evangelicals
and political behavior. The story goes something like this: evangelicals, the
main component of the Religious Right, emerged from a long slumber in the
1960s, upset by the secular courts and a perceived disintegration of moral and
family values. By the 1970s they began to mobilize politically; by the 1980s
they had earned a seat at the governing table of the Republican Party; and by
the 1990s they were running the party. Statistical analyses based on exit-poll
data confirm this arc. In 1960, for instance, evangelical Protestants accounted
for 19 percent of the GOP's voting bloc. By 2004, their share within the party
had grown to 40 percent.[62]

Of course not all evangelicals are conservative, and not all of the Christian
Right is made up of evangelicals, but the story of modern evangelicalism is tied
intimately to the development and demise of the spiritual-industrial complex.[63]
As in the political realm, America's religious war against Communism began as
an effort directed by a coalition of liberal, moderate, and conservative religious
leaders—from Oxnam to Niebuhr to Elson to Sheen. But by the late 1950s, conservative religious leaders had picked up the drooping banner of religious
anti-Communism and were carrying it in their own crusade.

Theological and cultural outsiders at the beginning of the Cold War, evangelicals did not figure as prominently in the formation of the spiritual-industrial
complex as more mainline faith traditions.[64] The National Association of Evangelicals, which provided the movement with an institutional framework, was
not founded until 1942. The Fuller Theological Seminary, which helped to provide an intellectual guidepost to the movement, was not founded until 1947.
And Billy Graham, who became the face of the new evangelicalism, did not
become nationally known until his 1949 revival in Los Angeles.[65] The emergence of evangelicals as a reinvigorated religious force coincided almost perfectly with the machinations of the spiritual-industrial complex. They came

forth at a moment in time when secular American institutions were conducting an all-out effort to promote religiosity. Few religious groups were better suited for this mission of revival.

Evangelical anti-Communism, if measured by its depth, surpassed its predecessors. The anti-Communist Christians of the late 1950s and 1960s did more than watch Fulton Sheen on television, attend church, and say a prayer for the nation each night before bed. They also traveled to attend lectures, subscribed to a variety of shoe-string-budget newsletters, discussed their beliefs with neighbors, and campaigned for the removal of anti-Christian, anti-American literature from library shelves. By its very nature, this second wave of anti-Communism had one disadvantage: relatively few people were willing to spend time and energy confronting a threat that most Americans no longer viewed as imminent. Its support, measured by breadth, was only a narrow band from the spectrum that once embraced religious anti-Communism. New leaders transformed anti-Communism from a cause that required the help of all religious groups into one that they alone were best equipped to handle. The holy war that once concerned all religious Americans became the province, and indeed the obsession, of a fraction of them.[66]

But Fred Schwarz, an Australian psychiatrist who became a lay preacher after moving to America, proved that a fraction of Americans, when assembled in one place, can still be formidable. Schwarz was one of several evangelical leaders who made up the second wave of religious anti-Communism. The label is at first glance misleading, since Schwarz, like his fellow leaders, were not newcomers to the battle. But their star rose at the precise moment the campaigns of religiously and politically moderate American leaders began to flag. Schwarz himself was an unlikely hero for the religious Right. Born into poverty in Brisbane, he was warmed at a young age by the charity of Christian missionaries. The first of two great turning points in the development of Schwarz's thought came in 1944 during a well-attended debate between Schwarz and a fellow undergraduate on the topic "Is Communism a science or a religion?" Not surprisingly, young Schwarz argued the latter, reciting the basic arguments made by religious leaders since the beginning of the 1930s. The second came when he met Billy Graham during a visit to America in 1952. Impressed by Schwarz's resolve and knowledge, Graham encouraged him to found an organization devoted to educating Americans on the spiritual dangers of Communism. Schwarz founded the Christian Anti-Communism Crusade the following year with $50.[67]

Of course in 1953 his message was hardly audible over the booming voices of Eisenhower, Luce, and the Congress. His first break came four years later with a round of testimony before HUAC. From there he built a following with pamphlets, newsletters, and word of mouth within the dwindling but dedicated minority of citizens who considered the spiritual threat of Communism paramount. But Schwarz was best known for his anti-Communist seminars, referred to as "schools." Short, intense, and well organized, the first was held in St. Louis in 1958, and from there they spread from state to state. Managed by Schwarz and a local citizens' committee, each lasted for a week and cost $20. The days were long, lasting from 8:30 a.m. to 10:00 p.m., and consisted of lectures, discussions, and film screenings. Schwarz assembled a "faculty" for each school made up of prominent Americans like Connecticut senator Thomas J. Dodd, Minnesota congressman Walter H. Judd, and University of California physicist Edward Teller. It was not uncommon for public schools to excuse students from classes so they could attend.[68]

Schwarz took his message across the country, but he found no more fertile ground than the sun-drenched valleys of Southern California when, in November 1960, he convened the first Greater Los Angeles School of Anti-Communism. He followed his first successful Southland school with another four months later in the shadow of Disneyland, and one more in the late summer of 1961 at LA's sports arena. Attended by thousands, touted by celebrities like Ronald Reagan, and even televised, the schools struck a nerve. Not all Americans were willing to declare a ceasefire in the holy war against Communism. It is impossible to know how many Arcadians attended the school or watched its proceedings on television, but if the arguments they made in the library controversy are any guide, they at least recognized a unity of purpose with those rallying to Schwarz.[69]

It is also impossible to know how many Arcadians, like many other religious Americans, joined in the crusades of Billy James Hargis, J. Vernon McGee, Bob Wells, or William Stuart McBirnie. Born into an impoverished Texas family, Hargis was ordained at the age of seventeen. He moved to Tulsa and in 1950 founded the fundamentalist ministry Christian Crusade. Hargis routinely decried what he perceived to be the disintegration of American culture, but he was most famous for his constant warnings against Communism. His influence grew exponentially in the 1950s, nourished by both the priority American leaders placed on anti-Communism and the advent of new media through which he could spread the word. By the end of the decade, Christian Crusade claimed 120,000 donating members and a network of four hundred radio stations. Hargis's books, pamphlets, and newsletters were widely disseminated, finding their way into Arcadia's conservative bookstore by the time of the library crisis.[70]

Evangelicals in Southern California could tune in to Hargis's broadcasts, but they could follow in person local preachers who took up the same cause. J. Vernon McGee, who, like Hargis, was born in Texas, moved to California at the start of World War II and assumed the pastorate of the Church of the Open Door in 1949. From his base in downtown Los Angeles, McGee regularly tied anti-Communism to both religious faith and the preservation of American democracy. During sermons he was fond of showing slides that depicted the places of his childhood—towns whose residents possessed the sort of wholesome, God-fearing values that were required to resist the Soviets. On Sunday afternoons he held regular discussion sessions with followers on the perils of Communism. And, like other political conservatives, he believed that the New Deal in particular and liberalism in general were refueling stops on the long road to a Marxist takeover. Much the same could be said of Bob Wells, who relocated to Orange County in 1956 where he founded the Central Baptist Church. Wells was known for eagerly digesting the religious, anti-Communist pronouncements of J. Edgar Hoover, so it was not surprising when he founded Heritage High School, a private institution devoted to the promotion of Christian patriotism with an emphasis on anti-Communist curriculum. William Stuart McBirnie, a Canadian by birth, moved to Glendale in 1961 and became a senior minister of the United Community Church. He also shared a belief in the primacy of religious anti-Communism. For decades to come he would make regular contributions to the radio program *Voice of Americanism,* warning all who listened that Communism was the anti-Christ foretold in Revelations.[71]

It was not uncommon for evangelical leaders to view the spiritual-industrial complex as an means to expand their ranks and gain a modicum of respectability. Before launching his Washington Crusade in 1952, Billy Graham knew that Truman's participation would increase the revival's legitimacy, and he tried desperately to secure the president's attendance. Truman refused, but his successor proved far more amenable to such endeavors. When, for example, in 1953 the National Association of Evangelicals conceived of a plan to stage a March for Freedom in the nation's capital, its leadership considered the event an invaluable opportunity to promote a specific evangelical cause under the aegis of the wider spiritual-industrial complex. For its ability to unify, focus, and provide a litmus test, religious anti-Communism was to the evangelical movement in the 1950s what opposition to abortion would become in the 1970s.[72]

American liberals and moderates denounced these exercises of the religious "extreme Right," but the better part of what they preached during the 1960s would have been considered acceptable or even wise ten or twenty years earlier, with two exceptions. Evangelicals in the religious Right differed from their more moderate contemporaries in their penchant for viewing the Cold War through the prism of biblical prophesy. Chambers had invoked the Garden of Eden in describing the earthly temptations that seduced Marx. Eisenhower had called the Cold War a struggle between good and evil, but he understood it as a system developed by misguided men. But some evangelicals looked at world events and saw unmistakable signs of the end-times. The future was bleak, a malignant system of belief was on the rise, and the nuclear age brought the real possibility of apocalypse. Yet in that moment of crisis there was a glimmer of hope for true believers, for with doomsday came the prospect of the millennium.[73]

Other anti-Communists had hinted at the infernal origins of Communism, but some evangelical leaders strove to make Satan a part of any Marxist equation. An associate of Schwarz put it best:

> Let's assume that you were Lucifer. . . . What would you do? I know what I would do if I were in his position. I would create something just as close to Christianity as I could, so that people would accept the counterfeit and not question it. . . . Communism is a religion spawned in Hell by Satan himself in his ruthless, relentless war against Christianity.[74]

McBirnie wrote that "The Christian explanation for the successful advances of communism . . . is SATAN!" Hargis proclaimed that "Communism, which is of Satan, hates America." Aspiring Christian folksinger Janet Greene, who sometimes performed at Schwarz's schools, wrote a ditty to the tune of "Jimmy Crack Corn" that began:

> When I was young it seemed to me
> The whole wide world would soon be free.
> But communism is on the rise
> And Satan has a new disguise.

California's attorney general labeled this growing evangelical belief the "Devil Theory" of anti-Communism.[75]

Second, some evangelical leaders, particularly fundamentalists, rejected the interfaith principle that had once served as a Constitutional safeguard in America's holy war. Truman, Eisenhower, Hoover, and others were careful to frame America's holy war as the joint exercise of all religious faiths. They were not promoting a specific religion but rather religion itself. Yet when leaders like Hargis called for a religious crusade against Communism, they envisioned its ranks populated with evangelicals. There has long been a strong separatist streak in American fundamentalism and evangelicalism.[76] The far more expansive battle against Communism in the early Cold War provided religious conservatives with some much-needed cover for attacking liberals. Fundamentalists signaled that they were willing to combat Communism but not in conjunction with mainline Protestants.

Carl McIntire best represented this attitude. Born in 1906 to a Presbyterian minister, he came of age during the height of the modernist-fundamentalist controversy and observed it from its epicenter at Princeton Theological Seminary. Having founded his own church during the Great Depression, he proceeded to publish a weekly newspaper, the *Christian Beacon*, and later in the 1950s he began a daily radio program. McIntire opposed Dulles's appointment as secretary of state, but he gained greater attention by targeting Methodist bishop G. Bromley Oxnam. He actively promoted HUAC's investigation of the bishop in 1953, citing his opposition to both the committee and Joe McCarthy. "As perhaps no other man," McIntire seethed, "Oxnam represents the popular, radical, pro-communistic element in religious circles in America." The bishop had echoed many of the spiritual-industrial complex's talking points since the late 1940s, but McIntire did not allow their common enemy to make them allies, nor did Hargis, who frequently scrutinized major societal institutions like the government, schools, and churches. Rather than seeing in them the spark of 1950s sacralization, he saw instead agents of Communism infiltration. Mainline religious groups like the National Council of Churches were among his favorite targets. This sectarian conception of anti-Communism led a group of Episcopalian bishops to a formal 1961 denunciation of religious "extremists" who stirred up "radical fear of communism." An official with the National Council of Churches attacked evangelical anti-Communists as "apostles of discord," and B'nai B'rith distributed a warning manual dissecting their tactics and aims.[77]

Though Arcadians recognized their shared goals, conservative Christianity and conservative politics did not instantly become allies on the national stage. After all, Jimmy Carter, America's first modern evangelical president, muddied the relationship by winning the conservative Christian vote in 1976. But Ronald Reagan would undo the electoral coalitions Carter assembled. Reagan, the figure modern conservatives saw as their political messiah—or at least their John the Baptist—brought political and religious conservatives, libertarians and traditionalists, into a muscular coalition.[78]

When Mayor Butterworth declared that holy war had come to Arcadia, he did not intentionally place his town's struggles within the broader context of the spiritual-industrial complex. But his assessment summed up in a handful of words the legacy of that endeavor. What began as a holy war against a theologically alien foe had become a holy war between Americans of different religious and political beliefs. What began as a project supported across the political and religious spectrum had become an organizing principle of religious and political conservatism.

The spiritual divisions imposed upon distant continents became political and cultural partitions in modern American life. Was America, in the words of the early Cold War U.S. Army, a covenant nation or a secular nation? The people of Arcadia could not reach a consensus. Neither could their fellow citizens across the country. They still cannot.

Epilogue

"It is simply unconscionable for activist judges and fanatical atheists to
intrude on the history of the United States."

—Bill O'Reilly, 2002

On March 8, 1983, President Ronald Reagan stood before the National Association of Evangelicals. Shortly after 3:00 p.m. in the Citrus Crown Ballroom of
Orlando's Sheraton Twin Towers Hotel, he delivered an address that would
define not only his view of the Cold War but his presidency as well. The pivotal
moment came with his description of the Soviet Union as an "evil empire."

The phrase, which quickly spread to newsrooms across the world, was not
necessarily intended to be the thematic cornerstone that historians and political
pundits would later fashion into an emblem of the death of détente. Rather, it
was something of a throwaway line, buried inside a paragraph. But it served to
underscore the president's larger point. "The struggle now going on for the world
will never be decided by bombs or rockets, by armies or military might," the
president explained. "The real crisis we face today is a spiritual one; at root, it is
a test of moral will and faith."[1] Just as his audience feted old-time religion, he
celebrated old-time anti-Communism. The Cold War was once again a struggle
"between right and wrong and good and evil." Nor did Reagan stop there. Like
an old scholar dusting off some misplaced tome, he paid his respects to the long-
dead Whittaker Chambers, reminding the crowd of Communism's most seductive promise: "Ye shall be as gods."[2]

It might be tempting to conclude that Reagan's words had brought the Cold
War full circle. But while his audience applauded, many in America and around
the world gasped. If the president thought the Soviets were evil, one strand of
popular thought held, then war with them would be inevitable. Reaction
against Reagan's choice of words was swift and savage. Eminent historian
Henry Steele Commager called it "the worst speech in presidential history"

and a "gross appeal to religious prejudice." *New York Times* columnist Anthony Lewis distilled his criticism into a rhetorical question: "What is the world to think when the greatest of powers is led by a man who applies to the most difficult human problem a simplistic theology?" Reagan did not stand firmly behind his "evil empire" assertion. Though he never admitted to regretting the comments, he softened considerably the moral and religious punch they appeared at first to deliver. In a March 18 interview with the *London Sunday Times*, the president explained that his use of the word "evil" was taken out of context and was never intended to imply that war between the United States and Soviet Union was inevitable. Several days later, he made the same argument during a press conference.[3]

In the years that have followed the 1983 speech, "evil empire" has been interpreted as a symbol of misguided bombast, a tribute to idiosyncratic leadership, and a bold sentiment in morally squishy times. The phrase was instead Reagan's articulation of a foreign policy framework as old as the conflict with Communism itself. Responding to the Orlando speech, the head of the Fuller Theological Seminary labeled it "an attempt to take us back to the '50s and deal with the Cold War as if it were a holy war."[4] He was right. The president's understanding of the Soviets and their worldview was indeed formed in the cauldron of the early Cold War, a time when religious ideas, institutions, and leaders exerted consequential influence upon the assumptions and implementation of U.S. foreign policy.

Reagan's 1980s shared some unmistakable similarities with Eisenhower's 1950s. They were times of relative peace and marked prosperity; the organization man and the yuppie stirred the concerns of social critics; and they were dominated by the anxiety of Cold War. Reagan himself shared something else with Eisenhower: a spiritual understanding of the battle against Communism. His political maturation occurred when the spiritual-industrial complex was at its peak. He fought Communists in Hollywood, then served on organizations like the CPL, and finally toured the nation under the conservative tutelage of an executive from General Electric.[5]

But times and assumptions had changed. Morality had become politicized. The attempt to view foreign policy through a religious prism was met with unease at best and bellowing denunciation at worst. What had been common, even expected, arguments from leaders across American society in the late 1940s and 1950s now seemed backward and even dangerous. Holy war was desired by some but decried by most.

Decades later the United States found itself locked in battle against an opponent that seemed tailor-made for the resurrection of holy war. The attacks of September 11, 2001, brought the world's foremost Christian republic into confrontation with Islamic terrorists. From the choking debris clouds of Manhattan,

Washington, and Pennsylvania, a holy battle cry might have risen. It did not. President George W. Bush announced America's inchoate plans for the coming "War on Terror" in an address before a joint session of Congress on September 20. Backed by the most united populace in a generation, Bush paused in the middle of his address to speak directly to the Muslim world. "We respect your faith," he proclaimed. "Its teachings are good and peaceful. . . . The terrorists are traitors to their own faith."[6] American leaders refused to fight a holy war, notwithstanding some neoconservatives labeling the enemy creed "Islamo-fascism." The Bush administration even forced a lieutenant general who called the Iraq War a battle against Satan to make a series of humbling apologies before a worldwide audience.[7] Fifty years earlier, such a statement may have resulted in an invitation to Valley Forge, a pat on the back from commanding officers, or a quotation in a USIA pamphlet.

When Eisenhower, Chambers, and Hoover passed into memory; when the schools let lapse their prayers; when the national faith drives ended; when the ink of millions on the Freedom Scroll faded with time; when the spiritual-industrial complex dissipated; when the spiritual threat of Communism waned into a mere recollection—did it also mark the end of this story?

Although the rhetoric of holy war is now shunned, the heritage of holy war is still embraced. America may, in the realm of foreign policy, look more like those "secular" nations the U.S. Army scorned in the 1950s, but in many ways its society has used the vestiges of the spiritual-industrial complex as evidence that it remains a "covenant" nation. What separates America from other industrialized nations is not only the extent of its religious beliefs but also the normative values Americans attach to those beliefs. The compulsion some Americans feel to exaggerate their own religiosity on opinion polls is an underappreciated curiosity.[8] Cold War sacralization is certainly not the only, or even the most significant, cause of this trend, but its prescriptive, religious residue has clung stubbornly to American life.

It clings there still. The Baylor Religious Survey was published with fanfare in June 2006. Its scope was unparalleled, but its contents merely confirmed what most people already seemed to know. Ninety-five percent of all Americans professed to believe in God; nine in ten had a specific religious affiliation; and nearly half considered themselves "Bible-believing."[9] The data confirmed two decades' worth of renewed religious vitality. Americans in the twenty-first century proudly proclaimed their religious beliefs. An old word—evangelical—was everywhere in print, television, and cultural conversation.[10] Tim F. LaHaye and Jerry B. Jenkins's ten-part fictionalization of the Rapture was a best-seller; Mel Gibson's controversial depiction of the crucifixion grossed over $370 million in box office receipts; and religiously inspired voters dominated discussions of the

2000 and 2004 presidential elections.[11] George W. Bush courted this emerging demographic and made religious faith a campaign issue. He cast himself as the prodigal son and lauded faith-based solutions to social problems. When asked in a debate to name his favorite political philosopher, he paused and then answered "Jesus Christ." Religious leaders applauded these developments, proclaiming the start of another Great Awakening, and though their claims were overstated, scholars and journalists had good reason to think something extraordinary was occurring in America.

The flexing of such spiritual muscles triggered the instinctive counter reflex of secularists and the bravado of atheists.[12] Outnumbered, the dissenters fought their battles in courtrooms and celebrated an early triumph in San Francisco in June 2002 when the Ninth Circuit Court of Appeals declared the Pledge of Allegiance unconstitutional for its inclusion of the words "under God." Public shock turned quickly into burning indignation. American political and religious leaders howled. They called the decision "junk justice" and "the worst ruling of any federal appellate court in history." The U.S. Senate cast its lot unanimously behind the words "under God," and the House passed the Pledge Protection Act, restricting judicial jurisdiction over the ritual. Hamlets across Tennessee scrambled to enact resolutions affirming their citizens' belief in God; the nation's most prominent newspapers chastised the judges; and most Americans found themselves in uncharacteristic consensus. Sixty percent reported being "very upset" at the circuit-court ruling, and 90 percent favored inclusion of "under God."[13] Nor was the battlefield limited to one courtroom or one issue. While the Pledge of Allegiance case worked its way through the courts, dozens more lawsuits sought removal of Ten Commandments plaques from public spaces across America. Outraged citizens guarded these displays with the same ferocity as they had the Pledge of Allegiance, and legislators in South Dakota, Indiana, and Kentucky responded by passing laws permitting public schools to display the Biblical laws.[14]

Those defending the convergenece of religion and secular culture enlisted history as an ally. With the Pledge of Allegiance controversy at the doors of the Supreme Court, a band of senators and representatives filed an amicus brief arguing that the phrase "under God" described an "indisputable historical fact." Into the brief they sprinkled quotes from the Founding Fathers declaring the importance of religion to society. Farther south, when the chief justice of the Alabama Supreme Court installed a three-ton replica of the Ten Commandments in his courthouse and then attempted to defy a federal court order for its removal, he rallied thousands of Christians who established a makeshift camp on the courthouse lawn. They proclaimed that America was a historically Christian nation, and they accused secularists of rewriting history. "Will you take our Bibles next?" the banner of an eight-year-old girl asked. Conservative commentator Bill O'Reilly summed up these sentiments best. "It is simply unconscionable," he wrote, "for activist judges and fanatical atheists to intrude on the history of the United States."[15]

It is curious that when Americans defend the place of religion within their society, they almost instinctively appeal to history books. They could just as easily point to countless polls revealing the breadth of American religiosity. These facts might provide justification enough for the claim that religion should rightfully exert a powerful influence upon society. America is, after all, a democracy, in which government and societal institutions ought to reflect popular sentiments. Perhaps supporters of this relationship worry that sheer numbers are an insufficient validation or that statistics alone cannot escape the long shadow of the establishment clause. By proving that religious influence and expression are enduring elements of American heritage—an inextricable part of the American way of life—religious and secular leaders make their arguments nearly unassailable. Defenders and opponents of religion's influence on modern society shrewdly focus on the colonial and Revolutionary periods, for demonstrating that America was God's country at the beginning as well as the present offers a powerful illusion of continuity. And so the debate centers on the true religious beliefs and intents of America's founders, as though these were the only positions that counted.[16]

But the two judges of the Ninth Circuit Court who ruled the Pledge of Allegiance unconstitutional, then aged seventy-one and seventy-nine, remembered something most Americans did not: a Pledge without the phrase "under God." Those words are relatively young. So are many of the Decalogue monuments under scrutiny, the national motto "In God We Trust," the printing of that slogan on paper currency, and the very public trips of presidents to their respective churches. When Americans now bristle at the thought of courts rewriting their cherished national history, they have in mind a more distant past, not occurrences within the lifespan of most baby boomers. The Cold War produced more than just religious flotsam and jetsam. It and its early leaders altered the relationship between sacred and secular in America by rallying to the belief—doubted once by secular prophets, religious leaders, and common folk—that religion could be of use not only to individuals but to society as well.

Ronald Reagan was not ad-libbing in 1983; he was reading from an old script.

NOTES

In citing works in the notes, some short titles have generally been used. These works have been identified by the following abbreviations:

APP   John Wooley and Gerhard Peters, eds. *The American Presidency Project.* University of California, Santa Barbara. http://www.presidency. ucsb.edu/.

CDT   *Chicago Daily Tribune*

Eisenhower Papers   *Public Papers of the Presidents of the United States: Dwight D. Eisenhower.* 8 vols. Washington, DC: Government Printing Office, 1960–61.

FDR Papers   *The Public Papers and Addresses of Franklin D. Roosevelt.* 13 vols. New York: Random House, 1938–50.

iPOLL Databank   iPOLL Databank. University of Connecticut, Roper Center for Public Opinion Research. http://www.ropercenter.uconn.edu/ipoll.html.

LAT   *Los Angeles Times*

NEA   *Addresses and Proceedings—National Education Association of the United States*

NYT   *New York Times*

PCRW Papers   Records of the President's Committee on Religion and Welfare in the Armed Forces, Harry S. Truman Presidential Library, Independence, MO.

Truman Papers   *Public Papers of the Presidents of the United States: Harry S. Truman,* 8 vols. Washington, DC: Government Printing Office, 1961–66.

WP   *Washington Post*

Introduction

1. *Chaplains' Character Guidance Manual for Training Divisions and Training Centers* (Carlisle Barracks, PA: The Chaplain School of the United States Army, n.d.), box 10, folder 8, PCRW Papers.
2. Decision of the Executive Committee of the Medyn District Soviet of Workers' deputies, no. 16–257, September 6, 1956, reprinted in *Religion in the Soviet Union: An Archival Reader,* ed. Felix Corley (New York: New York University Press, 1996), 201.
3. Paul Froese, *The Plot to Kill God: Findings from the Soviet Experiment in Secularization* (Berkeley: University of California Press, 2008), 32–33, 52, 58, 60; Michael Burleigh, *Sacred Causes: Religion and Politics from the European Dictators to Al Qaeda* (London: Harper, 2006), 42, 50, 52, 116; Philip Walters, "A Survey of Soviet Religious Policy," in *Religious Policy in the Soviet Union,* ed. Sabrina Petra Ramet (New York: Cambridge University Press, 1993), 13–14; Otto Luchterhandt, "The Council for Religious Affairs," in Ramet,

Religious Policy, 55–83; For an excellent study of organized resistance to religious institutions and beliefs in the Soviet Union, see Daniel Peris, *Storming the Heavens: The Soviet League of the Militant Godless* (Ithaca, NY: Cornell University Press, 1998).

4. These clubs sponsored 120,000 atheist lectures in 1954 alone. The best account of the devotion to Lenin is Nina Tumarkin, *Lenin Lives!: The Lenin Cult in Soviet Russia* (Cambridge, MA: Harvard University Press, 1983).

5. "Break Ground Soon for New Suburb Church," *CDT*, September 9, 1956; "Set Dedication Rites for New Church Today," *CDT*, September 9, 1956; "Break Ground for $575,000 Suburb Church," *CDT*, September 9, 1956; "Church Plans First Services in New Building," *CDT*, September 9, 1956.

6. Many religious histories note the revival of religion in the 1950s, though fewer contextualize it within the broader Cold War. Some place the 1950s religious revival in the context of the 1930s "religious depression," a term popularized in Robert T. Handy, "The American Religious Depression, 1925–1935," *Church History* 29, no. 1 (1960): 3–16. Winthrop S. Hudson and John Corrigan ascribe the revival to the trauma of World War II and call it "formless and unstructured" in *Religion in American Life: An Historical Account of the Development of American Religious Life*, 6th ed. (Upper Saddle River, NJ: Prentice Hall, 1999). Jon Butler, Grant Wacker, and Randall Balmer emphasize the "feel good" theology of Fulton Sheen and Norman Vincent Peale, and they pay excellent attention to the role of religion in civil rights, but they largely ignore the connection between anti-Communism and religion in *Religion in American Life: A Short History* (New York: Oxford University Press, 2003), and Donald C. Swift devotes little attention to Communism in *Religion and the American Experience: A Concise History* (Lanham, MD: Rowman & Littlefield, 1998). Some religious histories do pay significant attention to the connection between 1950s religiosity and anti-Communism, buy they often focus exclusively on the actions and understandings of religious leaders and their respective denominations. See Patrick Allitt, *Religion in America since 1945: A History* (New York: Columbia University Press, 2003); Robert S. Ellwood, *1950: Crossroads of American Religious Life* (Louisville, KY: Westminster John Knox, 2000); and Paul Harvey and Philip Goff, eds., *Religion in America since 1945* (New York: Columbia University Press, 2005). There are, of course, some notable exceptions. For an examination of the impact of the Cold War upon theology, see Ira Chernus, *Nuclear Madness: Religion and the Psychology of the Nuclear Age* (Albany: State University of New York Press, 1991). Martin E. Marty examines the relationship between Eisenhower, Communism, and civil religion in *Modern American Religion: Under God, Indivisible, 1941–1960*, vol. 3 (Chicago: University of Chicago Press, 1996). Some Catholic historians have done the same. See Patrick McNamara, *A Catholic Cold War: Edmund A. Walsh, S. J., and the Politics of American Anticommunism* (New York: Fordham University Press, 2005); Michael J. Epple, *American Crusader: Bishop Fulton J. Sheen's Campaign Against Communism* (PhD diss., University of Akron, 2001); Donald F. Crosby, *God Church, and Flag: Senator Joseph R. McCarthy and the Catholic Church, 1950–1957* (Chapel Hill: University of North Carolina Press, 1978).

7. Dwight D. Eisenhower, "Farewell Radio and Television Address to the American People," January 17, 1961, *Eisenhower Papers*, 8:1035–40.

8. For a brief but illustrative catalog of these highly visible markers of religious revival in the 1950s, see J. Ronald Oakley, *God's Country: America in the Fifties* (New York: Dembner, 1986), 319–27.

9. Nathan O. Hatch's work best represents this view in *The Democratization of American Christianity* (New Haven, CT: Yale University Press, 1989). See also Christine Leigh Heyrman, *Southern Cross: The Beginnings of the Bible Belt* (New York: Knopf, 1997).

10. Public opinion polls conducted in the 1950s consistently showed that while Americans openly professed religious beliefs, they possessed less tangible religious knowledge. For example, only 19 percent of respondents could name one biblical prophet. See Survey by the Gallup Organization, November 11–16, 1954, iPOLL Databank.

11. Survey by the Gallup Organization, February 22–24, 1965, iPOLL Databank.

12. Few cultural histories of Americans in the Cold War fail to mention its religious facet altogether. They include descriptions of Billy Graham's anti-Communist jeremiads or discussions of fanatics like Joe McCarthy who railed against "atheistic Communism." So too do they cite the addition of "under God" to the Pledge of Allegiance. But religion appears rarely in some celebrated cultural and social histories of the early Cold War. See, for instance, Elaine Tyler May, *Homeward Bound: American Families in the Cold War Era*, rev. ed. (New York: Basic Books, 1999) and Jeff Broadwater, *Eisenhower & the Anti-Communism Crusade* (Chapel Hill: University of North Carolina Press, 1992). Oakley's *God's Country* acknowledges the 1950s religious revival but ties it more to anxiety, identity, companionship, and reassurance than to Communism. Fewer works expressly address the place of religion in the Cold War. Stephen J. Whitfield, *The Culture of the Cold War* (Baltimore: Johns Hopkins University Press, 1991) discusses how Americans placed new "value" on religion during the 1950s through the use of ample examples and religious figures. Joel Kovel, *Red Hunting in the Promised Land: Anticommunism and the Making of America* (New York: Basic Books, 1994) situates religion more comprehensively in the culture of America's Cold War by showing how the former helped define the contours of America's postwar spiritual renewal.

13. Using religion as a category through which the Cold War, and foreign policy decisions in particular, can be explained, has become more popular among historians of foreign policy. See Andrew J. Rotter, "Christians, Muslims, and Hindus: Religion and U.S.–South Asian Relations, 1947–1954," *Diplomatic History* 24, no. 4 (2000): 593–622, which argues that "religious ideas infuse states"; Seth Jacobs, "'Our System Demands a Supreme Being': The U.S. Religious Revival and the 'Diem Experiment,' 1954–1955," *Diplomatic History* 25, no. 4 (2001): 589–624; and Andrew Preston, "Bridging the Gap Between the Sacred and the Secular in the History of American Foreign Relations," *Diplomatic History* 30, no. 5 (November 2006): 783–812. Another attempt at focusing on religion in the Cold War is Diane Kirby, ed., *Religion and the Cold War* (New York: Palgrave Macmillan, 2003), which examined not only the United States but events in Europe as well. More recently, a collection of works has emerged that focuses more narrowly on America. William Inboden, *Religion and American Foreign Policy, 1945–1960: The Soul of Containment* (New York: Cambridge University Press, 2008) shows how religious concerns weighed upon the consciences and, in turn, the policies of prominent politicians and policymakers in the international arena. For a treatment of civil religion in the Cold War, see T. Jeremy Gunn, *Spiritual Weapons: The Cold War and the Forging of an American National Religion* (Westport, CT: Praeger, 2009). Other works have addressed the religious nature of the Cold War, though as part of a larger historical sweep. See David S. Foglesong, *The American Mission and the "Evil" Empire* (New York: Cambridge University Press, 2007), which focuses upon the religious prism through which Americans understood Russia from the late nineteenth century to the present; Burleigh, *Sacred Causes*, which notes the quasi-religious qualities of both Nazism and Communism; and Robert Jewett, *Mission and Menace: Four Centuries of American Religious Zeal* (Minneapolis: Fortress, 2008), which devotes a chapter to Cold War American civil religion.

14. See Jon Butler, "Jack-in-the-Box Faith: The Religion Problem in Modern American History," *Journal of American History* 90, no. 4 (2004): 1357–78.

15. The study of religion at the societal level is contested ground between historians and sociologists. Historians often construct narratives where religion acts upon society. But in treating religion as the independent variable, historical analysis risks ignoring the power of the secular to shape the sacred. Unlike historians, sociologists often study how society acts upon religion. In this approach, religion is a malleable and constantly adapting entity—one whose survival and triumph is not guaranteed in a changing environment. But this methodology threatens to drown individual and religious agency in a sea of social forces. As a result, historians have been reluctant to draw upon it. A good example of this hesitancy is

George Marsden, "The Great Divide," *Reviews in American History* 17, no. 2 (1989): 284–88. Marsden critiques sociologist Robert Wuthnow's work for its lack of human initiative and overreliance on statistics to support a methodologically "biased" theory. Still, both methods have much to offer. Sociologists challenge the assumption that religion's role in and importance to society are constant, and historians demonstrate how individuals and specific decisions can alter the trajectories of history. For a discussion of the potential contribution of historical studies to the sociology of religion, see Kevin J. Christiano, "Clio Goes to Church: Revisiting and Revitalizing Historical Thinking in the Sociology of Religion," *Sociology of Religion* 69, no. 1 (2008): 1–28.

16. Peter Berger, *The Sacred Canopy: Elements of a Sociological Theory of Religion* (Garden City, NY: Doubleday, 1967). For an overview of differentiation, see Inger Furseth and Pal Repstad, *An Introduction to the Sociology of Religion* (Burlington, VT: Ashgate, 2006): 84–87.

17. See Hugh McLeod, *Secularisation in Western Europe, 1848–1914* (London: Macmillan, 2000). Callum Brown, *The Death of Christian Britain: Understanding Secularisation, 1800–2000* (London: Routledge, 2001) accepts the theory of secularization and argues that in Britain the trend did not become apparent until the 1960s and 1970s.

18. For finer delineations, see Steve Bruce, ed., *Religion and Modernization: Sociologists and Historians Debate the Secularization Thesis* (Oxford: Clarendon, 1992); Bryan Wilson, "Secularization: The Inherited Model," in *The Sacred in a Secular Age: Toward Revision in the Scientific Study of Religion*, ed. Phillip E. Hammond (Berkeley: University of California Press, 1985), 9–20; and Jeffrey K. Hadden, "Toward Desacralizing Secularization Theory," *Social Forces* 65, no. 3 (1987): 587–611.

19. "Old-school" secularization theorist Bryan R. Wilson recognized this in his first major work on the topic, *Religion in Secular Society: A Sociological Comment* (London: Watts, 1966). Rodney Stark and William Sims Bainbridge presented perhaps the strongest challenge to classical secularization theory by arguing that religion filled important social and psychological roles and would therefore continue to retain its societal significance. See Stark and Bainbridge, *The Future of Religion* (Berkeley: University of California Press, 1985) and Stark and Bainbridge, *A Theory of Religion* (New York: Peter Lang, 1987). Along these lines, Stephen R. Warner, "Work in Progress Toward a New Paradigm for the Sociological Study of Religion in the United States," *American Journal of Sociology* 98, no. 5 (1993): 1044–93, points to anomalous religious data and draws upon the religious-marketplace model to argue that secularization is no longer a valid theory. For an excellent overview of this debate, see David Yamane, "Secularization on Trial: In Defense of a Neosecularization Paradigm," *Journal for the Scientific Study of Religion* 36, no. 1 (1997): 109–22. See also Darren E. Sherkat and Christopher Ellison, "Recent Developments and Current Controversies in the Sociology of Religion," *Annual Review of Sociology* 25 (1999): 363–94. Admittedly, the historical profession has been reluctant to enter into this debate. Perhaps the foray into secularization most discussed across the profession was David A. Hollinger, "The 'Secularization' Question and the United States in the Twentieth Century," *Church History* 70 (2001): 132–43. In it, Hollinger suggested a better term for secularization in America would be "de-Christianization."

20. Mark Chaves, "Secularization as Declining Religious Authority," *Social Forces* 72, no. 3 (1994): 749–74. Chaves argues that secularization can be measured in terms of religious authority rather than religious attendance.

21. Christian Smith, "Future Directions in the Sociology of Religion," *Social Forces* 86, no. 4 (2008): 1561–90; Warren S. Goldstein, "Secularization Patterns in the Old Paradigm," *Sociology of Religion* 70, no. 2 (2009): 159–60.

22. Christian Smith, ed., *The Secular Revolution: Power, Interests, and Conflict in the Secularization of American Public Life* (Berkeley: University of California Press, 2003).

23. Rodney Stark and Roger Finke also use the term "sacralization," which they define as both a breakdown of the lines between sacred and secular as well as the suffusion of basic societal functions with religious symbols and belief. See Stark and Finke, *Acts of Faith:*

Explaining the Human Side of Religion (Berkeley: University of California Press, 2000), 193–217.

Chapter 1

1. See Andrew R. Murphy, *Prodigal Nation: Moral Decline and Divine Punishment from New England to 9/11* (New York: Oxford University Press, 2009), 7–10. Murphy chronicles the cyclical nature of the American jeremiad, paying special attention to Puritans, the Civil War, and the modern Christian Right. He identifies three basic traits of the jeremiad: (1) the claim of a decline relative to the past, (2) a clearly defined turning point, and (3) a call for reform or repentance. In this sense, Toynbee and those who made similar arguments after World War II were participating in this longstanding American tradition.
2. Arnold J. Toynbee, *A Study of History*, abridged (New York: Oxford University Press, 1947).
3. "The Challenge," *Time*, March 17, 1947, 71–79.
4. Toynbee's biographer discusses in detail the editorial decisions made by *Time* and highlights the discrepancies between authorial intent and reader reaction. See William H. McNeill, *Arnold J. Toynbee: A Life* (New York: Oxford University Press, 1989), 213–17.
5. "A Letter from the Publisher," *Time*, April 28, 1947, 17.
6. C. T. Lanham, "The Moral Core of Military Strength," February 16, 1949, box 33, folder 2–c, PCRW Papers.
7. David M. Kennedy, *Freedom from Fear: The American People in Depression and War, 1929–1945* (New York: Oxford University Press), 856–57.
8. This view is most forcefully articulated in Roger Finke and Rodney Stark, *The Churching of America, 1776–1990: Winners and Losers in Our Religious Economy*, 2nd ed. (New Brunswick, NJ: Rutgers University Press, 2005), though one can detect its currents in many other histories of American religion. In their work, for example, Finke and Stark argue that rates of religious adherence among Americans increased from 45 percent in 1890 to 56 percent in 1926.
9. Robert S. Lynd and Helen Merrell Lynd, *Middletown: A Study in American Culture* (New York: Harcourt, Brace, 1929), 518, 522.
10. For a discussion of these criticisms, see Richard Jensen, "The Lynds Revisited," *Indiana Magazine of History*, December 1979, 303–19.
11. Lynd and Lynd, *Middletown*, 358–59.
12. Charles Otis Gill and Gifford Pinchot, *The Country Church: The Decline of Its Influence and the Remedy* (New York: Macmillan, 1913), 77, 166; Edmund DeS. Brunner, "Sociological Significance of Recent Rural Religious Surveys," *American Journal of Sociology* 29, no. 3 (1923): 325–37; Benson T. Landis, *Sedgwick County Kansas: A Church and Community Survey* (New York: Doran, 1922), 55; Elizabeth R. Hooker, *Hinterlands of the Church* (New York: Institute of Social and Religious Research, 1931), 135; R. D. McKenzie, "The Neighborhood: A Study of Local Life in the City of Columbus, Ohio," *American Journal of Sociology* 27, no. 5 (1922): 588.
13. Lynd and Lynd, *Middletown*, 406.
14. Eduard C. Lindeman, *The Church in a Changing Community* (New York: Community Church of New York, 1929), 10–11.
15. Anton T. Boisen, "Factors Which Have to Do with the Decline of the Country Church," *American Journal of Sociology* 22, no. 2 (1916): 180–86.
16. Lynd and Lynd, *Middletown*, 316.
17. George Washington, "Farewell Address," 1796, in *The Writings of George Washington*, ed. John C. Fitzpatrick (Washington, DC: Government Printing Office, 1931), 229.
18. Gordon S. Wood discusses the role of religion as a moral glue for early American society in *The Radicalism of the American Revolution* (New York: Vintage Books, 1991), 330–35.

19. For background on Spencer's theory of social evolution and its impact, see David Wiltshire, *The Social and Political Thought of Herbert Spencer* (Oxford: Oxford University Press, 1978), 192–224; and J. D. Y. Peel, *Herbert Spencer: The Evolution of a Sociologist* (New York: Basic Books, 1971), 131–65.

20. William Graham Sumner, "Religion and the Mores," *American Journal of Sociology* 15, no. 5 (1910): 578–80.

21. See Christian Smith, "Secularizing American Higher Education," in Smith, *The Secular Revolution: Power, Interests, and Conflict in the Secularization of American Public Life* (Berkeley: University of California Press, 2003), 111–14.

22. Louis Wallis, "Biblical Sociology, I," *American Journal of Sociology* 14, no. 2 (1908): 1; Walter L. Sheldon, "The Evolution of Conscience as a Phase of Sociology," *American Journal of Sociology* 8, no. 3 (1902): 360–83; Simon N. Patten, "The Economic Causes of Moral Progress," *Annals of the American Academy of Political and Social Science* 3 (September 1892): 1–21.

23. Walter Lippmann, *A Preface to Morals* (1929; repr., New York: Time Life Books, 1964), 3, 11.

24. Ibid., 344, 348–49, 406.

25. Christian Gauss, "The Decline of Religion," *Scribner's Magazine*, April 1934, 241–46.

26. Bruce Barton, *The Man Nobody Knows: A Discovery of the Real Jesus* (Indianapolis: Bobbs-Merrill, 1925).

27. For an excellent account of Ford's celebrity and decision to implement the five-dollar day, see Steven Watts, *The People's Tycoon: Henry Ford and the American Century* (New York: Knopf, 2005), 173–98.

28. Ibid., 310.

29. Passage of the Eighteenth Amendment is often attributed to the zealous crusade of Protestants who controlled the Women's Christian Temperance Union and the Anti-Saloon League. Methodists and Baptists cheered its passage, Catholics cringed, and Billy Sunday held a mock funeral for John Barleycorn. See Sidney E. Ahlstrom, *A Religious History of the American People* (New Haven, CT: Yale University Press, 1972), 902–4. But though religious groups contributed to Prohibition, they do not deserve sole credit. Prohibition arrived not only because religious interests triumphed after a century of organized complaint, but also because America's business leaders entered the fray. Business titans sought a dependable and productive working class and believed that its creation required a liquor-free society. They donated generous sums of money to ensure passage of dry laws in state legislatures and Congress. For a detailed explanation of these arguments, see John J. Rumbarger, *Profits, Power, and Prohibition: Alcohol Reform and the Industrializing of America, 1800–1930* (Albany: State University of New York Press, 1989). Rumbarger argues that Prohibition was not the maniacal and irrational strand of progressive and evangelical thought that Richard Hofstadter alleges. Rather, he writes, "The roots of the temperance movement can be found in those social forces working together to develop the expansionist tendencies of the American economy."

30. Henry Ford, *My Philosophy of Industry* (New York: Coward-McCann, 1929), 18–19, 45, 101.

31. Lynd and Lynd, *Middletown*, 318.

32. Frank Luther Mott, *American Journalism: A History: 1690–1960* (New York: Macmillan, 1962), 488–90.

33. Malcolm M. Willey and Stuart A. Rice, "The Agencies of Communication," in *Recent Social Trends in the United States*, ed. Wesley C. Mitchell (New York: McGraw-Hill, 1933), 204–6. For a good description of the decline of religious journalism, see Edward Laird Mills, "Religious Journalism—Today and Tomorrow," in *The Church Looks Ahead: American Protestant Christianity*, ed. Charles E. Schofield (New York: Macmillan, 1933), 289–304.

34. Hornell Hart, "Changing Social Attitudes and Interests," in Mitchell, *Recent Social Trends*, 388–89.

35. Ibid., 399.

36. Ibid., 403–5.

37. Richard W. Flory, "Promoting a Secular Standard: Secularization and Modern Journalism, 1870–1930," in Smith, *Secular Revolution*, 395–433.

38. For a detailed portrait of Mencken, see Marion Elizabeth Rodgers, *Mencken: The American Iconoclast* (New York: Oxford University Press, 2005).

39. H. L. Mencken, *Treatise on the Gods* (New York: Knopf, 1930), 304, 324.

40. For a thorough treatment of the work's release and impact, see Richard R. Lingeman, *Sinclair Lewis: Rebel from Main Street* (New York: Random House, 2002), 282–304.

41. Ibid., 284.

42. For a narrative of the Scopes Trial, see Edward J. Larson, *Summer for the Gods: The Scopes Trial and America's Continuing Debate over Science and Religion* (New York: Basic Books, 1997). An excellent collection of primary source documents, including the court transcripts, can be found in Sheldon Norman Grebstein, ed., *Monkey Trial: The State of Tennessee vs. John Thomas Scopes* (Boston: Houghton Mifflin, 1960). The definitive biography of William Jennings Bryan, which includes a nuanced discussion of his religious beliefs, is Michael Kazin, *A Godly Hero: The Life of William Jennings Bryan* (New York: Knopf, 2006).

43. Marcel Chotkowski LaFollette, *Reframing Scopes: Journalists, Scientists, and Lost Photographs from the Trial of the Century* (Lawrence: University Press of Kansas, 2008), 6–10.

44. Charles McD. Puckette, "The Evolution Arena at Dayton," *NYT*, July 5, 1925. John Scopes wrote a memoir of the trial: "Reflections—Forty Years After," in *D-Days at Dayton: Reflections on the Scopes Trial,* ed. Jerry R. Tompkins (Baton Rouge: Louisiana State University Press, 1965), 17–34.

45. "Bryan in Dayton, Calls Scopes Trial Duel to the Death," *NYT*, July 8, 1925; "Commoner's Plea Sways Plain Folk," *NYT*, July 13, 1925.

46. As John T. Scopes noted forty years after the trial, "A court reporter cannot record what two people are saying at the same time, much less what six or seven screaming individuals are saying simultaneously." See Scopes, "Reflections," 27.

47. John T. Scopes, *The World's Most Famous Court Trial: Tennessee Evolution Case* (Cincinnati, OH: National Book Company, 1925), 284–304.

48. "2,000,000 Words Wired to the Press," *NYT*, July 22, 1925.

49. Rollin Lynde Hartt, "What Lies Beyond Dayton," *The Nation*, July 22, 1925, 111; "The Scopes Trial," *CDT*, July 17,1925; "Wronging Mr. Bryan," *NYT*, July 10, 1925.

50. H. L. Mencken, "July 11 Dispatch," in Tompkins, *D-Days at Dayton*, 39; Mencken, "July 18 Dispatch," in ibid., 51.

51. Larson, *Summer for the Gods*, 24.

52. Lynd and Lynd, *Middletown*, 183.

53. Warren A. Nord, *Religion and American Education: Rethinking a National Dilemma* (Chapel Hill: University of North Carolina Press, 1995), 63–75. The most complete and objective study of Horace Mann remains Jonathan Messerli, *Horace Mann: A Biography* (New York: Knopf, 1972).

54. Kraig Beyerlein, "Educational Elites and the Movement to Secularize Public Education: The Case of the National Education Association," in Smith, *Secular Revolution*, 163.

55. Ibid., 165.

56. For a detailed examination of faith in education and the evolution of education reform, see David Tyack and Larry Cuban, *Tinkering with Utopia: A Century of Public School Reform* (Cambridge, MA: Harvard University Press, 1995).

57. Vernon L. Bowyer, Olice Winter, and Gilbert H. Wilkinson, eds., *Character Education* (Chicago: Chicago Principal's Club, 1931), 3–4.

58. Edmund J. James, "The Relation of the Church to Higher Education in the United States," *NEA* 43 (1904): 69.

59. Read Bain, "Religious Attitudes of College Students," *American Journal of Sociology* 32, no. 5 (1927), 764.

60. Beyerlein argues that the secularization of public education was the result of a bitter struggle between elites. George M. Thomas, Lisa R. Peck, and Channin G. De Haan also portray the relationship between education and religion as more of a struggle, focusing on progressive educational elites in their chapter "Reforming Education, Transforming Religion, 1876–1931," in Smith, *Secular Revolution*, 355–94.

61. George M. Marsden concludes that the secularization of the American academy began around 1870, though he argues that it did not intensify until after World War I. Marsden concludes that secularization was the result of demands for a broader curriculum and fears that schools controlled by clerics could not produce the sort of scholars American society would need to compete on a world stage. See George M. Marsden, "The Soul of the American University: An Historical Overview," in *The Secularization of the Academy*, ed. George M. Marsden and Bradley J. Longfield (New York: Oxford University Press, 1992), 10–14.

62. Harry Pratt Judson, "Religion in the Public Schools," *Elementary School Teacher* 9, no. 5 (1909): 223, 226.

63. W. T. Harris, "The Separation of the Church from the School Supported by Taxes," *NEA* 42 (1903), 353.

64. George U. Wenner, *Religious Education and the Public School* (New York: American Tract Society, 1907), 1. One important, though impressionistic, indicator of evolving attitudes toward religion in American education was the progression of history textbooks, especially in their changing depictions of Puritans. Antebellum texts often portrayed Puritan society positively, emphasizing its virtue. Here the "Pilgrim Fathers" were "moved by religious devotion and sustained by Providence." One text informed students that reverence, intelligence, and morality were "things for which we have to thank the piety and wisdom of the Puritans." See Emma Willard, *History of the United States* (Philadelphia: Barnes, 1845), 29; and Samuel G. Goodrich, *The First Book of History* (New York: Collins and Hannay, 1833), 45. But these accounts set up New England's first European settlers for a textual fall from grace. By the turn of the twentieth century, textbooks were no longer celebratory of Puritanism. They focused upon Puritan intolerance, provincialism, and tyranny. "The Puritan mind seemed to revel in gloomy, bitter, and terrible thoughts," explained one 1904 textbook geared toward elementary schools. "The songs were sad and mournful. The sermons dwelt upon the horrors of everlasting punishment, the sinfulness of man, and the wrath of God." The same text devoted an entire chapter to the Salem witch trials, calling them "madness." See Henry Sabin and Elbridge H. Sabin, *Early American History for Young Americans* (Boston: Educational Publishing Company, 1904), 132. A textbook designed for high school and university students was even harsher, claiming that Puritan clergy ruled like tyrants, punishing or even killing those who disagreed and subverting the legal system for their own self-righteous ends. Nor did the Puritan spirit fade after the Revolutionary War. According to the text, in nineteenth-century New England, "amusements were largely frowned upon, dancing was not allowed, the theater was prohibited, and the players of football found little favor in the eyes of the rulers." See S. E. Forman, *Advanced American History*, rev. ed. (New York: Educational Publishing Company, 1924), 70–71. For more examples of this portrayal of Puritanism, see James Alton James and Albert Hart Sanford, *American History* (New York: Scribner's, 1909); and Fanny E. Coe, *Founders of Our Country* (New York: American Book Company, 1912). The Massachusetts Bay Colony became a moral foil—a piercing example of the dangers wrought by a society without freedom of religion. The contrast between Puritan society and the freedom of religion granted by the Founding Fathers could not have been lost on students or teachers. After discussing the Constitution, most texts abandoned discussions of religion altogether, except for an occasional mention of Mormonism or other sects created in antebellum America. Religion did appear again after the Civil War in one popular history textbook, but only in the context of secularization. "The church finds it difficult to compete with the many agencies clamoring for the leisure of the city dweller on Sunday mornings or weekday evenings," it explained in a line that could have been lifted directly from the Lynds. "Many complain that the church

and the home have surrendered their function of developing the character of citizens to the school." See William A. Hamm, *The American People* (Boston, Heath, 1938), 587.

65. Clifford W. Barnes, "Moral Training Thru the Agency of the Public School," *NEA* 45 (1907), 373.

66. Reed B. Tertrick and Henry G. Williams, "The School as an Instrument of Character-Building," *NEA* 46 (1908), 248.

67. Bowyer, Winter, and Wilkerson, *Character Education*, 5–12.

68. Ibid., 5–6; Wendell P. Garrison, *Parables for School and Home* (Boston: Longmans, Green, 1897).

69. Tertrick and Williams, "The School as an Instrument," 250; Department of the Interior, Bureau of Education, *Character Education: Report of the Committee on Character Education of the National Education Association*, no. 7 (1926): 13–15.

70. David Tyack and Elisabeth Hansot, *Managers of Virtue: Public School Leadership in America, 1820–1980* (New York: Basic Books, 1982), 114–15.

71. Wenner, *Religious Education*, 1; R. Freeman Butts, *The American Tradition in Religion and Education* (Boston: Beacon, 1950), 199–200.

72. *Report of the Committee on Character Education*, 13–15.

73. For explanations of the Baconian model, see George M. Marsden, *Fundamentalism and American Culture: The Shaping of Twentieth-Century Evangelicalism, 1870–1925* (New York: Oxford University Press, 1980), 109–18; and Walter J. Wilkins, *Science and Religious Thought: A Darwinism Case Study* (Ann Arbor: University of Michigan Research Press, 1987). George E. Webb provides a well-written account of Darwin's impact in *The Evolution Controversy in America* (Lexington: University Press of Kentucky, 1994), 1–5. See also Wilkins, *Science and Religious Thought*, 29.

74. Henry Ward Beecher, "Progress of Thought in the Church," *North American Review*, August 1882, 99–117; Charles Hodge, *What is Darwinism?* (New York: Scribner, Armstrong, 1874).

75. James H. Leuba, "Religious Beliefs of American Scientists," *Harper's*, August 1934, 296.

76. Charles E. Rosenberg attributes the surprising lack of conflict between religion and science throughout the nineteenth century to the fact that almost all Americans accepted the conclusions of Darwin. *No Other Gods: On Science and American Social Thought* (Baltimore: Johns Hopkins Press, 1961).

77. For an overview of these developments and the triumphal view of science, see Wendy R. Sherman and Trich Yourst Koontz, *Science and Society in the Twentieth Century* (Westport, CT: Greenwood, 2004).

78. Harry Emerson Fosdick, "Will Science Displace God?" *Harper's*, August 1926, 363.

79. See Clifford Kirkpatrick, *Religion in Human Affairs* (New York: Wiley, 1929).

80. John Herman Randall, Jr., *Our Changing Civilization: How Science and the Machine are Reconstructing Human Life* (New York: Stokes, 1929), 269; Mencken, *Treatise on the Gods*, 297–98.

81. For an account of this psychological impact, see Kennedy, *Freedom from Fear*, 164–66.

82. "U.S. Called in Grip of Spiritual Slump," *WP*, November 27, 1931.

83. "Has the Depression Brought People Back to the Church?" *LAT*, April 16, 1933; "Wagner Prescribes Faith to End Gloom," *NYT*, February 9, 1931; "Predicts Revival of Faith," *NYT*, November 24, 1930; "National Fast Day Urged on Hoover," *NYT*, July 27, 1931.

84. Though social scientists opened the door to a new conception of morality, national Progressive leaders pulled much of the nation across the threshold. From the comfort of their bully pulpits, Theodore Roosevelt and Woodrow Wilson appeared to toe George Washington's century-old line regarding the importance of faith in regulating public morality. They attended church regularly and often spoke of the power of religion. But they believed the state, and not the church, could be the primary instrument of justice, cleansing, and righteousness. For detailed and balanced overviews of the faith of both Wilson and Roosevelt, see Gary Scott Smith, *Faith and the Presidency: From George Washington to George W. Bush* (New York: Oxford University Press, 2006), 129–90. In his 1912 speech before the

Bull-Moose convention, Roosevelt deconstructed the traditional view that government power was inimical to liberty. Rather, he pleaded, increased government authority was needed to protect liberty and justice. See Theodore Roosevelt, "The New Nationalism," in *Progressivism: The Critical Issues*, ed. David M. Kennedy (Boston: Little, Brown, 1971), 51. Wilson refused to embrace "the cool process of mere science," but he too rejected the notion that the moral impulse was entirely reducible to religion. Like Roosevelt, Wilson sought to perfect the means "by which government can be put at the service of humanity." See Woodrow Wilson, "Inaugural Address," March 4, 1913, in *The Papers of Woodrow Wilson*, vol. 27, ed. Arthur S. Link (Princeton, NJ: Princeton University Press, 1978), 148–52. The pulpit may have been a sufficient instrument in the Jeffersonian world of the yeoman, but modern society required new agents. Some scholars who have studied the Progressive era conclude that religious institutions and leaders became displaced. Richard Hofstadter and Robert Wiebe offer substantially different interpretations of Progressive Era America, but both agree that religion was the one of the movement's greatest casualties. Hofstadter argues that America's religious leaders "were probably the most conspicuous losers from the status revolution" since secularization reduced their "capacity as moral and intellectual leaders." Wiebe contends that the developing professional class built a "new structure of loyalties to replace the decaying system of the nineteenth-century communities." Religion, associated with the old order, suffered. For Hofstadter, American reform was the progeny of status anxiety amongst America's once comfortable middle-class professionals, whereas Wiebe conceptualizes Progressivism as the rise of a new breed of professionals trying to impose a revolutionary order upon the rapidly disintegrating "island communities" of the nineteenth century. See Richard Hofstadter, *The Age of Reform* (New York: Knopf 1956), 150; and Robert Wiebe, *The Search for Order* (New York: Hill and Wang, 1967), 129, 150. This is not to obscure the ways that religion was deeply connected to the surge of Progressivism. The era provided a rich seedbed for reform-minded Christians—an environment where optimism flowed freely before such ideals foundered in the tempests of war and depression. Major reform groups like the Women's Christian Temperance Union wielded significant influence. Walter Rauschenbusch, who ministered to the misfortunate of New York's infamous Hell's Kitchen, became the foremost spokesman for the Social Gospel movement. His 1907 publication *Christianity and the Social Crisis* argued that Christians must take on the task of creating a new social order, and Washington Gladden, one of America's most recognized ministers, denounced the nation's rapacious system of free enterprise. In California, where Progressives managed a wide array of societal reforms, the movement's leaders shared three basic traits: they were white, middle class, and solidly Protestant. See Paul M. Minus, *Walter Rauschenbusch: An American Reformer* (New York: Macmillan, 1988); George E. Mowry, *The California Progressives* (Chicago: Quandrangle Books, 1963); and Ahlstrom, *Religious History*, 785–804.

85. "Faith Needed Now, Roosevelt Says," *NYT*, September 9, 1939; "President Extols Methodist Council," *NYT*, February 4, 1938.

86. Civil religion is a broad field of study. In his seminal essay on the subject, Robert N. Bellah argued that civil religion was "an understanding of the American experience in the light of ultimate and universal reality." Bellah, "Civil Religion in America," *Dædalus* 96, no. 1 (1967): 1–21. Donald G. Jones and Russell E. Richey identify five distinct forms of civil religion in "The Civil Religion Debate," in *American Civil Religion*, ed. Russell E. Richey and Donald G. Jones (New York: Harper and Row, 1974). Will Herberg contends that civil religion is best understood as the "American Way of Life," a system of values that constitute a common faith for all Americans. See Herberg, "America's Civil Religion: What It Is and Whence It Comes," in Jones and Richey, *American Civil Religion*, 77. Since these initial forays, historians have demonstrated a tendency to expand the category of civil religion. The danger, of course, is that every ritual, every mention of God, and every parade becomes part of this increasingly expansive concept.

87. Frank S. Adams, "President's Eucharistic Message Bases Peace on Sermon on Mount," *NYT*, October 18, 1938.

88. "Berle Sr. in Church Talk," *NYT*, February 12, 1934; "Churches Urged to Support NRA," *NYT*, August 28, 1933; "Fosdick Proposes a Personal Code," *NYT*, October 16, 1933; "Dr. Fosdick Says Our Refusal of New Deal Will Result in Fascism or Communism," *NYT*, January 8, 1934.

89. "Ickes Asks Church to Aid New Deal," *NYT*, May 24, 1934; "Recovery Drive Opened by 3 Faiths," *NYT*, September 23, 1935.

90. Ronald Isetti, "The Moneychangers of the Temple: FDR, American Civil Religion, and the New Deal," *Presidential Studies Quarterly* 26, no. 3 (1996): 688. Isetti provides an excellent examination of Roosevelt's use of religious imagery. See also "Roosevelt a New Moses," *NYT*, January 29, 1934.

91. This portrait of Hopkins is drawn from Robert E. Sherwood, *Roosevelt and Hopkins: An Intimate History* (New York: Harper, 1950).

92. William E. Leuchtenburg noted that "Franklin Roosevelt personified the state as protector" in *Franklin D. Roosevelt and the New Deal, 1932–1940* (New York: Harper Torchbooks, 1965), 331; Lizabeth Cohen, *Making a New Deal: Industrial Workers in Chicago, 1919–1939* (New York: Cambridge University Press, 1990), 285.

93. "Holds Roosevelt is Not a Messiah," *NYT*, December 6, 1933.

94. Cohen, *Making a New Deal*, 269–70.

95. "Peale Sees Nation in New Revolution," *NYT*, January 8, 1934.

96. Franklin D. Roosevelt, "Extemporaneous Address at the Hyde Park Methodist Episcopal Church," September 29, 1933, *FDR Papers*, 2:365–70.

97. Franklin D. Roosevelt, "Remarks at Thanksgiving Dinner, Warm Springs, Georgia," November 23, 1939, *FDR Papers*, 8:582–86.

98. Morris Markey, *This Country of Yours* (Boston: Little, Brown, 1932), 307–8.

99. U.S. Bureau of the Census, *Religious Bodies, 1936*, vol. 1 (Washington, DC: Government Printing Office, 1936), 51, 314–15. Not all denominations suffered losses. Catholics grew a steady 7 percent, and the Mormons grew a considerable 25 percent.

100. Robert S. Lynd and Helen Merrell Lynd, *Middletown in Transition: A Study in Cultural Conflicts* (New York: Harcourt, Brace, 1937), 297–318.

101. For a valuable overview of the immigrant Church see Jay P. Dolan, *The Immigrant Catholic Experience: A History from Colonial Times to Present* (Garden City, NY: Doubleday, 1985); James Stuart Olson, *Catholic Immigrants in America* (Chicago: Nelson-Hall, 1987); Randall M. Miller and Thomas Marzik, eds., *Immigrants and Religion in Urban America* (Philadelphia: Temple University Press, 1977). For more detailed examinations of immigrant Catholic parishes, see Edward Kantowicz, "Church and Neighborhood," *Ethnicity* 7 (1980): 349–66; Raymond Mohl and Neil Betten, "The Immigrant Church in Gary, Indiana: Religious Adjustment and Cultural Defense," *Ethnicity* 8 (1981): 2–3. For an excellent study of the immigrant Catholic laity, see David A. Gerber, "Modernity in the Service of Tradition: Catholic Lay Trustees at Buffalo's St. Louis Church and the Transformation of European Communal Traditions, 1829–1855," *Journal of Social History* 1, no. 4 (1982): 655–84. For an examination of immigrant conflict with the Catholic hierarchy, see Daniel S. Buczek, "Polish Americans and the Roman Catholic Church," *Polish Review* 21, no. 1 (1976): 39–61; Jonathan Herzog, "Our Sacred Lithuanian Word: St. Anthony's Thirst for Cultural Homogeneity," *Nebraska History* 84, no. 3 (2003):133–41; and Leslie Woodcock Tentler, "Who is the Church? Conflict in a Polish Immigrant Parish in Late Nineteenth-Century Detroit," *Comparative Studies in Society and History* 25, no. 2 (1983): 241–76.

102. For a detailed examination of the Catholic Church in Chicago during the Great Depression, see Cohen, *Making a New Deal*, which views the depression as a significant challenger to Catholic legitimacy and authority.

103. Frank D. Alexander, "Religion in a Rural Community of the South," *American Sociological Review* 6, no. 2 (1941): 341–51. Though it was not published until 1941, Alexander conducted his study in 1937.

104. James West, *Plainville, U.S.A.* (New York: Columbia University Press, 1945). West conducted his research in 1939.

105. Franklin D. Roosevelt, "State of the Union Address," January 6, 1942, *FDR Papers*, 11:32–42; Franklin D. Roosevelt, "Letter Accepting the Annual Award of the Churchman," June 8, 1942, *FDR Papers*, 11:258–59.

106. Franklin D. Roosevelt, "Christmas Greeting to the Nation," December 24, 1940, *FDR Papers*, 9:631–33; Franklin D. Roosevelt, "Christmas Eve Message to the Nation," December 24, 1941, *FDR Papers*, 10:593–95.

107. These statistics were drawn from Hadley Cantril, *Public Opinion, 1935–1946* (Princeton, NJ: Princeton University Press, 1951), 699–700, 742–45, 790–91, 1152.

108. "Imperialism of righteousness" comes from the best short account of religious leaders in the Spanish-American War: Julius Pratt, *Expansionists of 1898* (Chicago: Quandrangle Paperbacks, 1936), 279–316. William Archibald Karraker's *The American Churches and the Spanish-American War* (PhD diss., University of Chicago, 1940) carefully catalogs American religious opinion through each phase of the war, demonstrating the remarkable degree of avowed loyalty to the U.S. war effort across the entire spectrum of Christian faiths. To date, Frank Reuter, *Catholic Influence of American Colonial Policies, 1898–1904* (Austin: University of Texas Press, 1967) remains the best comprehensive account of American Catholic reaction to expansionism, though Reuter focuses primarily on the annexations that followed the initial conflict. Like Pratt and Karracker, he affirms the loyalty and patriotism of American Catholics and touches upon the Church's defensiveness in response to Protestant criticism. Winthrop Hudson, in his essay "Protestant Clergy Debate the Nation's Vocation, 1898–1899," *Church History* 42, no. 1 (1973): 110–18, departs from the "imperialism of righteousness" argument to contend that key Protestant leaders only reluctantly embraced the war with Spain and that their disillusionment with the war's aftermath led the U.S. to abandon its burgeoning imperialistic policies. Likewise, much has been written on the role of American religion during World War I. The classic account is Ray H. Abrams, *Preachers Present Arms* (Scottdale, PA: Herald, 1969). See also Elizabeth McKeown, *War and Welfare: American Catholics and World War I* (New York: Garland, 1988). McKeown argues that World War I was the first occasion when a large number of Catholics "learned to adopt a national outlook when the United States intervened in Europe." Perhaps the best institutional account is John F. Piper, Jr., *The American Churches in World War I* (Athens, OH: Ohio University Press, 1985). More recently, Richard Gamble has traced the attitudes and actions of American clergy during World War I, arguing that they not only abandoned previous pacifist tendencies in favor of confrontation but actively promoted the war from the pulpit as well. See Gamble, *The War for Righteousness: Progressive Christianity, the Great War, and the Rise of the Messianic Nation* (Wilmington, DE: Intercollegiate Studies Institute, 2003).

109. The most encompassing study of American religion during World War II is Gerald L. Sittser, *A Cautious Patriotism: The American Churches and the Second World War* (Chapel Hill: University of North Carolina Press, 1997). Sittser finds that American religious leaders remained remarkably restrained throughout the conflict, especially compared to World War I. For information on pacifism within American Christianity, see Cynthia Eller, *Conscientious Objectors and the Second World War* (New York: Praeger, 1991).

110. "War and Peace," *Fortune*, January 1940, 26–27; Abrams, *Preachers Present Arms*, 263; "The Church and the War," *Time*, February 3, 1941, 35; Cantril, *Public Opinion*, 790.

111. F. Ernest Johnson, "The Impact of the War on Religion in America," *American Journal of Sociology* 48, no. 3 (1942): 359.

112. Ibid., 355.

113. Nazism, like Communism, had undeniable religious properties, such as the propagation of paganism. See Burleigh, *Sacred Causes*, 116.

114. Quoted in Steven Merritt Miner, *Stalin's Holy War: Religion, Nationalism, and Alliance Politics, 1941–1945* (Chapel Hill: University of North Carolina Press, 2003), 221.

115. Franklin D. Roosevelt, "Excerpts from the Press Conference," September 30, 1941, *FDR Papers*, 10:399–403.

Chapter 2

1. Whittaker Chambers, *Witness* (New York: Random House, 1952), 83.
2. Ibid., 9.
3. Ibid., 11.
4. Walter Lippmann, *Drift and Mastery: An Attempt to Diagnose the Current Unrest* (New York: Kennerly, 1914).
5. Chambers, *Witness*, 449–50.
6. Richard Crossman, ed., *The God That Failed* (1949; repr., New York: Harper, 1972), 15–16.
7. Louis F. Budenz, *This Is My Story* (New York: McGraw-Hill, 1947), 347–71; Fulton J. Sheen, *Communism Answers Questions of a Communist* (Los Angeles: Tidings, 1945), 4–5; "Daily Worker Editor Renounces Communism for Catholic Faith," *NYT*, October 11, 1945; "Says Russia Plots to Rule the World," *NYT*, October 13, 1946.
8. Kathryn S. Olmsted, *Red Spy Queen: A Biography of Elizabeth Bentley* (Chapel Hill: University of North Carolina Press, 2002), 147; "Elizabeth Bentley, Former Soviet Spy, Becomes a Catholic," *CDT*, November 17, 1948.
9. See Elizabeth Bentley, *Out of Bondage* (New York: Devin-Adair, 1951); "Fools for Christ," *Time*, May 24, 1948, 56–57; Crossman, *The God that Failed I Was a Communist*; Alexei B. Liberov, *I Was a Communist* (New York: International Catholic Truth Society, 1936); Alexander Barmine, *One Who Survived* (New York: Putnam, 1945); and Victor Kravchenko, *I Chose Freedom* (Garden City, NY: Garden City Publishing, 1946). While *The God that Failed* certainly constructed Communism as a faith, some contributors like Richard Wright did not return to an organized religion after leaving.
10. Sam Tanenhaus, *Whittaker Chambers: A Biography* (New York: Random House, 1997), 461–62; "Best Sellers and Best Renters," *Retail Bookseller*, July 1952, 34.
11. Hundreds of these reviews, from large and small outlets, are collected in box 31 of the the Sam Tanenhaus Papers, Hoover Institution Archives, Stanford, CA (hereafter cited as Tanenhaus Papers).
12. Transcript, Robert Montgomery, "A Citizen Views the News," May 29, 1952, Tanenhaus Papers, box 31; Review, *Kansas City Star*, May 18, 1952; "A Witness—God Versus Communism," *Church Herald*, July 4, 1952; Paul Hutchinson, "Review," *Christian Century*, June 18, 1952; James M. Gillis, Review Press Release, June 2, 1952, box 31, Tanenhaus Papers; Irving Howe, "God, Man, and Stalin," *The Nation*, May 24, 1952, 502–4; "Chambers a Witness for Capitalism," *Weekly People*, July 19, 1952.
13. Some sociologists have expounded a broad definition of religion that includes scientific humanism, Marxism, and civil religion, but many others contend that a true religion must involve some concept of a higher power. As two noted sociologists of religion declared in 1985, "A religion lacking supernatural assumptions is no religion at all." Rejection of the supernatural is a central tenet of Communism, so in an academic sense it may not be a religion at all. See Rodney Stark and William Sims Bainbridge, *The Future of Religion* (Berkeley: University of California Press, 1985), 3–8.
14. See Peter G. Filene, *Americans and the Soviet Experiment, 1917–1933* (Cambridge, MA: Harvard University Press, 1967) for an excellent examination of the USSR and American political and popular opinion. Also see Filene, *American Views of Soviet Russia, 1917–1965* (Homewood, IL: Dorsey, 1968). The best treatment of the history of Communism and anti-Communism in America is Richard Gid Powers, *Not Without Honor: The History of American Anticommunism* (New York: Free Press, 1995). Powers offers a particularly compelling interpretation built upon the interactions of three groups in American society, which prevents the work from descending into a predictable

examination of reactionary anti-Communism: radicals, liberals, and conservative anti-Communists.

15. Martin E. Marty explores the religious facets of the Red Scare in *Modern American Religion*. Vol. 2, *The Noise of Conflict 1919–1941* (Chicago: University of Chicago Press, 1991), 66–79.

16. Russian Red Vents Hatred on Church," *NYT*, July 20, 1919; Harold Denny, "Slowly Religion is Starving in Russia," *NYT*, May 12, 1935. For a sample of period reports on the religious situation in Russia during the 1920s, see "Church in Soviet Russia," *American Review of Reviews*, November 1921; E. R. Hapgood, "Sermon, Soviet Style," *Independent*, April 23, 1921; "The Soviet War on Religion," *NYT*, April 8, 1922; "Red Church in Russia," *Literary Digest*, October 14, 1922; "How Bolshevism is Overwhelming the Russian Church," *Current Opinion*, June 1923; "Russia's Living Church," *NYT*, May 1, 1923; "Religious Melee in Russia," *Literary Digest*, May 26, 1923. It is important to note that American leaders had paid attention to the religious situation in Russia long before the Bolshevik Revolution. David Foglesong notes that in 1892 both the Republican and Democratic party platforms included criticisms of Russian hostility toward religion. See Foglesong, *The American Mission and the "Evil" Empire* (New York: Cambridge University Press, 2007), 25.

17. The best study of Laski's influence upon American thought is Gary Dean Best, *Harold Laski and American Liberalism* (New Brunswick, NJ: Transaction, 2005). Fulton Sheen quoted Laski more than two decades after his publication of *Communism* in his influential *Communism and the Conscience of the West* (Indianapolis: Bobbs-Merrill, 1948), as did Reinhold Niebuhr in *Moral Man and Immoral Society* (New York: Scribner's, 1932).

18. Harold J. Laski, *Communism* (New York: Holt, 1927), 159–61.

19. Little was written in English during this early period of conflict between the Bolshevik government and the Russian Orthodox Church. See Richard J. Cooke, *Religion in Russia Under the Soviets* (New York: Abingdon, 1924); and R. O. G. Urch, "Bolshevism and Religion in Russia," *Atlantic Monthly*, March 1923, 394–405.

20. "Russians Execute Mgr. Butchkavitch; Moscow Defiant," *NYT*, April 4, 1923; "Shot Vicar in Back of the Head," *NYT*, April 5, 1923. Peter G. Filene provides an excellent summary of the secular and religious newspaper reaction surrounding Buchkavich's death, noting that many Protestants and Jews were hesitant to directly assail the USSR throughout the 1920s and 1930s (Filene, *American Views*).

21. Francis McCullagh, "The Bolshevik War on Religion," *Commonweal*, January 28, 1925, 315–18; Lawrence Maynard Grey, "Religion in Russia Today," *Commonweal*, January 12, 1927, 266–68.

22. Sherwood Eddy, "Russia—Good and Evil," *Christian Century*, September 18, 1935, 1171–72. The two previous years produced three books of observations of the USSR and religion. See Sherwood Eddy, *Russia Today: What Can We Learn from It?* (New York: Farrar and Rinehart 1934); George Mecklenburg, *Russia Challenges Religion* (New York: Abingdon, 1934); and V. Ph. Martzinkovski, *With Christ in Soviet Russia* (Prague: Knihtiskárna V. Horák, 1933).

23. V. I. Lenin, *Religion* (New York: International Publishers, 1933). Few treatments of Communism and religion in the interwar years failed to mention some version of this famous quotation.

24. See James G. Ryan, *Earl Browder: The Failure of American Communism* (Tuscaloosa: University of Alabama Press, 1997).

25. Earl Browder, *Religion and Communism* (New York: Workers Library, 1935), 3.

26. Earl Browder, *What is Communism?* (New York: Workers Library, 1936), 146.

27. Ibid., 146; Earl Browder, *A Message to Catholics* (New York: Workers Library, 1938). The Foster quote is taken from Eugene Lyons, *The Red Decade: The Stalinist Penetration of America* (Indianapolis: Bobbs-Merrill, 1941), 170–82. Lyons, a former Communist himself, argued that in the 1930s Browder and others tried to Americanize Communism and make it appear that the movement was the true inheritor of the "Spirit of '76."

28. Harry F. Ward, "Christians and Communists," *Christian Century*, December 25, 1935, 1651–53. Ward was not the only Christian Communist contributing to the *Christian Century*. See also E. A. Havelock, "Must Christians Reject Communism?" *Christian Century*, October 16, 1935, 1307–8. Havelock referred to Communism as a "sublime faith" that could be reconciled with Christianity.

29. Special Committee on Un-American Activities, *Investigation of Un-American Propaganda in the United States*, vol. 1 (Washington, DC: Government Printing Office, 1938), 1.

30. Powers, *Not Without Honor*, 124–29.

31. Testimony of John P. Frey, *Investigation of Un-American Propaganda* 1:136–37.

32. Testimony of Walter S. Steele, *Investigation of Un-American Propaganda* 1:365–400; Statement of H. L. Chaillaux, *Investigation of Un-American Propaganda* 1:429–55; National Americanism Committee of the American Legion, *Isms: A Review of Alien Isms, Revolutionary Communism and their Active Sympathizers in the United States* (Indianapolis: American Legion, 1937), 246–65.

33. Martin Dies, *The Trojan Horse in America* (New York: Dodd, Mead, 1940), 4–7.

34. Ibid., 240; Martin Dies, "More Snakes Than I Can Kill," *Liberty Magazine*, February 10, 1940, 42.

35. Isaac F. Marcosson, "After Lenine—What? The Future Russia," *Saturday Evening Post*, February 14, 1925, 31, 129, 133.

36. For an outstanding examination of Niebuhr's life and the evolutionary of his theology, see Richard Wightman Fox, *Reinhold Niebuhr: A Biography* (New York: Pantheon Books, 1985).

37. Reinhold Niebuhr, "The Religion of Communism," *Atlantic Monthly*, April 1931, 462–70.

38. Ibid., 468. One year later Niebuhr refined some of these views in *Moral Man and Immoral Society*. He argued that Marxism combined a powerful sense of moral cynicism with equalitarian social idealism—a potent and intoxicating but altogether untenable formula. His 1932 book was more critical of Marxism than his 1931 article, demonstrating that his stance was hardening already.

39. Nicholas Berdyaev, "Russian Religious Psychology and Communistic Atheism," in *Vital Realities*, ed. Carl Schmitt et al., (New York: Macmillan, 1932), 105–49; Berdyaev, "The Religion of Communism," in ibid., 149–86.

40. Henry Black, "Religion and Communism—A Parallel," *Christian Century*, June 27, 1934, 861–62; H. G. Wood, *Christianity and Communism* (New York: Round Table, 1933), 3–4; F. J. Sheed, *Communism and Man* (New York: Sheed & Ward, 1938), 155.

41. Abba Gordin, *Communism Unmasked* (New York: Hord, 1940), 31, 50–51, 55–57. See also E. G. Lee, *Christianity in Chains* (London: Longmans, Green, 1939). Lee argued that Communism was actually a form of "secular mysticism."

42. Harry F. Ward, "Will Religion Survive in Russia?" *Christian Century*, February 12, 1945, 217.

43. Quoted from Doug Rossinow, "The Radicalization of the Social Gospel: Harry F. Ward and the Search for a New Social Order, 1898–1936," *Religion and American Culture* 15, no. 1 (Winter 2005): 79; for more examples of liberal Protestant admiration of the Soviet Union, see Foglesong, *American Mission*, 79.

44. Matthew Spinka, *Christianity Confronts Communism* (London: Religious Book Club, 1938), 165–95.

45. Pope Pius XI, *Atheistic Communism* (New York: Paulist Press, 1937).

46. Walter Reynolds to William F. Montavon, December 28, 1931, box 23, folder 19, National Catholic Welfare Conference Papers, American Catholic History Research Center, Catholic University, Washington, DC (hereafter cited as NCWC Papers); "Communism in the United States," 1937, box 23, folder 20, NCWC Papers.

47. "W. R. Hearst Lauds Catholic Church's Stand against Communism," *New York American*, December 11, 1935.

48. The *Commonweal*, a liberal Catholic journal, provided a platform for critiques of Communism, and rarely did an issue pass without some reference to that system. See William

Thomas Walsh, "Is Communism Dangerous?" *Commonweal*, February 8, 1935, 421. See also Catherine Radziwill, "Bolshevism—A Universal Danger," *Commonweal*, April 22, 1925, 653–55; Paul Scheffer, "Moscow and the Churches," *Commonweal*, April 23, 1930, 701–3; and F. J. McGarrigle, "The Soviet Religion," *Commonweal*, February 8, 1935, 177–79.

49. Eugene Kevane, "The Depths of Bolshevism," *Commonweal*, September 3, 1937, 433–35.

50. Pius XI, *Atheistic Communism*, 1; "Catholics Pledge Aid to Hitler Anew in War on the Reds," *NYT*, January 2, 1937; Fabian Flynn, *Catholicism, Americanism and Communism* (New York: Paulist Press, 1937), 14.

51. Pius XI, *Atheistic Communism*, 7; Joseph F. MacDonnell, *Religion and the Social Revolution* (New York: America, 1937), 234–35, Hoover Institution Pamphlet Collection on Religion and Communism, Hoover Institution, Stanford, California (hereafter cited as Hoover Pamphlet Collection). MacDonnell's speeches were also reprinted in the *Pilot*, Boston's predominant Catholic weekly.

52. Patrick McNamara, *A Catholic Cold War: Edmund A. Walsh, S. J., and the Politics of American Anticommunism* (New York: Fordham University Press, 2005), 10–106. Walsh contributed two important works to the burgeoning observations of religion in Soviet Russia. See Edmund A. Walsh, *The Fall of the Russian Empire* (New York: Blue Ribbon Books, 1928) and Walsh, *The Last Stand: An Interpretation of the Five-Year Plan* (Boston: Little, Brown, 1931).

53. Edmund A. Walsh, "The Challenge to Religion in a Changing World," *Annals of the American Academy of Political and Social Science* 180 (July 1935), 183–91. The Catholic Church in America seemingly settled the contentious issue of modernism in the late 1890s during the Americanism crisis fomented by Archbishop John Ireland, who argued that the Church should adapt to a changing society. In early 1899, Pope Leo XIII issued the apostolic letter *Testem Benevolentiae*, which effectively condemned all flirtations with liberal modernism. See Thomas T. McAvoy, *The Americanist Heresy in Roman Catholicism, 1895–1900* (South Bend, IN: University of Notre Dame Press, 1963); Robert D. Cross, *The Emergence of Liberal Catholicism in America* (Cambridge, MA: Harvard University Press, 1958); John T. McGreevy, *Catholicism and American Freedom* (New York: Norton, 2003), 105–12.

54. For a biography of Fulton Sheen that examines his anti-Communism, see Kathleen Riley Fields, *Bishop Fulton J. Sheen: An American Catholic Response to the Twentieth Century* (PhD diss., University of Notre Dame, 1988); Michael J. Epple, *American Crusader: Bishop Fulton J. Sheen's Campaign Against Communism* (PhD diss., University of Akron, 2001), 53; Fulton Sheen to Martin Dies, December 1, 1938, box 23, folder 21, NCWC Papers.

55. "Neglect of God Held Cause of Red's Rise," *NYT*, March 16, 1936; Fulton J. Sheen, preface to *The Philosophy of Communism*, by Charles J. McFadden (New York: Benzinger Brothers, 1939), vii–viii; Sheen, *Communism and the Conscience*, 49.

56. Fulton J. Sheen, *The Crisis in Christendom* (Washington, DC: National Council of Catholic Men, 1943), 15–20. See also Harry S. McDevitt, *Communism and American Youth* (New York: America, 1936), 1–3, Hoover Pamphlet Collection. Like Sheen, McDevitt argued that secularization had provided Communism "fertile ground in which to grow its seed."

57. Editorial, "Russia Passes into History," *Commonweal*, July 8, 1925, 217–18; Editorial, "Russia against Heaven," *Commonweal*, November 6, 1929, 6–7; McDevitt, *Communism and American Youth*, 1–5; Flynn, *Catholicism, Americanism and Communism*, 36–37; "Communist 'Faith' Defined by Sheen," *NYT*, March 25, 1935; "Religion is Held Antidote to Reds," *NYT*, June 3, 1935; "43,000 Hear Smith Assail Communism as Foe of Church," *NYT*, September 25, 1935; "World's Hope Seen in Catholic Dogma," *NYT*, February 4, 1935.

58. John La Farge, *Communism and the Catholic Answer* (New York: America, 1936), 6–8; "Proceedings form the Asheville Conference of Clergymen and Laymen," in *Moscow over Methodism*, ed. Rembert Gilman Smith (St. Louis, MO: Swift, 1936), 205; "Fight on Moscow Begun by Catholic," *NYT*, September 20, 1936; "Three Faiths Join for Loyalty Days," *NYT*, September 11, 1936.

59. Powers, *Not Without Honor*, 162–69.

60. Survey by the Gallup Organization, June 23–28, 1938, iPOLL Databank; Survey by the Gallup Organization, December 14–19, 1939, iPOLL Databank; Survey by the Gallup Organization, June 26–July 1, 1941, iPOLL Databank; Survey by the Gallup Organization, August 7–12, 1941, iPOLL Databank; Survey by the Gallup Organization, September 18–24, 1941, iPOLL Databank; Survey by the Gallup Organization, January 9–14, 1943, iPOLL Databank; Warren B. Walsh, "What the American People Think of Russia," *Public Opinion Quarterly* 8 (Winter 1944–45): 520.

61. Philip Burnham, "Russia as an Ally," *Commonweal*, February 6, 1942, 381; "Don't Let Anyone Confuse You," *Catholic Review*, July 11, 1941; "Fr. Walsh and Rep. Dies on Russian Religious Freedom," *WP*, October 2, 1941; George Sirgiovanni, *An Undercurrent of Suspicion: Anti-Communism in America During World War II* (New Brunswick, NJ: Transaction, 1990), 147–63.

62. See Peter C. Kent, *The Lonely Cold War of Pope Pius XII* (Montreal: McGill-Queen's University Press, 2002), 61.

63. John F. Cronin, "The Problem of Communism in 1945," box 24, folder 17, NCWC Papers.

64. For a decent overview of the Catholic leaders in Western Europe and their fight against Communism, see Thomas B. Morgan, *Faith is a Weapon* (New York: Putnam, 1952); "Poland Denounces Vatican Concordat," *NYT*, September 15, 1945; Herbert L. Matthews, "Papacy Strengthened to Resist Communism," *NYT*, February 24, 1946.

65. Donald F. Crosby, *God Church, and Flag: Senator Joseph R. McCarthy and the Catholic Church, 1950 – 1957* (Chapel Hill: University of North Carolina Press, 1978), 9–10; Marquis Childs, "Washington Calling," *WP*, February 27, 1946; Larry Allen, "Church Is Last Foe of Warsaw Regime," *WP*, March 14, 1948; "Bishops See Crisis for Polish Church," *NYT*, April 28, 1946; "Pole Back from Vatican," *NYT*, April 2, 1947.

66. "Poles Form New Illinois Group; Assail Stalin," *CDT*, January 8, 1945; "Priests Assail Lublin Rules as Reign of Terror," *CDT*, February 9, 1945; "Asserts F.D.R. Outsmarted in Grab of Poland," *CDT*, February 26, 1945; "Free Poland Demanded," *NYT*, May 12, 1945; Crosby, *God Church, and Flag*, 9–10.

67. Stepinac remained imprisoned until 1951, when Tito, after his famous break from Stalin, commuted the archbishop's sentence in a goodwill gesture to the West. The best account of the Stepinac case and the religious war in Eastern Europe is Kent, *Lonely Cold War*, 155–76. See also Morgan, *Faith is a Weapon*, 163–81. "Yugoslav Primate Seized as Traitor," *NYT*, September 18, 1946; "More Persecution Laid to Yugoslavs," *NYT*, September 22, 1946; "Yugoslavs Indict Bishop of Zagreb," *NYT*, September 26, 1946; Arthur M. Brandel, "Stepinatz Declared Guilty," *NYT*, October 12, 1946; Arnaldo Cortesi, "Officials in Stepinatz Case Excommunicated by Vatican," *NYT*, October 15, 1946.

68. John Cooney, *The American Pope: The Life and Times of Francis Spellman* (New York: Times Books, 1984), 152–54; "Fight Communism, Spellman Pleads," *NYT*, October 25, 1946; "Spellman Predicts Stepinatz Will Die," *NYT*, October 7, 1946; "140,000 Catholics March in New Jersey," *NYT*, October 14, 1946; "Stepinatz Protest Filed," *NYT*, January 12, 1947.

69. "U.S. Voices Worry at Yugoslav Trial," *NYT*, October 12, 1946; "Wagner Urges U.S. to Help Stepinatz," *NYT*, October 18, 1946; Cooney, *American Pope*, 153; Crosby, *God, Church, and Flag*, 10.

70. "Foreign Prelates at St. Patrick Mass," *NYT*, July 7, 1947; "Hungarian Cardinal Fights Seizure of Schools by the State," *CDT*, May 16, 1948; "Hungary Cardinal Seized as Plotter," *LAT*, December 28, 1948; "Cardinal Mindszenty Seized by Red Regime in Hungary," *NYT*, December 28, 1948.

71. "Father Cronin Charges," *WP*, March 11, 1946; "Bids Catholic Laity Put Faith to Work," *NYT*, September 24, 1946. For a detailed look at the role of lay organizations in Cold War America, see David L. O'Connor, *Defenders of the Faith: American Catholic Lay Organizations and Anticommunism, 1917 – 1975* (PhD diss., University of New York at Stony Brook, 2000).

72. "Miss Bentley Gets Position," *WP*, August 19, 1949; "Sheen Charges U.S. Banned Talks on Russia," *CDT*, January 20, 1947; "Sheen Asks Prayers to Win Communists," *NYT*, March 24, 1947; Sheen, *Communism and the Conscience of the West*, 15–47.

73. For a good overview of Our Lady of Fatima and American Anti-Communism, see O'Connor, *Defenders of the Faith*, 107–51. See also Thomas A. Kselman and Steven Avella, "Marian Piety and the Cold War in the United States," *Catholic Historical Review* 72, no. 3 (1986): 403–24.

74. William Thomas Walsh, *Our Lady of Fátima* (New York: Macmillan, 1947) helped introduce the Marian apparitions to the American public, and he situated them in a Cold War context; "Catholics on May Day to Pray for Russians," *NYT*, May 1, 1947; "Throng in Mass Prayer at Hollywood Bowl," *LAT*, May 3, 1948; Sheen, *Communism and the Conscience*, 207; O'Connor, *Defenders of the Faith*, 116–22.

75. "Text of Spellman Plea on Mindszenty," *NYT*, February 7, 1949.

76. Mindszenty escaped from prison during the Hungarian uprising in 1956 and was granted asylum by the U.S. embassy in Budapest, where he lived until leaving Hungary for good in 1971. "Spellman Assails Anti-Christ Trials," *LAT*, February 14, 1949; "Spellman Assails Mindszenty Arrest," *NYT*, December 29, 1948; "Mindszenty Upheld by City Paraders," *NYT*, February 14, 1949; Cooney, *American Pope*, 164–66; "Papal Decree against Communism," *NYT*, July 14, 1949.

77. Sermons Deplore Mindszenty Trial," *NYT*, Feburary 21, 1949; "Spellman Wins Praise," *NYT*, January 3, 1949; Culbert G. Rutenber to Truman, February 9, 1949, Official File, Mindszenty-226-MISC, Truman Presidential Library, Independence, MO (hereafter cited as Truman Official File).

78. "Fosdick at 68 Ends 43 Years in Pulpit," *NYT*, May 27, 1946. After his retirement Fosdick continued to speak out against Communism. See "Dr. Fosdick Sees Battle of Faiths," *NYT*, May 2, 1947; and "Fosdick Says Reds Ape Christianity," *NYT*, April 25, 1949.

79. Hugh S. Tigner, "Communism and Christianity," *Christian Century*, November 20, 1946, 1407; "Shadow of Evil Serious World Peril, Says Pastor," *LAT*, February 17, 1947; "Pagan Battle Line Opposed by La Roe," *NYT*, December 22, 1947; "Pastor Blamed Church Fire on Atheistic Reds," *CDT*, June 22, 1947.

80. "Bishop Oxnam Decries Force to Stop Reds," *CDT*, April 12, 1947; "Preaches on Communism," *NYT*, May 24, 1948; "Pagan Battle Line Opposed by La Roe," *NYT*, December 22, 1947; William A. Moses, "Pastor Decries Communist Force," *LAT*, January 17, 1949.

81. Clayton Kirkpatrick, "U.S. Protestant Leaders Join Battle on Reds," *CDT*, November 9, 1949; "Oxnam Says Bombs Cannot Win People," *NYT*, October 28, 1946; George Dugan, "Bishop Oxnam Asks Protestant Unity," *NYT*, April 29, 1948; Survey by the Gallup Organization, May 28–June 1, 1948, iPOLL Databank.

82. "Faith to Combat Communism Urged," *NYT*, October 22, 1947; Reinhold Niebuhr, "Can We Avoid Catastrophe?" *Christian Century*, May 26, 1948, 504–6.

83. "100 Churchmen Sail For World Assembly," *WP*, August 7, 1948; "Churchmen of World Meet in Holland Today," *CDT*, August 22, 1948; W. A. Visser 't Hooft, ed., *First Assembly of the World Council of Churches* (New York: Harper & Brothers, 1948).

84. "Text of Dulles' Address to Assembly of Council of Churches," *NYT*, August 25, 1948; "Report of Section III: The Church and the Disorder of Society," in *Man's Disorder and God's Design: The Amsterdam Assembly Series* (New York: Harper & Brothers, 1948), 194; "Bishop Oxnam Picked as One of 6 World Council Presidents," *CDT*, August 31, 1948.

85. "Power of Religion Urged as War Bar," *NYT*, March 6, 1949.

86. "Resigned Rabbi Urges Communism Check-up," *NYT*, November 15, 1947.

87. Executive Committee Meeting Minutes, June 7, 1948, American Jewish League Against Communism, Benjamin Gitlow Papers, box 7, folder 1, Hoover Institution Archives, Stanford, CA; *American Jewish League Against Communism, Inc.*, Gitlow Papers, box 7, folder 1, Hoover Institution Archives, Stanford, CA.

88. "Communism Seen as Peril to Jews," *NYT*, March 11, 1948; "Jewish League Formed to War on Communism," *CDT*, March 15, 1948; "Enslaved Jews Called Forgotten," *LAT*, May 3, 1948; "Jews Shipped to Siberia by Reds, U.N. Told," *CDT*, July 25, 1949; "Jews in U.S. Urged to Bar Communism," *NYT*, November 13, 1949; "Cultural Parley Is Scored by Rabbi," *NYT*, March 27, 1949; "1,700 Attend Rally to Fight Communism," *NYT*, June 17, 1948; "Rabbi to Get Legion Award," *NYT*, June 30, 1949.

89. Clare G. Fenerty, *The Red War on Religion* (New York: Tablet, 1946), 3, 11–12, Hoover Pamphlet Collection.

Chapter 3

1. For J. F. C. Fuller's statement see "Crusade for Freedom," *WP*, August 13, 1950.

2. Harry S. Truman to Reverend J. H. Allison, December 8, 1950, Vertical File, Truman Presidential Library, Independence, MO.

3. For background on Truman's religious beliefs, see Merlin Gustafson, "The Religion of a President," *Journal of Church and State* 10, no. 3 (1968): 379–87; and Alonzo L. Hamby, *Man of the People: A Life of Harry S. Truman* (New York: Oxford University Press, 1995), 12, 21. For an exploration of Truman's religious beliefs in the context of the evolving Cold War, see Elizabeth Edwards Spalding, "'We Must Put on the Armor of God': Harry Truman and the Cold War," in *Religion and the American Presidency*, ed. Mark J. Rozell and Gleaves Whitney (New York: Palgrave Macmillan, 2007), 95–118.

4. Billy Graham, *Just As I Am: The Autobiography of Billy Graham* (London: Harper Collins, 1998), xviii–xxi.

5. "Lovett Deplores Cardinal's Arrest in Budapest as a Sickening Sham," *NYT*, December 30, 1948; "Truman Condemns Arrest of Cardinal Mindszenty," *NYT*, December 30, 1948; "Acheson Calls Cardinal Case Soviet-Inspired Persecution," *LAT*, February 10, 1949; "President Assails Cardinal Sentence," *LAT*, February 11, 1949.

6. For a good overview of these events, see Richard Gid Powers, *Not Without Honor: The History of American Anticommunism* (New York: Free Press, 1995), 197–99.

7. Survey by the Gallup Organization, January 23–28, 1948, iPOLL Databank; Survey by the Gallup Organization, March 5–10, 1948, iPOLL Databank; Survey by the Gallup Organization, April 9–14, 1948, iPOLL Databank.

8. The Federal Council of Churches, led by Bishop G. Bromley Oxnam, protested Taylor's reappointment vigorously. See Merlin Gustafson, "Religion and Politics in the Truman Administration," *Rocky Mountain Social Science Journal* 3 (1966): 125–34.

9. This initial round of correspondence was reprinted by the White House in a press release, August 28, 1947, Secretary's Files, box 196, Truman Presidential Library, Independence, MO.

10. Harry S. Truman to Pius XII, March 26, 1948; Truman to Pius, April 24, 1948, Pius to Truman, July 19, 1948; Truman to Pius, August 11, 1948, Myron C. Taylor Papers, box 3, Truman Presidential Library, Independence, MO.

11. "Baptists Blast Truman-Pope Letter Writing," *CDT*, August 31, 1947.

12. Harry S. Truman, "Annual Message to the Congress on the State of the Union," January 7, 1948, *Truman Papers*, 4:1–10.

13. In his correspondence with Pius XII, Truman cited this particular State of the Union Address as proof of his religious resolve. See Truman to Pius, August 11, 1948.

14. Harry S. Truman, "Religion in American Life," October 30, 1949, Religion 76, Truman Official File.

15. Rights theorists distinguish between positive and negative rights. A negative right is generally the right *not to be* subjected to an action of another person or group of people, such as a state. A positive right, on the other hand, is a right guaranteed through the action of

another person or the state. In general, negative rights proscribe actions, and positive rights prescribe them. See Isaiah Berlin, *Two Concepts of Liberty* (Oxford: Clarendon, 1958).

16. For other examples of Truman emphasizing the positive right of religion, see Harry S. Truman, "St. Patrick's Day Address in New York City," March 17, 1948, *Truman Papers*, 6:186–90; Truman, "Address at Valley Forge Boys Scout Jamboree," June 30, 1950, *Truman Papers*, 6:513–16.

17. "Truman Says Faith is Best U.S. Weapon," *NYT*, December 25, 1950.

18. Harry S. Truman, "Address in Philadelphia at the Dedication of the Chapel of the Four Chaplains," February 3, 1951, *Truman Papers*, 7:139–41.

19. I owe much of this argument to Eric Foner, *The Story of American Freedom* (New York: Norton, 1998), 252–54.

20. The American Heritage Foundation's board of trustees was diverse and influential, including Reinhold Niebuhr, Henry R. Luce, John Foster Dulles, the president of Paramount Pictures, the heads of Standard Oil, General Electric, and U.S. Steel, and labor leaders. "Board of Trustees of the American Heritage Foundation," May 27, 1947, box 22, folder 10, Henry R. Luce Papers, Library of Congress, Washington, DC (hereafter cited as Luce Papers).

21. *American Heritage Program*, box 18, Tom C. Clark Papers, Truman Presidential Library, Independence, MO (hereafter cited as Clark Papers); American Heritage Foundation, *Documents of the Freedom Train*, box 22, folder 10, Luce Papers. To date the most comprehensive examination of the Freedom Train is found in Wendy Lynn Wall, *Inventing the "American Way": The Politics of Consensus from the New Deal to the Civil Rights Movement* (New York: Oxford University Press, 2008), 201–40. Wall argues that the project was supported by businessmen for the purpose of reselling Americans in the postwar period on the idea of free enterprise. See also Stuart J. Little, "The Freedom Train: Citizenship and Postwar Culture, 1946–1949," *American Studies* 34, no. 1 (1993): 35–67.

22. "Freedom Train Dedicated amid Attack on Reds," *CDT*, September 18, 1947; Foner, *Story of American Freedom*, 252; *American Heritage Program*, Clark Papers.

23. American Heritage Foundation, *Highlights of the National Rededication Program of the American Heritage Foundation*, box 22, folder 10, Luce Papers.

24. Surprisingly little has been written about Tom C. Clark's life. See A. Timothy Warnock, *Associate Justice Tom C. Clark: Advocate of Judicial Reform* (PhD diss., University of Georgia, 1972); and Jay Alan Sekulow, *Witnessing Their Faith: Religious Influence on Supreme Court Justices and Their Opinions* (Lanham, MD: Rowman & Littlefield, 2006), 249–51.

25. Tom C. Clark, "Statement on the American Legion Educational Program," box 18, Clark Papers; Tom C. Clark, "Address before the Chicago Bar Association," June 21, 1946, box 18, Clark Papers.

26. Tom C. Clark, "Address to the Second National Conference on Citizenship," May 10, 1947, box 18, Clark Papers; Tom C. Clark, "Address on the 215th Anniversary of the Birth of George Washington," February 22, 1947, box 18, Clark Papers.

27. Tom C. Clark, "Address before the National Conference on Catholic Youth Work," May 21, 1947, box 18, Clark Papers.

28. Tom C. Clark, "Address before the International Sunday School Convention," July 24, 1947, box 18, Clark Papers.

29. Ibid.

30. Two months after his Des Moines speech, Clark rehashed many of the same arguments in Cleveland. See "Clark to Continue War on Subversion," *NYT*, September 29, 1947.

31. The lack of solid records makes any biography of Hoover difficult, and many authors have produced conspiratorial works premised upon scant sources. For a well-researched and responsible biography on Hoover, see Richard Gid Powers, *Secrecy and Power: The Life of J. Edgar Hoover* (New York: Free Press, 1987).

32. Powers, *Secrecy and Power*, 265. Hoover's FBI compiled extensive intelligence reports on the internal workings of the Communist Party USA. See FBI, *The Communist Party, USA,*

Versus Earl Browder and Browderism (Washington, DC: Government Printing Office, 1953). For a detailed examination of FBI attempts to shape a Cold War anti-Communist consensus, see Kenneth O'Reilly, *Hoover and the Un-Americans* (Philadelphia: Temple University Press, 1983), 75–100.

33. John Cooney, *The American Pope: The Life and Times of Francis Spellman* (New York: Times Books, 1984), 146–48; J. Edgar Hoover, *Communism is a Menace* (New York: Constitutional Education League, 1946), 16.

34. Testimony of J. Edgar Hoover, March 26, 1947, *Hearings Before the Committee on Un-American Activities House of Representatives, 80th Cong., 1st sess.* (Washington, Government Printing Office, 1947), 37.

35. Ibid., 35, 43–44.

36. J. Edgar Hoover, "How to Fight Communism," *Newsweek,* June 9, 1947, 32.

37. House Committee on Un-American Activities, *One Hundred Things You Should Know About Communism* (Washington, DC: Government Printing Office, 1949), 35–50.

38. *Cong. Rec.* 95, 79th Cong., 2nd sess., 1946, pt. 13: A2230–31.

39. House Committee on Un-American Activities, *Hearings on Proposed Legislation to Curb or Control the Communist Party in the United States before the Subcommittee on Legislation of the Committee on Un-American Activities House of Representatives on H.R. 4422 and H.R. 4581, 80th Cong., 2d sess., 1948,* 2.

40. *Cong. Rec.* 95, 81st Cong., 1st sess., 1949, pt. 14: A4234–35; *Cong. Rec.* 95, 81st Cong., 1st sess., 1949, pt. 1: 1044.

41. *Cong. Rec.* 96, 81st Cong., 2nd sess., 1950, pt. 15: A3213; *Cong. Rec.* 95, 80th Cong., 2nd sess., 1949, pt. 8: 10844.

42. "Taft Urges A Crusade," *NYT,* October 22, 1947; *Cong. Rec.*96, 81st Cong., 1st sess., 1949, pt. 5: 6944–45; "Harris Defends Loyalty Inquiry," *NYT,* September 1, 1947.

43. *Cong. Rec.* 95, 81st Cong., 2nd sess., 1950, 95, pt. 15: A4159. For the best account of McCarthy's relationship with American Catholics and his reluctance to make religion a central issue in anti-Communism, see Donald F. Crosby, *God Church, and Flag: Senator Joseph R. McCarthy and the Catholic Church, 1950–1957* (Chapel Hill: University of North Carolina Press, 1978).

44. Eric Bentley, ed., *Thirty Years of Treason: Excerpts from Hearings before the House Committee on Un-American Activities, 1938–1968* (New York: Viking, 1971), 604.

45. Testimony of Bishop G. Bromley Oxnam, *Hearing Before the Committee on Un-American Activities, House of Representatives,* 83rd Cong., 1st sess., 1953 (Washington, DC: Government Printing Office, 1954), 3588.

46. Douglas B. Cornell, "Bishop Asks Velde Group to Retract 'Falsehoods'; House Committee Repeats Charges; 500 at Hearing Applaud Prelate 'False Witness' Rebuked by Oxnam," *WP,* July 22, 1953.

47. *Toomey v. Farley,* 156 N.Y.S. 2d 840 (1956).

48. This profile was constructed using Sylvia Jukes Morris, *Rage for Fame: The Ascent of Clare Boothe Luce* (New York: Random House, 1997).

49. Quoted in Stephen Shadegg, *Clare Boothe Luce: A Biography* (New York: Simon & Schuster, 1970), 210.

50. "Mrs. Luce Attends Class," *NYT,* October 10, 1946; Clare Boothe Luce, *Is Communism Compatible with Christianity?* (New York: Catholic Information Society, 1946), Catholic Pamphlet Collection, Catholic University of America, Washington, DC

51. *Cong. Rec.* 95, 81st Cong., 1st sess., 1949, pt. 13: A2092–93; *Cong. Rec.* 93, 80th Cong., 1st sess., 1947, pt. 11: A2185–87.

52. Arthur Edson, "Graham to Preach from Steps of Capitol Today," *NYT,* February 3, 1952.

53. Started in 1951, the Annual Washington Pilgrimage of Churchmen was the idea of Dr. and Mrs. Harold M. Dudley. The Dudleys conceived it as a public relations exercise for the rest of the world to see, and Voice of America covered each pilgrimage extensively. See Kenneth Dole, "Pilgrimage Date Set for May Weekend," *NYT,* January 12, 1952. For an example of

a speech given to the participants by the assistant national archivist in one such pilgrimage, see *Cong. Rec.* 100, 83rd Cong., 2nd sess., 1954, pt 19: A3975–77.

54. J. Edgar Hoover, "Could Your Child Become a Red?" *Parade*, May 11, 1952.

55. James Reston, "Eisenhower Opens 'Crusade' Amid His Boyhood Scenes; General Hews to Old-Fashioned Revivalist Line With Appeal for Frugality, Honesty," *NYT*, June 5, 1952; "Text of the Republican Party's 1952 Campaign Platform Adopted by National Convention," *NYT*, July 11, 1952; "Text of Democratic Party Platform for 1952 Race as Adopted by the Convention," *NYT*, July 24, 1952.

56. Franklin D. Roosevelt, "First Inaugural Address," March 4, 1933, *FDR Papers*, 2:11–16; Franklin D. Roosevelt, "Second Inaugural Address," January 20, 1937, *FDR Papers*, 6:1–6.

57. Edward L. R. Elson, *Wide Was His Parish* (Wheaton, IL: Tyndale House, 1986), 112.

58. Press Release, January 16, 1953, Inaugural Committee of 1953 Records, box 8, Eisenhower Library, Abilene, KS; "God's Float Will Lead the Inaugural Parade," *NYT*, January 19, 1953.

59. Marcosson, "After Lenine—What? The Future Russia."

60. Dwight D. Eisenhower, "First Inaugural Address," January 20, 1953, *Eisenhower Papers*, 1:1–8.

61. The prayer enjoyed publicity following the inauguration, often as the topic discussed first in news accounts. Many journalists reported that Eisenhower composed it shortly before the ceremony. See Willard Edwards, "Capital Celebrates with Ike," *CDT*, January 21, 1953.

62. Minutes, Cabinet Meeting, January 12, 1953, box 1, Ann Whitman File, Cabinet Series, Eisenhower Library, Abilene, KS (hereafter cited as AWF).

63. Edwards, "Capital Celebrates with Ike"; "Eisenhower Takes Over," *LAT*, January 21, 1953; Anne O'Hare McCormick, "Abroad; As a Solemn President Took the Oath," *NYT*, January 21, 1953.

64. Eisenhower, "First Inaugural Address."

65. Stephen E. Ambrose, *Eisenhower*, vol. 1, *Soldier, General of the Army, President-Elect, 1890–1952* (New York: Simon & Schuster, 1983), 24.

66. The best treatment of Eisenhower's personal faith is in Gary Scott Smith, *Faith and the Presidency: From George Washington to George W. Bush* (New York: Oxford University Press, 2006), 221–58.

67. The phrase is taken from William Lee Miller, *Piety on the Potomac: Notes on Politics and Morals in the Fifties* (Boston: Houghton-Mifflin, 1964).

68. Press Conference Transcript, May 3, 1948, box 156, Pre-Presidential File, Eisenhower Library, Abilene, KS (hereafter cited as Eisenhower PPF).

69. Graham to Eisenhower, December 3, 1951, box 44, Eisenhower PPF; Edward Elson, Oral History, vol. 3, Oral History File, Eisenhower Library, Abilene, KS. It would be a mistake to overemphasize the relationship between Eisenhower and Graham. The preacher was granted an occasional audience with the president, but these meetings were rarely more than five minutes in length. See Paul T. Carroll to Graham, October 3, 1953, box 966, folder 1052, Personal File, Eisenhower Presidential Library, Abilene, KS (hereafter cited as Eisenhower PF). When asked about his relationship with Graham in a 1956 press conference, Eisenhower acknowledged that the two shared some basic beliefs, but he downplayed any talk of Graham's inclusion in plans for national spiritual mobilization. See Press Conference Transcript, March 21, 1956, Press Conference Series, box 4, AWF.

70. Robert Cutler to Theodore G. Streibert, August 1, 1953, box 738, folder 144-G-1, Official File, Eisenhower Library, Abilene, KS (hereafter cited as Eisenhower OF).

71. Executive Summary of the Interim Report on Our Moral and Spiritual Resources for Brotherhood, Douglas Committee, 1954, box 738, folder 144-G-1, Eisenhower OF.

72. Statement on Religion to Episcopal Church News, September 8, 1952, Campaign Series, box 7, AWF.

73. Dwight D. Eisenhower, "Speech at Fort Worth," October 15, 1952, box 6, Stephen Benedict Papers, Eisenhower Library, Abilene, KS (hereafter cited as Benedict Papers).

74. Dwight D. Eisenhower, "Address before the National Council of Churches of Christ," November 18, 1953, Speech Series, box 4, AWF; Dwight D. Eisenhower, "Back to God Speech," February 20, 1955, Speech Series, box 11, AWF.

75. Dwight D. Eisenhower, "Remarks at the Dedication of the Washington Hebrew Congregation Temple," May 6, 1955, Speech Series, box 12, AWF.

76. Eisenhower Campaign Statement, n.d., Campaign Series, box 7, AWF; Eisenhower, "Speech at Fort Worth."

77. Dwight D. Eisenhower, "Speech in Boston," November 3, 1952, box 7, Benedict Papers.

78. Richard Nixon, "Campaign Statement for *Guideposts*," Campaign Series, box 7, AWF.

79. Dwight D. Eisenhower, Press Release to the American Legion, February 1, 1953, Speech Series, box 3, AWF.

80. Dwight D. Eisenhower, "Speech at Annapolis, MD," May 17, 1953, Speech Series, box 4, AWF.

81. Dwight D. Eisenhower, "Remarks of the President at Ceremonies in the Office of the Postmaster General," April 8, 1954, Speech Series, box 6, AWF.

82. "Trip to Dam is Arranged," *NYT*, June 5, 1953; Anthony Leviero, "Eisenhower Warns Soviet on Assault," *NYT*, June 12, 1953.

83. Dwight D. Eisenhower, "Address at the Sixth National Assembly of the United Church Women," October 6, 1953, box 4, AWF.

84. Dwight D. Eisenhower, "Garrison Dam Speech," June 11, 1953, Speech Series, box 4, AWF.

85. Dwight D. Eisenhower, "Remarks at the Dedication of the Washington Hebrew Congregation Temple."

86. Dwight D. Eisenhower, "Address to International Business Machines," June 26, 1948, box 195, Eisenhower PPF.

87. H. Meade Alcorn, Jr. to Walter Williams, n.d. [1952?], box 17, folder 1-A-9, Eisenhower PF. See folder 1-A-9 for other examples of letters from citizens regarding Eisenhower's church affiliation.

88. Edward L. R. Elson, *America's Spiritual Recovery* (Westwood, NJ: Revell, 1954), 9–29.

89. The best account of Eisenhower's baptism is in Elson, *Wide Was His Parish*, 115–17. For a sampling of front-page headlines reporting Eisenhower's baptism, see "Ike and Wife Join Church in Washington," *CDT*, February 2, 1953; "Eisenhower Baptized in Presbyterian Church," *LAT*, February 2, 1953; Morrey Dunie, "Eisenhowers Join Church in Rites Here," *WP*, February 2, 1953; "Eisenhowers Join Capital Church in Simple Presbyterian Ceremony," *NYT*, February 2, 1953.

90. Elson, *Wide Was His Parish*, 187.

91. Elson to Eisenhower, January 14, 1953, box 401, folder 101-P (2), Eisenhower OF; Minutes of Cabinet Meeting, February 6, 1953, Cabinet Series, box 1, AWF.

92. For Eisenhower's use of the National Day of Prayer, see Press Release, June 23, 1953, box 737, folder 144-F (1), Eisenhower OF; Proclamation, National Day of Prayer, June 17, 1952 and June 23, 1953, box 737, file 144-F (3), Eisenhower OF.

93. Frank Carlson, Oral History (OH-488), Oral Histories File, Eisenhower Presidential Library, Abilene, KS.

94. Eisenhower to William F. Knowland, September 20, 1954, box 737, folder 144-F (1), Eisenhower OF; Press Release, September 21, 1954, box 737, folder 144-F (1), Eisenhower OF.

95. The Prayer for Peace movement was the brainchild of State Department employee Hervé J. L'Heureux, who first floated the idea in 1948. By 1954 it had won the backing of not only Eisenhower but 5,241 religious, fraternal, and civic organizations. See Norman Lindhurst, "Prayers for Peace Catch on in Europe," *New Hampshire Sunday News*, September 19, 1954.

96. United States Department of Agriculture, Memorandum to Heads of Department, Agencies, and Employees, September 20, 1954, box 737, folder 144-F (2), Eisenhower OF.

97. See S Res. 1468 and HR 4423.

98. Kent B. Stiles, "Permanent Motto for All Future U.S. Issues is Advocated," *NYT*, April 12, 1953.

99. "New Stamp Gets Motto," *NYT*, February 26, 1954; "Stamp Dedicated by the President," *NYT*, April 9, 1954; Eisenhower, "Remarks of the President at Ceremonies in the Office of the Postmaster General."

100. The credit for authorship had been disputed by James Upham, a coworker of Bellamy's at the *Youth's Companion*, but in 1939 a committee appointed by the United States Flag Association ruled unanimously in Bellamy's favor. See "History of the Pledge of Allegiance: Its Origins and Changes through the Years," *Supreme Court Debates* 7, no. 5 (May 2004): 133.

101. Charles J. Russo and Ralph D. Mawdsley, "The Supreme Court and the Pledge of Allegiance: A Hollow Victory," *Education and the Law* 16 (December 2004): 261.

102. For a detailed and interpretative history of the pledge, see Richard J. Ellis, *To the Flag: The Unlikely History of the Pledge of Allegiance* (Lawrence: University Press of Kansas, 2005).

103. Supreme Knight Luke E. Hart distributed a self-congratulatory letter in July 1954 asserting his organization's contribution, and Eisenhower agreed in Eisenhower to Hart, August 6, 1954, box 824, folder 47, Eisenhower PF; *Cong. Rec.* 99, 83rd Cong., 1st sess., March 25, 1953, pt. 10: A1494; *Cong. Rec.* 99, 83rd Cong., 1st sess., 1953, pt 10: A2063.

104. George M. Docherty, "One Nation Under God," February 7, 1954, 6–7, in *New York Presbyterian Church Sermon Archive*, http://www.nyapc.org/congregation/Sermon_Archives/text/1954/under-god-sermon.pdf.

105. Ibid., 4.

106. Rabaut quickly adopted Docherty's arguments. See *Cong. Rec.* 100, 83rd Cong., 2nd sess., 1954, pt 5: 6077–78.

107. Docherty, "One Nation Under God," 9–10.

108. Ellis, *To the Flag*, 133.

109. Kenneth Dale, "Put God in Pledge, Pastor Urges," *WP*, February 8, 1954.

110. Senate Report No. 1287, *Cong. Rec.* 100, 83rd Cong., 2nd sess., 1954, pt. 5: 6231–32.

111. Louis C. Rabaut to Eisenhower, June 9, 1954, box 433, folder 102 C-2, Eisenhower OF. The additional resolutions were introduced by: John R. Pillion (R-NY), William E. Miller (R-NY), Charles G. Oakman (R-MI), Oliver P. Bolton (R-OH), Melvin R. Laird (R-WI), Peter W. Rodino (R-New Jersey), Francis E. Dorn (R-NY), Hugh J. Addonizio (D-NJ), William T. Granahan (D-PA), Barratt O'Hara (D-IL), Thomas J. Lane (D-MA), John P. Saylor (R-PA), John J. Rooney (D-NY), John E. Fogarty (D-RI), Homer D. Angell (R-Oregon), and Frazier Reams (D-OH).

112. It should be noted that both men made their strongest cases in Congress before the floor debate of June 7. See *Cong. Rec.* 100, 83rd Cong., 2nd sess., 1954, pt. 5: 6077–78; and *Cong. Rec.* 83rd Cong., 2nd sess., 1954, 100, pt. 6: 6919.

113. *Cong. Rec.* 100, 83rd Cong., 2nd sess., 1954, pt. 6: 7757–66. The only true debate in the House centered on a seemingly inconsequential difference between the Senate and House versions of the amendment. Ferguson's SJR 126 would have used the phrase, "one nation, indivisible under God." Rabaut's HJR 243 called for the wording: "one nation under God, indivisible." Rather than simply passing the Senate's version, Rabaut insisted upon the adoption of his wording, to the chagrin of many colleagues. Nonetheless, Rabaut prevailed, and Ferguson agreed to resubmit the House version to the Senate.

114. Ellis, *To the Flag*, 131, 135; James M. Haswell, "Public Wants 'Under God' Put in Pledge," *WP*, May 18, 1954; Clayton Knowles, "Big Issue in DC: The Oath of Allegiance," *NYT*, May 23, 1954.

115. Commonwealth of Massachusetts, "Resolutions Memorializing the Congress of the United States in Favor of the Adoption of the Resolution to Add the Words 'Under God' to the Pledge of Allegiance," May 24, 1954, box 10, folder 1-D, Eisenhower General File, Eisenhower Library, Abilene, KS (hereafter cited as Eisenhower GF).

116. "Under God," *New York Journal-American*, April 28, 1954.

117. "Congress Proposals Hit By Unitarians," *NYT*, May 22, 1954.

118. See "Letters to the Editor," *WP*, May 27, 1954; Kenneth H. Bonnell, "Pledge Wording," *LAT*, May 30, 1954; "Letters to the Times," *NYT*, June 18, 1954.

119. For a sampling of letters to the White House opposed to changing the pledge, see Eisenhower GF, box 10, folder 1-D.

120. "President Hails Revised Pledge," *NYT*, June 15, 1954; Catherine Harrington, "Ike Hails Pledge Revision," *WP*, June 15, 1954.

121. "Printing of Pledge is Backed," *NYT*, July 15, 1954; "Arlington Will Use New Pledge to Flag," *WP*, July 31, 1954; "Under God in Pledge to Flag," *NYT*, September 25, 1954; "Allegiance Pledge Given to DC Pupils," *WP*, April 15, 1955; "Flag Pledge Song to Get Premier," *WP*, June 12, 1955.

122. Bellamy's great-granddaughter claimed in 2002 that he was too strong a proponent of church-state separation to have ever supported adding "under God." See Sally Wright, "Writing the Pledge: The Original Intent," *NYT*, July 14, 2002.

123. Ellis, *To the Flag*, 122–24.

124. Ibid., 28, 31.

125. Anson Phelps Stokes and Leo Pfeffer, *Church and State in the United States*, (New York: Harper & Row, 1964), 571.

126. Louis Fisher and Nada Mourtada-Sabbah, "Adopting 'In God We Trust' as the U.S. National Motto," *Journal of Church and State* 44 (Autumn 2002): 672–74; Stokes and Pfeffer, *Church and State*, 568–69.

127. The Irish-born Augustus Saint-Gaudens was raised in New York and is perhaps best known for creating the Shaw Memorial in Boston Common and the Sherman Monument in New York. See Burke Wilkinson, *Uncommon Clay: The Life and Works of Augustus Saint Gaudens* (San Diego, CA: Harcourt Brace Jovanovich, 1985).

128. Fisher and Mourtada-Sabbah, "Adopting 'In God We Trust,'" 675–80; Willard B. Gatewood, "Theodore Roosevelt and the Coinage Controversy," *American Quarterly* 18, no. 1 (1966): 47, 49.

129. *Cong. Rec.* 101, 84th Cong., 1st sess., 1955, pt. 8: 10299.

130. On the reverse side of the seal appeared the phrases "Annuit Coeptis" (He has favored our undertakings) and "Novus Ordo Seclorum" (New order of the ages).

131. House Report No. 1959, 84th Cong., 2nd sess.

132. *Cong. Rec.* 102, 84th Cong., 2nd sess., 1956, pt. 11: 15302.

133. "In God We Trust Label Slated for All U.S. Money," *NYT*, June 8, 1955; "Inscription for All U.S. Money," *NYT*, July 12, 1955. Similarly, news of congressional votes on the national motto were buried deep inside the news section. See "House Asks U.S. Motto In God We Trust," *NYT*, April 17, 1956; "'In God We Trust' Voted as Official Motto of U.S.," *NYT*, July 24, 1956. The *Times* did, however, run a lengthier article on the history of the words "In God We Trust": Elizabeth M. Fowler, "Biography of an Old American Motto," *NYT*, July 28, 1956.

Chapter 4

1. Edward F. Willett, "Dialectical Materialism and Russian Objectives," January 14, 1946, in *Documentary History of the Truman Presidency*, vol. 7, ed. Dennis Merrill (Bethesda, MD: University Publications of America, 1996), 23–24.

2. Ibid., 49–50.

3. George F. Kennan, "Telegram 511 ['Long Telegram']," in Merrill, *Documentary History*, 68–103; John Lewis Gaddis, *Strategies of Containment* (New York: Oxford University Press, 1982), 19–24.

4. John Lewis Gaddis, who wrote perhaps the single best treatment of Kennan's "Long Telegram," also emphasized its psychological aspects. See Gaddis, *Strategies of Containment*, 36–37.

5. Kennan, "Long Telegram," 84–85, 91. Similarities between Kennan's formulation and Edmund Burke's observations during the French Revolution are surprisingly similar. Both men likened their opponents to a disease, both believed that alliance with their respective enemies was ideologically impossible, and both believed that domestic zeal could ensure victory. See Edmund Burke, "First Letter on a Regicide Peace," in *Empire and Community: Edmund Burke's Writings and Speeches on International Relations,* ed. David P. Fidler and Jennifer M. Welsh (Boulder, CO: Westview, 1999), 287–320.

6. A Gallup poll taken after the speech found that 68 percent of all Americans had read or heard of Churchill's famous speech. Survey by the Gallup Organization, March 15–20, 1946, iPOLL Databank.

7. Winston Churchill, "The Sinews of Peace," in *Churchill Speaks, 1897–1963,* ed. Robert Rhodes James (New York: Barnes & Noble Books, 1980), 877–84. Public opinion of the USSR, high during World War II, fell significantly in 1946.

8. John Foster Dulles, "Thoughts on Soviet Foreign Policy and What to do About It," *Life,* June 3, 1946, 113–26, and June 10, 1946, 118–30. For Dulles's life and, more importantly, its religious grounding, see Richard H. Immerman, *John Foster Dulles: Piety, Pragmatism, and Power in U.S. Foreign Policy* (Wilmington, DE: Scholarly Resources, 1999); Ronald W. Pruessen, *John Foster Dulles,* vol. 1 (New York: Free Press, 1982); and Mark G. Toulouse, *The Transformation of John Foster Dulles: From Prophet of Realism to Priest of Nationalism* (Macon, GA: Mercer University Press, 1985).

9. John Foster Dulles, "A Righteous Faith," *Life,* December 28, 1942, 49–51; Dulles, "Thoughts on Soviet Foreign Policy."

10. The Cold War forever altered U.S. conceptions of military force. Years before the capitulation of the Axis powers, FDR and other American leaders had grasped the lesson of World War I: the U.S. and its allies needed to develop a system of international organizations with mandates backed by American force. Given its new commitment to internationalism, the United States could not afford another quick round of demobilization and disengagement from world affairs. With a permanent army of five million troops, the USSR ensured that prewar American military levels would become an ever fainter memory. American dollars and troops were needed to fill the vacuum created by the withdrawal of old colonial powers. The U.S. military clung to its monopoly on nuclear weapons, but Truman and his advisers recognized that if the U.S. accepted the role of defender of the West, it needed a large, well-funded military. There was something profoundly un-American about maintaining a powerful standing military in times of peace. Since the Revolutionary War, Americans had been perfectly capable of military mobilization, with its logistical, economic, and political demands, but after each flare-up they and their leaders followed Cincinnatus in beating their swords into plowshares. Standing armies threatened liberty and smothered virtue. Americans preferred a small and, above all, cheap professional army augmented in times of crisis by a mass of citizen-soldiers. And of all the mobilizations of citizen-soldiers and industrial firepower in American history, World War II stood out. In 1940, with war a growing possibility, the U.S. spent less than $2 billion on a combined military roughly 500,000 strong. By 1945, military expenditures topped $80 billion, with almost twelve million men at arms. See Allan R. Millett and Peter Maslowski, *For the Common Defense: A Military History of the United States of America,* rev. ed. (New York: Free Press, 1994), 655–56. When the war ended, Americans understandably expected quick demobilization. In January 1946, as national-security experts were beginning to plan for the Cold War, 20,000 GIs rioted in Manila, demanding a speedy return home. On the home front, soldiers' wives organized "Bring Back Daddy" letter-writing campaigns and founded the Fathers' Release Association. When Eisenhower arrived on Capitol Hill to testify before the House in early 1946, an angry crowd of wives and mothers swarmed him, asking when their boys would return home. The general was visibly shaken by this emotional outpouring. See "Disturbance in Manila," *NYT,* January 9, 1946; Thomas J. Hamilton, "Wives of Soldiers Query Eisenhower," *NYT,* January 23, 1946.

11. Ten years earlier, in 1938, only 20 percent of servicemen were under twenty-one. See President's Committee on Religion and Welfare in the Armed Forces, *Community Responsibility to our Peacetime Servicemen and Women* (Washington, DC: Government Printing Office, 1949), 1, 6.

12. Ibid., 52.

13. Truman argued that UMT would "strengthen the spirit of democracy." He observed that when the ancient civilizations of Greece and Rome "turned to mercenary defense forces, they ended." See "Text of President Truman's Talk at Princeton Asking Universal Service," *NYT*, June 18, 1947; Felix Belair, Jr., "Unfit Nations Die, President Stresses to Training Group," *NYT*, December 21, 1946. This idea was not new. Military progressives in the early twentieth century had seen the same potential for universal training to regenerate society. The Boy Scouts operated with a similar aim, and army chief of staff Douglas MacArthur used the Civilian Conservation Corps as a test lab for character development and political indoctrination. The work of Lori Lyn Bogle has been particularly useful in contextualizing this examination of religion and the U.S. military. See Bogle, *The Pentagon's Battle for the American Mind* (College Station: Texas A&M University, 2004), 24–40.

14. Public Information Office, UMT Experimental Unit, *The Fort Knox Experiment*, 1947, box 41, folder 3, PCRW Papers.

15. Hanson W. Baldwin, "Army's Youth Unit Called a Success," *NYT*, May 18, 1947.

16. President's Committee on Religion and Welfare in the Armed Forces, *The Military Chaplaincy* (Washington, DC: Government Printing Office, 1950), 5–10; John M. Devine, *UMT Experimental Unit Interim Report*, 1947, box 41, folder 3, PCRW Papers.

17. John M. Devine, "Opening Conference UMT Cadre Courses," 1947, box 41, folder 3, PCRW Papers; Devine, *Interim Report*, 26.

18. Devine, *Interim Report*, 24–26; *Report of the sub-Committee of the Louisville Army Advisory Committee on Universal Military Training*, July 26, 1947, box 41, folder 2, PCRW Papers.

19. Devine, *Interim Report*, 11–20; "Report on Universal Military Training," *Army Information Digest*, June 1947, 12, 30–31.

20. President's Committee on Religion and Welfare in the Armed Forces, "The Universal Military Training Unit, III," 1947, box 23, folder 3A–8, PCRW Papers.

21. President's Advisory Commission on Universal Training, "A Program for National Security," 1947, box 41, folder 2, PCRW Papers.

22. Editorial, "Military Training," *NYT*, March 11, 1946. Belair, "Unfit Nations Die"; "Truman and Dewey Make Appeal for Universal Military Training As Legion Opens Convention Here," *NYT*, August 29, 1947.

23. Benjamin Fine, "219 College Heads Vote Against UMT," *NYT*, January 14, 1948; "War Not Inevitable, Methodists Declare," *NYT*, May 25, 1947; Walter W. Ruch, "Training Plan Hit by Presbyterians," *NYT*, May 29, 1947; "Petition Opposes Military Training," *NYT*, June 5, 1947.

24. "Taft Calls the Training Measure Obsolete, Wasteful, Un-American," *NYT*, June 27, 1947; Clayton Knowles, "Taft Assails UMT as Superficial," *NYT*, October 2, 1947; William S. White, "House GOP Leaders Put Aside UMT, Act to Add GI Benefits," *NYT*, January 29, 1948.

25. Hanson W. Baldwin, "Army To Extend UMT Experiment With First Camp Called a Success," *NYT*, May 17, 1947; "Religion Taught Troops," *NYT*, July 26, 1947.

26. In addition to Weil, Walsh, and Poling, the committee comprised the following: Milwaukee educator Dorothy Enderis, Chicago attorney Truman Gibson, Rockefeller Foundation vice president Lindsley F. Kimball, New York Board of Education member Mark A. McCloskey, American Red Cross president Basil O'Connor, Tennessee civic leader Mrs. Ferdinand Powell, Harvard Graduate School of Education dean Francis Keppell (added in 1950), and National Travelers Aid Association president Mrs. George H. Shaw (added in 1950).

27. Harry S. Truman, "Statement by the President," September 16, 1948, box 1, folder 2-b, PCRW Papers; Press Release, October 27, 1948, box 1, folder 2-a, PCRW Papers.

28. Meeting Transcript, December 3, 1948, box 3, folder B-1, PCRW Papers; Charles K. Brightbill to Committee, March 10, 1949, box 1, folder 1-B, PCRW Papers; Memorandum, February 25, 1949, box 1, folder 1-a-1, PCRW Papers.

29. PCRW, "Community Responsibility to our Peacetime Servicemen and Women," 16–17, 28.

30. *Warm Facts in a Cold War*, January 8, 1951, box 1 folder, 2-b, PCRW Papers.

31. Frederick H. Osborn, "Address before the Conference on Community Responsibility," May 25, 1949, box 1, folder 1B-2, PCRW Papers; Arthur J. Altmeyer, "The Civilian Opportunity," May 25, 1949, box 1, folder 1B-2, PCRW Papers; Proceedings, National Conference on Community Responsibility to Our Peacetime Servicemen and Women, Religious Needs and Church and Synagogue Responsibilities, 1949.

32. President's Committee on Religion and Welfare in the Armed Forces, *Military Chaplaincy*, 19; Wilma R. Lockhart to Frank L. Weil, November 16, 1950; Virginia Davies to Frank L. Weil, November 17, 1950; Newton A. Stearns to Frank L. Weil, November 16, 1950; and W. Kerr Scott to Frank L. Weil, November 20, 1950, box 10, Chaplaincy Report Folder, PCRW Papers.

33. Frank L. Weil, "Religious Resources of American Democracy," May 9, 1950, box 32, folder 2-a, PCRW Papers.

34. Mason L. Weems, *The Life of Washington*, ed. Marcus Cunliffe (Cambridge, MA: Belknap, 1962), 182. Bogle, *Pentagon's Battle*, 48–49; Freedoms Foundation, "Four Years Work for Freedom," August 1953, box 37, folder 6, Luce Papers.

35. Bogle, *Pentagon's Battle*, 78.

36. "Science without Conscience Menaces Man, Bradley Says," *WP*, November 11, 1948.

37. Omar N. Bradley, "Address before the Freedoms Foundation," February 22, 1951, box 37, folder 6, Luce Papers.

38. Anne C. Loveland, "Character Education in the U.S. Army, 1947–1977," *Journal of Military History* 64, no. 3 (July 2000): 795–96.

39. U.S. Army, *The Army Character Guidance Program*, 1950, 11, 17, box 8, folder 3-c, PCRW Papers; *Chaplains' Character Guidance Manual for Training Divisions and Training Centers* (Carlisle Barracks, PA: Chaplain School of the United States Army, n.d.), box 10, folder 8, PCRW Papers.

40. Office of Chief of Air Force Chaplains, *Report on the United States Air Force Character Guidance Program*, 1949, box 41, folder 14, PCRW Papers.

41. James Gilbert devotes an entire chapter to MIS and the U.S. Air Force in *Redeeming Culture: American Religion in an Age of Science* (Chicago: University of Chicago Press, 1997), 121–45; "Air Force to Show Religious Movies," *NYT*, December 18, 1949.

42. "Soldiers Rate Chaplains as Most Popular," *LAT*, June 3, 1951; Bess Furman, "Guidance Series a Best Seller," *NYT*, April 28, 1954.

43. Department of Defense, *Semiannual Report of the Secretary of Defense, January 1 to June 30 1951* (Washington, DC: Government Printing Office, 1951), 115–16; Department of Defense, *Semiannual Report of the Secretary of Defense, January 1 to June 30, 1952* (Washington, DC: Government Printing Office, 1952), 1.

44. World War I proved an early testing ground for the widespread use of propaganda in wartime. The British inflamed American opinion against Germany with fabricated stories of slaughtered babies, and Wilson massaged American opinion through George Creel's Committee on Public Information. America expanded its propaganda apparatus during World War II, when Roosevelt established the Office of the Coordinator of Inter-American Affairs and the Office of War Information. By 1942, the Voice of America was transmitting pro-American information into enemy-held regions of the South Pacific and Europe. Kenneth Osgood provides the best examination of the development of American propaganda and psychological operations during the Cold War in *Total Cold War: Eisenhower's Secret Propaganda Battle at Home and Abroad* (Lawrence: University of Kansas Press, 2006), 15–45.

45. Propaganda was hardly unknown in czarist Russia as well. Legend holds that the same year America ratified the Constitution, Prince Grigory Potemkin, an adviser and sometime lover of Catherine the Great, constructed a series of fake villages along the Dnieper River to make the newly conquered realm seem more impressive to the monarch as she visited it. "Potemkin villages" would later become synonymous with attempts to hide an embarrassing political or social reality. Lenin accepted the czarist penchant for propaganda without reservation, once informing a colleague that "to tell the truth is a petit bourgeois prejudice." See Marian Leighton, *Soviet Propaganda as a Foreign Policy Tool* (New York: Freedom House, 1991), 16.

46. NSC-4, December 17, 1947.

47. Edward P. Lilly, "Psychological Operations, 1945–1951," February 1952, box 1, folder 091.412, file 2, Psychological Strategy Board Files, Truman Library, Independence, MO (hereafter cited as PSB Files); Edward P. Lilly, "The Development of American Psychological Operations," folder 314.7, PSB Files.

48. NSC-68, April 7, 1950; John Lewis Gaddis's treatment of NSC-68 is quite useful. See *Strategies of Containment*, 90–117. For a discussion of the ways in which NSC-68 transcended the boundaries of a strategy document to frame the Cold War politically, socially, and culturally, see Ernest R. May, ed., *American Cold War Strategy: Interpreting NSC 68* (Boston: Bedford Books, 1993), 152–64.

49. Quoted in Edward P. Lilly, "Religious Factors in OCB," 1954, box 2, folder 000.3, file 2, Operations Coordinating Board Central Files, Eisenhower Library, Abilene, KS (hereafter cited as OCB Files). See also Gordon Gray, Oral History, Truman Oral Histories Files, Truman Library, Independence, MO; and Mallory Browne to Gordon Gray, February 15, 1952, box 1, folder 000.3, PSB Files.

50. Report, "Preliminary Estimate of the Effectiveness of U.S. Psychological Operations," 1952, box 15, folder 091.412, file 2, PSB Files; Draft Report, "Over-all Strategic Concept For Our Psychological Operations," 1952, box 15, folder 091.412, file 2, PSB Files; E. P. Lilly to William Gibbons, September 25, 1952, box 1, folder 000.3, PSB Files.

51. The committee comprised Monsignor Thomas J. McCarthy of the National Catholic Welfare Council, Reverend E. N. Pruden of the American Baptist Convention, and Isaac Franck of the Washington Jewish Council. Cardinal Spellman was also credited for assistance.

52. Department of State Policy Advisory Staff, *Moral and Religious Factors in the USIE*, 1951, box 1, folder 000.3, PSB Files.

53. Ibid.

54. Department of State, Press Release No. 94, February 4, 1952, Secretariat Series, box 5, OCB Files; Francis P. Keough, "Remarks for the Voice of America Broadcast by Archbishop Keough," November 8, 1951, box 35, folder 11, NCWC Papers; Laura A. Belmonte, *Selling the American Way: U.S. Propaganda and the Cold War* (Philadelphia: University of Pennsylvania Press, 2008), 103.

55. Roger Lyons, "The Problem of Religious Broadcasting to an International Audience," February 5, 1952, box 17, USIA Records, National Archives, College Park, Maryland (hereafter cited as USIA Records); Roger Lyons, "The Role of Religion on the Voice of America," n.d., box 17, USIA Records. Lyons was assisted by the USIE panel on Moral and Religious Factors, as well as by Albert J. McCartney. He benefited from guidance by Reinhold Niebuhr, who also contributed regularly to VOA programming.

56. Psychological Strategy Board, "U.S. Doctrinal Program," 1953, Secretariat Series, box 1, OCB Files; Agenda, Panel for Doctrinal Warfare, January 23, 1953, Secretariat Series, box 2, OCB Files; Stefan T. Possony to Edward P. Lilly, January 12, 1953, Secretariat Series, box 2, OCB Files; T. B. Larson, "Vulnerabilities of Soviet-Communist Ideology," 1952, Secretariat Series, box 2, OCB Files; Edward P. Lilly to Psychological Strategy Board, May 1, 1953, Secretariat Series, box 2, folder 5, OCB Files; Psychological Strategy Board, Doctrinal Warfare Panel, "National Doctrinal Program to Reduce Communist Influence," 1953, Secretariat Series, box 2, folder 5, PSB Files.

57. Gordon Gray notes the hostility of other agencies to the PSB in his oral history. See also Osgood, *Total Cold War*, 44–45.

58. Proceedings, Cabinet Meeting, January 12, 1953, Cabinet Series, box 1, AWF.

59. Although at first the USIA was still subject to State Department guidelines and policies, it would gain greater bureaucratic independence in coming years.

60. Murray G. Lawson, "The United States Information Agency: A History," 1970, box 6, USIA Records; *Operations Coordinating Board Handbook*, 1955, Central Files, box 100, folder OCB 334, OCB Files; Osgood, *Total Cold War*, 85–90. For an insider's perspective on the founding of the USIA, see Richard T. Arndt, *The First Resort of Kings: American Cultural Diplomacy in the Twentieth Century* (Washington, DC: Potomac Books, 2005), 264–87.

61. NSC 162/2, October 30, 1953. The same basic phrasing reappears in NSC 5440/1, released in December 1954, and in NSC 5602/1, released in March 1956.

62. Edward P. Lilly to Elmer B. Staats, March 3, 1954, Central Files, box 2, folder 000.3, OCB Files.

63. "Anti-Church Drive Seen," *NYT*, August 8, 1954; "Reds Winning Asia, Africa, Malik Says," *WP*, August 19, 1954; Chesly Manly, "Religious Hate in Many Lands Told at Parley," *CDT*, August 21, 1954; Chesly Manly, "Swing to Left Alarms Churches," *CDT*, August 8, 1954.

64. Richard Philbrick, "Thousands to Join in Prayer Sunday at Festival of Faith," *CDT*, August 12, 1954; Chesly Manly, "Faith Rally Draws 125,000," *CDT*, August 16, 1954.

65. Dwight D. Eisenhower, "Address to the World Council of Churches," August 19, 1954, *Eisenhower Papers*, Speech Series, box 8.

66. Joseph M. Gerrety to Elmer B. Staats, et al., August 27, 1954, Central Files, box 2, folder 000.3, OCB Files.

67. Lyons, "The Problem of Religious Broadcasting; "Elton Trueblood, "Work of Chief of Religious Information, USIA," December 1954, USIA Records Group 306, box 17; USIA, "U.S. Information Agency Output Highlights," August 1954, Central Files, box 2, file 000.3, OCB Files; Belmonte, *Selling the American Way*, 106–7; United States Information Agency, *First Report to Congress* (Washington, DC: Government Printing Office, 1953), 8.

68. Charles de Gaulle framed France's colonial battle in Indochina as a contest over Communism. When the U.S. ambassador to France questioned his motivations in 1945, the general snapped: "What are you driving at? Do you want us to become . . . one of the federated states under the Russian aegis?" Quoted in Andrew J. Rotter, "Chronicle of a War Foretold: The United States and Vietnam, 1945–1954," in *The First Vietnam War: Colonial Conflict and Cold War Crisis*, ed. Mark Atwood Lawrence and Frederik Logevall (Cambridge, MA: Harvard University Press, 2007), 289.

69. Seth Jacobs, *America's Miracle Man in Vietnam: Ngo Dinh Diem, Religion, Race, and U.S. Intervention in Southeast Asia, 1950–1957* (Durham, NC: Duke University Press, 2004), 40–43, 50–52.

70. "Moral Revival Pushed," *NYT*, June 10, 1954; *Foundation for Religious Action in the Social and Civil Disorder*, box 31, folder 1, Luce Papers.

71. Richard M. Nixon to Walter B. Smith, September 10, 1954, Central Files, box 2, folder 000.3, OCB Files; Foundation for Religious Action, Proposal to OCB, 1954, Central Files, box 2, folder 000.3, OCB Files.

72. "Spellman in Saigon," *NYT*, January 6, 1955; "Cardinal Upholds Aid," *NYT*, August 25, 1955; United States Information Agency, *A Primer on Communism* (Washington, DC: USIA Press Service, 1956), 39–40; USIA Broadcast, "Thanksgiving Day—For Creation and Redemption," November 11, 1954, USIA Record Group 306, box 17.

73. Lilly, "Religious Factors in OCB"; "Buddhists Fight Infiltration," *NYT*, July 17, 1954; "Caravans against Communism," *NYT*, July 8, 1956; Robert Alden, "Anti-Red Teams Stimulate Thais," *NYT*, May 18, 1956; Memo of Meeting, Committee on Buddhism, June 29, 1956, Central Files, box 2, folder 000.3 (3), OCB Files.

74. "President Appeals to Reds to Pray," *LAT*, September 22, 1954; Memorandum of Meeting, Ideological Subcommittee, June 8, 1955 and June 20, 1955, Central Files, box 2, file 000.3 (2), OCB Files.

75. For a discussion of this episode, see David E. Powell, *Antireligious Propaganda in the Soviet Union: A Study of Mass Persuasion* (Cambridge, MA: MIT Press, 1975), 39–40.

Chapter 5

1. "Town Deserts U.S. For Day in Soviet," *NYT*, May 2, 1950. This episode figured prominently in Richard M. Fried, *The Russians are Coming! The Russians are Coming! Pageantry and Patriotism in Cold War America* (New York: Oxford University Press, 1998).

2. "Reds Infiltrate Town in Wisconsin to Deride Mock May Day Seizure," *NYT*, May 1, 1950.

3. The most complete examination of the Cold War's impact on both the American classroom and debates among educators is Andrew Hartman, *Education and the Cold War: The Battle for the American School* (New York: Palgrave Macmillan, 2008).

4. "Clark Says Russia Aims for Our Youth," *NYT*, February 15, 1949.

5. William M. Blair, "Studebaker Maps War on Communism," *NYT*, November 29, 1947.

6. "U.S. Schools Program Drafted to Fight 'Isms,'" *WP*, January 18, 1948; Davis Taylor Marke, "Schools Progress in Americanism," *NYT*, June 6, 1948.

7. Elsie Carper, "Schools Deal Blow to Communism," *WP*, February 8, 1948.

8. Verne Paul Kaub, *Collectivism Challenges Christianity* (Winona Lake, IN: Light and Life, 1946), 2, 43, 70–75, 84, 125.

9. Francis Spellman, *Communism is Un-American* (New York: Constitutional Education League, 1946), 9; "Statement by Catholic Bishops on 'Man and the Peace,'" *NYT*, November 17, 1946; Richard Grinder, *The Red Terror and Religion* (New York: Catholic Information Society, 1947), 14, Hoover Pamphlet Collection.

10. Vera M. Butler, "Now is the Hour," *NEA* 86 (1948): 28–38.

11. Minutes of the Representative Assembly, *NEA* 86 (1948): 169–72.

12. *McCollum v. Board of Education*, 333 U.S. 203 (1948).

13. The true extent of release time is a matter of debate. The International Council of Religious Education claimed that more than two million students participated in released time while the NEA believed the number was actually much lower. Neither conclusion was backed by a systematic survey. See Butts, *The American Tradition*, 199–200; and V. T. Thayer, *The Attack Upon the American Secular School* (Boston: The Beacon, 1951), 181.

14. *McCollum v. Board of Education*, 210, 214–17, 237–38.

15. *Everson v. Board of Education of Ewing TP*, 330 U.S. 1 (1947).

16. "Miss Bentley Cites College Atheism," *NYT*, February 14, 1949; Benjamin Fine, "N.E.A. Adopts Red-Teacher Ban; 3,000 Delegates Shout Approval," *NYT*, July 7, 1949.

17. Mrs. John E. Haynes, "Within the Call of Duty," *NEA* 89 (1951): 45; Frank K. Weil, "Apathy—The Enemy of Democracy," *NEA* 89 (1951): 52–53.

18. Educational Policies Commission, *Moral and Spiritual Values in the Public Schools* (Washington, DC: National Education Association, 1951), 11–12.

19. Ibid., 18.

20. Educational Policies Commission, *Moral and Spiritual Values*, 71–80.

21. *Zorach v. Clauson*, 343 U.S. 306, 313–14 (1952).

22. Trying to reconcile the McCollum and Zorach decisions is an illustrative exercise. One possible solution rests in the key difference between the two: the Champaign public schools allowed religious leaders to teach inside public buildings, while in New York students left school for released time. This difference in circumstance was enough for Justices Douglas, Vinson, and Burton to rule differently. Justice Reed needed no convincing, since his was the lone dissenting vote in the McCollum decision four years earlier. But the differences between the two cases were lost on justices Black, Frankfurter, and Jackson. To them,

the New York schools still devoted classroom time to religious instruction. "Today's judgment will be more interesting to students of psychology . . . than to students of constitutional law," Jackson opined. While such interest to psychologists never materialized, the Zorach decision is indeed interesting to students of the Cold War. Jackson may have been hinting that something other than strict constitutional interpretation was at play in the decision. Ibid., 325.

23. Drew Pearson, "A Prayer Dissolves Party Lines," *WP*, February 5, 1950.
24. "Schools Plan New Stress on Moral Values," *LAT*, June 19, 1952; "L.A. High PTA Will Hear Talk," *LAT*, October 19, 1952.
25. California Association of Secondary School Administrators, *Moral and Spiritual Values in the Curriculums of California High Schools* (Sacramento: California State Department of Education, 1952), 14.
26. Joan DelFattore, *The Fourth R: Conflicts over Religion in America's Public Schools* (New Haven, CT: Yale University Press, 2004), 70.
27. Leonard Buder, "Regents' Prayer Adopted Slowly," *NYT*, October 12, 1952.
28. "Stanza of 'America' Naming God Ordered into Daily School Ritual," *NYT*, January 16, 1953.
29. Charles P. Taft, "Religion and the Public Schools," *NEA* 90 (1952): 81–85; Gene Currivan, "Teaching about Religion Is to Be the Subject of a Project in Teacher-Training Institutions," *NYT*, August 16, 1953.
30. Bella V. Dodd, *School of Darkness* (New York: Kennedy, 1954), 233, 244, 250.
31. Editorial, "Religion and the Schools," *WP*, December 15, 1952.
32. California Association of Secondary School Administrators, *Moral and Spiritual Values*, 3; San Diego City Schools, *Spiritual Values* (San Diego, CA: San Diego Public School District, 1948), 1.
33. Department of Education of the National Catholic Welfare Conference, *Moral and Spiritual Values in the Public Schools*, 1952, box 28, folder 3, NCWC Papers.
34. Henry R. Luce, "Address at College of Idaho—A Presbyterian Institution," October 6, 1951, box 74, folder 4, Luce Papers.
35. Hornell Hart, "Changing Social Attitudes and Interests," in *Recent Social Trends in the United States*, ed. Wesley C. Mitchell (New York: McGraw-Hill, 1933), 388–403.
36. Brooks Atkinson, "Socialist World Soviet Aim, Times Moscow Writer Says," *NYT*, July 8, 1946.
37. *Cong. Rec.* 92, 79th Cong., 2nd sess., 1946, pt. 12: A4337–9; Anne O'Hare McCormick, "The War on the Side of Angels," *NYT*, April 5, 1947; "A Struggle for Men's Souls," *NYT*, November 23, 1949; "Church Unity," *WP*, August 29, 1948; "The Godless Religion's New Crusade," *CDT*, February 23, 1949; "Communism and Christianity," *Wall Street Journal*, February 14, 1949; Walter Lippmann, "U.S.S.R. vs. West Is Like Islam vs. Christendom," *LAT*, February 4, 1949. One should note, however, that Lippmann argued that no struggle on this scale could be solved ideologically. Instead he believed that the only solution was reconciliation.
38. David Segal, "From Billy Graham-A Big Tent Revival," *WP*, June 26, 2005.
39. James L. Baughman, *Henry R. Luce and the Rise of the American News Media* (Boston: Twayne, 1987), 2.
40. Henry R. Luce, "The American Century," *Life*, February 17, 1941, 61–65.
41. Henry R. Luce, "A New Measure of Patriotism," June 6, 1944, box 72, folder 2, Luce Papers; Henry R. Luce, "The Human Situation," July 2, 1944, box 72, folder 3, Luce Papers; Henry R. Luce, "The World's Need for a Church," December 10, 1944, box 72, folder 5, Luce Papers.
42. Though Luce faced a near revolt by staffers over Whittaker Chambers, he remained loyal until nearly the end, even paying some of Chambers's legal fees during the famous Hiss trial. See Robert E. Herzstein, *Henry R. Luce* (New York: Scribner's, 1994), 198–206, 346–58.
43. Karl E. Mundt to Henry R. Luce, February 5, 1945, box 2, folder 18, Luce Papers.

44. Henry R. Luce, "Address at United Congregational Church, Bridgeport, CT," March 26, 1950, box 74, folder 1, Luce Papers; Henry R. Luce, "Address at the Alumni Dinner of the Union Theological Seminary," May 17, 1948, box 73, folder 6, Luce Papers; Henry R. Luce, "Remarks Before the Laymen's Movement," November 30, 1949, box 73, folder 11, Luce Papers.

45. W. A. Swanberg, *Luce and His Empire* (New York: Scribner's, 1972), 303.

46. For a description of Luce's religious beliefs (and his constant questioning of his own faith), see Alan Brinkley, *The Publisher: Henry Luce and His American Century* (New York: Knopf, 2010), 437–39.

47. Henry R. Luce, "The Ethical Problems Facing America," February 12, 1946, box 72, folder 6, Luce Papers.

48. Luce repeated this basic theme in other addresses. See Henry R. Luce, "Address at United Congregational Church," March 26, 1950, box 74, folder 1, Luce Papers; and Henry R. Luce, "The American Proposition," November 29, 1953, box 75, folder 10, Luce Papers.

49. John K. Jessup, ed., *The Ideas of Henry Luce* (New York: Atheneum, 1969), 70.

50. "Destiny's Men," *Time*, July 15, 1946, 60–62; "Dr. Crankley's Children," *Time*, February 23, 1948, 30–34.

51. "The Road to Religion," *Life*, April 7, 1947, 36.

52. Luce, "Address at United Congregational Church"; Luce, "Address at the Alumni Dinner of the Union Theological Seminary."

53. "Honored by Christian Education Group," *NYT*, April 21, 1948; "Warns on Communism," *NYT*, March 21, 1947.

54. David M. Potter, *People of Plenty: Economic Abundance and the American Character* (Chicago: University of Chicago Press, 1954), 166–88.

55. Advertising Council, *The Advertising Council: What it is and What it Does*, 1950, box 52, folder 11, Luce Papers; "Go-to-Church Ads Win Wide Support," *NYT*, December 5, 1949.

56. Harry S. Truman, "Religion in American Life," October 30, 1949, Religion 76, Truman Official File. For a detailed description of the Advertising Council's various Cold War campaigns, including RIAL, see Daniel L. Lykins, *From Total War to Total Diplomacy: The Advertising Council and the Construction of the Cold War Consensus* (Westport, CT: Praeger, 2003).

57. Advertising Proofs, Advertising Council, 1949, box 52, folder 11, Luce Papers.

58. "Religion's Revival Sought for Nation," *NYT*, October 29, 1950.

59. "Church Advertising Raises Attendance," *NYT*, February 8, 1952; The Committee on Religion in American Life, *Annual Report*, 1956, box 38, folder R, James M. Lambie Papers, Eisenhower Library, Abilene, KS; "Wilson is Praised for Religious Gain," *NYT*, January 19, 1951.

60. "So. Cal Set for July Fourth Dedication to Liberty," *Los Angeles Herald-Express*, July 2, 1951; Committee to Proclaim Liberty, *Proclaim Liberty*, 1953, box 737, folder 144-F (1), Eisenhower OF; James C. Ingebretsen, "Hailing Freedom Under God," *LAT*, June 18, 1951; "Committee to Proclaim Liberty Formed to Celebrate July 4," *LAT*, June 8, 1951.

61. Committee to Proclaim Liberty, "The Story Behind the Committee to Proclaim Liberty," n.d., series I, box 69, folder 10, James C. Ingebretsen Papers, Special Collections and University Archives, University of Oregon (hereafter cited as Ingebretsen Papers).

62. Earl Warren, Proclamation, June 29, 1953, box 737, folder 144-F (1), Eisenhower OF; Committee to Proclaim Liberty, *Proclaim Liberty*, 1953; Committee to Proclaim Liberty, *New Meaning for July 4th*, 1957, series I, box 69, folder 10, Ingebretsen Papers; Committee to Proclaim Liberty, Press Release, July 1, 1951, series I, box 69, folder 10, Ingebretsen Papers.

63. Ingebretsen, "Hailing Freedom Under God"; "Committee to Proclaim Liberty Formed to Celebrate July 4," *LAT*, June 8, 1951; Committee to Proclaim Liberty, *Proclaim Liberty*.

64. See Len Travers, *Celebrating the Fourth: Independence Day and the Rites of Nationalism in the Early Republic* (Amherst: University of Massachusetts Press, 1997), 107–54. One could

make the case that the Fourth of July was an example of civil religion, but this conception nevertheless was not what CPL had in mind.

65. Diana Karter Appelbaum, *The Glorious Fourth: An American Holiday, An American History* (New York: Oxford University Press, 1989), 20.

66. "A Spiritual Airlift," *NYT*, October 22, 1950; National Crusade for Freedom Council, Report, July 24, 1950, box 33, folder 11, Luce Papers.

67. Radio Free Europe was formed by a splinter group of the American Heritage Foundation called the National Committee for a Free Europe. It was funded by a coterie of powerful businessmen disillusioned with the government's Voice of America. See Sig Mickelson, *America's Other Voice: The Story of Radio Free Europe and Radio Liberty* (New York: Praeger, 1983).

68. "Freedom Crusade Will Begin September 4," *NYT*, July 28, 1950; National Crusade for Freedom Council, *Join the Crusade for Freedom*, 1950, box 33, folder 11, Luce Papers.

69. "Freedom Crusade Seeks Volunteers," *NYT*, August 31, 1950; "Crusade For Freedom Petitions Draw Area Signatures," *WP*, October 3, 1950; "Scrolls At Fire Houses," *NYT*, October 13, 1950.

70. Editorial, "Crusade for Freedom," *NYT*, July 28, 1950; Editorial, "Crusade for Freedom," *WP*, August 13, 1950; Editorial, "Enlist in the Crusade for Freedom," *LAT*, August 23, 1950; "Text of Eisenhower Call for Crusade," *NYT*, September 5, 1950.

71. Crusade for Freedom, "Crusade for Freedom Statement of Purpose," 1950, and "Crusade for Freedom Fact Sheet," 1950, box 33, folder 11, Luce Papers; "Sermons to Stress Religious Liberty," *NYT*, October 8, 1950; "Freedom Sunday is Set," *NYT*, October 6, 1950.

72. "Crusade for Freedom Petitions Draw Area Signatures," *WP*, October 3, 1950.

73. For a discussion of voluntary associations and their growth from World War II through the 1950s, see Robert D. Putnam, *Bowling Alone: The Collapse and Revival of American Community* (New York: Simon & Schuster, 2000), 54–58.

74. "Cavallaro Hailed For Anti-Red Fight," *NYT*, October 19, 1953; John T. Frederick, "Speaking of Books," *The Rotarian*, March 1953, 35; Dan L. Thrapp, "Communism Held Foe of Religion," *LAT*, October 11, 1952.

75. For a history of the American Legion and its Americanism Committee, see Thomas A. Rumer, *The American Legion: An Official History, 1919 – 1989* (New York: Evans, 1990); and Rodney Glisan Minott, *A History of the National Americanism Commission of the American Legion, 1919 – 1954* (master's thesis, Stanford University, 1956).

76. Address by Philadelphia mayor Bernard Samuel, *Proceedings of the 31st National Convention of the American Legion*, 1951 (Washington, DC: Government Printing Office, 1952), 6–8 (hereafter cited as *Legion Proceedings*); Address by Clarence Manion, *Legion Proceedings* (1951): 16–18.

77. "Report of the National Chaplain," *Legion Proceedings* (1952): 359–61.

78. These editorial excerpts appeared in "Spiritual Reawakening," *San Bernardino Telegram*, March 7, 1952; *Cong. Rec.* 99, 83rd Cong., 1st sess., 1953, pt. 9: A652.

79. "Report of the National Chaplain," *Legion Proceedings* (1953): 311–12.

80. "Back to God Drive Enlists President," *NYT*, February 2, 1953.

81. "U.S. Will Hear President on 'Back to God' Appeal," *NYT*, January 28, 1954. For a script from the 1954 *Back to God* telecast, see *Cong. Rec.* 100, 83rd Cong., 2nd sess., February 16, 1954, pt. 16: A1204–6; Dwight D. Eisenhower, "Address for the American Legion Back to God Program," February 7, 1954, Speech Series, box 6, AWF.

82. *To Make You Think* (St. Paul, MN: Catechetical Guild Education Society, 1947), Religion 76, Truman OF; *The Truth Behind the Trial of Cardinal Mindszenty* (St. Paul, MN: Catechetical Guild, 1949), box 25, folder 1, NCWC Papers.

83. National Council of Catholic Men, *And Some Fell Upon Good Ground*, 1950, box 35, folder 8, NCWC Papers; Fulton J. Sheen, "Why I Am on Television," *TV Guide*, April 11, 1952, 8.

84. Robert Healey, *Awake or Perish* (Washington, DC: National Council of Catholic Men, 1950), Catholic Pamphlet Collection, Catholic University of America.

85. "New Crusade Post Taken by Wanger," *LAT*, August 21, 1950; "Film Alliance Backs Crusade for Freedom," *LAT*, September 8, 1950; "Film Workers Hear Communism Assailed," *NYT*, September 28, 1950.

86. Powers, *Not Without Honor*, 218–21. For select transcripts of HUAC film industry investigations, see Bentley, *Thirty Years of Treason*, 110–246. See also John Joseph Gladchuk, *Hollywood and Anticommunism: HUAC and the Evolution of the Red Menace, 1935 – 1950* (New York: Routledge, 2007).

87. Mae Tinee, "Movie Inspired by Mindszenty Case is Graphic," *CDT*, February 23, 1950; Philip K. Scheuer, "Cardinal Mindszenty's Trial Film-Dramatized," *LAT*, March 20, 1950.

88. Edwin Schallert, "Quo Vadis Triumphant as Great Film Spectacle," *LAT*, November 30, 1951.

89. "DeMille Speech Stresses World Crisis on Reds," *LAT*, September 20, 1950.

90. Tony Shaw, "Martyrs, Miracles and Martians: Religion and Cold War Cinematic Propaganda in the 1950s," *Journal of Cold War Studies* 4, no. 2 (2002): 10. For another article examining Hollywood and religion in the early Cold War, see Robert Torry, "The Wrath of God: Hollywood Religious Epics and American Cold War Policy," *Arizona Quarterly* 61, no. 2 (Summer 2005): 67–86.

91. Statement, Foundation for Religious Action, box 738, folder 144-G-1, Eisenhower OF; *National Conference on the Spiritual Foundations of American Democracy*, box 37, folder 1, Luce Papers; *Highlights of the First National Conference on the Spiritual Foundations of American Democracy*, box 738, folder 144-G-1, Eisenhower OF; Edward L. R. Elson to Eisenhower, October 3, 1954, box 738, folder 144-G-1, Eisenhower OF.

92. "Spirit Linked to Power," *NYT*, May 14, 1956; Foundation for Religious Action in Social and Civil Order, *FRASCO's Program of Action in the Struggle Against Atheism and Tyranny*, 1960, series I, box 69, folder 2, Ingebretsen Papers; Foundation for Religious Action in Social and Civil Order, *FRASCO's New Program of Action*, [1959?], series I, box 69, folder 2, Ingebretsen Papers; Foundation for Religious Action in Social and Civil Order, *FRASCO's New Program of Action*, [1960?], series I, box 69, folder 2, Ingebretsen Papers.

Chapter 6

1. "Religious Revival Runs at Flood Tide," *WP*, May 14, 1952; "Churchmen See Spiritual Gains," *WP*, January 12, 1955; George Dugan, "American Data on Organized Faiths Emphasizes New Widespread Growth in This Country," *NYT*, April 12, 1954; Dan L. Thrapp, "20,000 See Dawn at Hollywood Bowl," *LAT*, April 14, 1952; James Hudnut-Beumler, *Looking for God in the Suburbs: The Religion of the American Dream and its Critics, 1945–1965* (New Brunswick, NJ: Rutgers University Press, 1994), 48.

2. Seymour Korman, "Is Hollywood Getting Religion?" *CDT*, June 6, 1954.

3. Edward P. Morgan, ed., *This I Believe* (New York: Simon & Schuster, 1952), xvii, 30, 44, 76, 89; Raymond Swing, ed., *This I Believe: 2* (New York: Simon & Schuster, 1954), 42, 140, 142, 150, 152.

4. "A New Harvard Center," *NYT*, February 11, 1952;

5. Stanley Rowland, Jr., "Religious Interest on Campuses Takes Place Outside Churches," *NYT*, October 24, 1955; "Rise of Religion in U.S. Analyzed," *NYT*, October 21, 1956.

6. For a good overview of prayer during the 1950s, see Hudnut-Beumler, *Looking for God*, 44–47; Gerald Weales, "A Family That Prays Together Weighs Together," *New Republic*, March 25, 1957, 19–20.

7. "Phone Devotions Shared by Thousands," *WP*, February 25, 1956.

8. Survey by the Gallup Organization, June 16–21, 1951, iPOLL Databank.

9. Survey by Ben Gaffin and Associates, June 1952, iPOLL Databank.

10. "Commandments Ad Honored by Eagles," *NYT*, September 1, 1956; Delores R. Jeffords, "The Mountain that Quotes the Bible; Decalogue is Spelled Out on Slope in Carolina Hill

Country," *NYT*, May 18, 1952; "Decalogue Held Need of America; Rabbi Proposes Having the Ten Commandments in Schools and in Newspapers as Part of 'Common Heritage,'" *NYT*, January 28, 1951.

11. This profile was constructed using Carol V. R. George, *God's Salesman: Norman Vincent Peale and the Power of Positive Thinking* (New York: Oxford University Press, 1993).

12. Norman Vincent Peale, *The Power of Positive Thinking* (Englewood Cliffs, NJ: Prentice-Hall, 1956), viii; George, *God's Salesman*, 131.

13. Roger Bruns, *Billy Graham: A Biography* (Westport, CT: Greenwood, 2004), 34; Marshall Frady, *Billy Graham: A Parable of American Righteousness* (Boston: Little, Brown, 1979).

14. George Dugan, "American Data on Organized Faiths Emphasize New Widespread Growth in This Country," *NYT*, April 12, 1954; "Report Church Membership at All-Time High, *CDT*, September 6, 1955.

15. Surveys by the Gallup Organization, February 24–March 1, 1939; November 21–26, 1940; June 1–7, 1942; May 2–7, 1954; March 15–20, 1957, iPOLL Databank. One should note that the results of such polls vary according to the time they were taken. But despite these minor variations, it is clear when examining the polls from 1939 to 1958 that self-reporting of religious attendance among Americans climbed by 10–15 percent.

16. See C. Kirk Hadaway, Penny Long Marler, and Mark Chaves, "Overreporting Church Attendance in America: Evidence That Demands the Same Verdict," *American Sociological Review* 63, no. 1 (February 1998): 122–30; and Hadaway, Marler, and Chaves, "What the Polls Don't Show: A Closer Look at U.S. Church Attendance," *American Sociological Review* 58, no. 6 (December 1993): 741–52.

17. Surveys by the Gallup Organization, November 7–12, 1947; March 28–April 2, 1953, iPOLL Databank.

18. James West, *Plainville, U.S.A.* (New York: Columbia University Press, 1945), 142; Art Gallaher, Jr., *Plainville: Fifteen Years Later* (New York: Columbia University Press, 1961), 169.

19. Surveys by the Gallup Organization, February 24–March 2, 1939, March 15–March 20, 1957, iPOLL Databank.

20. Surveys by the Gallup Organization, October 24–29, 1947, July 22–28, 1949, iPOLL Databank.

21. Surveys by the Gallup Organization, November 11–16, 1954, August 25–August 30, 1955, IPOLL Databank.

22. George Gallup, "Religious 'Revival' May be Losing Surge," *LAT*, April 18, 1962; Survey by the Gallup Organization, February 19–24, 1965, iPOLL Databank.

23. For example, when polled in 1966, 70 percent of Americans opposed the Supreme Court's ruling against school prayer. See Survey by Louis Harris & Associates, November 1966, iPOLL Databank.

24. Paul L. Montgomery, "Religion Revival Found Leveling," *NYT*, December 27, 1963.

25. Richard Mathison, "Elmer Gantry Likely to Stir Furor as a Movie," *LAT*, October 25, 1959; Murray Schumach, "Hollywood T.N.T.," *NYT*, October 11, 1959; Richard Brooks, "Film Conversion of a Controversial Novel," *NYT*, July 3, 1960.

26. "He's Unqualified for Top Job, Says Neely," *CDT*, March 29, 1955; "Senator Neely Lashes Out at Eisenhower," *LAT*, March 29, 1955; "Ike Denounced for Golfing, Church Going; Two G.O.P Senators Reply to Criticism," *CDT*, March 29, 1955.

27. W. H. Lawrence, "G.O.P. Chiefs Push Eisenhower Draft; He Merely Smiles," *NYT*, February 18, 1955; "Pastors Defend Ike's Church Record," *WP*, March 3, 1955; "Ike Denounced for Golfing, Church Going," *CDT*; "White House Ridicules Charge," *NYT*, March 29, 1955; Walter Trohan, "Neely Slur on Ike's Religion Stirs Capital," *CDT*, March 30, 1955; Editorial, "The Season's Low," *CDT*, March 31, 1955; Editorial, "Neely's Slippery Ground," *WP*, March 31, 1955.

28. William Lee Miller, *Piety on the Potomac: Notes on Politics and Morals in the Fifties* (Boston: Houghton-Mifflin, 1964), 34, 41–42, 44.

29. Ibid., 43.

30. The only work devoted solely to probing this confluence is Hudnut-Beumler, *Looking for God in the Suburbs*. For history of American suburbanization during the 1950s, see Kenneth Jackson, *Crabgrass Frontier: The Suburbanization of the United States* (New York: Oxford University Press, 1985); and Barbara M. Kelly, *Expanding the Dream: Building and Rebuilding Levittown* (Albany: State University of New York Press, 1993).

31. Stanley Rowland, Jr., "Suburbia Buys Religion," *The Nation*, July 28, 1956, 78–80. See also Stanley Rowland, Jr., *Land in Search of God* (New York: Random House, 1958).

32. Gibson Winter, "The Church in Suburban Captivity," *Christian Century*, September 28, 1955, 1112–14; "Last Train to Babylon," *Time*, October 10, 1955, 73–76; William H. Whyte, *The Organization Man* (Garden City, NY: Doubleday Anchor Books, 1957), 407.

33. "Clergy Skeptical Over Revivalism," *NYT*, September 12, 1955; "Church Leader Says Revival Isn't Genuine," *WP*, May 19, 1955; "'Juke Box' Religion Hit by Adventist Speaker," *WP*, June 9, 1956.

34. Kenneth Dole, "News of the Churches," *WP*, February 19, 1955; Harry C. Meserve, "The New Piety," *Atlantic Monthly*, June 1955, 35.

35. David G. Dalin, ed., *From Marx to Judaism: The Collected Essays of Will Herberg* (New York: Wiener, 1989), xiii–xvii. See also Harry J. Ausmus, *Will Herberg: From Right to Right* (Chapel Hill: University of North Carolina Press, 1987).

36. Will Herberg, *Protestant–Catholic–Jew: An Essay in American Religious Sociology* (Garden City, NY: Doubleday, 1955), 26.

37. Ibid., 88–104.

38. Ibid., 279–80.

39. Reinhold Niebuhr, "Is There a Revival of Religion?" *NYT*, November 19, 1950.

40. Reinhold Niebuhr, "Varieties of Religious Revival," *New Republic*, June 6, 1955, 13–16; Reinhold Niebuhr, *Pious and Secular America* (New York: Scribner's, 1958), 1–23.

41. Editorial, "Patriotism and Religion," *Commonweal*, September 2, 1955, 531–32; Editorial, "Patriotism and Religion," *St. Louis Register*, September 16, 1955.

42. John C. Bennett, "A Condition for Coexistence," *Christianity and Crisis*, April 28, 1958, 1–2.

43. Martin E. Marty, *The New Shape of American Religion* (New York: Harper & Brothers, 1958), 7, 34, 67–71.

44. Ibid., 37–40.

45. Dean M. Kelley, *Why Conservative Churches Are Growing: A Study in Sociology of Religion* (New York: Harper & Row, 1972), viii. Roger Finke and Rodney Stark argue that when the cost of membership increases, the net gains of membership increase as well, and such religious traditions grow. They warn that costs alone do not determine growth or failure. See Finke and Stark, *The Churching of America, 1776–1990: Winners and Losers in Our Religious Economy*, 2nd ed. (New Brunswick, NJ: Rutgers University Press, 2005), 250–51.

46. Rodney Stark and Roger Finke call this process "sacralization," which they define as a breakdown of differentiation between sacred and secular and the suffusion of basic societal functions with religious symbols and belief. See Stark and Finke, *Acts of Faith: Explaining the Human Side of Religion* (Berkeley: University of California Press, 2000), 193–217.

47. *Cong. Rec.*101, 84th Cong., 1st sess., 1955, pt. 18: A4456–57.

48. Editorial, "Spotting Communists," *NYT*, June 14, 1955; "Army Cancels Booklet Linking Words to Reds," *NYT*, June 15, 1955.

49. Operations Coordinating Board, "Psychological Aspects of United States Strategy," Office of the Special Assistant for National Security Affairs, Records 1952–61, NSC Series, Subject Subseries, box 10, Eisenhower Library, Abilene, KS.

50. "Deterrence and Survival in the Nuclear Age," *Foreign Relations of the United States, 1955–1957: National Security Policy*, vol. 19 (Washington, DC: Government Printing Office), 639–61.

51. Philip Benjamin, "Arms Rise Urged Lest Reds Seize Lead in 2 Years," *NYT*, January 6, 1958.

52. Dwight D. Eisenhower, "Second Inaugural Address," January 20, 1957, *Eisenhower Papers*, 5:60–35.

53. Dwight D. Eisenhower, "Farewell Radio and Television Address to the American People," *Eisenhower Papers*, 8:1035–40.

54. James F. King, "Sputnik Could Be a Spy-in-Sky," *WP*, October 7, 1957.

55. "Sputnik on Stamp," *WP*, November 29, 1957.

56. James Reston, "Nixon's Moscow Arrival Clouded by Many Events," *LAT*, July 24, 1959.

57. The most complete and contextualized account of the American Exhibition can be found in Walter L. Hixson, *Parting the Curtain: Propaganda, Culture, and the Cold War, 1945–1961* (New York: St, Martin's, 1997), 151–214.

58. The founder of All-State Properties returned to the United States and founded Leisurama, a company specializing in the construction of new model homes.

59. For a printed record of the "Kitchen Debate," see "The Two Worlds: A Day-Long Debate," *NYT*, July 25, 1959.

60. James Reston reported that Ambassador Llewellyn E. Thompson, Jr. and Milton Eisenhower were "standing outside wondering whatever became of diplomacy and why didn't somebody pull a plug on the whole thing." See "A Debate of Politicians," *NYT*, July 25, 1959.

61. Harrison E. Salisbury, "U.S. Cars and Models Distract Soviet Workmen at Fairgrounds," *NYT*, July 24, 1959.

62. John F. Kennedy, "Speech in Alexandria, VA," August 24, 1960, *APP*.

63. John F. Kennedy, "Speech at the VFW Convention," August 26, 1960, *APP*. It is interesting to note that Kennedy did not mention Laika.

64. John F. Kennedy, "Speech in Portland, OR," September 7, 1960, *APP*.

65. John F. Kennedy, "Speech in Bowling Green, KY," October 8, 1960, *APP*.

66. John F. Kennedy, "Questions and Answer Period, Springfield, IL," October 3, 1960, *APP*.

67. John F. Kennedy, "Pathways to Peace," September 9, 1960, *APP*; John F. Kennedy, "Speech at Zembo Mosque Temple, Harrisburg, PA," September 15, 1960, *APP*.

68. Richard M. Nixon, "The Meaning of Communism," August 21, 1960, *APP*.

69. Richard M. Nixon, "Speech at VFW Convention," August 24, 1960, *APP*.

70. For example, in a speech at the Mormon Tabernacle in Salt Lake City, Kennedy said the following:

> This is not a struggle for supremacy of arms alone—it is also a struggle for supremacy between two conflicting ideologies: Freedom under God versus ruthless, godless tyranny. The contest, moreover, is not merely to gain the material wealth of other nations—it is a contest for their hearts and minds. And the challenge to all Americans now is not merely the extent of our material contribution as taxpayers—but the extent to which we can find greater strength for the long pull in our traditions. September 23, 1960, *APP*.

71. Though Kennedy never acknowledged it, he applied the principles of Abraham Maslow's hierarchy of needs to the Cold War in the developing world. Eisenhower and Nixon often emphasized those values at the pinnacle of the hierarchy—values that could only be achieved after more basic needs were satisfied. Kennedy, on the other hand, believed that high concepts like morality meant less to starving people than food or education. Maslow, a Brooklyn College psychologist, had published the article "A Theory of Human Motivation" in 1943. From this work grew the famous "hierarchy of needs," which divided human wants into an ascending scheme of importance from physiological (food, shelter, sex) to the more elusive needs of self-actualization (morality, problem solving, creativity). See Edward Hoffman, *The Right to be Human: A Biography of Abraham Maslow* (New York: McGraw-Hill, 1999), 139–61.

72. Robert N. Bellah used the inaugural as the basis for his influential essay on civil religion. See Bellah, "Civil Religion in America," *Dædalus* 96, no. 1 (1967): 1–21.

73. Theodore C. Sorensen, *Kennedy* (New York: Harper & Row, 1965), 19.

74. For an excellent overview of Kennedy and religion, see Gary Scott Smith, *Faith and the Presidency: From George Washington to George W. Bush* (New York: Oxford University Press, 2006), 259–92.

75. John F. Kennedy, "Address before the Greater Houston Ministerial Association," September 12, 1960, *APP*.

76. For a more detailed analysis of the Fulbright Memorandum and its political context, see Donald T. Critchlow, *Phyllis Schlafly and Grassroots Conservatism: A Woman's Crusade* (Princeton, NJ: Princeton University Press, 2005), 96–103; Cabell Phillips, "Right-Wing Talks By Officers Curbed," *NYT*, July 21, 1961.

77. Roy R. Silver, "5 L.I. Parents Who Started Suit Hail Decision," *NYT*, June 26, 1962.

78. Jonathan Spivak, "The Fourth R," *Wall Street Journal*, May 7, 1962.

79. *Engel v. Vitale*, 370 U.S. 421, 432, 445–47 (1962).

80. "Top Court Ban on School Prayer Stirs Congress Ire," *CDT*, June 26, 1962; Jack Smith, "Graham Urges National Vote on School Prayer," *LAT*, July 15, 1962; Howard James, "Legion Backs School Prayer Amendment," *CDT*, August 4, 1962; Helen Dewar, "Theologian Sees Public Revolt Over School Prayer Ban," *WP*, July 4, 1962.

81. For a compilation of editorials on *Engel v. Vitale* by newspapers across the country, see "Excerpts from Editorials on School Prayer Decision," *NYT*, June 29, 1962; Editorial, "Prayer is Personal," *NYT*, June 27, 1962; Editorial, "In Behalf of Religion," *WP*, June 26, 1962.

82. Editorial, "The Court on Prayer," *Commonweal*, July 13, 1962; Editorial, "Prayer Still Legal in Public Schools," *Christian Century*, July 4, 1962.

83. For a quick overview of congressional reaction, see Joseph Hearst, "Battle Ban on Prayers in Schools," *CDT*, June 27, 1962; *Cong. Rec.* 108, 87th Cong., 2nd sess., 1962, pt. 9: 11675, 11707–10, 11713, 11718, 11775, 11778.

84. John F. Kennedy, "The President's News Conference of June 27, 1962," *APP*.

85. *School District of Abington Township v. Schempp*, 374 U.S. 203 (1963).

86. *Cong. Rec.* 109, 88th Cong., 1st sess., 1963, pt. 8: 11122; *Cong. Rec.* 110, 88th Cong., 2nd sess., 1964, pt. 6: 8117–19; "Congress Reacts Mildly to Ban; Some Ask Amendment to Kill it," *NYT*, June 18, 1963; Laurence Stern, "Most Religious Leaders Support High Court Rule on School Prayer," *WP*, June 18, 1963; "Religious Leaders in L.A. Differ Widely on School Prayer Ruling," *LAT*, June 18, 1963; Jay Alan Sekulow, *Witnessing Their Faith: Religious Influence on Supreme Court Justices and Their Opinions* (Lanham, MD: Rowman & Littlefield, 2006), 242.

87. *Abington v. Schempp*, 203.

88. Anne C. Loveland, "Character Education in the U.S. Army, 1947–1977," *Journal of Military History* 64, no. 3 (July 2000): 806–8.

89. William H. McNeill, *Arnold J. Toynbee: A Life* (New York: Oxford University Press, 1989), 243–44.

90. Billy Graham, *Just As I Am: The Autobiography of Billy Graham* (London: Harper Collins, 1998), 205.

Chapter 7

1. Edward L. Butterworth, "Statement before the Arcadia City Council," December 4, 1962, box 3, folder 2, Margaret Meier Collection of Extreme Right Ephemeral Materials, University Archives, Stanford University (hereafter cited as Meier Collection).

2. Nikos Kazantzakis, *The Last Temptation of Christ*, trans. P. A. Bien (New York: Simon & Schuster, 1960).

3. Using a city or region as a case study for understanding the development of modern American conservatism is common in some of the most impressive contributions to the field. California in particular has been a rich area for such endeavors. The best known is Lisa McGirr, *Suburban Warriors: The Origins of the New American Right* (Princeton, NJ: Princeton University Press, 2001). See also Darren Dochuk, *From Bible Belt to Sunbelt: Plain Folk, Religion, Grassroots Politics, and the Southernization of Southern California* (PhD diss., Notre Dame, 2005). For examples of localized studies that explore other elements of California

politics in the postwar period, see Robert O. Self, *American Babylon: Race and the Struggle for Postwar Oakland* (Princeton, NJ: Princeton University Press, 2003); and Becky M. Nicolaides, *My Blue Heaven: Life and Politics in the Working-Class Suburbs of Los Angeles* (Chicago: University of Chicago Press, 2002).

4. James M. Beasley to James L. Young, August 21, 1962, box 2, folder 15, Meier Collection.

5. J. Davis Barnard to Arcadia Library Board, August 26, 1962, box 2, folder 15, Meier Collection.

6. Arcadia Americanism Committee, General Statements 1 and 2, box 3, folder 8, Meier Collection.

7. Mrs. Bear to J. L. Young, November 2, 1962, box 2, folder 15, Meier Collection; The Church of Jesus Christ of Latter Day Saints also became involved early in the controversy. See R. S. Summerhays to Library Board, October 26, 1962, box 2, folder 15, Meier Collection.

8. Homer L. Fletcher, Statement, November 10, 1962, box 2, folder 18, Meier Collection.

9. Jean Winslow to Arcadia City Council, November 26, 1962, box 5, folder 2, Meier Collection.

10. Mortensen and Meier, "Speech before the International Freedom Committee, Los Angeles," November 2, 1964, box 3, folder 2, Meier Collection.

11. "Book Protests Rock Southland Libraries: Novel Called Blasphemous," *Independent* (Pasadena), November 30, 1962.

12. Mortensen and Meier, "Speech before the International Freedom Committee, Los Angeles."

13. Advertisement, "The Truth in the Library Issue," *Arcadia Tribune*, December 16, 1962.

14. Mrs. William Aerick Bear to President of the Library Board of Trustees, November 2, 1962, box 2 folder 15, Meier Collection; Irma K. Bethune to Homer Fletcher, July 14, 1962, box 2, folder 17, Meier Collection.

15. Mr. and Mrs. Robert S. Johnson to Library Board, December 6, 1962, box 2, folder 15, Meier Collection.

16. "Text of Letters Read at Council Meeting," *Arcadia Tribune*, July 21, 1963.

17. Thomas Jefferson may have disapproved of O'Keeffe's program.

18. O'Keeffe to Arcadia City Council, February 5, 1963, box 2, folder 10, Meier Collection.

19. H. Warren Anderson, "Statement in Regard to the Book Controversy," February 5, 1963, box 2, folder 10, Meier Collection.

20. "Church Council in Policy Quarrel on Book Banning," *Arcadia Tribune*, January 11, 1963.

21. Meredith to Butterworth, December 3, 1962, box 2, folder 10, Meier Collection.

22. Editorial, "The Banning of a Book," *Independent Star-News*, December 2, 1962.

23. Louis Berger to City Council, December 26, 1962, box 2, folder 13, Meier Collection.

24. Geo. M. Richter to John L. Young, December 31, 1962, box 2, folder 13, Meier Collection.

25. "5,000 Urge Removal of Controversial Book: Protestant Council Submits Petition to City Council," *Daily News-Post* (Monrovia), February 6, 1963

26. Minutes, City Council of the City of Arcadia, March 19, 1963, box 3, folder 15, Meier Collection.

27. "Council Supports Book Circulation," *Arcadia Tribune*, March 21, 1963.

28. Advertisement, "Over 5,000 Petitioners Refused by Arcadia City Council," *Arcadia Tribune*, March 24, 1963.

29. "Library Board Votes 3–2 against Special Shelf," *Arcadia Tribune*, June 23, 1963.

30. Mortensen and Meier, "Speech before the International Freedom Committee, Los Angeles."

31. "Book Ban Advocates Eye Arcadia Election," *Pasadena Independent*, November 5, 1963.

32. Editorial, "Campaign in Arcadia," *Independent Star-News*, June 2, 1963.

33. Advertisement, *Arcadia Tribune*, April 12, 1964. See also Campaign letter from Budd Garretson and Robert J. Considine, n.d., box 4, folder 4, Meier Collection.

34. Mortensen and Meier, "Speech before the International Freedom Committee, Los Angeles."

35. Ibid.

36. Survey by the Gallup Organization, February 3–8, 1937, iPOLL Databank; Survey by the Gallup Organization, April 2–7, 1959, iPOLL Databank.

37. Survey by the Gallup Organization, February 10–February 15, 1937, iPOLL Databank; Survey by the Gallup Organization, December 10–15, 1959, iPOLL Databank.

38. Survey by the Gallup Organization, July 30–August 4, 1958, iPOLL Databank.

39. See John T. McGreevy, *Catholicism and American Freedom* (New York: Norton, 2003), 167–88; John Wicklein, "Warning to Jews Issued by Jesuits," *NYT*, August 27, 1962.

40. *Cong. Rec.* 101, 84th Cong., 1st sess., April 26, 1955, pt. 4: 5060–61; Norman Vincent Peale, "Five Ways You Can Help Your Church Fight Communism," *Women's Home Companion*, October 1954, 115.

41. There now exists a solid collection of historical works on the birth, growth, and dominance of conservatism. See Mary C. Brennan, *Turning Right in the Sixties: The Conservative Capture of the GOP* (Chapel Hill: University of North Carolina Press, 1995); Donald T. Critchlow, *The Conservative Ascendancy: How the GOP Right Made Political History* (Cambridge, MA: Harvard University Press, 2007); Matthew Dallek, *The Right Moment: Ronald Reagan's First Victory and the Decisive Turning Point in American Politics* (New York: Free Press, 2000); Laura Jane Gifford, *The Center Cannot Hold: The 1960 Presidential Election and the Rise of Modern Conservatism* (DeKalb: Northern Illinois University Press, 2009); Jerome L. Himmelstein, *To the Right: The Transformation of American Conservatism* (Berkeley: University of California Press, 1990); Godfrey Hodgson, *The World Turned Right Side Up: A History of the Conservative Ascendancy in America* (Boston: Houghton Mifflin, 1996); Kim Phillips-Fein, *Invisible Hands: The Making of the Conservative Movement from the New Deal to Reagan* (New York: Norton, 2009); Gregory L. Schneider, *The Conservative Century: From Reaction to Revolution* (Lanham, MD: Rowman & Littlefield, 2009); Jonathan M. Schoenwald, *A Time for Choosing: The Rise of Modern American Conservatism* (New York: Oxford University Press, 2001); Bruce J. Schulman and Julian E. Zelizer, eds., *Rightward Bound: Making America Conservative in the 1970s* (Cambridge, MA: Harvard University Press, 2008); Sean Wilentz, *The Age of Reagan: A History, 1974–2008* (New York: Harper, 2008).

42. George H. Nash, *The Conservative Intellectual Movement in America Since 1945* (New York: Basic Books, 1976).

43. Not all conservatives rooted the movement in religious ground. Ayn Rand, for instance, was an avowed atheist. See Jennifer Burns, "Godless Capitalism: Ayn Rand and the Conservative Movement," *Modern Intellectual History* 1, no. 3 (2004): 1–27.

44. Richard Hofstadter, "The Psuedo-Conservative Revolt—1955," in *The Radical Right*, ed. Daniel Bell (Garden City, NY: Doubleday, 1963), 63–80; Lionel Trilling, *The Liberal Imagination: Essays on Literature and Society* (New York: Viking, 1950), ix.

45. Russell Kirk, *The Conservative Mind: From Burke to Santayana* (Chicago: Regnery, 1953), 9. See also W. Wesley McDonald, *Russell Kirk and the Age of Ideology* (Columbia: University of Missouri Press, 2004).

46. Kirk, *Conservative Mind*, 7–8.

47. Richard M. Weaver, *Ideas Have Consequences* (Chicago: University of Chicago Press, 1949), 5–17.

48. Clarence Manion, *The Key to Peace: A Formula for the Perpetuation of Real Americanism* (Chicago: Heritage Foundation, 1950), 35; Joseph Alsop and Stewart Alsop, "Matter of Fact . . . The Case of Dr. Manion," *WP*, January 29, 1954; "Manion Blasts Ike's Policies as Socialistic," *Washington Post and Times-Herald*, March 7, 1955. For a refinement of Manion's views, situated within the emerging conservative movement, see Clarence Manion, *The Conservative American: His Fight for National Independence and Constitutional Government* (New York: Devin-Adair, 1964).

49. Peter Viereck, "Conservatism under the Elms," *NYT*, November 4, 1951.

50. Milton Bracker, "Yale Survey Finds No Influence or Threats to Academic Freedom," *NYT*, Feburary 18, 1952.

51. William F. Buckley, Jr., *God and Man at Yale: The Superstitions of "Academic Freedom"* (Chicago: Regnery, 1951), xiii–xix, 17, 25, 29.

52. Kirk, *The Conservative Mind*, 9; Weaver, *Ideas Have Consequences*, 6.

53. Clare Boothe Luce, *Is Communism Compatible with Christianity?* (New York: Catholic Information Society, 1946); Sheen, *Communism and the Conscience of the West*, 49; Whittaker Chambers, *Witness* (New York: Random House, 1952), 9–11; Manion, *Key to Peace*, 37.

54. Whittaker Chambers, "The Devil," *Life*, February 2, 1948, 76–85. Chambers recalled his submission of "The Devil" to the editors at *Life*, who regarded it skeptically. "Like so many others," he noted, "[they] did not know that the American people is, above all, a religious people." Chambers, *Witness*, 508.

55. Committee to Proclaim Liberty, "The Story Behind the Committee to Proclaim Liberty," n.d., series I, box 69, folder 10, James C. Ingebretsen Papers, 5.

56. The best treatment of the CMF, and indeed the role of anti-Communism in the early conservative movement, is Donald T. Critchlow, *Phyllis Schlafly and Grassroots Conservatism: A Woman's Crusade* (Princeton, NJ: Princeton University Press, 2005), 80–83, 104; "Mindszenty Foundation Plans Freedom Seminar," *CDT*, November 21, 1960; Editorial, "Red Plans," *CDT*, March 1, 1961.

57. See Jonathan M. Schoenwald, "We Are an Action Group: The John Birch Society and the Conservative Movement in the 1960s," in *The Conservative Sixties*, ed. David Farber and Jeff Roche (New York: Lang, 2003), 21–36.

58. John Birch Society, *The Blue Book of the John Birch Society*, 6th ed. (Belmont, MA: John Birch Society, 1961), 39, 58, 60, 144.

59. Robert Welch, *The Life of John Birch: In the Story of One American Boy, the Ordeal of His Age* (Chicago: Regnery, 1954), 86, 91, 99, 109–10.

60. Schoenwald, "We Are an Action Group," 27–28.

61. Kirk, *The Conservative Mind*, 399–400, 414.

62. Lyman Kellstedt, John Green, Corwin Smidt, and James Guth, "Faith Transformed: Religion and American Politics from FDR to George W. Bush," in *Religion and American Politics: From the Colonial Period to the Present*, 2nd ed., ed. Mark A. Noll and Luke E. Harlow (New York: Oxford University Press, 2007), 281.

63. Not all explorations of modern evangelicalism note its connection to spiritual anti-Communism. See William Martin, *With God on Our Side: The Rise of the Religious Right in America* (New York: Broadway Books, 1996). Martin's book was groundbreaking, but it rarely mentions the early importance of Communism to the Religious Right.

64. It is true that not all evangelicals are fundamentalists, but nonetheless modern evangelicalism has emerged out of the debates between fundamentalists and liberals/modernists.

65. The best account of fundamentalism and, by extension, evangelicalism in the decades before the Cold War is Joel A. Carpenter, *Revive Us Again: The Reawakening of American Fundamentalism* (New York: Oxford University Press, 1997).

66. Axel R. Schafer deftly connects the emergence of American evangelicalism to the growth of the federal government during the early Cold War. See Schafer, "The Cold War State and the Resurgence of Evangelicalism," *Radical History Review* 99 (Fall 2007): 19–50.

67. "School against Communism Opens Monday," *LAT*, November 6, 1960; Frederick Schwarz, *Beating the Unbeatable Foe: One Man's Victory over Communism, Leviathan, and the Last Enemy* (Washington, DC: Regnery, 1996), 15–16, 21–22, 104.

68. Ibid., 162–69; Christian Anti-Communism Crusade, *The Southern California School of Anti-Communism*, 1961, box 31, folder 1, Meier Collection.

69. "1,000 Enrollment Expected; Anti-Communism School Series Will Open Monday in Anaheim," *LAT*, March 5, 1961; "Anti-Red School Opens Monday at Sports Arena," *LAT*, August 27, 1961; "Anticommunism School on KTTV," *LAT*, August 28, 1961.

70. Adam Bernstein, "Evangelist Billy James Hargis Dies; Spread Anti-Communist Message," *WP*, November 30, 2004; Billy James Hargis, *Communist America . . . Must it Be?* (Tulsa,

OK: Christian Crusade, 1960), 154; Hargis, *The Far Left* (Tulsa, OK: Christian Crusade, 1964), 227.

71. For a fuller discussion of the life and contributions of McGee and Wells, see Darren Dochuk, "They Locked God Outside the Iron Curtain:' The Politics of Anticommunism and the Ascendancy of Plain-Folk Evangelicalism in the Postwar West," in *The Political Culture of the New West*, ed. Jeff Roche (Lawrence: University Press of Kansas, 2008), 97–134; William Steuart McBirnie, *The Real Power Behind Communism* (Glendale, CA: Center for American Research and Education, n.d.), Hoover Collection of the Far Right, Box 34, Hoover Institute Archives.

72. Nancy Gibbs and Michael Duffy, *The Preacher and the Presidents: Billy Graham in the White House* (New York: Center Street, 2007), 28–29; Anne C. Loveland, *American Evangelicals and the U.S. Military, 1942–1993* (Baton Rouge: Louisiana State University Press, 1996), 37–39; Scott Flipse, "Below-the-Belt Politics: Protestant Evangelicals, Abortion, and the Foundation of the New Religious Right, 1960–75," in Farber and Roche, *The Conservative Sixties*, 127.

73. The best work on this aspect of Cold War evangelical belief is Angela M. Lahr, *Millennial Dreams and Apocalyptic Nightmares: The Cold War Origins of Political Evangelicalism* (New York: Oxford University Press, 2007).

74. W. P. Strube, Jr., *Communism—A Religion* (n.p.: Christian Anti-Communism Crusade, 1962), box 31, folder 2, Meier Collection.

75. McBirnie, *The Real Power Behind Communism*; "Crusaders' Anti-Red Folk Song Pays Off," *LAT*, October 14, 1964; "Right Wing Errs on Reds, Mosk Says," *LAT*, April 21, 1963.

76. Billy Sunday, for instance, the best known evangelist of the early twentieth century, used the occasion of the first Red Scare not only to win converts but also to attack Protestant modernists. See Martin E. Marty, *Modern American Religion*. Vol. 2, *The Noise of Conflict 1919–1941* (Chicago: University of Chicago Press, 1991), 75.

77. Marty, *Modern American Religion*, 3:362–63; Heather Hendershot, "God's Angriest Man: Carl McIntire, Cold War Fundamentalism, and Right-Wing Broadcasting," *American Quarterly* 59, no. 2 (June 2007): 373–96; "Bishops Hit Both Reds, Far Right," *WP*, September 28, 1961; "Church Council Aide Denounces Extremist Groups of Far Right," *NYT*, February 26, 1962; Solomon S. Bernards, *The Radical Right and Religion* (New York: Anti-Defamation League of B'nai B'rith, 1965).

78. For an excellent treatment of Reagan's religious beliefs and their intersection with politics, see Gary Scott Smith, *Faith and the Presidency: From George Washington to George W. Bush* (New York: Oxford University Press, 2006), 325–63.

Epilogue

1. Ronald Reagan, "Speech before National Association of Evangelicals," March 8, 1983, *Public Papers of the Presidents of the United States: Reagan*, (Washington, DC: Government Printing Office, 1982–91), 1983 vol., book 1, 359–64 (hereafter cited as *Reagan Papers*.

2. Ibid.

3. Bill Peterson, "Reagan's Use of Moral Language to Explain Policies Draws Fire," *WP*, March 23, 1983; Anthony Lewis, "Onward, Christian Soldiers," *NYT*, March 10, 1983; Ronald Reagan, "Interview With Henry Brandon of the London Sunday Times and News Service on Domestic and Foreign Policy Issues," March 18, 1983, APP; Ronald Reagan, "Question-and-Answer Session With Reporters on Domestic and Foreign Policy Issues," March 29, 1983, *Reagan Papers*, 1983 vol., book 1, 464.

4. John Dart, "Reagan Wants a Quid Pro Quo: Sermons vs. Arms Freeze and Red Evil," *LAT*, March 12, 1983.

5. See Thomas E. Evans, *The Education of Ronald Reagan: The General Electric Years and the Untold Story of His Conversion to Conservatism* (New York: Columbia University Press, 2006)

6. "President Bush's Address on Terrorism before a Joint Meeting of Congress," *NYT*, September 21, 2001.

7. Michael R. Gordon, "The Struggle for Iraq," *NYT*, April 24, 2007; Sheryl Gay Stolberg, "Islamo-Fascism Had Its Moment," *NYT*, September 24, 2006; Douglas Jehl, "U.S. General Apologizes for Remarks About Islam," *NYT*, October 18, 2003.

8. This has been a trend at least since researchers returned to Plainville, Missouri, in the early Cold War and found that, while the number of unbelievers had remained unchanged, the residents were increasingly reticent to share their disbelief publicly. See Art Gallaher, Jr., *Plainville: Fifteen Years Later* (New York: Columbia University Press, 1961), 169. Recent sociological studies have also demonstrated a marked trend by Americans toward exaggerating measures like religious attendance. See C. Kirk Hadaway, Penny Long Marler, and Mark Chaves, "What the Polls Don't Show: A Closer Look at U.S. Church Attendance," *American Sociological Review* 58, no. 6 (December 1993), 741–52; and Hadaway, Marler, and Chaves, "Overreporting Church Attendance in America: Evidence That Demands the Same Verdict," *American Sociological Review* 63, no. 1 (February 1998): 122–30.

9. Baylor Institute for Studies of Religion, *Select Findings from the Baylor Religious Survey* (Waco, TX: Baylor Institute for Studies of Religion, 2006), 7–24.

10. A good indication of this trend was *Time's* listing of the twenty-five most influential evangelicals in America, which appeared in its February 7, 2005, issue. America's newfound faith has been a rich topic of documentary film as well. Some treat American religious expression as an object of ridicule, such as Heidi Ewing and Rachel Grady's *Jesus Camp* (2006). Others, like PBS's *With God on Our Side* (1996), take a more balanced look at the rise of the religious right. Evangelicalism and fundamentalism now comprise the bulk of late twentieth-century American religious history. See Monique El-Faizy, *God and Country: How Evangelicals Have Become America's New Mainstream* (New York: Bloomsbury, 2006); Jeffery L. Sheler, *Believers: A Journey Into Evangelical America* (New York: Viking, 2006); Douglas A. Sweeney, *The American Evangelical Story: A History of the Movement* (Grand Rapids, MI: Baker Academic, 2005); Heather Hendershot, *Shaking the World For Jesus: Media and Conservative Evangelical Culture* (Chicago: University of Chicago Press, 2004); and Randall Herbert Balmer, *Mine Eyes Have Seen the Glory: A Journey Into the Evangelical Subculture in America*, 3rd ed. (New York: Oxford University Press, 2000).

11. Tim F. LaHaye and Jerry B. Jenkins, *Left Behind: A Novel of Earth's Last Days* (Wheaton, IL: Tyndale House, 2000). Mel Gibson's *The Passion of the Christ* (2004) was the highest-grossing R-rated film of all time. Even before the election of 2000, some observers noted the infusion of religious rhetoric. A detailed *New York Times* exposé began: "Whatever else it achieves, the presidential campaign of 2000 will be remembered as the time in American politics when the wall separating church and state began to collapse." Jeffrey Rosen, "Is Nothing Secular?" *NYT*, January 30, 2000. The election of 2004 spawned a conference on the influence of religion on politics at Notre Dame University that culminated in David E. Campbell, ed., *A Matter of Faith: Religion in the 2004 Presidential Election* (New York: Brookings Institution Press, 2007).

12. A coterie of popular neo-atheists has emerged in both Great Britain and the United States, publishing bestsellers and fomenting an earnest discussion of the place of religion within modern society. Their advocacy has taken on elements of a religious faith itself. See Sam Harris, *Letter to a Christian Nation* (New York: Knopf, 2006); Richard Dawkins, *The God Delusion* (Boston: Houghton-Mifflin, 2006); Daniel C. Dennett, *Religion as a Natural Phenomenon* (New York: Viking, 2006); and Christopher Hitchens, *God is Not Great: How Religion Poisons Everything* (New York: Twelve, 2007).

13. Derek H. Davis, "The Pledge of Allegiance and American Values," *Journal of Church and State* 45 (September 2003): 657; "Pro-God Resolutions 'Spreading like Wildfire' in Tennessee," *Journal of Church and State* 45 (December 2003): 3; Survey by CNN and USA Today, March 26–28, 2004, iPOLL Databank.

14. Michael Janofsky, "Colorado Asks: Is 'In God We Trust' a Religious Statement?" *NYT*, July 3, 2000.

15. Brief Amici Curiae of Senators George Allen and Sam Brownback et al. and Representatives Robert Aderholt et al., 02–1624, 13–15 (2003); Jeffrey Gettleman, "Supporters of Ten Commandments Rally On," *NYT*, August 24, 2003; Bill O'Reilly, "Believe it or Not," *Jewish World Review*, July 8, 2002.

16. Debating the religious beliefs and intents of America's founders is a popular cottage industry for historians and journalists. Philip Hamburger argues that the Founding Fathers never intended strict separation of church and state, and his work has been marshaled by those supporting the Pledge of Allegiance. See Hamburger, *Separation of Church and State* (Cambridge, MA: Harvard University Press, 2002). See also Frank Lambert, *The Founding Fathers and the Place of Religion in America* (Princeton, NJ: Princeton University Press, 2003).

INDEX

Printed in the USA/Agawam, MA
June 18, 2018

676982.035